MW01054794

Northeastern
Technical College Library

Archaeology of Food

Volume 2: L–Z

Archaeology of Food

An Encyclopedia

Volume 2: L–Z

EDITED BY
KAREN BESCHERER METHENY
AND
MARY C. BEAUDRY

ROWMAN & LITTLEFIELD
Lanham • Boulder • New York • London

Published by Rowman & Littlefield
A wholly owned subsidiary of The Rowman & Littlefield Publishing Group, Inc.
4501 Forbes Boulevard, Suite 200, Lanham, Maryland 20706
www.rowman.com

Unit A, Whitacre Mews, 26-34 Stannary Street, London SE11 4AB, United Kingdom

Copyright © 2015 by Rowman & Littlefield

All rights reserved. No part of this book may be reproduced in any form or by any electronic
or mechanical means, including information storage and retrieval systems, without written
permission from the publisher, except by a reviewer who may quote passages in a review.

British Library Cataloguing in Publication Information Available

Library of Congress Cataloging-in-Publication Data
Archaeology of food : an encyclopedia / edited by Karen Bescherer Metheny and Mary C.
Beaudry.
    volumes cm
  Includes bibliographical references and index.
  ISBN 978-0-7591-2364-9 (cloth : alkaline paper) — ISBN 978-0-7591-2366-3 (electronic)
    1. Prehistoric peoples—Food—Encyclopedias. 2. Food habits—History—Encyclopedias.
3. Diet—History—Encyclopedias. 4. Excavations (Archaeology)—Encyclopedias. 5. Social
archaeology—Encyclopedias. I. Metheny, Karen Bescherer, 1960– II. Beaudry, Mary Carolyn,
1950–
  GN799.F6A73 2015
  394.1'209—dc23
                                                                                    2014049892

∞™ The paper used in this publication meets the minimum requirements of
American National Standard for Information Sciences—Permanence of
Paper for Printed Library Materials, ANSI/NISO Z39.48-1992.

Printed in the United States of America

In memory of our colleagues

Klaus Schmidt
1953–2014

Sharon Zuckerman
1965–2014

CONTENTS

THEMATIC CONTENTS

FIGURES AND TABLES

FIGURES

TABLES

ABBREVIATIONS

aDNA	ancient DNA
AMS	accelerator mass spectrometry radiocarbon dating
BSR	Broad Spectrum Revolution
^{14}C	Carbon-14 or radiocarbon
cDNA	complementary DNA
cf.	confer or compare (taxonomic nomenclature)
CIEP	crossover immunoelectrophoresis
CT	computed tomography
DEM	digital elevation model
DISH	diffuse idiopathic skeletal hyperostosis
DNA	deoxyribonucleic acid
EBA	Early Bronze Age
EDX	energy dispersive X-ray analysis
ESA	Early Stone Age
FCR	fire-cracked rock
FTIR	Fourier transform infrared spectroscopy
GC/C/IRMS	gas chromatography–combustion–isotope ratio mass spectrometry
GC/GC-MS	gas chromatography/gas chromatography–mass spectrometry
GIS	geographic information system
HBE	human behavioral ecology
HPLC	high performance liquid chromatography
ICP-AES	inductively coupled plasma–atomic emission spectroscopy
ICP-MS	inductively coupled plasma–mass spectrometric analysis
INAA	instrumental neutron activation analysis
kcal	kilocalories
LAB	lactic acid bacteria
LBA	Late Bronze Age
LC-MS/MS	liquid chromatography–mass spectrometry/mass spectrometry
LEH	linear enamel hypoplasias
LiDAR	light detection and ranging
LP	lactase persistence
LSA	Late Stone Age
micro-CT	micro-computed tomography or microtomography
MNI	minimum number of individuals
MRI	magnetic resonance imaging

MSA	Middle Stone Age
mtDNA	mitochondrial DNA
n=	number equals
NAA	neutron activation analysis
NGS	next generation sequencing
NISP	number of identified specimens
PCR	polymerase chain reaction
PPNA	Pre-Pottery Neolithic A
PPNB	Pre-Pottery Neolithic B
pXRF	portable X-ray fluorescence
qPCR	quantitative polymerase chain reaction
RNA	ribonucleic acid
ROV	remotely operated vehicle
RT-PCR	reverse-transcription polymerase chain reaction
SAGE	serial analysis of gene expression
SEM	scanning electron microscopy
sp./spp.	one or several species unknown or unspecified (taxonomic nomenclature)
USO	underground storage organ
var.	variety (taxonomic nomenclature)
VHR	very high resolution satellite imagery
VLM	visible-light microscopy
WTSS	whole transcriptome shotgun sequencing
XRF	X-ray fluorescence

DATES

BP	before present
cal AD	calibrated years AD
cal BC	calibrated years BC
cal BP	calibrated years BP
cal KYA	thousand years ago calibrated
KYA	thousand years ago
MYA	million years ago

SYMBOLS

ca.	circa
~	similar to
<	less than
>	greater than
±	plus or minus

INTRODUCTION

An egg. A ceramic bowl. A stone pestle. Charred grains of wheat. Seemingly ordinary objects that nonetheless have profound implications for understanding past human culture and society. Food procurement is essential to human survival, and changes to diet have been intimately connected with human evolutionary and social development. Ancient populations developed a multitude of strategies (of which food production, or agriculture, is only the most recent) to procure, process, and consume foods for their subsistence. But food is more than diet and nutrition. Food and foodways are central to cultural practice, social organization, and a range of intersecting identities and belief systems.

In editing the first reference work devoted to the fundamental connection between food and archaeology, our chief goal has been to assemble into two volumes entries that succinctly encapsulate current scientific knowledge about the archaeology of food. The encyclopedia's 284 entries, contributed by 236 archaeologists and scholars from across the globe, are a reflection of the interest in and breadth of food-related inquiries in our field. The encyclopedia spans diverse geographical and temporal contexts, as well as an array of topics related to the archaeological study of food, including eras, places, cultural groups, specific foodstuffs, landmark sites, analytical techniques, methodology, pioneers in the field, innovations, theories, issues, controversies, and more. Entries such as *Bioarchaeological Analysis* or *Food and Capitalism* provide broad overviews of research using examples from different sites, cultures, or eras. More narrowly focused entries, for example, on specific analytical techniques, and site-focused entries provide greater detail.

Because the archaeological study of food is a dynamic and growing area of interest, the encyclopedia also features recent discoveries alongside the results of decades of research that have shaped the course of debate on issues such as the origins of agriculture, the role of technological advances in human development, and the role of food and foodways in creating identity or communicating meaning. Many entries are explicitly multi- and interdisciplinary in content and approach, a reflection not only of the intersection of food and foodways with many aspects of daily life, but also of the value of blending scientific and humanistic analyses to understand both the content and context of food consumption in the past.

The entries in the encyclopedia are of necessity brief. They are not intended to provide comprehensive discussions but rather to offer summaries that will allow the reader to gain a broad overview of the nature and importance of the research related to a particular topic, key research questions, types of evidence, types of sites, and methods of analysis. Further, each entry directs interested readers to the relevant literature through the recommendation of key publications on each topic. The recommended readings will provide an entry point into the vast body of work that has been published on each topic, and readers are encouraged to use this tool to learn more about a particular area of interest.

This encyclopedia is timely, as it reflects not only increased interest in past diet and foodways within archaeology but also the coalescence of a wide range of disciplines, including food studies, that are bringing food to the forefront of academic study. The reasons for this rising interest are many—from the acknowledgment of food as a legitimate and vastly important topic of academic study, to public fascination with food and cuisine. Attention to food and foodways, both scholarly and popular, acknowledges food's centrality to our daily lives and affirms the need to understand the choices humans make and have made about food, diet, and subsistence, and why they make the choices they do. It also reflects current concerns about the effects of globalization, the loss of biodiversity, and the need for sustainability and food security. The archaeological evidence of past food consumption is surprisingly rich, and archaeologists have much to contribute to a dialogue on these important issues.

We hope that this encyclopedia will serve as a reference for scholars and students in archaeology, food studies, and related disciplines, as well as an introduction to the archaeology of food for culinary historians, food historians, food writers, and food and archaeology enthusiasts. By synthesizing and summarizing the vast archaeological literature about food and foodways in the past, the encyclopedia provides an exciting, broad-ranging, and useful introduction to this fascinating field of study. We hope that it also serves to develop awareness of the importance of this research for contemporary food-related issues and interests.

We thank Andrea Kendrick and Leanne Silverman, our editors at Rowman & Littlefield, for their support. We also thank Wendi Schnaufer, now of University of Alabama Press, who initiated this project. Most of all, we thank our many contributors who responded with enthusiasm to our invitations and who have prepared their entries with such care. It has been a tremendous pleasure to work with so many of our colleagues. The connections we have forged with these scholars serve to emphasize the global relevance of food-related studies as well as the interdisciplinary nature of such research. We are excited to be able to offer these two volumes as a testament to our mutual interest in and curiosity about the archaeology of food.

Karen Bescherer Metheny
Mary C. Beaudry

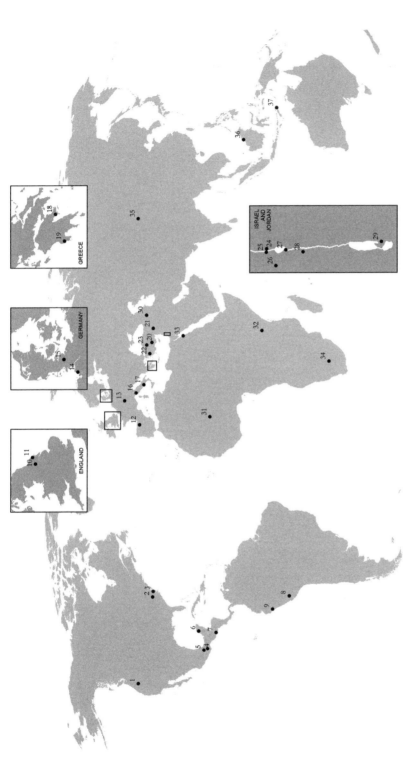

Featured archaeological sites. Robinson Projection, WGS 1984. *Data source:* Natural Earth (naturalearthdata.com). Map by Laura E. Masur. *Key:* **United States:** (1) Paisley Caves, Oregon; (2) Poplar Forest, Virginia; (3) Jamestown, Virginia. **Mexico:** (4) Guilá Naquitz; (5) Tehuacán Valley; (6) Kabah. **El Salvador:** (7) Joya de Cerén. **Peru:** (8) Conchopata; (9) Ñanchoc Valley. **England:** (10) York; (11) Star Carr. **Spain:** (12) Gran Dolina. **France:** (13) Oedenburg. **Germany:** (14) Feddersen Wierde; (15) Haithabu. **Italy:** (16) San Genesio, Medieval Tavern Site (San Miniato, Pisa); (17) Herculaneum and Pompeii. **Greece:** (18) Franchthi Cave; (19) Palace of Nestor. **Turkey:** (20) Çatalhöyük; (21) Göbekli Tepe; (22) Sardis; (23) Gordion. **Israel:** (24) Gesher Benot Ya'aqov; (25) Hazor; (26) Hilazon Tachtit; (27) Ohalo II; (28) Tel Reḥov. **Jordan:** (29) Dhra'. **Armenia:** (30) Areni. **Mali:** (31) Gao. **Tanzania:** (32) Olduvai Gorge. **Egypt:** (33) Quseir al-Qadim. **South Africa:** (34) Wonderwerk Cave. **China:** (35) Subeixi Cemeteries. **Malaysia:** (36) Niah Caves. **East Timor:** (37) Jerimalai Cave.

L

LACTASE PERSISTENCE AND DAIRYING

The development of agricultural societies, dating back to around 10,000 years ago, is a recent innovation in the timeline of human evolution. It has led, however, to fundamental changes in human ecology, involving new ways of living and eating, and is associated with a number of innovations, many of which have reshaped the adaptive landscape of humans. Among these, lactase persistence (LP) is probably the best studied. Lactase is the enzyme that enables the digestion of the milk sugar lactose. Its expression decreases after the weaning period is over in most mammals, including most humans. In some humans, however, particularly in those populations that have a history of dairying, lactase is expressed throughout adulthood. In Africa and the Middle East, several variants have been found to associate with LP, while a single variant ($-13,910{\star}T$) has been identified in Europe and the Indian subcontinent. It is possible to obtain estimates of the age of specific LP-associated variants by studying genetic variation in surrounding regions. Interestingly, they all bracket the time when dairying began in the corresponding regions. For variants to be so recent and yet so frequent, natural selection is very likely to be involved. The estimated selection strengths required to explain the age/frequency distributions of $-13,910{\star}T$ and $-14,010{\star}C$ are indeed among the highest estimated for any human genes in the last ~30,000 years (1.4–19 percent and 1–15 percent, respectively). While the selective advantages of drinking milk without symptoms of lactose intolerance are still a matter of debate, evidence from dairy fat residues detected in potsherds and from allele frequencies in ancient European populations indicates dairying was practiced before LP arose or became common. A spatially explicit simulation modeling approach suggested selection on the $-13,910{\star}T$ allele originated in central Europe about 7,500 years ago.

See also BIOMOLECULAR ANALYSIS; CATTLE; DIGESTION AND HUMAN EVOLUTION; MILK AND DAIRY PRODUCTS; RESIDUE ANALYSIS, DAIRY PRODUCTS; SECONDARY PRODUCTS REVOLUTION

Further Reading

Evershed, Richard P. 2008. Experimental Approaches to the Interpretation of Absorbed Organic Residues in Archaeological Ceramics. *World Archaeology* 40(1):26–47.

Gerbault, Pascale, Anke Liebert, Yuval Itan, et al. 2011. Evolution of Lactase Persistence: An Example of Human Niche Construction. *Philosophical Transactions of the Royal Society of London, Series B, Biological Sciences* 366(1566):863–77. doi:10.1098/rstb.2010.0268.

■ PASCALE GERBAULT AND MARK G. THOMAS

LAKE VILLAGES (EUROPE)

Lake villages or lake dwellings, prehistoric settlements built on the water or the shores of lakes and rivers, are known from several archaeological periods. Most famous are the Neolithic lake dwellings of Europe, especially those in the circum-Alpine region (Switzerland, Germany, France, Italy, Austria, and Slovenia), named to the UNESCO World Heritage list in 2011. The earliest circum-Alpine dwellings date to around 4200 cal BC. This type of settlement continued until the Late Bronze Age, ending around 800 cal BC. There are earlier Neolithic lake dwellings such as the site of La Draga in northeast Spain, however, that date to around 5300 cal BC. In the Baltic region and in Scotland and Ireland lake dwellings (*crannogs* or artificial islands) are mostly dated to the Late Bronze/Iron Age (around 1200 until 500 cal BC).

In lake villages, archaeological deposits or cultural layers are often well preserved in a waterlogged state. Plant remains are particularly well preserved. Macroremains such as seeds, fruits, and cereal chaff are typically recovered. This gives archaeologists considerable insight into the diversity of plant use. People in the lake villages were farmers, cultivating plants and keeping domestic animals. Gathering and hunting also played an important role, however.

Very important cultivated plants in the Neolithic circum-Alpine lake villages were wheat (a mostly tetraploid naked wheat, emmer, and, more rarely, einkorn) (figure 37), barley (a multirowed form), flax, and opium poppy. Rarely represented are peas. Inhabitants also relied on hazelnuts, crab apples, acorns, and many other species of gathered wild plants. Direct evidence of diet has been recovered from residues adhering to cooking pots (figure 38) and from human excrement. A popular dish was a sort of stew containing cereals, wild plants, and meat.

See also ARCHAEOBOTANY; BARLEY; BIOMOLECULAR ANALYSIS; CEREALS; COOKING VESSELS, CERAMIC; MACROREMAINS; PALEOFECAL ANALYSIS; USE-WEAR OR USE-ALTERATION ANALYSIS, POTTERY; WHEAT

Further Reading

Jacomet, Stefanie. 2007. Neolithic Plant Economies in the Northern Alpine Foreland (Central Europe) from 5500–3500 BC cal. In *The Origins and Spread of Domestic Plants in Southwest Asia and Europe*, edited by Sue Colledge and James Conolly, 221–58. Walnut Creek, CA: Left Coast Press.

———. 2009. Plant Economies and Village Life in Neolithic Lake Dwellings at the Time of the Alpine Iceman. *Vegetation History and Archaeobotany* 18(1):47–59.

Jacomet, Stefanie, Malgorzata Latalowa, and Felix Bittmann, eds. 2014. The Potential of Palaeoecological Studies in Archaeological Wetland Sites of the Southern Baltic Sea Regions. *Vegetation History and Archaeobotany* 23(4):339–40.

Menotti, Francesco, and Aidan O'Sullivan. 2013. *The Oxford Handbook of Wetland Archaeology*. Oxford: Oxford University Press.

■ STEFANIE JACOMET

Figure 37. Imprint of a wheat ear, possibly *Triticum durum*, on the bottom of a ceramic pot from the site of Arbon-Bleiche 3, a late Neolithic circum-Alpine, pile-dwelling settlement (dated by dendrochronology between 3384 and 3370 BC) on the southeast shore of Lake Constance, Canton Thurgau, Switzerland. Photograph by Daniel Steiner. Courtesy of Amt für Archäologie Thurgau, Switzerland.

Figure 38. Organic materials, including food remains such as seeds, fruit stones, and cereal chaff, are often preserved in a waterlogged state. Excavations of a Neolithic pile-dwelling at the site of Riedmatt, Canton Zug, Switzerland (3230 cal BC), revealed broken pottery, charcoal, and faunal remains among the preserved posts. Photograph by Rolf Glauser (†) (Archiv Archäologie). Courtesy of Amt für Denkmalpflege und Archäologie, Kanton Zug, Direktion des Innern, Switzerland.

LANDSCAPE AND ENVIRONMENTAL RECONSTRUCTION

Landscape in archaeology refers most fundamentally to the physical or natural world that is the backdrop for human activities. Landscape is also defined as the relationship between people and the places they inhabit, especially the ways people conceptually organize space and give meaning to their surroundings. Landscapes are physical (landforms and vistas), biological (plants and animals), and ideological (imbued with cultural meaning). The role that landscape plays in food and foodways is profound, as the production of food is intricately linked to both the physical environment and people's beliefs about their relationships with the land. Because landscapes of food production are anthropogenic (human created), reconstruction of these environments is an important tool for understanding past cultures.

Some food plants may have originated in people's unconscious activities in the landscape. For example, a domesticated form of goosefoot (*Chenopodium berlandieri* ssp. *jonesianum*), which provided nutritious seeds and greens, was domesticated in northeastern North America by 2,500 BP. It underwent genetic modification as a result of human activities and likely began the domestication process as a weedy camp follower—a plant whose germination and growth was encouraged by disturbed ground. The seedbed hypothesis suggests that competition for faster germination among weedy plants that are associated with disturbed areas, such as those around human settlements, facilitated humans' use and led to plant domestication.

Deliberate management of vegetation was a common way people engaged and modified landscapes for food. Prior to the arrival of Europeans, native peoples of North America burned brush-filled environments to increase deer populations and to encourage certain plants such as nut-bearing trees or plants that yield fruits or tubers. This management technique created the parklike landscape noted by early European explorers. In swidden, or slash-and-burn, agriculture, people clear areas of dense forests for small gardens or fields. This practice is common in tropical areas and transforms plant communities in ways that leave traces for generations.

Some food production activities have left highly visible, enduring impacts on the geophysical landscape. People in the Andes, throughout Southeast Asia, and in the Philippines constructed extensive terraces for fields of rice, barley, wheat, and maize. These terraces reduced the angle of slopes and greatly increased agricultural productivity in mountainous regions. One complex of terraces in the Philippines has been in use for 2,000 years and has been designated a World Heritage Site. The Peruvian Andes has particularly extensive and complex systems of land and water control features: raised fields, rain-fed and irrigated terraces, and irrigation canals. Other anthropogenic features raised the productivity of landscapes, including *chinampas* in the Valley of Mexico and gravel mulch gardens created by ancestral Pueblo peoples.

People's relationship with the landscape is not limited to altering their environment. For some societies, features of the landscape provide cues for food-producing or food-gathering activities. For example, the Wampanoag peoples of New England told 17th-century French explorer Samuel de Champlain that they planted corn (maize) when oak leaves were the size of a squirrel's foot, and the Arrernte of Australia use the acacia to indicate when game animals are good to hunt.

Embedded in anthropogenic landscapes are social and political meanings. During the 17th century, native peoples of New England planted orchards as one way of demonstrating ownership and control over traditional lands in the face of an encroaching colonial government. Environmental reconstruction of the spaces surrounding historic-period house lots in New England has allowed researchers to explore changes to food production that accompanied urbanization and the development of a middle class.

The broad range of activities relating food and landscape calls for the application of a variety of analytical tools. Methods may include geophysical and topographic mapping surveys. Satellite imagery and LiDAR (light detecting and ranging) not only map the geophysical aspects of terrain such as topography and terraces but also can be used to analyze vegetation cover to identify anthropogenic ecosystems. Sedimentation rates in lake cores from central Mexico were used to explore the impact of different land-use regimes: maize agriculture under the Aztecs and animal husbandry and plow agriculture under Spanish colonists. Studies of domestication and food production use a variety of botanical and faunal methods. Macrobotanical (seeds and larger plant parts) analysis is typically used to explore the morphological changes that accompany plant domestication. Palynology (pollen analysis) has been used to identify the production of crops and ritually important plants such as cotton in gravel mulch gardens in the American Southwest. Microscopic wood charcoal from sediments provides evidence of the use of fire as a land management tool.

Environmental reconstructions frequently employ botanical analyses to re-create past vegetation as a proxy for the environment as a whole. Palynology is perhaps the most common tool, but phytoliths (silicate deposits in plant cells) have been important for identifying grasslands and in tropical areas where pollen may not preserve well. Starch grains are used to specifically identify food components as well as general vegetation. Microfauna (e.g., snails and insects) are useful for reconstructing localized environments. Because of the highly specific niches they occupy, some beetles are particularly helpful for determining anthropogenic environments associated with food, such as storerooms or house interiors, or determining the presence or the condition of foods such as spoiled grains.

Recent trends in landscape analysis emphasize methodological advances for mapping the physical environment, such as LiDAR. GIS (geographic information system) has become an important tool for examining agricultural features, such as irrigation canals, gravel mulch gardens, and terraces, and their relationship to the landscape. Recent work has concentrated on increasing temporal and spatial resolution to provide more precise reconstructions and employing cross-disciplinary analyses. Combinations of methods, pollen, charcoal, chironomids (midges), fauna, and sediments have been particularly useful for examining the dramatic changes in landscapes associated with the Viking occupation of Iceland. Research questions also focus on social aspects, exploring such issues as the construction of landscapes to provide visible manifestations of social power and the creation of sacred and profane spaces.

See also AGRICULTURAL FEATURES, IDENTIFICATION AND ANALYSIS; AGRICULTURAL/HORTICULTURAL SITES; ARCHAEOBOTANY; IRRIGATION/HYDRAULIC ENGINEERING; MULTI- AND

Interdisciplinary Approaches; Palynology; Phytolith Analysis; Plant Domestication; Soil Microtechniques; Spatial Analysis and Visualization Techniques;
Zooarchaeology

Further Reading

Anschuetz, Kurt F., Richard H. Wilshusen, and Cherie L. Scheick. 2001. An Archaeology of Landscapes:
   Perspectives and Directions. *Journal of Archaeological Research* 9(2):157–211.
Bain, Allison. 1998. A Seventeenth-Century Beetle Fauna from Colonial Boston. *Historical Archaeology*
   32(3):38–48.
Chase, Arlen F., Diane Z. Chase, John F. Weishampel, et al. 2011. Airborne LiDAR, Archaeology, and the
   Ancient Maya Landscape at Caracol, Belize. *Journal of Archaeological Science* 38(2):387–98.

■ HEATHER B. TRIGG AND DAVID B. LANDON

LATRINES AND SEWER SYSTEMS

Throughout history, as groups of people came to live together by the hundreds and then
thousands, close living conditions increased the risk of epidemics and water pollution,
making efficient waste disposal essential. As human settlements became larger and more
complex, the problem of disposing of liquid and solid waste became ever more pressing.
Latrines and sewer systems represent intentional and more permanent efforts to deal with
this issue. These sites are primary sources of evidence for the foodways, dietary practices,
and health of past populations. Related features, such as drainage ditches, also hold considerable evidence of these food-related practices.

Some of the earliest evidence of organized waste disposal comes from the Palace of
Knossos (2000–1700 BC), the center of Minoan civil and religious power. Both a water
supply system and sewage disposal system were constructed. Rainwater was stored in
cisterns and was then made available, via terra-cotta pipes, for a variety of uses including
flushing latrines, while wastewater was channeled out into the river. It was not until the
rise of the city of Rome that another such complex sewage system was created, this time
on a larger scale. By the sixth century BC, channels had been dug to drain the marshland
on the edge of the settlement; residents also used these ditches to dispose of their waste.
Conduits were constructed along main roads within the city to allow water to empty
into the Cloaca Maxima, the huge drain that led to the Tiber River. Over the centuries,
the Romans became ever more accomplished at hydraulic engineering, organizing their
towns with complex water supply systems, including aqueducts built both below and
above ground. In parallel, they organized water drainage via sewer systems that ran under
the streets, and although these were created primarily to service public buildings, they
were eventually connected to many private houses.

The cities destroyed by the eruption of Vesuvius in AD 79 provide unique insight into
many aspects of daily life in the Roman period, including the problem of waste disposal.
The recently excavated sewer under the Cardo V street in Herculaneum was the repository
for waste from an entire urban block, known as the Insula Orientalis II (figure 39). Chutes
from latrines and kitchens were channeled into it, not only from the ground floor but also
from at least three upper floors that made up the Insula Orientalis II building. The absence

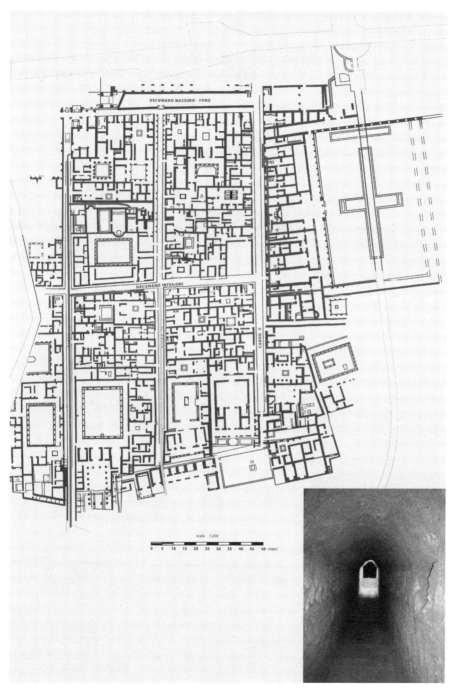

Figure 39. Plan of the archaeological site of Herculaneum. Branches of the town's sewer that have been investigated are shown in dark gray; the hypothesized sewer branch under Cardo IV is indicated in light gray; the water drainage channels that ran along the sides of the Decumanus Maximus are indicated by a solid black line. Drawing by D. Camardo based on A. Maiuri, *Ercolano*, Tav. V (Rome 1958). Inset: The sewer under Herculaneum's street known as Cardo III. Photograph by D. Camardo/Herculaneum Conservation Project.

of an outlet toward the sea suggests that it was a closed system, more like a large septic tank. Built in the Claudian period, the sewer gathered material via a system of chutes, tunnels, and precisely calculated sloping surfaces. Sewage would have built up in a large conduit that must have been periodically emptied by gaining entry via inspection hatches located within many of the insula's ground-floor shops. The sediment that built up beneath the Cardo V was 80–135 centimeters deep and was formed mainly of organic material and kitchen waste that was probably used to fertilize agricultural land. This deposit was sealed by the volcanic material of the AD 79 eruption. In total, 775 sacks of organic sediment were excavated, each one containing about 15 liters of material. A first campaign of wet sieving of nearly 10 percent of the sediment revealed eggshells, poppy seeds, fig seeds, olive pits, fish scales and bones, small animal and bird bones, sea urchin spines, and seafood shells.

Various types of latrines, preserved by the volcanic eruption, were connected to the Herculaneum sewer system, and parallels can be found with the latrines at Pompeii. In Herculaneum, 83 latrines have been identified in the houses, shops, and public buildings of the excavated area (figure 40). Latrines seem to have been an important feature of the Romans' homes, given that almost every house in Herculaneum had one or more of them. The most common type of latrine found on the ground floor was a small cubicle in which a seat (a wooden board with a central hole cut into it) was installed. In most cases the cubicle was built within a larger room used as a kitchen, with which it shared waste chutes. This type of latrine had a floor paved with tiles that sloped down toward

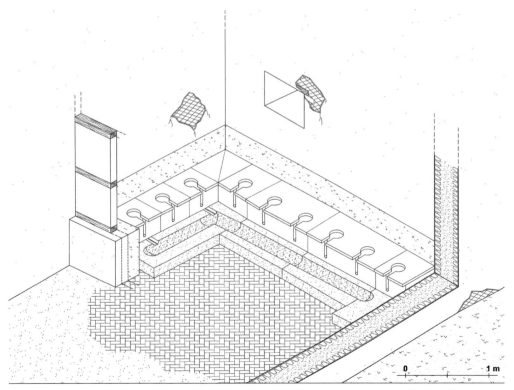

Figure 40. Reconstruction of the public latrine found in Herculaneum's Central Baths. Drawing by Mario Notomista/Herculaneum Conservation Project.

the chute. Buckets of water would have been used to wash the waste down the chute and into the public sewer or cesspit. On the upper floors, a niche latrine was most commonly used. In this case the wooden toilet seat was installed within a small niche. The hole in the seat was placed directly above the waste chute so that the excrement would have fallen directly down the chute to a sewer or cesspit. These latrines would also have needed water to work properly. Along with traces of organic remains that line the route down to the sewer, lime-scale buildup can be seen within the downpipes, a clear sign that water constantly flowed down them. Further analysis of the material collected from the excavation of the sewer beneath Cardo V and the town's many latrines, both private and public, is expected to produce significant information on the diet and health of the ancient population of Herculaneum.

See also ARCHAEOBOTANY; FLOTATION; HERCULANEUM AND POMPEII; MANURING AND SOIL ENRICHMENT PRACTICES; MIDDENS AND OTHER TRASH DEPOSITS; PALEODIETARY ANALYSIS; PALEOFECAL ANALYSIS; PALEONUTRITION; WATER SUPPLY AND STORAGE

Further Reading

Camardo, Domenico. 2006. Water Supply and Drainage at Herculaneum. In *Cura Aquarum in Ephesus*, vol. 1, edited by Gilbert Wiplinger, 183–191. Leuven: Peeters.

Hobson, Barry. 2009. *Latrinae et Foricae: Toilets in the Roman World*. London: Gerald Duckworth.

Jansen, Gemma C. M., Ann Olga Koloski-Ostrow, and Eric M. Moormann, eds. 2011. *Roman Toilets: Their Archaeology and Cultural History*. Leuven: Peeters.

Maiuri, Amedeo. 1958. *Ercolano*, Tav. V. Rome: Instituto Poligrafico della Stato.

■ DOMENICO CAMARDO

LEGUMES AND PULSES

Legumes, plants belonging to the Leguninosae family, and pulses, or legumes that are grown primarily for their seeds, have formed staples for human societies since prehistoric times. Pulse seeds are a frequent find at archaeological sites, while pod preservation is extremely rare. Pulse seed consumption has provided human populations with plant protein, complementing starch intake from cereals, while cultivation of pulses in rotation with cereals has helped to secure soil nutrient availability.

Near Eastern hunter-gatherers of the Paleolithic were harvesting wild lentils at Kebara (50,000 BP) and wild bitter vetch at Ohalo (23,000 BP) (Israel). Wild pulses also were harvested by early cultivators of the region around 12,000 years ago. Most specialists consider cultivation of wild pulses a prerequisite of domestication, though Ladizinsky has argued that domestication traits in some wild pulse species like lentils could have developed prior to cultivation. For most pulse species of western Asia and Europe, the wild progenitors and their modern geographic distribution are known. Some, like wild pea, are thought to have originated within the Fertile Crescent; others extended farther north, or had a narrow geographical distribution (e.g., wild chickpea). Wild pulses were also harvested by Mesolithic inhabitants of prehistoric sites of the Mediterranean such as Franchthi Cave (Greece) and Grotta del Uzzo (Sicily).

Morphological traits, including a very gradual increase of seed size and reduction of seed-coat thickness, are used to identify the transition from wild to domesticated species. Domesticated lentils (*Lens culinaris*), peas (*Pisum sativum*), chickpeas (*Cicer arietinum*), and bitter vetch (*Vicia ervilia*) are considered to be components of the Near Eastern Neolithic "package" that spread with agriculture from the Near East to Europe (seventh millennium BC onward) and other areas of the Old World. Divergences from this model occur, however, such as the near absence of chickpea and the common presence of grass pea, which is not a "package" species, in Neolithic southeastern Europe. Celtic beanlike seeds (*Vicia faba*), either a wild form or in incipient cultivation, were harvested 11,000 years ago in northwest Syria and Israel; this species is also known from Mesolithic and Early Neolithic settlements of the western part of the Mediterranean but is absent from the Neolithic of Greece and Bulgaria. In the Bronze Age (third to early first millennium BC), it was cultivated in Greece and parts of central Europe but not in Bulgaria. During the Bronze Age, systematic cultivation of Cyprus vetch (*Lathyrus ochrus*) and Spanish vetchling (*Lathyrus clymenum*) was practiced on the Aegean islands, and the use of the latter is also attested in the Levant. Today these are minor food crops of the Aegean. Other pulse species that were brought into cultivation in the Near East and the Mediterranean include fenugreek, lupins, and common vetch.

In South Asia indigenous pulse species were brought into cultivation from the third millennium BC onward, around the same time that pulses of western Asian origin appear in parts of India. Mung bean (*Vigna radiata*) was a major Neolithic crop in south India and perhaps the western Himalayan foothills. Other Indian pulses encountered in the archaeobotanical record include horsegram (*Macrotyloma uniflorum*, 2500 BC), moth bean (*Vigna aconitifolia*), urd bean (*Vigna mungo*), and pigeonpea (*Cajanus cajan*, mid- to late second millennium BC). Some of the pulses of South Asia, such as cowpea (*Vigna unguiculata*) and hyacinth bean (*Lablab purpureus* [L.] Sweet), may have originated in Africa, though adequate archaeobotanical data are lacking at present. Cowpea has been found in Ghana as early as the second millennium BC. Cowpea and horsegram probably spread from India to Southeast Asia. Southeast Asian pulses, including soybean (*Glycine max*) and the azuki bean (*Vigna angularis*), are encountered in the archaeobotanical records of prehistoric Korea, China, and Japan. Their exploitation goes back to approximately 9,000 years and 5,000 years ago, respectively; both were domesticated in several locations in East Asia.

In America various bean species, including common bean (*Phaseolus vulgaris*) and lima bean (*P. lunatus*), appear to have been domesticated independently in both Mexico and the Andes, as indicated by analyses of modern cultivated and wild populations of this species. AMS (accelerator mass spectrometry) dates from Mesoamerican common beans do not provide evidence for their cultivation prior to 2,500 years ago in Mexico, while earlier dates are available for domesticated common and lima beans in the Peruvian Andes and coastal Peru (3,500–5,600 BP).

Evidence for processing and cooking pulses for human consumption is usually inferred by the properties of the different species, from modern culinary practice, and from ethnographic accounts. Ancient Greek and Roman texts also provide information on the status of pulses as food, methods of cooking, and their use in soups, as roasted snacks, or as flour for bread making. Grass pea and bitter vetch (usually considered a fodder crop) were probably detoxified by soaking or boiling in water, as well as by removal of the seed coat through grinding. Split bitter vetch seeds, probably treated with hot water, have been identified at the Early Bronze Age (third millennium BC) site of Agios Athanasios in northern Greece, while pulse flour has been identified at Bronze Age Akrotiri (mid-second millennium BC) on the island of Santorini. Splitting of pulses reduces both toxicity and cooking time and increases digestibility. The resulting mushy dish is still consumed in different parts of the Old World (*fava*, modern Greece; *dhal*, India).

See also ARCHAEOBOTANY; BEAN/COMMON BEAN; CULTIVATION; FRANCHTHI CAVE; MACRO-REMAINS; NEOLITHIC PACKAGE; PLANT DOMESTICATION; PLANT PROCESSING; WILD PROGENITORS OF DOMESTICATED PLANTS

Further Reading

Castillo, Cristina, and Dorian Q Fuller. 2010. Still Too Fragmentary and Dependent upon Chance? Advances in the Study of Early Southeast Asian Archaeobotany. In *50 Years of Archaeology in Southeast Asia: Essays in Honour of Ian Glover*, edited by Bérénice Bellina, Elisabeth A. Bacus, Thomas Oliver Pryce, and Jan Wisseman Christie, 92–111. Bangkok: River Books.

Flint-Hamilton, Kimberly B. 1999. Legumes in Ancient Greece and Rome: Food, Medicine or Poison? *Hesperia* 68(3):371–85.

Fuller, Dorian Q, and Emma L. Harvey. 2006. The Archaeobotany of Indian Pulses: Identification, Processing and Evidence for Cultivation. *Environmental Archaeology* 11(2):219–46.

Kislev, M. E. 1989. Origins of the Cultivation of *Lathyrus sativus* and *L. cicera* (Fabaceae). *Economic Botany* 43(2):262–70.

Lee, Gyoung-Ah. 2013. Archaeological Perspectives on the Origins of Azuki (*Vigna angularis*). *Holocene* 23(3):453–59.

Lee, Gyoung-Ah, Gary W. Crawford, Li Liu, et al. 2011. Archaeological Soybean (*Glycine max*) in East Asia: Does Size Matter? *PLoS ONE* 6(11):e26720. doi:10.1371/journal.pone.0026720.

Valamoti, Soultana Maria, Aikaterini Moniaki, and Angeliki Karathanou. 2011. An Investigation of Processing and Consumption of Pulses among Prehistoric Societies: Archaeobotanical, Experimental and Ethnographic Evidence from Greece. *Vegetation History and Archaeobotany* 20(5):381–96.

Zohary, Daniel, Maria Hopf, and Ehud Weiss. 2012. *Domestication of Plants in the Old World*. 4th edition. Oxford: Oxford University Press.

■ SOULTANA MARIA VALAMOTI

LIPIDS
See BIOMOLECULAR ANALYSIS

LITHICS
See TOOLS/UTENSILS, STONE; USE-WEAR ANALYSIS, LITHICS; WEAPONS, STONE

LOW-LEVEL FOOD PRODUCTION
See CULTIVATION; PLANT HUSBANDRY

M

MACROBOTANICAL REMAINS
See MACROREMAINS

MACROFLORAL REMAINS
See MACROREMAINS

MACROREMAINS

Macroremains are remnants of plants that are recovered from archaeological contexts and can be observed by the naked eye or under low-power magnification. They range from tiny seeds to large wooden beams, and include a wide array of resources such as wood, bark, stems, leaves, nutshells, fruits, seeds, and tubers, as well as other plant parts and tissues. Today it is widely recognized that macroremains provide the kind of data needed to answer questions about diet, origins of food production, diffusion of cultigens, biodiversity, land-use strategies, medicinal and ritual practices, and technological and economic uses of plants.

Macroremains become a part of archaeological matrices through discard, loss, or abandonment. They can survive the physical and chemical ravages of time if carbonized, desiccated, frozen, or waterlogged. These natural processes inhibit the growth of decomposers like bacteria or saprophytic fungi, slow the rate of enzyme action, and lower the speed at which chemical reactions occur. Desiccation, quick-freezing, and waterlogging are remarkable for the types of plant tissue preserved, if not for the sheer abundance of material. Most macrobotanical remains are derived from open-air archaeological sites in mesic or moderately moist contexts, however, where they are subjected to a host of small organisms that facilitate decomposition and to oscillations between wet and dry regimes that increase their susceptibility to chemical decomposition.

Prior to excavation, decisions need to be made on how much and from what contexts macrobotanical samples will be collected. Sampling strategies keep processing and analysis from reaching unmanageable proportions, while affording an assemblage that is representative of the total population of plant remains at a site. A thorough consideration of research questions should guide one's choices. Sampling strategies can be combined into two basic groups: sediment column sampling, used to establish broad, diachronic trends, and horizontal sampling, used to answer synchronic questions about diet and nutrition.

A decision needs to be made about how the macroremains will be recovered. Macroremains can be retrieved by hand, in the screen, or via flotation samples (i.e., block units of sediment are removed and taken to the lab for processing). When choosing a retrieval method or combination of methods, the biases of each should be considered. For example, hand collection and screening are biased toward larger, readily visible plant remains. In the case of field screening, the collected remains will be those pieces with a minimum dimension greater than the size of the mesh. Flotation, although not without its own biases, makes it possible to collect even the tiniest of macroremains. Because macrobotanical remains can be preserved in different states—carbonized, desiccated, frozen, waterlogged—one also needs to consider preservation when planning for the collection of remains. While it may be acceptable to "float" carbonized macrobotanical remains, the water used in the flotation process may cause desiccated tissues to expand and fracture. To facilitate the separation of desiccated plant remains from their dirt matrix, it may be wiser to dry-screen samples through a nest of progressively smaller geological sieves. When handling waterlogged remains, it becomes essential to prevent them from drying out; drying can create conditions for decay and cause distortions that can impede identification. For similar reasons, the thawing of frozen macroremains requires special treatment.

Identification of macrobotanical remains requires access to comparative collections, as classification to botanical families, genera, species, and subspecies is accomplished mostly by visually comparing archaeological specimens to known specimens. Moreover, identification depends on the condition of the remains (how eroded or fragmented they may be) and on the abilities of the researcher to discern diagnostic attributes.

Quantification can be problematic. For example, how does one quantify fragments of seeds or wood? Counts and weights are often used, despite the fact that absolute measures are heavily influenced by factors such as preservation and sampling. While they do not necessarily alleviate all the biases, manipulations of counts and weights (e.g., conversion factors, diversity indices, rankings, ratios, and ubiquity measure) do help to standardize the remains. Even more sophisticated statistics like multivariate analysis, while useful, do not preclude the biasing of plant assemblages by cultural, natural, or analytical processes that may ultimately influence interpretations.

Problem orientation and subsequent interpretations are project-specific and are structured as much by theoretical perspectives as by available time and money. While one may never realize all the nuances of past human-plant interrelationships, studies of macroremains, especially when combining other analyses (e.g., pollen, phytoliths, starch grains, DNA, and residues), can result in sophisticated understandings of the dynamic relationship between past peoples and plants.

See also ARCHAEOBOTANY; FEDDERSEN WIERDE; FLOTATION; HAITHABU/HEDEBY; LAKE VILLAGES; OEDENBURG; QUSEIR AL-QADIM

Further Reading

Beck, Wendy. 2006. Plant Remains. In *Archaeology in Practice: A Student Guide to Archaeological Analyses*, edited by Jane Balme and Alistair Paterson, 296–315. Malden, MA: Blackwell.

Fritz, Gayle J. 2005. Paleoethnobotanical Methods and Applications. In *Handbook of Archaeological Methods*, vol. 2, edited by Herbert D. G. Maschner and Christopher Chippindale, 773–834. Lanham, MD: AltaMira Press.

Lennstrom, Heidi A., and Christine A. Hastorf. 1995. Interpretation in Its Context: Sampling and Analysis in Paleoethnobotany. *American Antiquity* 60(4):701–21.

Pearsall, Deborah M. 2000. *Paleoethnobotany: A Handbook of Procedures*. 2nd edition. San Diego, CA: Academic Press.

Sobilik, Kristin D. 2003. *Archaeobiology*. Archaeologist's Toolkit 5. Walnut Creek, CA: AltaMira Press.

Van Zeist, Willem, Krystyna Wasylikowa, and Karl Ernst Behre, eds. 1991. *Progress in Old World Paleoethnobotany*. Rotterdam: A. A. Balkema.

Wright, Patti J. 2010. On Methodological Issues in Paleoethnobotany: A Consideration of Issues, Methods, and Cases. In *Integrating Zooarchaeology and Paleoethnobotany*, edited by Tanya M. Peres and Amber M. VanDerwarker, 37–64. New York: Springer.

■ PATTI J. WRIGHT

MAIZE

Maize, beans, squash, chili peppers, and tomatoes have been the primary staples of New World foodways for millennia. Archaeologists have long maintained that maize, the major Mesoamerican food staple, played a central role in the shift to agricultural subsistence, sedentism, social stratification, and precocious ceramic innovation throughout the Americas. The economic importance of maize has been linked to processing technologies and associated material culture in the archaeological record. Isotopic signatures from the bones of ancient skeletons document the earliest evidence of maize-based subsistence economies and long-term economic dependence.

Maize or corn (*Zea mays* L.) is monophyletic. It arose from a single domestication event ca. 7,000 years ago, a direct descendant of an annual grass, teosinte (*Zea mays* ssp. *parviglumis*), a wild grass native to the Balsas River drainage in southern Mexico. The genus *Zea* includes cultivated maize (*Z. mays* ssp. *mays*), and the various subspecies of teosintes are classified as members of the grass family *Poaceae*. The fruit of *Poaceae* is a caryopsis, that is, it has the appearance of a seed. All taxa of *Zea* have a central spike or terminal branch, which is a continuation of the central inflorescence axis or rachis. Teosinte has male and female flowers on the same branch and kernels encased in a hard outer casing called a glume. Maize is highly branched, with a male inflorescence (tassel) on its central branch and female inflorescences (cobs) on auxiliary branches. Maize male inflorescences (tassels) are distinguished by a stiffer, stronger, and more densely beset central terminal spike, with more highly exaggerated and slender lateral branches than subspecies of other *Zea* taxon. While maize seed dispersal is totally dependent upon humans, teosinte fruit cases are not. Maize is highly mutagenic; kernel color and ear morphology are directly affected by wind pollen from maize cultivated in surrounding fields.

The origins of maize have been a matter of considerable scientific debate, largely because of its phenotypic characteristics versus those of teosinte and its importance as a food crop. While theories of a wild maize ancestor have been largely discarded, there is no archaeological evidence from early cave and rockshelter sites such as Guilá Naquitz or those in the Tehuacán Valley to suggest that teosinte fruit cases were exploited for food.

Some archaeologists maintain that instead teosinte was exploited initially for its stalk sugar for use as a condiment or for fermentation, and archaeological evidence indicates that early on maize stalks were chewed and perhaps used to make intoxicants such as *pulque*. The Tehuacán Valley sequences show that maize subsequently became an important food source and a staple by ca. 1500 BC.

The domestication of food crops like maize represents a process of evolutionary change involving the genetics of plant populations. These changes are primarily in response to human influence or conscious selection for certain favorable traits, or unconscious selection—that is, genetic responses to human modification of the environment or management of reproduction. The gradual interdependence and changes in adaptation associated with plant domestication involve a shift to sedentary, permanent settlements associated with rivers and streams and away from the mobile lifestyles of hunters and gatherers. Archaeologists have long maintained that ceramic technology and grinding stones (*manos*, *metates*) at New World archaeological sites developed simultaneously and that these material forms and technologies are emblematic of maize-based agricultural economies. Ceramic containers and processing stones were seen as essential for processing this food crop into flour for mass consumption. With the advent of ^{14}C dating, however, multidisciplinary research at numerous Mexican rockshelters and caves indicates that maize appeared long before the associated processing tools.

Recent advances in scientific analyses and increased understanding of the plant itself suggest the role of maize as a food source was more complex than previously understood. In Mesoamerica, maize cultivation was accompanied by the adoption of nixtamalization. *Nixtamal* is a Nahuatl term that refers to the preparation of maize kernels by soaking or cooking in an alkali solution using limewater (calcium hydroxide) and wood ash (potassium hydroxide). Processing releases enzymes and niacin (vitamin B3) that enhance the absorption of amino acids. Mycotoxins such as molds and fungi are reduced by 90–94 percent. Thus maize consumed as tamales, tortillas, hominy, and so on is significantly more nutritious, with an improved and enhanced flavor and aroma. Maize as flour (i.e., tamales or tortillas) is indigenous to Mesoamerican cuisines. Recent stable carbon isotope, molecular, and ethnobotanical evidence indicates that previous assumptions regarding the economic importance of unprocessed maize to prehistoric cultures needs to be reassessed, however, particularly theories that processed maize was necessary for the development of complex societies in Mesoamerica.

Research surrounding the origins of maize has been critical to understanding the shift from hunting and gathering to agricultural economies. Our current perceptions regarding its economic importance are largely based upon scientific research on the plant itself. New analytical techniques, however, including isotopic analysis of bone collagen and residue analysis of ancient pottery, now allow us to look directly at diet and foodways, adding to our understanding of the complexity of this human–plant relationship. Future research will be able to directly document the economic importance and various roles of maize in ancient economies throughout the Americas, and to more precisely determine its importance to the development of social complexity and the sudden collapse of Pre-Columbian cultures.

See also AGRICULTURE, ORIGINS OF; ARCHAEOBOTANY; BEAN/COMMON BEAN; *CHICHA*; DNA ANALYSIS; FOOD PRODUCTION AND THE FORMATION OF COMPLEX SOCIETIES; GUILÁ NAQUITZ; MESOAMERICAN ARCHAIC-PERIOD DIET; NIXTAMALIZATION; PLANT DOMESTI-CATION; PLANT PROCESSING; *PULQUE*; QUIDS; RESIDUE ANALYSIS, STARCH; STABLE ISOTOPE ANALYSIS; TEHUACÁN VALLEY

Further Reading

Byers, Douglas S., ed. 1967. *The Prehistory of the Tehuacán Valley.* Vol. 1, *Environment and Subsistence.* Austin: University of Texas Press.

Flannery, Kent V., ed. 1986. *Guilá Naquitz: Archaic Foraging and Early Agriculture in Oaxaca.* San Diego, CA: Academic Press.

MacNeish, Richard S. 1992. *The Origins of Agriculture and Settled Life.* Norman: University of Oklahoma Press.

Staller, John E. 2010. *Maize Cobs and Cultures: History of Zea mays L.* Berlin: Springer.

Staller, John E., Robert H. Tykot, and Bruce F. Benz, eds. 2006. *Histories of Maize: Multidisciplinary Approaches to the Prehistory, Linguistics, Biogeography, Domestication, and Evolution of Maize.* Walnut Creek, CA: Left Coast Press.

■ JOHN E. STALLER

MANIOC/CASSAVA

Cassava or manioc (*Manihot esculenta* Crantz, Euphorbiaceae) is the third most important source of calories in the tropics after rice and maize. A woody shrub grown for its starchy, tuberous roots, the cassava plant is tolerant of drought and acidic, nutrient-poor soils, making it a cheap and reliable source of carbohydrates for some of the world's poorest populations. While native to the New World, cassava is grown throughout the humid tropics worldwide. Plants are propagated by stem cuttings, with roots typically harvested several months after planting. Cassava varieties are numerous and vary tremendously in growth habit, leaf and root morphology, and agroecological adaptation, as well as in levels of potentially toxic cyanogenic glucosides. Varieties have traditionally been classified as either "sweet" (low cyanide) or "bitter" (high cyanide); the former may be consumed after simply boiling the root, while the latter require additional processing (including grating and soaking in water or fermentation) prior to consumption. There is little evidence that the bitter/sweet classification reflects genetically distinct subgroups within the crop. Once harvested, cassava roots are highly perishable, and as a consequence the crop tends to be grown either by subsistence farmers for local consumption or industrially for processing into tapioca and other starch products.

Until the last two decades, very little was known about cassava's center of domestication or early cultivation history. As a crop of humid lowlands, archaeobotanical preservation is poor, and well-preserved remains tend to come from arid sites that do not reflect the crop's earliest use. A compounding problem is that archaeobotanical data, where available, have suggested an early and rapid spread following cassava's domestication, further hindering efforts to trace its origin and diffusion. Traditional botanical data (e.g., morphological characters) offered little resolution in identifying cassava's closest wild relatives or likely center of domestication. The genus *Manihot* comprises approximately 98 species distributed from the southern United States to Argentina—many of which, like cassava, are highly variable morphologically. In the absence of a readily recognized direct wild ancestor, researchers proposed multiple hybridization events, potentially involving species distributed throughout the neotropics.

Advances in our understanding of cassava's origin and early history have come from two complementary areas of research: evolutionary genetics and archaeobotanical analysis. Beginning in the 1990s, molecular genetic data were used to examine cassava's evolutionary relationship to wild *Manihot* species. Comparisons of DNA sequences and other genetic markers between cassava and wild *Manihot* species revealed that the crop is not a hybrid but rather is derived from a single wild species in South America, *M. esculenta* ssp. *flabellifolia* (Pohl) Ciferri, and that domestication most likely occurred in a region along the southern border of the Amazon basin.

Documentation of the crop's postdomestication diffusion has been greatly facilitated by methodological developments in archaeobotanical starch grain analysis. These have permitted the recovery and identification of cassava starch grains, even in the absence of recognizable macrobotanical remains. Starch grain data provide clear evidence that cassava was already widely cultivated throughout Mesoamerica and Central and South America by 6,500 BP. At sites in the Peruvian coastal zone (e.g., Quebrada de las Pircas in the Zaña Valley), cassava remains have been dated to ca. 7,950 ± 180 BP; this suggests that cassava's earliest cultivation in the Amazonian lowlands must have been even earlier. Further from the center of origin, cassava starch grains recovered from grinding stones in the Porce and Cuaca Valleys of north-central Colombia have been dated to ca. 7,500 BP. In Central America, cassava starch grains from the Aguadulce site in Panama are approximately 6,900 years old. Within the Caribbean, cassava starch grains isolated from processing tools in Puerto Rico have been dated to ~3,300–2,900 BP. Pollen grains also indicate an early diffusion, with pollen that is likely to be from domesticated cassava dating to ~5,800 BP and 4,500 BP in archaeological contexts along the Gulf Coast of Mexico and Belize, respectively. Thus, while archaeological evidence within cassava's Amazonian center of origin remains scarce, data from outside this region leave little doubt as to this crop's early domestication and rapid dissemination throughout the New World tropics.

See also ARCHAEOBOTANY; BIOMOLECULAR ANALYSIS; DNA ANALYSIS; PALYNOLOGY; PLANT DOMESTICATION; PLANT PROCESSING; RESIDUE ANALYSIS, STARCH; ROOT CROPS/TUBERS; STARCHES, ROLE OF; TOOLS/UTENSILS, GROUND STONE

Further Reading

Isendahl, Christian. 2011. The Domestication and Early Spread of Manioc (*Manihot esculenta* Crantz): A Brief Synthesis. *Latin American Antiquity* 22(4):452–68.

Olsen, Kenneth M., and Barbara A. Schaal. 1999. Evidence on the Origin of Cassava: Phylogeography of *Manihot esculenta*. *Proceedings of the National Academy of Sciences USA* 96(10):5586–91.

Piperno, Dolores R. 2006. Identifying Manioc (*Manihot esculenta* Crantz) and Other Crops in Pre-Columbian Tropical America through Starch Grain Analysis: A Case Study from Central Panama. In *Documenting Domestication: New Genetic and Archaeological Paradigms*, edited by Melinda A. Zeder, Daniel G. Bradley, Eve Emshwaller, and Bruce D. Smith, 46–67. Berkeley: University of California Press.

■ KENNETH M. OLSEN

MANURES AND OTHER FERTILIZERS, IDENTIFICATION AND ANALYSIS

Aside from the reliance on ethnographic and written records, the use of fertilizers in archaeological contexts can largely be assessed in two ways. The first relies on the artifactual or morphological evidence of the deposition of soil amendments into contexts that are believed to have been gardens or agricultural fields. The second relies on chemical or molecular proxies that are indicative of the addition of particular amendments to the soil; these proxies may be applied to the cultivated areas (i.e., soils), to botanical materials, or to the tissues of humans or animals.

By virtue of their capacity to dissolve and release nutrients—characteristics that make them valuable in agriculture—fertilizers are unlikely to persist in the soil over archaeological timescales. Nevertheless, the presence of animal excreta in archaeological contexts has been deduced on the basis of a number of indicators: clear physical presence of the excreta (coprolites), spherulites (crystalline structures that form in animal guts), plant and arthropod remains (mites, dung beetles), spores of coprophilous fungi, and eggs of internal parasites. These indicators are generally consistent with the presence of animal waste but not necessarily of its use as a fertilizer. As such, they are highly dependent on solid contextual data.

The practice of amending the soil may take on a very specific tone, with the addition of fertilizers from particular sources, or it may be more generalized, incorporating a broad range of domestic refuse. In the latter case, fertilization may be identified by the presence of materials that are not necessarily fertilizers but are associated with domestic spaces. The wide dispersal of ceramic sherds or charred plant remains across large areas in the immediate vicinity of human occupations may represent the utilization of domestic refuse (including animal waste products) in intensive agriculture. Similarly, the wide distribution of highly fragmented bone is suggestive of the use of bone meal as a fertilizer (although the use of general household debris is also possible).

Several chemical or molecular markers have been employed to detect fertilization practices. Soil phosphate content is a general indicator of anthropogenic activity, including the deposition of organic fertilizers, but it cannot be unequivocally associated with the activity of fertilization. More specific animal fecal biomarkers have recently been employed, focusing on the detection of sterols and bile acids in sediments from archaeological contexts. These markers are excreted in the feces of mammals and are relatively resistant to degradation in comparison to other organic components of animal manure. In addition to detecting the presence of animal feces, the use of multiple biomarkers has the potential to distinguish fecal products derived from specific sources (e.g., cow and sheep vs. human, pig vs. human, mammal vs. bird).

Isotopic studies offer several potential means with which to detect prehistoric fertilization practices. The application of animal manures to agricultural fields tends to increase the nitrogen isotopic composition ($d^{15}N$) of plants. The magnitude of this difference varies strongly with the type and amount of fertilizer applied. The difference in $d^{15}N$ values between fertilized and unfertilized plants is relatively modest for manure derived from ruminant herbivores such as cattle, larger for manures derived from pigs and poultry, and extremely large for manure derived from seabird guano. Nitrogen isotopic analysis of human or animal remains can provide evidence of the use of fertilizers, but this is only clear when the fertilizer causes a large effect on plant $d^{15}N$ values and there are no other foods with similar carbon isotopic compositions (as is the case for C_3 plants fertilized with seabird guano). Where fertilizers cause more modest effects on plant $d^{15}N$ values, it is difficult to differentiate between the consumption of animal protein and fertilized plant protein on the basis of bulk isotopic data derived from animal tissues such as bone collagen. Nitrogen isotopic data have the potential to provide clearer evidence of past fertilization practices via the analysis of sediment profiles or archaeobotanical remains, provided that it can be demonstrated that the isotopic signature is not the product of post-depositional processes. Such data would be extremely valuable because they would provide very clear evidence that manures actually were used to fertilize crops, rather than simply documenting the local presence of manure.

See also AGRICULTURAL FEATURES, IDENTIFICATION AND ANALYSIS; BIOMOLECULAR ANALYSIS; LANDSCAPE AND ENVIRONMENTAL RECONSTRUCTION; MANURING AND SOIL ENRICHMENT PRACTICES; SOIL MICROTECHNIQUES; STABLE ISOTOPE ANALYSIS

Further Reading

Bogaard, A., T. H. E. Heaton, P. Poulton, and I. Merbach. 2007. The Impact of Manuring on Nitrogen Isotope Ratios in Cereals: Archaeological Implications for Reconstruction of Diet and Crop Management Practices. *Journal of Archaeological Science* 34(3):335–43.

Bull, Ian D., I. A. Simpson, P. F. van Bergen, and R. P. Evershed. 1999. Muck 'n' Molecules: Organic Geochemical Methods for Detecting Ancient Manuring. *Antiquity* 73(279):86–96.

Canti, M. G. 1999. The Production and Preservation of Faecal Spherulites: Animals, Environment and Taphonomy. *Journal of Archaeological Science* 26(3):251–58.

Holliday, Vance T., and William G. Gartner. 2007. Methods of Soil P Analysis in Archaeology. *Journal of Archaeological Science* 34(2):301–33.

Jones, Richard, ed. 2012. *Manure Matters: Historical, Archaeological and Ethnographic Perspectives.* Farnham, UK: Ashgate.

Miller, Naomi F., and Kathryn L. Gleason. 1994. Fertilizer in the Identification and Analysis of Cultivated Soil. In *The Archaeology of Garden and Field*, edited by Naomi F. Miller and Kathryn L. Gleason, 25–43. Philadelphia: University of Pennsylvania Press.

Shahack-Gross, Ruth. 2011. Herbivorous Livestock Dung: Formation, Taphonomy, Methods for Identification, and Archaeological Significance. *Journal of Archaeological Science* 38(2):205–18.

Szpak, Paul, Jean-Francois Millaire, Christine D. White, and Fred J. Longstaffe. 2012. Influence of Seabird Guano and Camelid Dung Fertilization on the Nitrogen Isotopic Composition of Field-Grown Maize (*Zea mays*). *Journal of Archaeological Science* 39(12):3721–40.

■ PAUL SZPAK

MANURING AND SOIL ENRICHMENT PRACTICES

Farmers have always drawn upon a wide array of materials to improve soil fertility and yields. The generation of human excreta, animal dung, and plant residues by all agrarian communities has ensured their universal application as manures irrespective of time and place. The precise quantities and ratios applied might vary considerably, however, depending on the balance and output of farming regimes, population size, cultural mores, religious tenets (resulting, for instance, in the avoidance or favoring of dung from particular animals), the sophistication of scientific knowledge, and health concerns. Furthermore, individual access to manure has always been influenced by social status, affluence, and size of landholding.

Across time, most agrarian economies have supplemented their basic manure supplies with other locally sourced materials including household detritus and food waste, although much of the latter often would be fed directly to animals. Lime and marl were favored dressings wherever geological deposits occurred. Peat and stubble were commonly burned and plowed into the soil. In coastal areas sand, shell, seaweed, and fish were regularly applied. The use of nitrogen-fixing plants such as lupins and clover is recorded from at least the Roman period; so too the application of bird guano. More recently, byproducts of industrial processes such as soap ashes, shoddy (waste wool clippings), malt dust, furriers' chippings, horn shavings, and fellmongers' cuttings (pieces of hides or skins that are being prepared for tanning) have added to the variety of manuring admixtures.

Historical documentation and ethnographic examples are extensive and warn against viewing manure as a simple fertilizer. From Poland to India, the size of one's manure heap has been used historically as an indicator of relative affluence. Biblical references associating dunghills with the salvation of the poor or places to which the rich fall have ensured that manure has carried a unique social and theological significance in Judeo-Christian contexts. Hindus understand the product of the sacred cow to be imbued with powers over and above its nutritional value. For Roman and medieval farmers (both Christian and Muslim), manure was spread according to elemental principles. Hot and moist animal dungs helped to balance cold and dry soils; fertilizers such as hearth ashes and pottery were applied to cold and wet soils, while cold and moist vegetal matter best enriched hot and dry fields. The timing of application also was dictated by season, by wind direction, and by the phases of the moon, the former since these too affected the balance between hot, cold, wet, and dry, the latter because the moon was thought to affect whether the nutritional value of the manure was drawn into (waning) or up from (waxing) the ground.

Until recently, it was difficult to augment these sources with archaeological data. Most manures are organic and rapidly degrade; few leave a visible trace in the archaeological record, although soil darkening can signal the application of humic-rich matter. The durability of inorganic materials such as pottery does allow the extent and timing of plowing episodes to be mapped where sherds have become integrated into the manure mix although the interpretation of this evidence remains problematic. In recent decades biological and geochemical analyses have begun to reveal the previously invisible signs of manuring. These include lipid and isotopic analyses, which hold the potential to identify the presence of human and animals fecal matter or the growing of nitrogen-fixing crops, respectively, and the study of plant and insect macrofossils, which has helped to pinpoint the use of stable manures and to locate midden sites. Dirt DNA, magnetic susceptibility, soil micromorphology, and total phosphate concentration, when used in combination with ethnographic and historical sources, have enabled geoarchaeologists to tease out local methods of manuring and the materials used. The potential of dirt DNA has recently been demonstrated in a study in Greenland proving the contribution of feces and urine from domestic animals in the preparation of cropping areas. Combinations of these methods have been deployed on the Scottish mainland and isles, as well as in the Netherlands, to investigate the creation of anthropogenic and plaggen soils (rich soils comprising peat and rotted stable bedding). Given cultural preferences as well as socioeconomic factors, health beliefs, and other influences on manuring practices, these scientific approaches offer new and exciting insights into the complex decisions taken by farmers in the past to maintain soil fertility.

See also AGRICULTURAL FEATURES, IDENTIFICATION AND ANALYSIS; DNA ANALYSIS; DOCUMENTARY ANALYSIS; ETHNOGRAPHIC SOURCES; FOODWAYS AND RELIGIOUS PRACTICES; LANDSCAPE AND ENVIRONMENTAL RECONSTRUCTION; MANURES AND OTHER FERTILIZERS, IDENTIFICATION AND ANALYSIS; SOIL MICROTECHNIQUES

Further Reading

Forbes, Hamish. 2013. Off-Site Scatters and the Manuring Hypothesis in Greek Survey Archaeology: An Ethnographic Approach. *Hesperia* 82(4):551–94.
Jones, Richard, ed. 2012. *Manure Matters: Historical, Archaeological and Ethnographic Perspectives.* Farnham, UK: Ashgate.
Kenward, Harry, and Allan Hall. 1997. Enhancing Bioarchaeological Interpretation Using Indicator Groups: Stable Manure as a Paradigm. *Journal of Archaeological Science* 24(7):663–73.

■ RICHARD JONES

MARINE MAMMALS

Marine mammals (e.g., whales, seals, porpoises, dolphins, and walruses) were a valuable source of meat and fats in hunter-gatherer-fisher populations. Sea mammals provide a large supply of meat (a single humpback whale providing 40 tons of meat) and blubber. Marine mammals represent a high calorific return per individual captured and therefore were a valuable resource for archaeological populations through time in coastal regions across the world. Farming populations also exploited marine mammals, as seen in zooarchaeological assemblages from the Neolithic onward in the Scottish Atlantic islands. Ethnographic studies of the Topnaars in Namibia have demonstrated that whale meat can be boiled, dried, or consumed raw. Dried whale meat can be stored, making it a valuable resource when alternative nutrition is unavailable.

Marine mammal exploitation can be difficult to identify archaeologically as whale meat is often butchered on-site and taken back to settlements without any bone being removed. Indirect techniques can be used to try to understand whale consumption. The presence and abundance of other prey species may indicate whether specialized economies were being practiced. New techniques also have been developed to identify marine mammal fats in pottery vessels and have potential to inform on archaeological marine mammal consumption.

Marine mammals can be procured through active hunting of targeted species using harpoons and other paraphernalia, or through passive procurement such as beachcombing as seen in the Scottish North Atlantic islands. Procurement can be assessed by analyzing species representation at sites. The homogenous nature of marine mammal bone fragments makes species identification difficult, however, and thus it is also difficult to determine active versus passive whaling.

See also BIOARCHAEOLOGICAL ANALYSIS; BUTCHERY; ETHNOGRAPHIC SOURCES; FORAGING; HUNTER-GATHERER SUBSISTENCE; STABLE ISOTOPE ANALYSIS; WEAPONS, BONE/ANTLER/ IVORY; WEAPONS, METAL; WEAPONS, STONE; ZOOARCHAEOLOGY

Further Reading

Cramp, Lucy, and Richard P. Evershed. 2013. Reconstructing Aquatic Resource Exploitation in Human Prehistory Using Lipid Biomarkers and Stable Isotopes. In *Treatise on Geochemistry*. Vol. 14, *Archaeology and Anthropology*, edited by Thure Cerling, 319–39. 2nd edition. Oxford: Elsevier.
Mulville, Jacqui. 2002. The Role of Cetacea in Prehistoric and Historic Atlantic Scotland. *International Journal of Osteoarchaeology* 12(1):34–48.
Smith, Andrew B., and John Kinahan. 1984. The Invisible Whale. *World Archaeology* 16(1):89–97.
Yesner, David R. 1980. Maritime Hunter-Gatherers: Ecology and Prehistory. *Current Anthropology* 21(6):727–50.

■ JENNIFER R. JONES

MARKETS/EXCHANGE

Until recently, most archaeologists afforded little role to either exchange or markets when it came to the procurement of food. In preindustrial contexts, most households historically have been viewed as largely self-sufficient, only moving toward food transfers when pushed by population/environmental imbalances or pulled by tribute-seeking elites. Now, based on new conceptual and empirical advances, this perspective is being revised through the recognition that interhousehold cooperation, including exchanges of food (and other goods), has had a much more central role in human history than was previously envisioned. Around the world, the sharing of comestibles and associated food preferences underpins social identities and cohesion. Intensified cultivation of olives and grapes in the Mediterranean world and xerophytic plants such as agaves in Mexico constructed new human niches that fostered intensified food exchanges in those regions.

As archaeologists long have recognized, face-to-face reciprocal exchanges as well as top-down tribute exactions have served as important modes to distribute food in many historical contexts. Yet in addition to these means of transfer, marketplace exchanges have also been shown to have long-standing significance in many regions of the world. For example, in both pre-Hispanic Mexico and ancient Rome, food exchanges in marketplaces were central features of their economies. Yet given their scope and diversity, these impressive market systems and others known historically, such as in Classical Greece and Byzantium and from the Warring States period in China, did not develop without historical antecedents. Those marketplace exchanges almost certainly had much deeper histories than many social scientists have presumed.

On a theoretical level, the long-held, rather stark theoretical dichotomies drawn between command and free economies as well as primitive and modern economic systems are now under rigorous challenge and are being reframed. No longer can it be presumed that preindustrial economies were always centrally controlled or administered. Likewise, it is becoming apparent that all economic systems are embedded in their broader societal contexts, even those associated with contemporary nation-states. Thus, when it comes to the comparative investigation of economic systems, whether past or present, the question is not whether or not they were state/politically controlled but how economic practices, including food procurement, were intertwined and shaped by political and other societal institutions, including definitions of property, modes of revenue generation, means and networks of commodity distribution, as well as other considerations.

Although textual data still provide the firmest evidence for preindustrial markets, archaeologists have refined a series of procedures to identify marketplaces based on spatial analyses as well as chemical studies of sediments. Other investigations have examined intrasettlement and regional distributions of goods as indicators of market-based exchanges. Ultimately, the strongest empirical evidence (and the best avenue to avoid equifinality) that archaeologists can employ to identify marketplace exchanges is implemented through multiscalar research designs that examine several of the aforementioned indicators while ruling out alternative hypotheses that favor large-scale redistribution (such as massive central storage facilities).

Through reciprocity, redistribution, marketplace exchanges, and other modes of economic transfer, people across time have been remarkably active in moving food products long distances and then adopting the introduced comestibles into their core culinary practices. Few people are aware that the potato was not native to Ireland, or the tomato to Italy, or sugarcane to the Caribbean. All of these foods were carried halfway across the globe before profoundly affecting the histories of the regions where they were brought.

Available transport technologies do have a limiting effect when it comes to the movement of staple foods in bulk. If more calories are needed to move heavy loads than are retrieved from the burden's consumption, then it is unlikely that such movements will often occur. Until the advent of large-scale seaborne vessels and motorized transport, high-status and lighter-weight foods (such as spices) were exchanged over much longer distances than were large amounts of staple foods (such as grains). The maize in the diet of the Aztec ruler Moctezuma II was almost entirely grown in central Mexico surrounding his capital, Tenochtitlán, yet the cacao from which his frothy beverage was made is said to have been brought regularly to him and his court from coastal Veracruz where it was harvested. Thus, although exchanges of food are subject to real constraints, both environmental and transport, people have been remarkably creative when it comes to circumventing both of these impediments, moving their preferred foods across the world.

See also Archaeology of Household Food Production; Columbian Exchange; Consumption; Food and Capitalism; Food and Politics; Food as a Commodity; Food Production and the Formation of Complex Societies; Globalization; Informal Economic Exchange; Shipwrecks; Soil Microtechniques; Spatial Analysis and Visualization Techniques; Trade Routes

Further Reading

Blanton, Richard, and Lane Fargher. 2008. *Collective Action in the Formation of Pre-Modern States.* New York: Springer.

Feinman, Gary M. 2013. Crafts, Specialists, and Markets in Mycenaean Greece: Reenvisioning Ancient Economies; Beyond Typological Constructs. *American Journal of Archaeology* 117(3):453–59.

Feinman, Gary M., and Christopher P. Garraty. 2010. Preindustrial Markets and Marketing: Archaeological Perspectives. *Annual Review of Anthropology* 39:167–91.

Feinman, Gary M., and Linda M. Nicholas. 2012. The Late Prehispanic Economy of the Valley of Oaxaca, Mexico: Weaving Threads from Data, Theory, and Subsequent History. *Research in Economic Anthropology* 32:225–58.

Garraty, Christopher P., and Barbara L. Stark, eds. 2010. *Archaeological Approaches to Market Exchange in Ancient Societies*. Boulder: University Press of Colorado.

Morrisson, Cécile, ed. 2012. *Trade and Markets in Byzantium*. Dumbarton Oaks Byzantine Symposia and Colloquia 4. Washington, DC: Dumbarton Oaks.

Temin, Peter. 2013. *The Roman Market Economy*. Princeton, NJ: Princeton University Press.

■ GARY M. FEINMAN

MATERIAL CULTURE ANALYSIS

The archaeological material culture of food is rich. It encompasses landscapes, built environments, features, and artifacts. Archaeologists often deal with agricultural landscapes but may analyze any type of cultural landscape where humans interacted with food. On a colonial plantation, for instance, in addition to gardens, pastures, and fields, they also may consider the connections that tie the kitchen to its outdoor surroundings, the main house, and any relevant outbuildings, such as a coop or smokehouse. The archaeological remains of food mills, root cellars, kitchens, storerooms, dining rooms, banquet halls, or feasting structures are a few of the food-related architectural elements found in excavation. Examples of archaeological features that are linked to food include hearths, ovens, storage pits, or middens. Yet food-related artifacts constitute the bulk of this ensemble, from agricultural tools to storage containers, cooking utensils, and the objects that people used for eating and drinking. Finally, some researchers consider that the body itself and the remains of plants and animals are part of this ensemble.

Following social anthropologists such as Jack Goody, archaeologists find it convenient to conceptualize the relationship between food and people as a series of practices organized into five main groups. These steps are generally defined as food production or acquisition, distribution or storage, preparation, consumption, and disposal. One of the strengths of material culture is that it is present at all of these stages and can therefore shed light on each of them. Artifacts alone may support the collection and production of food, as well as its transport and storage. They tend to play a crucial role during its transformation and consumption. Even when artifacts do not have a specific function in regard to food discard, they may influence how leftovers are handled and often enter the archaeological record together with food refuse. Feasting practices, in particular, can generate as many material culture remains as food waste.

Materials matter because they determine how things are preserved in the ground. It is likely that in many societies—from contexts as diverse as most Paleolithic cultures to pre-1950 Iceland—a significant proportion of food-related artifacts were made of organic materials such as wood, grass, leather, bone, or even foodstuffs themselves. In most of medieval Europe, for example, food was served and consumed on trenchers made of stale bread. Yet the conditions necessary for the preservation of organic remains are not common at archaeological sites. Furthermore, metals are often recycled. Glassware tends to be specialized—in particular, for serving and drinking cold liquids—and food-related stone vessels or stone tools, such as mortars or grinders, are relatively rare. Pottery thus receives the bulk of attention and best exemplifies the diversity of data that can be culled from artifacts. Archaeologists may study its composition, morphology, decoration, markings, physical properties such as its reaction to thermal shock, use-wear, repairs, or, increasingly, the food residues found within it. In addition, what often distinguishes these analyses from other types of inquiries is the special attention archaeologists pay to issues of quantification and provenience.

In archaeology, the context in which an object, a feature, a construction, or a landscape exists is as informative as the intrinsic attributes of those objects or features. Contexts stem first from provenience, or the precise location where something is found, and run the gamut of food-related cultural practices—some food artifacts, for example, are recovered as grave goods or as trash in cemeteries. Contextual studies can be done at different levels, from a single household or a community to the intersocietal scale, but the most in-depth approaches often try to combine several kinds of data—for instance, architecture, artifacts, and food remains. In many cases, this archaeological context also can be enriched through other lines of evidence, in particular, history, ethnography, and ethnohistory. In order to write detailed, contextualized, and culturally specific reviews of material culture, archaeologists may therefore rely on a wide array of sources, including documents, artwork, oral informants, or modern archaeological experiments. Each kind of source is complementary and only needs to be critically assessed for its relevance to the study, the types of data it will yield, as well as its inherent biases and limits.

The research themes archaeologists explore through the material culture of food are extremely varied. Using tableware alone, historical archaeologists have examined issues of identity in relation to gender, age, race, ethnicity, religious beliefs, socioeconomic status, taste, or other sociocultural constructs such as gentility. They have also considered notions of aestheticism, agency, class formation, colonialism, consumption, and domesticity. In doing so, they have borrowed a long list of sociocultural theses, including several Marxist concepts, Pierre Bourdieu's cultural capital and *habitus*, Thorstein Veblen's conspicuous consumption, Norbert Elias' civilizing process, Neil McKendrick's consumer revolution, or Michel Foucault's reflections on power. Moreover, the growing body of archaeological research carried out about one general theme—feasting practices—showcases the multifaceted nature of the material culture of food. Since feasting often entailed special serving vessels, cooking utensils, and locations, this topic has led to the discussion of sites as diverse as chiefly residences in Hawai'i, imperial open patios in the Central Andes, Maya settlements in Honduras, elite houses of the Aztecs in Mexico, platform mounds in North America, Neolithic henge enclosures in Britain, Iberian *oppida* in Spain, Gaulish sanctuaries in France, palatial architecture in the Aegean, and prehistoric burials throughout the world, from Norway to Greece, the Near East, Egypt, the Philippines, and China. It is also this ubiquity, combined with a great variety, which makes the material culture of food such a potent line of study.

See also AGRICULTURAL/HORTICULTURAL SITES; AGRICULTURE, PROCUREMENT, PROCESSING, AND STORAGE; ARCHAEOLOGY OF COOKING; ARCHITECTURAL ANALYSIS; COOKING VESSELS, CERAMIC; COOKING VESSELS, METAL; COOKING VESSELS, OTHER MATERIALS; DOCUMENTARY ANALYSIS; ETHNOGRAPHIC SOURCES; EXPERIMENTAL ARCHAEOLOGY; FEASTING; FOOD AND DINING AS SOCIAL DISPLAY; FOOD AND IDENTITY; HOUSEHOLD ARCHAEOLOGY; MIDDENS AND OTHER TRASH DEPOSITS; OFFERINGS AND GRAVE GOODS; STORAGE FACILITIES; TOOLS/UTENSILS, DECORATED; TOOLS/UTENSILS, GROUND STONE; TOOLS/UTENSILS, METAL; TOOLS/UTENSILS, ORGANIC MATERIALS; TOOLS/UTENSILS, STONE; WEAPONS, BONE/ANTLER/IVORY; WEAPONS, STONE

Further Reading

Hicks, Dan, and Mary C. Beaudry, eds. 2010. *The Oxford Handbook of Material Culture Studies*. Oxford: Oxford University Press.

Pennell, Sara. 1998. "Pots and Pans History": The Material Culture of the Kitchen in Early Modern England. *Journal of Design History* 11(3):201–16.

Twiss, Katheryn C. 2012. The Archaeology of Food and Social Diversity. *Journal of Archaeological Research* 20(4):357–95.

■ MYRIAM ARCANGELI

MEAD

Mead is among the contenders for the oldest fermented beverage, possibly even preceding the Neolithic. Produced with honey as the carbohydrate source and with a variety of yeasts (most often *Saccharomyces cerevisiae*) as the fermenting agent, mead leaves traces in the archaeological record via residues containing pollen or beeswax in excavated ceramic vessels and metal cauldrons. Archaeological evidence is reinforced by the appearance of mead in mythology and folklore, historical writings, etymologies from ancient languages, and paleolinguistic analyses. Given that ancient peoples often added honey when fermenting cereal grains or grapes and other fruits, however, interpretations of residues should be made with caution. Archaeological reports of mead based on residues in drinking vessels encompass the Bell Beaker culture (Copper to Bronze Age Europe), Hallstatt and La Tène cultures (Iron Age Europe), and Germanic societies (AD 100, Skudstrup, Denmark). Drinking horns, the archetypical vessels for mead consumption, have been excavated from various locations in the British Isles and northern Europe and are represented in the Bayeux Tapestry and various Viking-era figurines and stone carvings. Mead halls, venues for consumption of mead by Anglo-Saxon and Teutonic kings and chieftains, also have been excavated, their construction and contents analyzed, and their ritual and social functions deduced in detail. Premodern woodcuts, chapbooks (short tracts that often included recipes and recommendations for gardening or housekeeping), and artifacts attest to production and consumption of mead into modern times.

See also CARVINGS/CARVED REPRESENTATIONS OF FOOD; DOCUMENTARY ANALYSIS; FERMENTATION; HONEY AND NECTAR; MATERIAL CULTURE ANALYSIS; ORAL AND FOLK NARRATIVES; WINE; YEAST

Further Reading

Crane, Eva. 1999. *The World History of Beekeeping and Honey Hunting*. New York: Routledge.

Dugan, Frank M. 2008. *Fungi in the Ancient World: How Mushrooms, Mildews, Molds and Yeast Shaped the Early Civilizations of Europe, the Mediterranean, and the Near East*. St. Paul, MN: APS Press.

———. 2009. Dregs of Our Forgotten Ancestors: Fermentative Microorganisms in the Prehistory of Europe, the Steppes and Indo-Iranian Asia, and Their Contemporary Use in Traditional and Probiotic Beverages. *Fungi* 2(4):16–39.

Hornsey, Ian S. 2003. *A History of Beer and Brewing*. Cambridge: Royal Society of Chemistry.

McGovern, Patrick E. 2009. *Uncorking the Past: The Quest for Wine, Beer, and Other Alcoholic Beverages*. Berkeley: University of California Press.

Pollington, Stephen. 2003. *The Mead Hall: The Feasting Tradition in Anglo-Saxon England*. Norfolk, UK: Anglo-Saxon Books.

■ FRANK M. DUGAN

MEAT

Meat has been a fundamental component of human diet since our origin as a species. Humans can survive without eating meat, as widespread vegetarianism in current and past cultures demonstrates, but they are omnivorous, and as such they will opportunistically seek any source of food—including meat. Early hominids exploited animal flesh, though the extent to which this was the product of hunting or scavenging is still the subject of debate. Although most primates predominantly eat plants, fruits, and insects, their consumption of meat is well documented. Chimpanzees, the closest relatives to humans, hunt on a regular basis and also have been known to predate on juvenile humans.

For most of the Paleolithic, human societies relied on hunting animals and gathering plants. The relative proportion of meat in the diet varied by time period and region, but the consumption of the flesh of wild animals was vital for the survival of many Paleolithic communities. In the Upper Paleolithic some human groups specialized in the consumption of the flesh of specific preys. Examples include reindeer (*Rangifer tarandus*) in Europe, horses (*Equus ferus*) in central Asia, gazelles (*Gazella* sp.) in western Asia, bison (*Bison bison*) in North America, and guanacos (*Lama guanicoe*) in South America. In Africa the great variety of ungulates (hoofed animals) has led to a greater diversification of human preys.

Archaeological evidence indicates that toward the end of the Paleolithic, prey specialization gave way to a much broader spectrum of hunted animals. While in earlier times hunters had been interested mainly in large game, by the end of the Paleolithic (and Mesolithic) smaller mammals and birds were consumed more frequently. It has been argued that this transition marked a period of resource crisis, for climatic, ecological, or demographic reasons, eventually leading to the domestication of animals and the onset of the Neolithic (about 10,000 years ago).

Though archaeologists initially believed that in the Early Neolithic, domestic animals were exploited only for meat production rather than secondary products (e.g., milk, wool, traction), this view has gradually been revised, mainly in light of the evidence of organic residues from pottery that demonstrates the early exploitation of milk. Nevertheless, the consumption of the meat of important food animals such as cattle (*Bos taurus*), sheep (*Ovis aries*), goat (*Capra hircus*), and pig (*Sus domesticus*) was fundamental for life in the

Neolithic—and in later times. These animals spread out from their original centers of domestication in the Old World, and by early modern times, their meat was consumed everywhere in the world. The meat of wild animals was still consumed, but in most communities it became of secondary importance to that of domestic livestock.

The chicken (*Gallus domesticus*) is the only other animal to have ever matched the importance of these early domesticates as a meat resource, providing humans around the world with a common and reliable source of food. Other birds, such as goose (*Anser anser*) and duck (*Anas platyrhynchos*) in the Old World and turkey (*Meleagris gallopavo*) in the New World, were also, in later times, domesticated for meat, but never assumed the importance of chicken. Domesticates of regional importance include Old and New World camelids, the yak (*Bos mutus*) in southern central Asia, and the reindeer (*Rangifer tarandus*) in the Arctic area.

Given the right circumstances, humans have basically eaten (and still do) any animal whose flesh is not toxic or otherwise threatening to human health. Meat consumption has been dictated not only by subsistence needs, however, but also by social rules and religious beliefs. Meat taboos are widespread and have been attested archaeologically. Some cases, such as the Hindu repulsion for eating beef and the Jewish and Muslim refusal of pork, are particularly well known. The archaeological evidence has highlighted other cases in which apparently available meat sources were deliberately avoided. The meat of the domestic horse (*Equus caballus*) has never been a staple, for example, unlike its wild counterpart. In several cultures the consumption of horse meat has been and is deliberately avoided.

In historical times the consumption of meat has maintained its great dietary importance for human societies but is increasingly embedded in patterns of social distinction. Archaeological and historical sources from classical times suggest that meat was mainly consumed in a ritualized form, particularly in Archaic and Classical Greece. Lavish, meat-based banquets notoriously characterize the excesses of the Roman aristocracy, though archaeological evidence suggests that the much-discussed consumption of suckling pigs was almost exclusively an Italian phenomenon. While in Italy the consumption of pork predominated, in all other areas of the Roman Empire mutton or beef were the most commonly consumed meats.

In medieval times, meat consumption was a key criterion of social differentiation. The lower classes ate meat only very occasionally, while the aristocracy could dine lavishly on great meat-based banquets. The type of meat that was eaten was an important social indicator, with venison and the meat of many other wild mammals and birds being the privilege of the upper classes. By and large poor people mainly ate meat in a preserved form (e.g., bacon). The consumption of fresh meat was regarded as a luxury and, in rural areas, was probably limited to occasional feasting events. Increased urbanization went hand in hand with a higher consumption of meat and the gradual development of a market economy. It was, however, not until the second half of the 20th century that meat consumption reached, in the wealthy Northern Hemisphere, the levels that we are used to today. After aiming, for most of their histories, to maximize their access to meat resources, human societies, ironically, now face the challenge of reducing their dependence on meat.

See also ANIMAL DOMESTICITY; ANIMAL HUSBANDRY AND HERDING; BUTCHERY; CATTLE; CHICKEN; HUNTER-GATHERER SUBSISTENCE; PIG; PREFERENCES, AVOIDANCES, PROHIBITIONS, TABOOS; SECONDARY PRODUCTS REVOLUTION; SHEEP/GOAT; ZOOARCHAEOLOGY

Further Reading

Clutton-Brock, Juliet. 2012. *Animals as Domesticates: A World View through History*. East Lansing: Michigan State University Press.

Harris, Marvin. 1998. *Good to Eat: Riddles of Food and Culture*. Long Grove, IL: Waveland Press.

Milner, Nicky, and Preston Miracle, eds. 2002. *Consuming Passions and Patterns of Consumption*. McDonald Institute Monograph. Cambridge: McDonald Institute for Archaeological Research.

Woolgar, Chris, Dale Serjeantson, and Tony Waldron, eds. 2006. *Food in Medieval England: Diet and Nutrition*. Oxford: Oxford University Press.

■ UMBERTO ALBARELLA

MEDICINAL PLANTS
See GREENS/HERBS; PLANTS

MESOAMERICAN ARCHAIC-PERIOD DIET

Mesoamerica is one of the three most important centers for plant domestication and the emergence of agriculture in the world. One of its more important and distinctive cultural elements is the *milpa*, the complex agroecosystem based on maize, beans, squashes, and chili peppers to which other wild, domesticated, and semidomesticated species (e.g., tomato, tomatillo, and agaves) are added, depending of the region. One of the central questions concerning the high cultural development of this region is how successive Mesoamerican cultures achieved the alimentary, agronomic, and ecological complementarities of the species upon which the *milpa* is based. It has been hypothesized that the basic Mesoamerican diet could have been shaped in the Archaic period (7000–2400 BC), before the invention of ceramics and before the domestication of the plants upon which it is based. This has been suggested by the fact that populations of the putative wild ancestors of these species can be consumed in at least 20 different dishes that remain part of the contemporary foodways of poor peasants and are still prepared with tools and techniques that were available in the Archaic: sun drying, roasting, toasting, baking, cracking, grinding, crushing, fermenting, and soaking in plain water and water with ashes and using three-stone fireplaces, stone toasters, crushers, grinders, rock pits, and at least three types of earth ovens. The Mesoamerican Archaic-period diet could be based on at least 68 plant species, the nutritional complementarity of which could be one of the incentives for their domestication and for the development of the *milpa* agricultural system. Cooking in water and vapor, nixtamalization (soaking and cooking with water that contains lime), and possibly distillation were the most important innovations following the development of ceramics. They facilitated the transformation of the ingredients, raised their quality and the number of dishes, and introduced new selective pressures on the cultivated plants, all of which probably had an impact on their diversification, domestication, and productivity, and on the complexity of the agro-food system. The persistence of many of these dishes in Mexican foodways today shows the biocultural importance of the Mesoamerican diet.

See also AGRICULTURE, ORIGINS OF; ARCHAEOLOGY OF COOKING; BEAN/COMMON BEAN; CHILI PEPPERS; CULTIVATION; MAIZE; NIXTAMALIZATION; PLANT PROCESSING; SQUASH/GOURDS

Further Reading

Zizumbo-Villarreal, Daniel, Alondra Flores-Silva, and Patricia Colunga-GarcíaMarín. 2012. The Archaic Diet in Mesoamerica: Incentive for Milpa Development and Species Domestication. *Economic Botany* 66:328–43.

Zizumbo-Villarreal, Daniel, and Patricia Colunga García-Marín. 2010. Origin of Agriculture and Plant Domestication in West Mesoamerica. *Genetic Resources and Crop Evolution* 57(6):813–25.

■ PATRICIA COLUNGA-GARCÍAMARÍN
AND DANIEL ZIZUMBO-VILLARREAL

MESOLITHIC DIET

The Mesolithic period in northwestern Europe extended from ca. 9,500 BP to 5,500 BP. In southern Scandinavia, where it is referred to as the Late Mesolithic Ertebølle Culture, it continued until ca. 5,200 BP. The vegetation of temperate Europe went through some major changes during this period, from forests dominated by pine and pine-birch during the Pre-Boreal and Boreal, to the development of mixed deciduous forests during the Atlantic, with trees such as oak, hazel, elm, lime, and ash.

Studies of Mesolithic subsistence diet have long focused on animal and fish resources. This is mainly a factor of the abundance of bone remains and artifacts associated with hunting and fishing found at archaeological sites. Among many Mesolithic sites excavated in Europe, there are four with outstanding preservation of organic material: Star Carr in England, Tybrind Vig in Denmark, and Hardinxveld-Giessendam and Rotterdam Yangtzehaven in the Netherlands. These sites provide information about the economic aspects of Mesolithic Europe. Terrestrial animals such as red deer, elk, roe deer, wild pig, and aurochs were regarded as important game animals in the Mesolithic. Various small, fur-bearing mammals such as beaver, otter, and marten were hunted or trapped. There is evidence also for fowling and fishing. A wide range of fish species from both marine and freshwater habitats were incorporated into the Mesolithic diet. Evidence for subsistence activities is particularly abundant at coastal Late Mesolithic Ertebølle sites. Artifacts associated with fishing, such as hooks, leisters (three-pronged spears), weirs, bone points, nets, boats, and paddles, are well preserved from this period. Shell middens from coastal sites in southern Scandinavia document use of shellfish (mainly oysters and mussels) in the Late Mesolithic period.

Although there were some early attempts to emphasize the importance of plant foods during the Mesolithic, the lack of archaeobotanical evidence, or at least the limited range of encountered species, prevented a direct assessment of the relationship between animal sources and plant food components. Even when the recovery of plant remains was part of archaeological research, it often resulted in a rather limited spectrum of plant foods, mainly hazelnuts, complemented by acorns, water chestnut, and fleshy fruits such as wild strawberry, crab apple, sloe plum, hawthorn, raspberries, and rowanberries. Recently, the deployment of scanning electron microscope (SEM) techniques to identify charred remains of vegetative plant tissue derived from underground storage organs, also known as storage parenchyma, has shown that starchy root foods, including true roots, tubers, rhizomes, and bulbs of various plant species, are among the food resources that contributed substantially to the Mesolithic diet.

Roots and tubers likely formed the most abundant and readily available source of starch in the increasingly forested environment of Mesolithic temperate Europe. Individual groups of hunter-gatherers probably exploited 20–30 species of edible roots in the course of their annual rounds. The few examples of nonvegetative starchy foods in Mesolithic Europe would have included oak acorns, water chestnuts, inner bark tissue of birch and pine, and water lily seeds (*Nymphaea* spp. and *Nuphar lutea*).

Recent analysis of plant remains shows diversity in the resources exploited by Mesolithic groups. One of the members of the buttercup family, lesser celandine (*Ranunculus ficaria*), was a well-known root vegetable among Mesolithic groups in temperate Europe. Lesser celandine often grows in extensive stands and can provide a plentiful harvest of starchy tubers from just one plant. The tubers, however, contain toxins and have to be processed (dried, cooked, or baked in hot ashes) before they can be eaten. Charred tuber remains of lesser celandine were found at a number of Middle to Late Mesolithic sites, including Hardinxveld-Giessendam Polderweg, Hardinxveld-Giessendam De Bruin, and Rotterdam Yangtzehaven, all in the Netherlands, and at Staosnaig on Colonsay Island in Scotland. Another starchy root food well known to many if not to all groups living along the North Sea coast in early prehistory was the sea beet (*Beta vulgaris* ssp. *maritima*) (figure 41). The plant occurs naturally on shingle beaches, tidal drift deposits, and the drier areas of salt marshes. Numerous charred root remains recovered from occupation deposits at the Late Mesolithic Ertebølle site at Tybrind Vig in Denmark indicate that sea beet roots formed part of the local diet. Charred remains of sea beet roots were also found at Early to Middle Mesolithic sites in the Dutch province of Groningen, and charred fruits (*perianths*) were found at the Ertebølle site Møllegabet II in Denmark.

Two additional examples of root foods dated to the Late Mesolithic Ertebølle period come from the site of Halsskov in Denmark. These are bulbs of ramsons (*Allium* cf. *ursinum*) (figure 41) and tubers of pignut (*Conopodium majus*); both were found in a charred state. *Allium ursinum* is a perennial herb with the strong smell and flavor of garlic; it often forms extensive patches in shady, damp, deciduous forests. Both the leaves and the bulbs are edible. At Halsskov the bulbs would have been gathered and used as main food or cooked as flavoring with other foods. Cooking would convert the bulb's major carbohydrate, inulin, which is neither easily digestible nor very palatable, into sweet-tasting fructose. For the inhabitants of Halsskov and perhaps other sites, ramsons would have been the first root as well as green vegetable to appear in spring. The tubers of pignut (*Conopodium majus*), a member of the Apiaceae family, can be found in open woodland and grasslands. They grow at the base of the stem and have a mildly nutty flavor when cooked. Interestingly, the tubers cannot be harvested by pulling the stem of the plant, as it is thin and breaks very easily. This suggests that the tubers at Halsskov

Figure 41. Evidence of plant consumption during the Mesolithic period includes the sea beet root and bulbs of ramsons. Top left: SEM micrograph of a charred fragment of parenchyma derived from the sea beet root (*Beta vulgaris* ssp. *maritima*) from a Late Mesolithic Ertebølle site at Tybrind Vig in Denmark, showing concentric rings of xylem and broad bands of storage parenchyma between each ring; top right: collecting sea beet roots on the Dutch North Sea coast near Bergen in August; bottom left: charred bulb of ramsons (*Allium* cf. *ursinum*) from the Late Mesolithic Ertebølle site at Halsskov in Denmark; bottom right: bulbs of ramsons dug out in April before flowering. Courtesy of Lucy Kubiak-Martens, BIAX Consult.

were dug out with some kind of digging tool, after which they were brought to the site, where they were most likely used as food.

Mesolithic hunter-gatherers were consistently attracted to marsh and water plants as sources of starchy food. The charred remains of arrowhead tubers (*Sagittaria* cf. *sagittifolia*) found at the Early Mesolithic site of Całowanie in Poland suggest that tubers were deliberately dug up and brought to the site; arrowhead tubers grow in shallow water or swampy ground and they are rather deeply buried in the mud. Exposure to a domestic fire must have been part of their preparation prior to consumption. The presence of charred rhizome remains of the common club-rush (*Schoenoplectus lacustris*) at the Early to Middle Mesolithic site Rotterdam Yangtzehaven in the Netherlands suggests that the people who visited the dune site collected the starchy rhizomes of this marsh plant. Interestingly, the transverse section of one of the specimens revealed a very smooth, clear-cut surface, suggesting that the rhizome was cut prior to becoming charred—an obvious sign of processing by humans. The interpretation of rhizomes of this species as food is supported by archaeobotanical finds from other Early to Middle Mesolithic sites in the Netherlands.

Tubers of various horsetail species (*Equisetum* spp.) may have provided a starchy food source. Although horsetails are rarely considered as a food source because of their high silica content, it is mainly the stems that are rough and silicon-impregnated, while the tubers contain much starch and have a sweet taste. Charred remains of *Equisetum* sp. tubers found at various Early to Late Mesolithic sites across temperate Europe may therefore have been part of the diet. It is likely that several knotgrass species (*Polygonum*) as well as the closely related dock species (*Rumex*) were collected in Mesolithic Europe for their edible rhizomes and for their greens. The charred rhizome remains of knotgrass (*Polygonum* sp.) found at the Early Mesolithic site at Całowanie in Poland reflect some food processing methods.

The examples of starchy foods discovered in the last two decades and presented here have considerable implications for the way we view the plant component of Mesolithic diet. There are clear indications that starchy foods were frequently gathered, implying that starch was a significant dietary energy source in Mesolithic Europe. Mesolithic groups explored and used a broad range of plant species and many ecological zones in their search for vegetative and nonvegetative starchy foods. The finds of charred archaeological parenchyma from Mesolithic sites will continue to hold our interest. Although it is difficult, and perhaps still too early, to estimate the complex proportion between animal protein and plant foods (starchy foods in particular), it is clear that a more balanced view of the Mesolithic diet is emerging from archaeological sites.

See also ARCHAEOBOTANY; FISH/SHELLFISH; FORAGING; HUNTER-GATHERER SUBSISTENCE; PALEODIETARY ANALYSIS; PLANT PROCESSING; ROOT CROPS/TUBERS; SCANNING ELECTRON MICROSCOPY; SHELL MIDDENS; STAR CARR; STARCHES, ROLE OF; ZOOARCHAEOLOGY

Further Reading

Clarke, David L. 1976. Mesolithic Europe: The Economic Basis. In *Problems in Economic and Social Archaeology*, edited by Gale de Giberne Sieveking, Ian H. Longworth, and K. E. Wilson, 449–81. London: Duckworth.

Kubiak-Martens, Lucy. 2002. New Evidence for the Use of Root Foods in Pre-Agrarian Subsistence Recovered from the Late Mesolithic Site at Halsskov, Denmark. *Vegetation History and Archaeobotany* 11:23–31.

Mason, Sarah L., Jon G. Hather, and Gordon C. Hillman. 2002. The Archaeobotany of European Hunter-Gatherers: Some Preliminary Investigations. In *Hunter-Gatherer Archaeobotany: Perspectives from the Northern Temperate Zone*, edited by Sarah L. Mason and Jon G. Hather, 188–96. London: Institute of Archaeology, University College of London.

Price, Douglas T. 1989. The Reconstruction of Mesolithic Diets. In *The Mesolithic in Europe: Papers Presented at the Third International Symposium, Edinburgh, 1985*, edited by Clive Bonsall, 48–59. Edinburgh: John Donald Publisher.

Zvelebil, Marek. 1994. Plant Use in the Mesolithic and Its Role in the Transition to Farming. *Proceedings of the Prehistoric Society* 60:35–74.

■ LUCY KUBIAK-MARTENS

MICROFLORAL REMAINS
See PALYNOLOGY; PHYTOLITH ANALYSIS

MICROMORPHOLOGY
See SOIL MICROTECHNIQUES

MICROSCOPY
See SCANNING ELECTRON MICROSCOPY

MIDDENS AND OTHER TRASH DEPOSITS

The term *midden* has traditionally been used to define a "trash" deposit, broadly consisting of waste occupation debris, ranging from single dumps to long-term buildups of material from sedentary communities. Deposits classified as midden can be incredibly diverse and heterogeneous, however, and it is generally acknowledged that even within a single site, all "midden" deposits are not necessarily the same thing. At some sites, the term *midden* may not be used at all, with such deposits being referred to simply as trash, domestic waste, or discard deposits. The term *trash pit* has been used to describe shorter-lived features, deposited within pits rather than mounds or spreads of debris. As human activity invariably produces waste byproducts, it is fair to say that most types of archaeological sites will be associated with a form of midden, though not all middens are composed exclusively of food waste. Fuel byproducts are another major waste component, for example.

Midden debris may include plant remains, animal bones, pottery and stone tool debris, decayed organic remains, human and animal dung, and artifacts. As such they are incredibly useful repositories of information on diet and subsistence. In some cases they may be the primary source of information on these activities. For example, at the Neolithic settlement of Çatalhöyük, Turkey, primary activity residues in buildings are rare, thus it is the midden deposits that provide the vast majority of ecofacts. Human remains also have been found in some middens. Middens may be dominated by a single class of material—for example, shell middens. Shell middens are found all over the world, often but not always associated with coastal populations. They are some of the most extensively studied types of midden deposits and are sometimes treated as archaeological sites in themselves. These single-material middens are linked to a more limited range of activities than those composed of more diverse deposit types, but even here there is diversity in their composition and interpretation. The shell middens of Denmark (*køkkenmødding* or kitchen mound) consist of food processing waste. The Pacific Northwest coast of the United States is also notable for its extensive shell midden deposits.

The literature on midden deposits is as diverse as the deposits themselves, and several key areas of research can be identified. Several studies are concerned with midden formation processes. As a subcategory of site-formation processes, this is a means of understanding human activity in the past. For all types of middens, consideration of taphonomy and formation processes is crucial to understand the deposits fully and must occur before cultural inferences can be made. Dietary reconstruction and analysis of resource exploitation are also major areas of research. The overall assemblage of mollusks or animal bones gives information on species exploitation at a site. More detailed analyses of different contexts and strata within middens enable reconstruction of how this exploitation changes over time. Measurements of the change in size of shellfish species have been used to infer human impact on these populations, for example. Studies of midden composition can provide information on wider questions of trade and ecology, as well as localized activity, and isotopic analysis of faunal remains from feasting middens has provided insight into animal husbandry practices. Plant remains in middens also provide information on diet. Plant remains are typically found as charred remains but also may be present as silica phytoliths and mineralized remains. Although charred plants may typically be a result of fuel use, dietary information also can be obtained from plant processing waste or the discard of food that is accidentally burned.

Midden deposits can be approached at a range of scales, from macro- to microlevel. Analytical methods vary depending on the research questions, the type of midden deposit, and level of preservation. For example, middens dominated by shells or other faunal remains require a zooarchaeological approach. Oxygen isotope analysis is frequently applied to shell middens alongside species assessments to interpret seasonality of coastal resource exploitation. During excavation, it is often necessary to divide middens into broad stratigraphic layers because of the apparent homogeneity at the macroscale or complexity that precludes excavation of individual layers. The latter is preferred when possible to separate material from different episodes of deposition. Depth of accumulation may give insight into whether deposits were formed rapidly or gradually over time, though in some cases deep deposits can be a result of relatively short-lived activities.

At the macroscale, the clustering and spatial arrangement of different components within the midden (e.g., faunal remains, charred macrobotanical remains, ceramics) may be studied. It is often useful to consider different classes of material together to reconstruct activities, and to assess long-term changes in disposal patterns. Middens are especially useful for this type of integrated research, as they may contain several classes of material in association. The sediments themselves, and the depositional relationships between the different components, are also significant. The use of microarchaeological methods such as thin section micromorphology can reveal information that is otherwise invisible—for example, the presence of ard marks provides evidence that middens in prehistoric Britain were used for small-scale agriculture.

All of these studies rely on the development of appropriate sampling strategies, which can impact the interpretation of species compositions. Ethnoarchaeological research also provides useful insights into the motivations behind disposal behavior for different classes of material.

See also AGRICULTURAL FEATURES, IDENTIFICATION AND ANALYSIS; ARCHAEOBOTANY; ÇATAL-HÖYÜK; ETHNOARCHAEOLOGY; SHELL MIDDENS; SOIL MICROTECHNIQUES; STABLE ISOTOPE ANALYSIS; ZOOARCHAEOLOGY

Further Reading

Guttman, E. B. A. 2005. Midden Cultivation in Prehistoric Britain: Arable Crops in Gardens. *World Archaeology* 37(2):224–39.

Hayden, Brian, and Aubrey Cannon. 1983. Where the Garbage Goes: Refuse Disposal in the Maya Highlands. *Journal of Anthropological Archaeology* 2(2):117–63.

Schiffer, Michael B. 1987. *Formation Processes of the Archaeological Record*. Albuquerque: University of New Mexico Press.

Shillito, Lisa-Marie, Wendy Matthews, Matthew J. Almond, and Ian D. Bull. 2011. The Microstratigraphy of Middens: Capturing Daily Routine in Rubbish at Neolithic Çatalhöyük, Turkey. *Antiquity* 85(329):1024–38.

Stein, Julie. 1992. *Deciphering a Shell Midden*. San Diego, CA: Academic Press.

■ LISA-MARIE SHILLITO

MILITARY SITES

A good soldier is well fed. In 1795 Napoleon Bonaparte famously stated that "an army marches on its stomach," and this accurately reflects the importance—and the difficulty—in provisioning a fighting force that is far from home and far from safe, predictable sources of supply. Soldiers' diaries, officers' orderly books, and letters sent home have always made references to food and drink, and historical sources such as these give archaeologists clues as to what evidence for food we might hope to find when we dig at military encampments.

Archaeology has been conducted at many of the military sites created over the past several thousand years, but no matter the time period, similar questions may be asked regarding the foods consumed by armies. Was the food fresh or preserved by salting, smoking, or drying? Was it prepared by roasting or boiling, or eaten raw? Did officers and their men eat essentially the same foods, and did men in the field eat the same foods as their families back home? Can the remnants of cooking pans and pots reveal the size of the group that was dining together, whether in huts, barracks, or tents? And can food remains reveal the ethnicity or country of origin of the soldiers?

Soldiers almost invariably have foraged for food to supplement their often-meager rations, and thus archaeologists search for evidence of wild foods that would not have been documented in military records, as well as alternative foods that might have been purchased from civilian merchants (sutlers) who were attached to most military camps. The quantification of faunal remains can be difficult, however, because of off-site butchering. In a classic cautionary study, John Guilday discovered relatively few butchered animal bones at the British site of Fort Ligonier (1758–66) in western Pennsylvania (USA). Only through the use of historical records was he able to determine that most butchering was done off-site, and most of the meat ration (salt pork) left no archaeological record at the site.

Battlefields typically lack food remains, and it is the forts and encampments that have substantial food middens, built up over months or years of habitation. Some of the best evidence for food along military frontiers comes from the Roman forts positioned along Hadrian's Wall in northern England. Vindolanda is the best-documented of these, with abundant archaeological evidence that includes masses of animal bones in ditches at the fort from the consumption of beef, pork, venison, goat, chicken, whooper swans, and even oysters and mussels. Archaeological finds, coupled with references in some well-preserved writing tablets, also indicate the consumption of grain, cabbages, beans, fruit, nuts, honey, eggs, wine, beer, olive oil, various sauces and olives, as well as exotic condiments such as pepper. Roman-style dining and drinking vessels of pottery, glass, and bronze were recovered. Ovens for baking bread and hearths for roasting meat also were exposed. Archaeology thus supports the interpretation that soldiers on Rome's northern frontier dined quite well. Though the presence of Roman foods and foodways is strong, there is nonetheless some suggestion of the ethnicity of soldiers. Along the Antonine Wall on the northwest frontier, for example, locally made pottery similar to that from North Africa was recovered.

In more recent times, a dependence upon sutlers to add variety to the military diet has been amply demonstrated by the excavation of a sutling house on the Hudson River in Fort Edward, New York (USA), where a merchant, Edward Best, maintained a tavern and sold supplies to the British army during the French and Indian War. In a period when the military chiefly ate beef and pork, much of it salted, the burned remains of Mr. Best's house (1757–58) contained sheep and fish bones and a wide range of wine glasses and other drinking vessels. The broken remains of wine bottles were ubiquitous, with well over 10,000 fragments, reinforcing the popular assumption that alcohol was the favorite vice of the British army. Regular rations, typically transported over long distances, resulted in a fairly monotonous diet at most military camps. Sutlers clearly provided a welcome variety of alternative foods and dining experiences and, above all, a great deal of liquor.

Archaeological sites from the American Civil War in the 1860s have provided rich evidence for food and foodways. The ditches at the U.S. Army depot at Camp Nelson in Kentucky (1863–66) included remains of beans, cowpeas, lentils, beef (especially ribs and hind shanks) and pork (hams and hocks), ceramic storage and serving vessels, plus ample bottle glass. The presence of sheep and rabbit bones suggests some variation in the meat portion of the diet. Historical records indicate that sutlers' stores provided a great variety of food and drink, including onions, potatoes, canned condensed milk, butter, hardtack, cookies, fried pies, canned meats and oysters, dried beef, sausages, dried and salted fish, sardines, eggs, flour, coffee and tea, beer, wine, and whiskey. Bottles for alcoholic beverages provide evidence of social status, with wine and whiskey often reflecting a higher status.

The analysis of skeletal remains also provides direct evidence for the types of food that soldiers consumed. Dietary deficiencies are often reflected in bones, suggesting inadequate nourishment or vitamin deficiencies that would have undercut the effectiveness of any fighting force. It cannot be overemphasized that military leaders are keenly aware of the importance of properly feeding their soldiers, contributing to good troop morale and, ultimately, to victory.

See also ARCHAEOBOTANY; BIOARCHAEOLOGICAL ANALYSIS; BUTCHERY; DISTILLED SPIRITS; FOOD AND IDENTITY; FOOD AND STATUS; MATERIAL CULTURE ANALYSIS; MIDDENS AND OTHER TRASH DEPOSITS; OEDENBURG; PALEODIETARY ANALYSIS; PALEONUTRITION; ZOOARCHAEOLOGY

Further Reading

Birley, Robin. 2009. *Vindolanda: A Roman Frontier Fort on Hadrian's Wall.* Gloucestershire, UK: Amberley.
Delo, David M. 1998. *Peddlers and Post Traders: The Army Sutler on the Frontier.* Helena, MT: Kingfisher Books.
Geier, Clarence R., David G. Orr, and Matthew B. Reeves, eds. 2006. *Huts and History: The Historical Archaeology of Military Encampment during the American Civil War.* Gainesville: University Press of Florida.
Guilday, John E. 1970. Animal Remains from Archaeological Investigations at Fort Ligonier. In *Archaeological Investigation of Fort Ligonier, 1960–1965* by Jacob L. Grimm, 177–86. Pittsburgh: Carnegie Museum.
McBride, W. Stephen, Susan C. Andrews, and Sean P. Coughlin. 2000. "For the Convenience and Comforts of the Soldiers and Employees at the Depot": Archaeology of the Owens' House/Post Office Complex, Camp Nelson, Kentucky. In *Archaeological Perspectives on the American Civil War,* edited by Clarence R. Geier and Stephen R. Potter, 99–124. Gainesville: University Press of Florida.
Starbuck, David R. 2010. *Excavating the Sutlers' House.* Hanover, NH: University Press of New England.

■ DAVID R. STARBUCK

MILK AND DAIRY PRODUCTS

Dairying is a prehistoric, Old World technology, depicted in representational art and textual sources. Until recent advances in residue analysis and the interpretation of faunal remains, however, milk and dairy products were notoriously difficult to detect in the archaeological record. Consequently, there has been little record of their use prior to the first urban societies in Mesopotamia. Milk and dairy products are part of a range of secondary animal products that were hypothesized to have revolutionized the economy of Europe in the Late Neolithic/Early Bronze Age. The identification of dairy lipids on a range of earlier ceramic cooking pots from southwestern Asia (northwest Anatolia, ca. 9,000 BP) and southeastern Europe (ca. 8,000 BP) has challenged the idea of a "secondary products revolution," however. It now appears that dairy foods were exploited to some extent as soon as domesticated animals became available in the Early Neolithic period, and dairy residues continue to be widely detected on later prehistoric pottery. Similarly, residue analysis has confirmed that dairying was practiced among emerging pastoralists in the North African Sahara ca. 8,000 BP.

While the analysis of pottery residues confirms a very early culinary use of dairy products, it cannot reveal the scale and specificity of milk production. In this respect, information from animal bones has been more successful. Accurate age determinations of ruminant skeletal remains from Early Neolithic faunal assemblages have been used to reconstruct mortality profiles. In many cases, these match kill-off patterns expected for economies centered on dairying of both caprines and cattle, rather than meat exploitation.

The identification of dairying in the Early Neolithic period raises the question of whether humans were actually able to digest the sugars (lactose) in milk at such an early time. The enzyme (lactase) needed to break down lactose is absent in many of the world's adult populations although it is common in people with European ancestry. The evolution of adult lactase persistence is therefore closely linked with the history of dairying. Based on DNA analysis of modern and ancient populations, it appears that this genetic trait has been under strong selection since the start of the Neolithic period, possibly originating in central Europe. The actual selective advantage that was conferred by dairy products is unknown; dairy may have been beneficial to diet and health or enhanced social standing and reproductive success. Interestingly, fermenting milk into yogurts and cheeses significantly decreases the amount of lactose present. Therefore, in many societies (e.g., in southern Europe), fermented dairy products were important foodstuffs despite a relatively high frequency of lactose intolerance in the population. The identification of 7,000-year-old cheese strainers in northern Europe may suggest that this technological solution was also available to some Neolithic communities from a very early time.

See also ANIMAL HUSBANDRY AND HERDING; BIOMOLECULAR ANALYSIS; DNA ANALYSIS; FERMENTATION; FOOD STORAGE; LACTASE PERSISTENCE AND DAIRYING; RESIDUE ANALYSIS, DAIRY PRODUCTS; SECONDARY PRODUCTS REVOLUTION; ZOOARCHAEOLOGY

Further Reading

Itan, Yuval, Adam Powell, Mark A. Beaumont, et al. 2009. The Origins of Lactase Persistence in Europe. *PLoS Computational Biology* 5(8):e1000491. doi:10.1371/journal.pcbi.1000491.

Salque, Mélanie., Peter I. Bogucki, Joanna Pyzel, et al. 2013. Earliest Evidence for Cheese Making in the Sixth Millennium BC in Northern Europe. *Nature* 493(7433):522–25.

Sherratt, Andrew. 1997. *Economy and Society in Prehistoric Europe: Changing Perspectives*. Edinburgh: Edinburgh University Press.

■ OLIVER CRAIG

MILLETS

Millets are a genetically diverse group of cereals that typically produce small grains. They have been classified as domesticated grasses (in the family Poaceae), not including species of wheat (*Triticum*), barley (*Hordeum*), oats (*Avena*), maize (*Zea*), and rice (*Oryza*). Millets are also categorized as large or major (e.g., pearl millet, *Pennisetum glaucum*) and small or minor millets (e.g., foxtail millet, *Setaria italica*), based on grain size and economic importance. Although millets can be highly productive under ideal agricultural conditions, they are also drought tolerant and survive when higher-yielding crops, such as maize and wheat, fail. They are fast-maturing plants and able to produce dependable yields on impoverished soils, with minimal use of fertilizers and irrigation. Today millets rank as some of the most significant crops by global standards of production. Major producers of millet typically include India, Nigeria, Mexico, Argentina, Niger, and Ethiopia. While millets tend to be underutilized by developed nations, apart from their use as livestock fodder and bird seed, these highly nutritious crops are of immense importance to millions of small-scale farming households across semiarid and arid regions of the world.

Wild progenitors of millet were domesticated in several regions. In Africa, domesticated varieties include pearl millet, sorghum, finger millet (*Eleusine coracana*), fonio (*Digitaria exilis*), and t'ef (*Eragrostis tef*). Domesticates in India include browntop millet (*Brachiaria ramosa*), bristly foxtail (*Setaria verticillata*), kodo millet (*Paspalum scrobiculatum*), and sawa millet (*Echinochloa frumentacea*). East Asian crops include foxtail millet, broomcorn millet (*Panicum miliaceum*), and barnyard millet (*Echinochloa utilis*). In the Americas, mango (*Bromus mango*) and sauwi millet (*Panicum sonorum*) were grown until the time of European contact.

Millets were domesticated in northern China by 11,000 years ago, in southern India by 4,700 years ago, and in West Africa by 4,500 years ago. In these regions, they later formed the agricultural foundations of early complex societies, including Meroë and Aksum in eastern Africa, the Nok culture of West Africa, the Indus Valley Harappan civilization, and the Xia and other early states of northern China. Millets have been identified in the archaeological record through remains of charred grains, phytoliths, ceramic impressions, and starch granules. Large numbers of charred pearl millet grains were recovered at the Birimi site in West Africa, suggesting that Kintampo cultures were growing the crop by 4,000 years ago. Starch granules were identified at the sites of Nanzhuangtou and Donghulin in northern China, indicating the presence of domesticated foxtail millet more than 11,000 years ago.

Sorghum and pearl millet, also known as major millets, normally rank in the top five or six cereals in terms of global production and have a long history of use and multiple cultural associations based on archaeological and ethnographic evidence. For example, sorghum is consumed in the form of boiled, roasted, or popped grains and in fermented and nonfermented porridges, flat breads, dumplings, and beverages in Africa and India. Pearl millet is consumed in the same regions as porridges, flat breads, and fermented and nonfermented beverages.

In arid zones, minor millets constitute highly nutritious sources of human food and fodder and are of immense cultural importance. They improve the resilience of small communities by enhancing food security, and millet growing persists despite high labor inputs required in nonmechanized processing. A good example is t'ef, which is indigenous to the Ethiopian highlands where it is used to make a staple bread known as *injera*. T'ef is widely recognized as the most important cereal in Ethiopia and Eritrea, where it plays a fundamental role in regional economies, cultures, and cuisines. In West Africa, fonio grains are boiled and consumed as porridge and popped grain and are ground with other flours to make breads and pastries. Although the use of millet is an ancient practice, it is considered a prestige food and a gourmet item in some circles. Finger millet is a significant grain in India, where it is ground into *ragi* flour and used in making porridges and flatbreads, including unleavened *roti*. It is also malted to produce various foods and beer. In northern China, foxtail and broomcorn millet grains are similarly consumed as porridge and boiled grain. The use of millet flour in making noodles is known in northwestern China from at least 4,000 years ago.

The immense diversity seen in millets today is the result of more than 10,000 years of careful selection and breeding by generations of subsistence farmers. As such, they represent a storehouse of genetic diversity and a valuable ecological heritage. Ironically, millets, in particular small millets, tend to be neglected by scientists and agricultural policy makers despite their critical role in enhancing food security in rural areas around the world. This may soon change, however, with the growing appetite for gluten-free foods and the realization of the potential of millets to prosper in the face of increasing aridity and global climate change.

See also AGRICULTURE, ORIGINS OF; ARCHAEOBOTANY; ARCHAEOLOGY OF COOKING; BREAD; CEREALS; PLANT DOMESTICATION; PLANT PROCESSING; RESIDUE ANALYSIS, STARCH; STARCHES, ROLE OF; SUSTAINABILITY; WILD PROGENITORS OF DOMESTICATED PLANTS

Further Reading

D'Andrea, A. C. 2008. T'ef (*Eragrostis tef*) in Ancient Agricultural Systems of Highland Ethiopia. *Economic Botany* 62(4):547–66.

D'Andrea, A. C., and J. Casey. 2002. Pearl Millet and Kintampo Subsistence. *African Archaeological Review* 19(3):147–73.

Fuller, Dorian, Ravi Korisettar, P. C. Venkatasubbalah, and Martin K. Jones. 2004. Early Plant Domestication in Southern India: Some Preliminary Archaeobotanical Results. *Vegetation History and Archaeobotany* 13(2):115–29.

Manning, Katie, Ruth Pelling, Tom Higham, et al. 2011. 4500-Year-Old Domesticated Pearl Millet (*Pennisetum glaucum*) from the Tilemsi Valley, Mali: New Insights into an Alternative Cereal Domestication Pathway. *Journal of Archaeological Science* 38(2):312–22.

National Research Council, Board on Science and Technology for International Development. 1996. *Lost Crops of Africa*. Vol. 1, *Grains*. Washington, DC: National Academy Press.

Seetharama, A., Ken W. Riley, and G. Harinarayana, eds. 1989. *Small Millets in Global Agriculture*. New Delhi: Oxford and IBH.

Weber, Steven A., and Dorian Q Fuller. 2008. Millets and Their Role in Early Agriculture. *Prāgdhārā* 18:69–90.

Yang, Xiaoyan, Zhiwei Wan, Linda Perry, et al. 2012. Early Millet Use in Northern China. *Proceedings of the National Academy of Sciences USA* 109(10):3726–30.

■ A. CATHERINE D'ANDREA

MILLING

Milling is a process that breaks solid material into smaller pieces and, in terms of food preparation, is one of mankind's greatest technological inventions. There are various foodstuffs that contain a hard outer husk that must be removed before the softer inner portion can be eaten. This can be done by hand, and grain in the form of a stew or porridge can be eaten without the use of milling. The process is much easier and substantially faster, however, if two stones are used for crushing. The resulting ground flour can be mixed to bake bread that, in one form or another, is a staple of most diets.

Although grain will keep, flour has a comparatively short shelf life, and in early societies this generally meant daily milling for domestic use. Milling stones such as saddle querns and rotary querns and, later, millstones driven either by animal, water, or wind have all played a vital role in food processing. The saddle quern used two stones, a stationary lower stone, usually concave in shape (the "saddle"), and a smaller, active, upper stone (the "rubber"). Once the grain was dehusked, probably by separate pounding, the process used a forward-and-back motion of the rubber on the saddle to crush. A fairly crude form of the saddle quern can probably be dated back to the Paleolithic. This essentially domestic process came into its own during the Neolithic, however, when settled communities grew a range of grain, primarily wheat, maize, and rice, and milling played a vital role in a subsistence economy.

The addition of a handle to the rubber allowed the use of larger, flatter lower stones; this led to the development of the slab mill. The handle was lengthened and subsequently anchored one end to a fixed pivot to produce the lever or Olynthus mill, larger versions of which could produce flour in quantity and were probably intended for mill bakeries, with bread as a commercial product. The oscillatory Olynthus mill was common in the east, especially during the Hellenistic period. Rotary querns seem to have been in general use in western Europe by the middle Iron Age, and they quickly superseded, although did not entirely replace, the less efficient saddle quern. The rotary quern was a major innovation and consisted of a fixed lower stone and a rotating upper stone (figure 42). A central hole in the upper stone allowed grain to be poured in, while a *rynd*, a piece of metal or wood bridging the hole and pivoting on a spindle set in the lower stone, allowed a crude means of regulating the fineness of the flour. The grinding surfaces of both stones were dressed with a series of grooves that allowed the grain to be cut open by a shearing action rather than just by the pressure of the upper stone. Also, dehusking could be done at the same time, as the hulls were crushed with the flour and the chaff was released, much of which could be separated by sieving.

Figure 42. Quern stone (top and bottom views of the upper stone) for milling, found during excavations of the Bar Hill Fort along the Antonine Wall near Twechar, Scotland. This Roman fortification dates to AD 142–180. The stone, which features a notch for a wooden handle, is 0.35 meters in diameter and was made of lava from Andernach, Germany (former site of the Roman settlement of Antunnacum). Photographs © The Hunterian Museum, University of Glasgow, 2014.

Pompeian-style mills ("donkey mills") represent a revolution in flour production, providing the means of grinding greater quantities of grain with far less effort. They consist of two large millstones, one cone shaped, positioned upright and stationary (*meta*), and the other hollow, hourglass-shaped, and positioned on top (*catillus*). Grain was poured into the top of the *catillus*, which was rotated in a circular motion either by manpower or with a donkey or horse, thereby greatly increasing output over the smaller domestic rotary quern. The most celebrated groups of Pompeian millstones are those from the bakeries of first century AD Pompeii, where milling and baking were combined. Water-powered mills also are common from the Roman period; a channeled hydraulic force drove a large flat millstone on top of a stationary one. Windmills are known in the east from the seventh century AD, although they were not seen in Europe until the medieval period. Both of these technologies allowed a sharp increase in flour output over mills turned by animal or human power, and milling and baking were of necessity separated.

Not every type of stone is suitable for querns or millstones. Volcanic basalts, in particular, were prized because of the gas vesicles in the rock, which retain sharp edges. These and other hard rocks were quarried where they occurred and then widely traded. Petrological and chemical techniques have been used to characterize and identify sources, while recent scientific study on millstones has been concerned with identifying organic residues and phytoliths, trapped in the surface vesicles of the rock, which will tell us what actually was being ground.

See also BAKERIES; BEDROCK FEATURES; BREAD; CEREALS; FACTORIES; FOOD STORAGE; HERCULANEUM AND POMPEII; INDUSTRIALIZATION OF FOOD AND FOOD PRODUCTION; PHYTOLITH ANALYSIS; RESIDUE ANALYSIS, STARCH; STARCHES, ROLE OF; TOOLS/UTENSILS, GROUND STONE

Further Reading

Frankel, Rafael. 2003. The Olynthus Mill, Its Origin, and Diffusion: Typology and Distribution. *American Journal of Archaeology* 107(1):1–21.

Langdon, John. 2004. *Mills in the Medieval Economy, England 1300–1540*. Oxford: Oxford University Press.

Peacock, D. P. S. 1980. The Roman Millstone Trade: A Petrological Sketch. *World Archaeology* 12(1): 43–53.

———. 2013. *The Stone of Life: The Archaeology of Querns, Mills and Flour Production in Europe up to c. 500 AD*. Southampton, UK: Highfield Press.

Ross, Julie M. 2004. Phytoliths from a Norse Greenlandic Quern Stone: A Preliminary Investigation. *Environmental Archaeology* 9(1):99–106.

Wikander, Örjan. 2000. The Water-Mill. In *Handbook of Ancient Water Technology*, edited by Örjan Wikander, 371–400. Leiden: Brill.

Williams, David F., and David Peacock, eds. 2011. *Bread for the People: The Archaeology of Mills and Milling*. Oxford: Archaeopress.

Williams-Thorpe, Olwen, and Richard S. Thorpe. 1993. Geochemistry and Trade of Eastern Mediterranean Millstones from the Neolithic to Roman Periods. *Journal of Archaeological Science* 20(3): 263–320.

■ DAVID WILLIAMS

MOLECULAR ANALYSIS
See Biomolecular Analysis

MORTARS
See Bedrock Features; Tools/Utensils, Ground Stone

MORTUARY COMPLEXES
In this entry, *mortuary complex* refers to groups of tombs and associated architecture, including temples, mounds, and other monuments, though the term has also been used to describe a set of culturally related funerary practices (e.g., the Eastern Woodlands mortuary complex in North America). Food remains can help archaeologists reconstruct activities performed in spaces dedicated to celebrating or remembering the dead. Because it was a key component of offerings placed in graves and at funerary feasts, food can also help us understand cultural views of death and the dead, as well as social divisions in life that shaped celebrations of death.

Because they contain multiple culturally and often chronologically associated tombs, mortuary complexes allow archaeologists to infer broader mortuary patterns, including the intentional and patterned selection of food for placement with the dead. Some foods may be particularly meaningful or appropriate in funerary contexts. For example, Lambayeque burials at Farfán in coastal Perú commonly contained foods like maize, beans, fish, and chili peppers in bowls and cooking pots placed alongside individuals. Associated jars may have contained *chicha* (maize beer). Maize was a favorite offering; it was present in 90 percent of the burials that contained food, which made it almost three times as ubiquitous in burials as in samples from contemporaneous households at a nearby agricultural village. Species common in households, including fruits such as cherimoya, were rare in burial offerings. This example suggests that food placed with the dead is likely to have been selected for this purpose from within the broader cuisine.

Remains of food and drink encountered in mortuary complexes may be offerings for the dead, or they may represent the remnants of feasts consumed by the living. Feasts are an important component of ancestor veneration ceremonies at which the living commemorate the dead, though cultural views of death varied widely in antiquity. For ancient Mesopotamians, offering the proper libations at death and periodically continuing to provide food and drink to the deceased established a commensal relationship between living and dead, but also helped fend off misery in the afterlife and kept malevolent dead at bay. In contrast, in early China, food and wine were consumed at graveside feasts that helped convert honored dead into helpful ancestors by ensuring their continued attention and allegiance. In Bronze Age cemeteries in China, roasted meat and drinking vessels were left in niches alongside the bodies of the deceased. Pitchers were generally placed on their sides, suggesting that they were emptied during funerary feasts. By the Late Shang Dynasty, graveside feasting became more elaborate and more focused on royal ancestors, and funeral rituals expanded beyond the graveside to include processions and ceremonies at ancestral temples. In each case, the living shared food and drink with the dead, but the meaning of these offerings was shaped by cultural views of death and the proper relationship between the living and the dead.

The commemoration of ancestors through collective rituals and repeated offerings of food, drink, and other goods at mortuary complexes was one way to reinforce territorial claims and reaffirm shared identity among populations that were dispersed or mobile. Mortuary complexes were meaningful places on ancient landscapes, and the performance of rituals and especially the consumption of alcohol and other special-occasion foods helped to emphasize this meaning for participants. For example, the impressive earthwork-mound complexes constructed by the Hopewell in the Ohio Valley (USA) have been interpreted as periodic gathering places where the dead from the surrounding region were interred and celebrated at large community feasts. In this way, funerary feasts can reinforce community solidarity and identity in the face of a disruptive event such as death.

Where socioeconomic inequality was present, mortuary complexes and the feasts that took place within them often reflected and reinforced social distinctions. Emphasizing particular ancestors through continued offerings and rituals legitimized elite claims to power. In ancient Mesopotamia, textual sources indicate that food and drink such as dates, fish, and wine were consumed at most funerals, but elite funerary feasts were distinguished by the quality of vessels and by the number of guests who could be served. In this case, graveside consumption was one arena for the ostentatious display of wealth, while at the same time the experience of commensality at funerary feasts and in other social contexts helped to unite Mesopotamians of different classes.

Some mortuary complexes contained kitchens where food was prepared for feasts and rituals. For example, Egyptian mortuary temples often had attached bakeries and breweries where foods such as bread, beer, goat, and fruits were prepared for offerings to the pharaoh's statue. In this case, funerary ritual overlapped with the other economic activities of the state; food prepared in these kitchens also fed the temple staff and provided the local workforce with wages in kind. Not all mortuary complexes had dedicated food preparation facilities, however. At Farfán in coastal Peru, the relatively small quantities of food placed in each burial and the use-wear present on most vessels suggest that food was prepared in households using quotidian cooking pots.

Food remains are an important line of evidence for understanding the range of activities that took place within mortuary complexes, but also for reconstructing the social experience of death, beliefs about the afterlife, and social organization within a wide range of ancient societies.

See also CARVINGS/CARVED REPRESENTATIONS OF FOOD; *CHICHA*; COMMENSALITY; FEASTING; FOOD AND IDENTITY; FOOD AND RITUAL; FOOD AND STATUS; FOODWAYS AND RELIGIOUS PRACTICES; OFFERINGS AND GRAVE GOODS; REPRESENTATIONAL MODELS OF FOOD AND FOOD PRODUCTION

Further Reading

Carr, Christopher, and D. Troy Case, eds. 2006. *Gathering Hopewell: Society, Ritual, and Ritual Interaction.* New York: Springer.

Cutright, Robyn E. 2011. Food for the Dead, Cuisine of the Living: Mortuary Food Offerings from the Jequetepeque Valley, Perú. In *From State to Empire in the Prehistoric Jequetepeque Valley, Peru*, edited by Colleen M. Zori and Ilana Johnson, 83–92. BAR International Series 2310. Oxford: British Archaeological Reports.

Nelson, Sarah Milledge. 2003. Feasting the Ancestors in Early China. In *The Archaeology and Politics of Food and Feasting in Early States and Empires*, edited by Tamara L. Bray, 65–89. New York: Kluwer Academic/Plenum Publishers.

Pollock, Susan. 2003. Feasts, Funerals, and Fast Food in Early Mesopotamian States. In *The Archaeology and Politics of Food and Feasting in Early States and Empires*, edited by Tamara L. Bray, 17–38. New York: Kluwer Academic/Plenum Publishers.

Smith, Vanessa. 2006. Food Fit for the Soul of a Pharaoh. *Expedition Magazine* 48(2):27–30.

■ROBYN E. CUTRIGHT

MTDNA ANALYSIS (MITOCHONDRIAL DNA)

The analysis of mtDNA was once the dominant method for tracing the origins and affinities of animals. Mitochondrial DNA is found in the mitochondria, the energy-generating organelles of most eukaryotic cells (cells with a membrane-bound nucleus). The mtDNA genome is circular and in most animals has between 16,000 and 17,000 paired nucleotide bases or base pairs. While every cell typically has two copies of each nuclear chromosome, some cells can have up to 8,000 copies of mtDNA. Both egg and sperm have mtDNA; during fertilization, however, the mitochondria of the sperm, concentrated in the tail, is excluded from the egg. Therefore the mitochondria of the zygote, a fertilized ovum, contain only mtDNA from the female line and reflect maternal lineages. MtDNA generally has more resolution over shorter timescales than nuclear DNA because of its higher mutation rate.

The mitochondrial genome is small, has an accelerated mutation rate, rarely undergoes recombination, and is relatively abundant when compared to nuclear DNA. These traits have made it a more attractive target for ancient DNA analyses of archaeological material. It is considered by many to be preferable for tracking geographic and historical relationships between specific groups of animals associated with human migration and interaction. Despite its accelerated mutation rate, the coding regions of mtDNA are believed to be sufficiently conserved to show clear links between domesticated animals and their wild ancestors, and between specific sets of sequences, or haplogroups, and geographic regions.

The noncoding segments of mtDNA, often referred to as the hyper-variable or control region, contain most of the informative mutations for reconstructing relationships. These regions not only accumulate more mutations but also are more easily damaged in living organisms and after death and deposition in the ground and thus require more critical analysis for their interpretation. In addition, mtDNA mutation rates vary between species and species groups, and universal application of mutation rates for mtDNA may complicate the calculation of divergence times.

See also ANIMAL DOMESTICATION; BIOMOLECULAR ANALYSIS; DNA ANALYSIS; ZOO-ARCHAEOLOGY

Further Reading

Brown, Terry, and Keri Brown. 2011. *Biomolecular Archaeology: An Introduction*. Chichester, UK: Wiley-Blackwell.

Matisoo-Smith, Elizabeth, and K. Ann Horsburgh. 2012. *DNA for Archaeologists*. Walnut Creek, CA: Left Coast Press.

■ ALICE STOREY

MULTI- AND INTERDISCIPLINARY APPROACHES

While the nature of archaeological practice has generally necessitated the use of over-lapping research questions, methods, and analytical frameworks, the archaeological study of food in particular requires the collective interest of multiple disciplines to address the complex research questions that are increasingly the focus of inquiry. Indeed, such cross-disciplinary study is essential, and food-related research in archaeology today not only draws from a large body of work being produced in other disciplines but involves the creation of research designs in cooperation with scholars in related fields to generate questions, determine appropriate research methods, and interpret findings.

The advances brought through the application of the biological, chemical, and molecular sciences in archaeology are wide ranging, from the identification of food residues preserved on the surface or absorbed into the body of cooking vessels and the identification of the chemical signatures of agricultural practices such as manuring or the disposal of food waste, to changes to the morphological features of certain grains through exposure to different cooking techniques and, especially, the identification (with increasing precision and accuracy) of wild and domestic plant and animal species. These contributions make it possible to investigate and identify the vast range of human behaviors associated with food procurement and consumption in the past.

Because food consumption is not limited to the biological needs of humans, but also pertains to cultural, economic, and social aspects of consumption—to questions about family, households, and communities, the role of gender and hierarchy, or the influence of religious beliefs or cultural identity, for example—archaeologists increasingly work with and draw upon the analytical tools and theoretical frameworks of anthropology, history, sociology, psychology, folklore, art history, material culture and architectural studies, feminist theory, and gender studies, as well as the emerging fields of food studies and gastronomy. In addition to the vast body of social, behavioral, and anthropological theory about food consumption, these related disciplines provide insight into foodways as a highly complex cultural system with both sensorial and communicative aspects.

Finally, cross-disciplinary research and discussion have implications beyond the reconstruction of past subsistence and food-related practices. The archaeological study of food, and of the changing relationships between humans and their environment, including patterns of land-use, is poised to contribute to current discussions about globalization, industrialization, sustainability, loss of biodiversity, and food security.

See also AGRICULTURE, ORIGINS OF; ARCHAEOBOTANY; BIOARCHAEOLOGIAL ANALYSIS; BIOMOLECULAR ANALYSIS; DOCUMENTARY ANALYSIS; ETHNOARCHAEOLOGY; ETHNOGRAPHIC SOURCES; EXPERIMENTAL ARCHAEOLOGY; FOODWAYS; LANDSCAPE AND ENVIRONMENTAL RECONSTRUCTION; ORAL AND FOLK NARRATIVES; PALEODIETARY ANALYSIS; PALEONUTRITION; PALEOPATHOLOGY; SUSTAINABILITY; ZOOARCHAEOLOGY

Further Reading

Carballo, David M., Paul Roscoe, and Gary W. Feinman. 2014. Cooperation and Collective Action in the Cultural Evolution of Complex Societies. *Journal of Archaeological Method and Theory* 21(1):98–133.

Counihan, Carole M. 2002. Interdisciplinarity, Food, and Power. *Appetite* 38:73–74.

Zarger, Rebecca K. 2009. Mosaics of Maya Livelihoods: Readjusting to Global and Local Food Crises. *NAPA Bulletin* 32(1):130–51.

■ KAREN BESCHERER METHENY AND MARY C. BEAUDRY

MUMMIES

Mummies are ancient human or animal remains still containing preserved skin or even internal soft tissues such as ligaments, muscles, or organ tissue. Mummified human remains can be found in all parts of the world. The earliest mummy to date, Acha Man, was recovered from the Atacama Desert in South America and has been radiocarbon dated to 8,970 BP (7020 BC). The preservation of the soft tissue varies between mummies considerably, ranging from excellently preserved whole bodies or body parts to poorly preserved specimens where only some soft-tissue remains cover the skeleton. Various mummification processes that reduce or stop postmortal body decay can cause soft-tissue preservation. Rapid dehydration of a body in a hot or cold, very dry environment prevents tissue decomposition by intracellular lysosomes (cellular organelles that enzymatically break down cellular debris), bacteria, and insects. In ancient Egypt, the removal of body fluids to preserve the body was further enhanced by the addition of natron salt. Heavy metals such as mercury (Hg) or arsenic (As) and low pH values also preserve soft tissue by suppressing enzymatic action.

In general, three different types of mummification processes exist: spontaneous mummification, anthropogenic mummification, and natural-intentional mummification. Spontaneous mummification is induced by nature and without the intervention of humans. Spontaneously mummified bodies can be further grouped into three subclassifications according to the natural environment contributing to the mummification process: ice mummies, bog bodies, and dry mummies.

A prominent example of an ice mummy is the Iceman, one of the oldest human mummies discovered. His body was preserved for more than 5,300 years in an Italian Alpine glacier before he was discovered in 1991 by two German mountaineers at an altitude of 3,210 meters above sea level. The Iceman contains a considerable amount of humidity in his cells that was retained while he was naturally mummified by freeze-drying. The mummified body, various tissue types, and even intestinal contents are therefore still extraordinary well preserved. Analysis of the food remains in the stomach indicates a fat-rich last meal, including a mix of grain material and meat fibers of wild animals.

Bog bodies are spontaneously mummified individuals found in the peat bog waters of northern Europe. The low pH values and the presence of the swamp moss product called "sphagnan" (a pectin-like carbohydrate polymer) in the peat bog water result on the one hand in the degradation of the bone matrix but on the other hand perfectly preserve the skin and other soft tissue by chemically cross-linking biomolecules. Most bog bodies like the famous Grauballe Man from Denmark were found in modern times while harvesting peat, which is used in a dried form as fossil fuel. Food remnants preserved in the gut and stomach of bog bodies provide a unique opportunity to describe their diet and subsistence practices during their lifetime.

In the hyperarid areas of the world such as the Atacama Desert in northern Chile or the Taklamakan Desert in China, deceased individuals spontaneously mummify via desiccation to dry mummies. About half of the famous Chinchorro mummies from Chile can be regarded as spontaneous dry mummies. Analysis of the bone chemistry and gut contents of spontaneously mummified Chinchorros showed a seafood-rich diet. The remaining Chinchorro individuals, however, were actively mummified by humans by removing the internal organs and replacing them with vegetable fibers or animal hair. This active mummification process induced by humans is termed anthropogenic mummification. Ancient Egyptians believed in the concept of eternal life and that death marked the beginning of a journey to the fields of eternity. This desired afterlife was linked to the active preservation of the deceased body. Increasing development of mummification techniques such as evisceration of the body and the use of embalming agents resulted in thousands of mummified human remains. Even today most of them display perfectly preserved body features. In Egypt, mummification was initially an exclusively royal privilege and was used to enhance the authority and power of the king's throne by displaying the deceased ruler's body during his funeral and by the periodic performance of mummy-related rituals. Thus, dietary information extracted from these mummies provides a narrow view of elite dietary practices, in contrast to later Egyptian mummification of non-royal elite and, finally, of members of the public.

Natural-intentional mummification refers to all mummies that were mummified naturally but were placed intentionally in a mummification-favoring environment (arid, cold). Most prominent examples are mummies in churches and catacombs or the Inca mummies from the Andes in South America. Interestingly, natural-intentional mummification refers also to mummified individuals who actively started the mummification process during life. Japanese priests of the 17th century, for example, are reported to have reduced the intake of nutrition toward the end of their life, becoming extremely thin and dehydrated, thereby favoring their natural mummification after death.

See also BIOARCHAEOLOGICAL ANALYSIS; BOGS; GUT ANALYSIS; ICEMAN; PALEODIETARY ANALYSIS; PALEONUTRITION; PALEOPATHOLOGY; PARASITOLOGICAL ANALYSIS

Further Reading

Aufderheide, Arthur C. 2003. *The Scientific Study of Mummies*. Cambridge: Cambridge University Press.
Lynnerup, Niels. 2007. Mummies. *American Journal of Physical Anthropology* 134(S45):162–90.

■ FRANK MAIXNER AND ALBERT R. ZINK

MURALS
See WALL PAINTINGS/MURALS

MUSHROOMS
See FUNGI

ÑANCHOC VALLEY (PERU)

As a result of major environmental and climatic changes, plant and animal communities were altered considerably throughout the Late Pleistocene and Middle Holocene period (~11,000–5,000 BP) in most regions of South America. For this time period, there is scant evidence for plant foods in the archaeological record. In localities where organic remains are preserved, there is macrobotanical evidence (e.g., burned seeds) of the domestication of squash (*Cucurbita moschata*) in Colombia, Ecuador, and Peru by at least 10,000 BP and the use of palm nuts (*Arecaceae* sp.) and other plants in Colombia by 9,200 BP. At the end of the Pleistocene period, when climate conditions were generally warm and stable, intentional plant manipulation was under way in several areas, but primarily in the neotropics and the central Andes.

Some of the best-documented archaeological evidence for the early adoption of plant foods comes from the multiple resource zones of the western slopes of the Andes in northern Peru, where macro- and microfossils, the latter from the calculus of human teeth, reveal the presence of several food crops. In the Ñanchoc Valley in northern Peru, several major crops were adopted between at least 9,500 and 7,000 BP, including squash (*C. moschata*), peanuts (*Arachis* sp.), common bean (*Phaseolus*), pacay (a tree fruit; *Inga feuillei*), quinoa (*Chenopodium*), coca (*Erythroxylum novogranatense* var. *truxillense*), and industrial cotton (*Gossypium*). Archaeobotanical remains and the bones of various large and small animal species provide evidence for a broad-spectrum subsistence economy in the tropical dry forest of the valley. The evidence also indicates that by 6,500 BP an effective agricultural system employing a wide range of wild and domesticated seed, tree, vegetable, and root crops provided balanced, nutritious, and stable diets to the inhabitants of the valley. This system exploited small but fertile alluvial patches along the Ñanchoc River.

Three archaeological phases in the valley record these developments. The early El Palto Phase (~11,500–10,000 BP) resulted in a pattern of scheduled, possibly seasonal movements between coastal and upland locations on the western Andean slopes, where various plants, animals, and seafood were available during all or at different times of the year. Regional and local variation in stone tools, dated between 10,500 and 9,000 BP, and the use of small domestic structures and local raw lithic material suggest the economic exploitation of circumscribed local territories and possibly semi-sedentism. Domesticated squash (*C. moschata*) was adopted at this time. The constriction of territory, reduced mobility, and localization of populations continued and accelerated past ~9,000 years ago into the Las Pircas and Tierra Blanca phases. In some areas of the valley, this pattern of resource exploitation began to change rapidly between ~8,500 and 6,000 years ago.

Las Pircas hunters and gatherers began a local permanent or perhaps sedentary life at higher elevations between 8,000 and 7,000 BP, with small organized settlements, burial of the dead, domestic circular houses, and subtle social differences. Unifacial tools, a varied ground stone technology, simple food storage, and a food economy based primarily on the exploitation of a wide variety of plants and animals dominated the technology. Las Pircas sites yielded wild and cultivated squash, chenopodium (cf. quinoa), peanut, yucca, manioc, and several unidentified wild fruits. Low frequencies of exotic materials (e.g., marine shell, carved stingray spines, quartz crystals, and raw stone material) suggest minor contact with distant coastal and highland areas.

During the Tierra Blanca Phase (~7,000–4,500 BP), settlements aggregated closer to the valley floor and its fertile soils. House styles changed (from small, circular structures to larger, multiple-room, rectangular structures); cotton, beans, and coca were added; and residents constructed an artificial agricultural system associated with irrigation canals and sedentism. Although exotics disappeared, the separation of public and private or domestic space was pronounced, as evidenced by dual, stone-lined, multitiered earthen mounds at the Cementerio de Ñanchoc site in the Ñanchoc Valley. Lime was produced here in a controlled, presumed public ritual context for probable use with coca leaves or as a food supplement. This site was located in an area separate from but also accessible to all households. For reasons not fully understood, sedentism did not occur everywhere in this valley. Some groups continued practicing a mobile foraging lifeway well after cultigens were introduced. Between ~6,000 and 4,500 BP, farmers and foragers coexisted and were codependent on one another.

The development of more permanent and extensive forms of sedentism and small, complex societies in the Ñanchoc Valley and in a few other areas on the Peruvian coast and in the highlands occurred between ~4,500 and 3,500 BP. During this period, maritime and agricultural villages along the coast increased in size, and the first example of large-scale, monumental, nondomestic architecture appeared in the form of stone platform mounds and small ceremonial pyramids. A few examples are Huaca Prieta, Alto Salaverry, Áspero, Huaynuna, Caral, and Garagay.

Although many of the cultural transformations from the Late Pleistocene to the middle Holocene period are understood in terms of different climate and environmental changes, others can be comprehended only in terms of social and cultural processes. A paradox is that just when cooler or arid climatic conditions are thought to have been unfavorable in northern Peru during this period, people in the Ñanchoc Valley moved toward sociocultural complexity, transitioning from mobile foraging to less mobile and eventually sedentary agriculture in the Ñanchoc Valley, and taking steps toward plant and possibly animal domestication in other areas of the Andes.

See also AGRICULTURE, ORIGINS OF; BROAD SPECTRUM REVOLUTION; COCA; CULTIVATION; IRRIGATION/HYDRAULIC ENGINEERING; LANDSCAPE AND ENVIRONMENTAL RECONSTRUCTION; SEDENTISM AND DOMESTICATION

Further Reading

Balter, Michael. 2007. Seeking Agriculture's Ancient Roots. *Science* 316(5833):1830–35.

Dillehay, Tom D. 2011. *From Foragers to Farmers in the Andes: New Perspectives on Food Production and Social Organization.* Cambridge: Cambridge University Press.

Dillehay, Tom D., Jack Rossen, Thomas C. Andres, and David E. Williams. 2007. Preceramic Adoption of Peanut, Squash, and Cotton in Northern Peru. *Science* 316(5833):1890–93.

Hastorf, Christine A. 1999. Cultural Implications of Crop Introductions in Andean Prehistory. In *The Prehistory of Food: Appetites for Change,* edited by Chris Godsen and James Hather, 35–56. London: Routledge.

Piperno, Dolores R. 2006. The Origins of Plant Cultivation and Domestication in the Neotropics: A Behavioral Ecological Perspective. In *Behavioral Ecology and the Transition to Agriculture,* edited by Douglas J. Kennett and Bruce Winterhalder, 137–66. Berkeley: University of California Press.

Piperno, Dolores R., and Tom D. Dillehay. 2008. Starch Grains on Human Teeth Reveal Early Broad Crop Diet in Northern Peru. *Proceedings of the National Academy of Sciences USA* 105(5):19622–27.

■ THOMAS D. DILLEHAY

NATIVE AMERICAN ETHNOBOTANY

Native American people were omnivores, eating anything from wild rice to a mammoth. Evidence of food plant use is found in archaeological contexts but is also derived from a large body of ethnographic accounts and from a large database of Native American plant use known as Native American Ethnobotany (NAE). The focus of this entry is on native species only; although archaeologically known peoples quickly adopted many introduced European plants, they only did so after about AD 1500.

Determining which plants were consumed as foods is a significant challenge. Even plant parts found in coprolites might not have been eaten as food but might have been taken as medicines or ingested in some other accidental way. Ethnographic and ethnohistorical evidence shows beyond a doubt that in many areas in North America, acorns were a very important food, for example. NAE has 302 different records showing the Native American use of some sort of oak as food, though 484 additional records report the use of oak leaves, bark, wood, and fruit for nonfood purposes, from medicinal treatments, dyes, fibers, and building materials to game pieces, musical instruments, and fuel. Ethnographic accounts indicate that acorn meal also was used to repair cracked clay pots. The archaeological context is therefore critical for determining a food-related use.

As this example demonstrates, one dilemma in the study of the plants used as foods by archaeologically known peoples is determining the role of plant remains found at a site. Similar challenges exist for an array of additional plants such as sunflowers, beans, roses, bearberry or manzanita, biscuit root, currant, and many others that have a broad range of uses as both foods and drugs, dyes, fibers, and other nonfood uses. One approach that may be used to overcome this challenge is to consider plants at a higher taxonomic level—the family level—and gain some patterns at the expense of detail. There are, in North America, 238 families of native plants recognized in the most recent classification of the orders and families of flowering plants. For each family, the NAE database includes a total number of species in the region, the number utilized as foods, and the number utilized for something else. For example, Asteraceae, the sunflower family, has 3,291 native species in North America, of which 154 are reportedly used as foods while 417 have other uses (e.g., drug, dye, fiber).

A scatterplot analysis allows an archaeologist in North America to put a probability on the use of a particular plant as a food or for other purposes (figure 43). First utilized in 1996, this method involves two regression analyses, first of the food plants, second of the "other use" plants. The residuals are then calculated for each case; the residual is the observed (actual) value of the variable minus the predicted value obtained in the regression analysis. In this case, if the residual for a family in the food regression is large and positive, it means that the family is disproportionately used by people for food. If it is large and negative, it means the family is only rarely selected for food use. To complete the analysis, the residuals are plotted in an XY graph with the food plant residuals along the horizontal axis and the "other use" residuals on the vertical axis. Note that the positions of the zero level are exaggerated in both directions, giving the graph four quadrants. The upper right quad shows families that have high

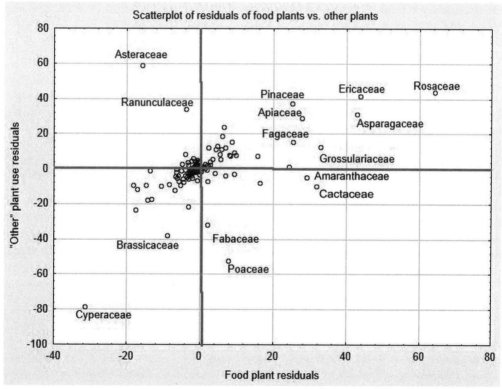

Figure 43. Scatterplot analysis of plants found in the Native American Ethnobotany (NAE) database showing the probability of a particular plant's use as a food or for other, nonfood purposes. In this figure, the horizontal axis shows residuals for the number of species per family used for foods in the NAE database, and the vertical axis shows the residuals for the number of all other utilized species (except foods) in the NAE. The families in the upper right quadrant are used very frequently by native peoples for *both* these purposes; those in the lower right are most likely to be used for food and not for other purposes (for a detailed discussion, see Moerman 1996; Prendergast et al. 1998). Figure by Daniel E. Moerman.

residuals on both regressions; they are families with disproportionate use in both categories. These include Rosaceae, Ericaceae, Asparagaceae, Grossulariaceae, and so on; these are very likely to be food plants but are equally likely to be "other use" plants. The lower left quad shows families that are likely to be rare in archaeological collections since they are broadly underutilized for everything, including foods and "other uses." The upper left quad showing Asteraceae and Ranunculaceae (the buttercups) represents plants that are widely utilized for nonfood purposes; both of them are very commonly utilized sources of drug plants. The most interesting quad from an archaeological perspective is the lower right where families low on "other uses" but high on food uses are located. These include the labeled points for Cactaceae, Amaranthaceae, Poaceae, and Fabaceae. While all of these families have some nonfood uses, they tend to have very few. Most archaeological remains from these families are probably foods. The remaining five families in this quad that are not labeled, and not in the central scrum are, right to left, Amaryllidaceae (e.g., onions and garlic), Montiaceae (bitterroot), Polygonaceae (rhubarb), Loasaceae (blazing star), and Onagraceae (evening primrose). Perhaps the two most interesting of these families are the Fabaceae, the beans, and the Poaceae, the grasses. The latter, of course, is the source of the great bulk of modern food, the food grains wheat, rice, maize, barley, sorghum, millet, sugarcane, oats, and rye; and the former, the beans, includes soybeans, peanuts, beans (*Phaseolus* spp.), chickpeas, and cowpeas.

See also ARCHAEOBOTANY; ETHNOGRAPHIC SOURCES; NUTS; PLANT HUSBANDRY; PLANT PROCESSING; PLANTS

Further Reading

Bremer, Birgitta, Kåre Bremer, Mark W. Chase, et al. 2009. An Update of the Angiosperm Phylogeny Group Classification for the Orders and Families of Flowering Plants: APG III. *Botanical Journal of the Linnean Society* 161(2):105–21.

Etkin, Nina L., ed. 1994. *Eating on the Wild Side: The Pharmacologic, Ecologic, and Social Implications of Using Noncultigens.* Tucson: University of Arizona Press.

Kuhnlein, Harriet V., and Nancy J. Turner. 1991. *Traditional Plant Foods of Canadian Indigenous Peoples: Nutrition, Botany and Use.* Amsterdam: Gordon and Breach.

Moerman, Daniel E. 1996. An Analysis of the Food Plants and Drug Plants of Native North America. *Journal of Ethnopharmacology* 52(1):1–22.

———. 1998. *Native American Ethnobotany.* Portland, OR: Timber Press.

———. 2003. *Native American Ethnobotany Database: A Database of Foods, Drugs, Dyes and Fibers of Native American Peoples, Derived from Plants.* http://herb.umd.umich.edu.

Prendergast, H. D. V., N. L. Etkin, D. R. Harris, and P. J. Houghton, eds. 1998. *Plants for Food and Medicine: Proceedings of the Joint Conference of the Society for Economic Botany and the International Society for Ethnopharmacology, London, 1–6 July 1996.* Richmond, UK: Royal Botanic Gardens, Kew.

■ DANIEL E. MOERMAN

NEANDERTHAL DIET

The abundance of Neanderthal fossil remains makes them the best understood of the extinct hominin species, yet important aspects of their behavior, including diet, are still under debate. These studies are complicated by the frequent use of Neanderthals as foils for our own, "more advanced," species. For many years, we debated whether Neanderthals were capable hunters or merely scavengers. Though they are now accepted as proficient hunters, Neanderthals are still thought to have a single, restricted, and "primitive" dietary pattern, comprised almost exclusively of meat and fat from large animals. Data from four main research areas now indicate that Neanderthal diets were diverse, more like that of early modern humans.

The environments in which Neanderthals lived determined the kinds of foods available to them. Though exclusively Eurasian, Neanderthals were exposed to a large array of environments and climates. Their full geographic range included everything from steppe to closed forest, with each habitat having its own contingent of flora and fauna. In the roughly 100,000 years that they occupied this region (ca. 150–40 KYA), Neanderthals experienced long glacial periods as well as several, albeit short, warm climatic cycles. Different Neanderthal populations therefore had access to a large number of plant and animal foods, which varied through time and across space.

New analyses of the fossil remains of Neanderthals have provided more information about their diets. Of the handful of studied Neanderthals, most have nitrogen isotope signals like those of foxes and bears, indicating that most of their dietary protein came from meat and that they were relatively high on the food chain. The carbon isotope signals of these individuals suggest they did not eat aquatic foods. Dental macro- and microwear patterns in Neanderthals, when broadly compared with early modern humans, are indicative of more meat consumption. The patterns of dental wear vary among Neanderthal populations, however, with groups from more wooded environments having dental wear indicating more plant consumption than those from open environments. Microscopic particles of food and other food residues are sometimes preserved in the dental calculus, or plaque, on teeth. These microremains and residues show that Neanderthals from several different environments ate a wide range of plant foods, including some starch-rich tubers at Spy Cave in Belgium and possibly some medicinal plants, like yarrow and chamomile, at Sima de los Huesos in Spain. Modified plant microremains found in Neanderthal calculus from Shanidar Cave, Iraq, suggest that they cooked some plants.

The tools that Neanderthals employed can indicate how they procured and processed their food. Though Neanderthals made a variety of stone tools, they made fewer types than did early modern humans. There is no evidence of grindstones or other advanced plant processing technologies, or harpoons or other fishing tools. Neanderthal stone points were shaped for use as the tips of thrusting or throwing spears, and not for projectiles like arrows or atlatl darts. This suggests that Neanderthals focused primarily on large game and did not invest in more advanced technology for consuming plants or for capturing small, fast, and hard-to-catch game like birds and fish. Residues on a few Neanderthal stone tools from Payre and La Quina, France, and from Starosele, in the Crimea, come from starchy and woody plants as well as from birds and mammals, however. Overall, the tools suggest Neanderthals hunted large game with heavy spears, and occasionally ate smaller game and plant foods, even if they did not have specialized tools to access these foods.

The direct remains of Neanderthals' food are the best evidence of their diet. Bones with butchery marks indicate that Neanderthals hunted a range of animal species, including large game like reindeer, red deer, horse, bison, wooly rhinoceros, and mammoth and small game like birds, rabbits, and hares. In many Neanderthal sites in north-central and northwestern Europe, the animal bones come almost exclusively from a single species of large game like reindeer or horse, though the exact species varies from place to place. In other sites, often in the Mediterranean region, the bones indicate that Neanderthals ate a large array of animals and did not focus on a single species. In those places where Neanderthals ate small game, there is diversity in the kinds of small game they hunted. In some sites, they only harvested slow, easy-to-catch small game like tortoises, while in other areas they also hunted fast and hard-to-catch small game like birds and rabbits. Overall, the way Neanderthals hunted and the species they ate varied from place to place. Because plant remains do not fossilize as readily as animal remains, there is less evidence for plant use. Charred seeds from legumes, grasses, and pistachios have been found at Kebara Cave, Israel, and phytoliths from grass seed husks and other plants have been found at Amud Cave, Israel, suggesting that in the Near East, at least, Neanderthals consumed a variety of plant foods. Similar remains have not been discovered at other Neanderthal sites, but it is difficult to tell whether this is a preservation bias or a true dietary difference.

The overall pattern suggested by the archaeological data is that Neanderthals consumed different foods in different habitats. Animal meat was consistently a large component of their diets, but the relative importance of large game, small game, and plant foods varied from place to place. Therefore, Neanderthals likely behaved more like modern human foragers, who also modify their diets depending on the abundance and value of the foods in their particular environment.

See also ARCHAEOBOTANY; DENTAL ANALYSIS; FORAGING; HUNTER-GATHERER SUBSISTENCE; PALEOLITHIC DIET; PLANT PROCESSING; RESIDUE ANALYSIS, STARCH; STABLE ISOTOPE ANALYSIS; WEAPONS, STONE; ZOOARCHAEOLOGY

Further Reading

Conard, Nicholas J., ed. 2006. *When Neanderthals and Modern Humans Met.* Tübingen: Kerns Verlag.

Conard, Nicholas J., and Jürgen Richter, eds. 2011. *Neanderthal Lifeways, Subsistence and Technology: One Hundred Fifty Years of Neanderthal Study.* Dordrecht: Springer.

Henry, Amanda G., Alison S. Brooks, and Dolores R. Piperno. 2011. Microfossils in Calculus Demonstrate Consumption of Plants and Cooked Foods in Neanderthal Diets (Shanidar III, Iraq; Spy I and II, Belgium). *Proceedings of the National Academy of Sciences USA* 108(2):486–91.

Hovers, Erella, and Steven L. Kuhn, eds. 2006. *Transitions before the Transition: Evolution and Stability in the Middle Paleolithic and the Middle Stone Age.* New York: Springer.

■ AMANDA G. HENRY

NECTAR
See HONEY AND NECTAR

NEOLITHIC PACKAGE
The terms *Neolithic package* or *Neolithic bundle* refer to a set of innovations that marked the transition from hunter-gatherer subsistence to agriculture during the Neolithic period.

Polished stone tools, the domestication of animals and plants, and sedentism have been seen as key elements of the "Neolithic package" that developed during the late tenth and ninth millennia BC in the so-called Fertile Crescent of the Near East. These transitions were followed by the introduction of pottery in the seventh millennium BC. These innovations would then have spread northward, arriving in central Europe around 5500 BC.

Recent research has outlined two main problems regarding this process. The first applies to the specific criteria for the Neolithic package itself, while the second, more contentious, question centers on the formation and the mode by which these innovations spread.

Detailed regional studies substantiate the fact that not all elements of the package were present in every region, and others were around much earlier than hitherto believed. A semi-sedentary lifestyle seems to have evolved in the Near East as early as the Epipaleolithic; at sites like Abu Hureyra (Syria) or Ohalo II (Israel), there is evidence for large-scale gathering of nondomesticated plants as a basis for year-round occupation. Most researchers now agree that a sedentary way of life and long-term acquaintance with wild plant and animal forms were essential to domestication processes. Pottery, on the other hand, was not invented yet when the key changes toward a new lifestyle took place in the Fertile Crescent, and thus was not part of the initial package transmitted to other regions in the Pre-Pottery Neolithic. The insight that there are several differently packaged Neolithic bundles has left only the presence of food production as a secure, ubiquitous indicator for the Neolithic stage.

Further, ideas on the location and reasons for the start of the Neolithic have seen paradigmatic changes over the last decades. Following the work of Kathleen Kenyon at Jericho, Israel, the roots of food production initially were sought in the Southern Levant. With the research of Linda and Robert Braidwood at Jarmo in northern Iraq, however, the focus shifted to the northeast of the Fertile Crescent, or its "hilly flanks." Recently, it has become clear that the region between the middle and upper reaches of the Euphrates and Tigris and the foothills of the Taurus Mountains (Upper Mesopotamia) has the potential to be the cradle of agriculture in the Near East. In this region the wild forms of several domesticated plants (the "founder crops": emmer wheat, einkorn wheat, hulled barley, lentil, chickpea, bitter vetch, and flax) overlap.

At the same time, research on the reasons for this important change has undergone further development. Initially a direct relationship between the material needs of people and the advent of agriculture had been drawn. In his model of what he termed the *Neolithic Revolution*, V. G. Childe proposed climate change as the main driving force for people to settle down permanently as farmers. In his view, aridity drove people to concentrate in oases, and population pressure forced them to adopt new ways of food production.

Starting with the Braidwoods' research in Upper Mesopotamia, it became clear that this region had the environmental features and wild biota necessary for the Neolithization process. In addition, nearly every site from the tenth and ninth millennia BC excavated at the appropriate scale shows a spatial division into residential and specialized workshop areas, and special buildings or open courtyards for communal and ritual purposes as well as evidence for extensive feasting. This evidence suggests a degree of social complexity that was hitherto unsuspected for hunter-gatherers. The rich iconography and the monumentality of buildings related to cult are especially striking. One of the key sites in this respect is the hilltop sanctuary of Göbekli Tepe in the Turkish Euphrates region. Excavations conducted there since 1995 have revealed monumental architecture and rich iconography dating to the early and middle Pre-Pottery Neolithic (9600–8000 cal BC). This indicates that the mentality of the hunter-gatherers who visited Göbekli Tepe and their social structures were changing before and not after the shift to food production as a way of life, as argued by Jacques Cauvin.

Another paradigm shift in recent years concerns the dispersion and emergence of Neolithic packages in several parts of the Old World. Three main hypotheses have been proposed. The first one sees the Neolithization of Europe as the result of the migration of people from areas with an already developed Neolithic society; parallel autochthonous invention of key innovations and the diffusion of ideas, food, and technology form the other poles of explanation. Genetic evidence as well as the analyses of strontium isotope ratios in bones seem to hint at the first possibility, the movement of people and domesticated animals, as the most important factor. Formation, content, and distribution of the "Neolithic package" are still under intense scientific debate, however.

See also AGRICULTURE, ORIGINS OF; ARCHAEOBOTANY; BIOMOLECULAR ANALYSIS; CEREALS; DNA ANALYSIS; FOOD TECHNOLOGY AND IDEAS ABOUT FOOD, SPREAD OF; GÖBEKLI TEPE; OLD WORLD GLOBALIZATION AND FOOD EXCHANGES; PALEODEMOGRAPHY; PLANT DOMESTICATION; SEDENTISM AND DOMESTICATION; STABLE ISOTOPE ANALYSIS

Further Reading

Bentley, R. Alexander, Lounès Chikhi, and T. Douglas Price. 2003. The Neolithic Transition in Europe: Comparing Broad Scale Genetic and Local Scale Isotopic Evidence. *Antiquity* 77(295):63–65.
Çilingiroğlu, Çiler. 2005. The Concept of "Neolithic Package": Considering Its Meaning and Applicability. *Documenta Praehistorica* 32:1–13.
Dietrich, Oliver, Manfred Heun, Jens Notroff, et al. 2012. The Role of Cult and Feasting in the Emergence of Neolithic Communities: New Evidence from Göbekli Tepe, South-Eastern Turkey. *Antiquity* 86(333):674–95.
Lev-Yadun, Simcha, Avi Gopher, and Shahal Abbo. 2000. The Cradle of Agriculture. *Science* 288(5471):1602–3.
Lichter, Clemens, ed. 2005. *How Did Farming Reach Europe? Anatolian-European Relations from the Second Half of the 7th through the First Half of the 6th Millennium cal BC.* Istanbul: Yayınları.
Schmidt, Klaus. 2012. *Göbekli Tepe: A Stone Age Sanctuary in South-Eastern Anatolia.* Berlin: ExOriente.
Watkins, Trevor. 2010. New Light on Neolithic Revolution in South-West Asia. *Antiquity* 84(325):621–34.

■ OLIVER DIETRICH, JENS NOTROFF, AND KLAUS SCHMIDT

NEOLITHIC REVOLUTION/NEOLITHIZATION
See AGRICULTURE, ORIGINS OF

NIAH CAVES (MALAYSIA)
The Niah Great Cave is the most iconic and comprehensively studied archaeological site in Island Southeast Asia. The cave system of Niah is part of the Gunung Subis limestone

massif, located southwest of the city of Miri, within the main eastern outcrop of Bukit Bekajang in what is now Sarawak, Malaysia. Niah as a site is highly significant because it is one of two places in Island Southeast Asia where archaeologists have recovered the earliest evidence of anatomically modern human remains and artifacts dated to ca. 50,000 years ago (the other site is Tabon Cave in central Palawan, Philippines). Moreover, the study of the archaeological deposits (50,000 to 4,500 BP) at Niah has led to a rich understanding of people–environment relationships during this early period.

As a result of systematic, long-term archaeological exploration and research that began within the cave's huge west mouth in the early 1950s, we know more of the transformation of subsistence strategies at this site. This knowledge is based on a thorough application of current paleoenvironmental methods, including palynology, zooarchaeology, archaeobotany, soil micromorphology, ecology, and lithics use-wear analysis, all of which contribute to a better understanding of foraging practices on-site and in the surrounding areas.

At around 50,000 to 35,000 years ago we know that the subsistence strategy of human communities around Niah was wholly foraging. There was no evidence of any domesticated plants or animals. Forest clearing was not substantial. Mollusks were gathered and small and large animals were exploited; butchering marks are found on most of these animal remains. There is also evidence for bone tool manufacture using the remains of consumed animals. Use-wear marks on stone tools suggest the cutting and slicing of soft and hard materials. Simultaneously, people also gathered nuts and tubers, and had the capacity to process and detoxify poisonous plants for consumption, such as the nuts of the tree *Pangium edule* Reinw.

Paleoenvironmental and archaeological data from 11,500 to 4,500 years ago suggest the presence of a subsistence system that may not be considered purely foraging, however. The domestication of bananas in the region, the management of tree crops, and the cultivation of various yams and aroids (plants from the Araceae family, e.g., taro [*Colocasia esculenta*], but other species from the forest, including some that are eaten by humans even today, though only as famine food), together with the nonpackaged spread of animals such as the domestic pig, are among the mid- to early Holocene subsistence practices documented archaeologically at Niah. The collective data speak to the complexity of the strategies applied by human communities to access and manage their food sources.

Niah also has contributed to our pan–Island Southeast Asian understanding of rice agriculture. Current thinking puts rice introduction at ca. 4,000 years ago in the region, but its dominance as a subsistence food only occurred in the last 2,000 years. Evidence of rice utilization at Niah supports this interpretation but leaves unresolved the question of whether rice served as a subsistence food or more as a ritualized and status-bearing managed crop.

See also AGRICULTURE, ORIGINS OF; ARCHAEOBOTANY; CULTIVATION; FORAGING; HUNTER-GATHERER SUBSISTENCE; PACIFIC OCEANIC EXCHANGE; PALEODIETARY ANALYSIS; PLANT HUSBANDRY; RICE; SUBSISTENCE MODELS; TOOLS/UTENSILS, ORGANIC MATERIALS; TOOLS/UTENSILS, STONE; USE-WEAR ANALYSIS, LITHICS; ZOOARCHAEOLOGY

Further Reading

Barker, Graeme, ed. 2013. *Rainforest Foraging and Farming in Island Southeast Asia: The Archaeology of the Niah Caves, Sarawak.* Vol. 1. Cambridge: McDonald Institute for Archaeological Research.

Harrisson, Tom, and Barbara Harrisson. 1971. *The Prehistory of Sabah.* Kota Kinabalu, Malaysia: Sabah Society.

■ VICTOR PAZ

NIXTAMALIZATION

Nixtamalization is the process of boiling *Zea mays* L. (maize) kernels in an alkali solution. Nixtamalization, as it is known in Mesoamerica, is also called hominy production in the Eastern Woodlands. The traditional process creates an alkali solution using wood ash, burnt shell, lye, or a lime solution. Maize kernels are then boiled and steeped in the solution. Finally, the kernels are washed in clean water to remove the hulls. Removal of the hulls allows for the kernels to be ground into a wet dough, *masa*, that either can be stored or used fresh in the production of tortillas. The act of boiling maize kernels in an alkali solution changes the phenotypic and chemical structures, which are beneficial in terms of health and increase the storage capacity of the kernels. Nixtamalization enhances the availability of niacin and its precursors, including tryptophan, which decreases the risk of pellagra.

Recent studies suggest that the act of nixtamalization decreased morphological distortion during carbonization and increased the probability of archaeological preservation. Because nixtamalization softens the pericarp (the fruit wall) and increases water uptake, the kernel is able to swell without splitting, allowing it to maintain its shape. Alkali-processed maize kernels, when carbonized, lose their pericarps, their points of attachment, and their embryos, giving them a distinct bean shape. This shape resembles those kernels found at archaeological sites. Current research is centered on determining if maize found at archaeological sites was, in fact, alkali-processed. Although archaeologists have determined that nixtamalization was widely used, future research should investigate when diffusion occurred between Mesoamerica and North America and what varieties of maize were commonly used. Its widespread usage in the New World suggests nixtamalization's importance as a food processing technique for past and present societies, and it is a significant tool for aiding archaeologists in understanding prehistoric uses of maize.

See also ARCHAEOBOTANY; EXPERIMENTAL ARCHAEOLOGY; FOOD TECHNOLOGY AND IDEAS ABOUT FOOD, SPREAD OF; MACROREMAINS; MAIZE; MILLING; PALEONUTRITION; PLANT PROCESSING

Future Reading

Dezendorf, Caroline. 2013. The Effects of Food Processing on the Archaeological Visibility of Maize: An Experimental Study of Carbonization of Lime-Treated Maize Kernels. *Ethnobiology Letters* 4:12–20.

Goette, Susan, Michele Williams, Sissel Johannessen, and Christine A. Hastorf. 1994. Towards Reconstructing Ancient Maize: Experiments in Processing and Charring. *Journal of Ethnobiology* 14(1):1–21.

Katz, S. H., M. L. Hediger, and L. A. Valleroy. 1974. Traditional Maize Processing Techniques in the New World. *Science* 184(4138):765–73.

■ CAROLINE A. DEZENDORF

NUTRITION
See PALEONUTRITION

NUTS

Nuts can serve as an additional source of protein in the diet or as a dietary staple, depending on their availability and abundance. Hunter-gatherer groups were more likely to rely on nuts as a staple food source, but agrarian societies made use of nut resources also, sometimes collecting them from locally available sources and sometimes bringing them into cultivation in gardens and orchards. Most nut remains found in archaeological contexts are preserved by charring, but waterlogged nut remains have been recovered. Pollen and starch grains are also key sources of evidence.

Acorns (*Quercus* spp.) are known from both archaeological and ethnographic evidence to have been a dietary staple in many areas of the world such as eastern North America, California (USA), and Japan. Acorns can be a very abundant food source, but harvest from a given species of oak can vary greatly from year to year and therefore reliance on acorns as a staple is possible only in areas with a variety of different oak species. Acorns also may have been used as food in Europe, but the archaeobotanical record is poorer and more ambiguous. At Çatalhöyük, a Neolithic village in southern central Turkey, acorns and almonds were found together with other stored foods, suggesting that these nuts were probably collected as food. Starch grains and wear analysis of grinding stones from early Neolithic sites in the middle Yellow River Valley (China) demonstrated the use of acorns (*Lithocarpus* sp., *Quercus* sp., and *Cyclobalanopsis* sp.).

A rich ethnographic record suggests that acorns were ground or crushed into a flour, then leached to remove the water-soluble tannins before cooking. Stone mortars and pestles, used to grind acorns and other seeds, are sometimes found on archaeological sites. Though in historical times acorns have been perceived in many cultures as famine food or fit only for the poor, in other areas they are seen as a culturally significant and valued food source.

See also ARCHAEOBOTANY; ÇATALHÖYÜK; ETHNOGRAPHIC SOURCES; FAMINE; FOOD STORAGE; NATIVE AMERICAN ETHNOBOTANY; PALYNOLOGY; PLANT HUSBANDRY; PLANT PROCESSING; RESIDUE ANALYSIS, STARCH; TOOLS/UTENSILS, GROUND STONE; USE-WEAR ANALYSIS, LITHICS

Further Reading

Bogaard, Amy, Michael Charles, Katheryn C. Twiss, et al. 2009. Private Pantries and Celebrated Surplus: Storing and Sharing Food at Neolithic Çatalhöyük, Central Anatolia. *Antiquity* 83(321):649–68.

Liu, Li, Judith Field, Richard Fullagar, et al. 2010. What Did Grinding Stones Grind? New Light on Early Neolithic Subsistence Economy in the Middle Yellow River Valley, China. *Antiquity* 84(325):816–33.

Mason, Sarah. 1995. Acornutopia? Determining the Role of Acorns in Past Human Subsistence. In *Food in Antiquity*, edited by John Wilkins, David Harvey, and Mike Dobson, 12–24. Exeter: University of Exeter Press.

■ LISA MOFFETT

O

OEDENBURG (FRANCE)

The Roman settlement of Oedenburg was founded at the beginning of the first century AD in the lower plains of the Rhine River, between the present-day communities of Biesheim and Kunheim in Alsace, France. The archaeology of the Roman settlement comprises two successive first-century AD military camps, a civil agglomeration including a large temple complex (first to fourth century AD), and a late Roman occupation. Much of the archaeological site is located under the present groundwater level, resulting in excellent preservation through waterlogging. The archaeobotanical analysis has revealed a rich and diverse plant spectrum of cultural and wild plants. In total, 303 plant taxa have been identified, preserved through waterlogging (n=292), mineralization (n=57), and charring (n=58). The plant assemblage illustrates that the inhabitants of Roman Oedenburg had access to a wide variety of vegetable food. The main part of their basic diet consisted of cereals and pulses; their dishes were seasoned with typically Roman condiments, while fruits and nuts from both local and foreign sources were regularly consumed. In comparison to other sites in the Upper Rhine region and the north of Switzerland, the list of food plants in Oedenburg is extensive and varied. This can be linked to the military occupation of the site and, after that, to its function as a center of distribution.

Many plants were imported from the Mediterranean region, while others were traded over greater distance (e.g., black pepper, black cumin, olive, date, and stone pine). The spectrum of wild plants demonstrates a settlement area characterized by a moist environment with open and slowly flowing water, an open landscape of cereal fields, meadows, and pastures in the vicinity. Archaeobotanical remains provide additional evidence for the exploitation of garden plots, used for the cultivation of vegetables, spices, and pulses; the management of grassland; and the cultivation of both summer and winter cereals.

See also ARCHAEOBOTANY; CONDIMENTS; FRUITS; MILITARY SITES; NUTS; SPICES; TRADE ROUTES; VEGETABLES

Further Reading

Vandorpe, Patricia, and Stefanie Jacomet, 2011. Plant Economy and Environment. In *Oedenburg, Vol. 2, L'agglomération civile et les sanctuaires: Vol. 2, Matériel et études*, edited by Michel Reddé, 3–72. Band 79/2. Mainz: Monographien des RGZM.

■ PATRICIA VANDORPE

OFFERINGS AND GRAVE GOODS

Death is one of the most profound experiences for humans, and it is therefore not surprising that rituals surround the burial and memory of the dead, many of which incorporate food. Burials may include foods as grave goods or as offerings for the dead, or food may be part of a ceremony in which the living take leave from the dead (such as wakes). Funeral feasting may also serve to enhance the status of the descendants or successors by offering lavish hospitality. For example, the Arabic traveler Ibn Fadhlan described an encounter with a band of Rus in the tenth century AD in which he observed a funeral feast that included heavy drinking and animal sacrifice.

Examples of food offerings date as far back as ancient Mesopotamia, and feasts and banquets are described in early texts such as *Gilgamesh*. Roman sources offer details of *sacrificia mortuorum*—sacrifices for the dead—that could include food and were clearly practiced in late antiquity. Writers such as Augustine tried to persuade Christians to invest in prayers rather than actual offerings to the dead (see also Psalm 106:28 where the Egyptians are said to have eaten the sacrifices for the dead). Food offerings from pharaonic Egypt are perhaps the best-known archaeological examples, but the practice of including food and drink spans many cultures. Offerings are sometimes representational in form—for example, carved wooden models of food, paintings, or reliefs of feasts. Food remains, though less common because of preservation issues, also have been recovered. Celtic and Anglo-Saxon graves contain grains, bones, or residue of drinks, for example.

Food in graves is often understood to be an offering for an afterlife, but in archaeological examples of burial sites from the early medieval West, some of the bones seem to have been gnawed, such as at Castledyke, Lincolnshire (UK), Grave 195, or were located in the backfill, such as Butler's Field, Gloucestershire (UK), Grave 74, suggesting they may have been eaten as part of the funeral ritual. Special edifices, so-called *cellae memoriae*, were erected in continental cemeteries, so that the living could hold a meal in memory of the dead. Wooden structures and buildings found in many Anglo-Saxon cemeteries may have had the same function. Pits and burnt stone features found at cemeteries such as Snape, Suffolk (UK), have been associated with food preparation. Therefore food residues may be the remnants of last meals that were celebrated with the dead. This practice continued even after the conversion to Christianity, despite prohibitions against *dadsisas* (literally, "sitting with the dead," or vigils for the dead) and *sacrificia mortuorum*. The written injunctions of clerics tell us that graves continued to be places where feasts—including singing and other performances—occurred.

Both skeletal and cremated remains of numerous domesticated animal species have been recovered from graves. At the Anglo-Saxon site of Sancton, East Yorkshire (UK), almost half of the urns contained animal bone. The sixth-century cemetery at Holywell Row, Suffolk (UK), contained the inhumation of a girl with a pot containing several duck eggs placed in front of her face. In northern Europe, pieces of meat were included in important burials such as Burial 7 at Valsgärde, Sweden. The ninth-century Oseberg ship, Westfold, Norway, in which two women were buried, contained two whole oxen and an array of foodstuffs including a bucket of crab apples. On the Continent, Frankish row graves often included containers with food, and in the Alemannic region many graves contained eggs, the legs and feet of pigs, beef joints, and fowl. The same species types have been recorded from Anglo-Saxon burials. Often the food remains are merely symbolic parts of the overall animal, and many burials contain only the remnants of edible parts, such as a pig mandible in Grave 56 at Butler's Field.

The detection of grain and plant produce, such as bread, is more complex because these foodstuffs are highly perishable and may not be easily detected. Such remains were often overlooked in the past by archaeologists. Textual and archaeological evidence clearly links grains to burial rituals, however. A decree by Theodore of Tarsus, who was archbishop of Canterbury from AD 668 to 690, forbade the burning of grain *ubi mortus est homo*, or "where a man has died." Grain has been found in the posthole of a chapel close to a group of ninth-century graves at Yarnton in the Upper Thames Valley (UK).

Food vessels also are informative. Some contain residues or soot, denoting their use as cooking vessels. Others contain residues of lipids or other substances from prepared foods. Drinking vessels with residues of alcoholic beverages are frequently found. Symbolic meals and feasting are implicit in the deposition of some food vessels. At sites such as Snell's Corner, Hampshire (UK), vessels follow a strict, gendered choreography, such as a placement on one side of the head.

The recently discovered burial of a woman and a cow at the early Anglo-Saxon cemetery of Oakington, Cambridgeshire (UK), serves as an example of the complexity of interpreting food remains in graves. It is unclear whether the cow is a food offering or a grave good. The cow may be an indication of this woman's wealth, or it may symbolize a type of foodstuff enjoyed by the deceased. The cow also may be part of a ritual deposit, indicating, for example, a belief that the demise of the woman was caused by the animal.

Food offerings in graves, however small, must be viewed as deliberate deposits. Some may indicate ritual feasting occurred at the graveside. Others may indicate gendered, political, or socioeconomic status and hierarchy. All reflect belief systems of past cultures. The complexities of potential foodstuffs, as in the Oakington cow burial, make the distinction between offering and grave good difficult. Every inclusion in the grave is deliberate, however. Careful recording is necessary so that meaningful comparisons can be drawn.

See also Bread; Carvings/Carved Representations of Food; Food and Gender; Food and Ritual; Food and Status; Foodways and Religious Practices; Gordion; Mortuary Complexes; Representational Models of Food and Food Production; Subeixi Cemeteries; Zooarchaeology

Further Reading

Baker, Jill L. 2012. *The Funeral Kit: Mortuary Practices in the Archaeological Record*. Walnut Creek, CA: Left Coast Press.

Baker, Sera, Martyn Allen, Sarah Middle, and Kristopher Poole, eds. 2008. *Food and Drink in Archaeology*. Vol. 1. Totnes, UK: Prospect Books.

Bullough, Donald. 1983. Burial, Community and Belief in the Early Medieval West. In *Ideal and Reality in Frankish and Anglo-Saxon Societies*, edited by Patrick Wormald, with Donald Bullough and Roger Collins, 177–201. Oxford: Blackwell.

Effros, Bonnie. 2002. *Creating Community with Food and Drink in Merovingian Gaul*. New York: Palgrave Macmillan.

Lee, Christina. 2007. *Feasting the Dead: Food and Drink in Anglo-Saxon Burial Rituals*. Woodbridge, UK: Boydell Press.

■ CHRISTINA LEE

OHALO II (ISRAEL)

Ohalo II is a 23,000-year-old submerged fisher-hunter-gatherers' camp located in the Sea of Galilee, Israel. It is unique for the excellent preservation of organic materials, and is particularly important for reconstructing diet, subsistence, and camp life toward the end of the last Ice Age. The site was excavated between 1989 and 1991 and 1999 and 2001 when the water level in the lake dropped and the site was temporarily exposed. The lakeshore camp covered an area of at least 2,000 square meters, with a nearby creek and a wide variety of food and raw material resources in the immediate vicinity.

Camp Structure

The camp remains include six brush huts, several adjacent open-air hearths, a grave, and additional features. A wealth of in situ remains was found in all features. These comprise charred seeds, animal bones, flints, grinding stones, stone bowls, bone tools, and beads. Most of the loci were directly dated by ^{14}C, with a total of 45 dates, indicating that the entire range of features is contemporaneous. A human grave was found in the camp, with the skeleton of a right-handed male about 40 years old.

Diet, Subsistence, and Seasonality

In most contemporaneous sites, plant remains are rare if present at all. At Ohalo II a sample of ca. 150,000 seeds and fruits was analyzed, representing ca. 150 species. These provide unprecedented data regarding the vegetal component of the diet, indicating heavy reliance on large grain cereals such as wild barley, wild wheat, and wild oats. Their remains were found all over the site, with a patterned concentration of grains around a grinding stone set on a brush hut floor. Microscopic starch granules were also found on the stone surface. Small grain grasses such as *Bromus*, as well as acorns, pulses, and wild fruits, were also consumed at the camp, in descending order of importance.

In the 1960s, Kent Flannery proposed that prior to the transition to farming in southwest Asia, there was a period during which hunter-gatherers broadened their resource base by utilizing a wider range of animal and plant species. It was impossible to study the vegetal component of this Broad Spectrum Revolution, however, until the Ohalo II floral remains were analyzed. The latter not only support the model but show that this economic shift was much wider and began earlier than previously conceived.

A variety of mammals were commonly hunted and brought to the site for consumption and other uses. The most important was the gazelle, followed by fallow deer and low frequencies of fox, hare, wild pig, deer, and wild cattle. Fish bones from the Cyprinidae and Cichlidae families were abundant at the site, reflecting their dietary importance; they were probably retrieved by the use of nets. Birds were also captured, with 83 species identified so far; the most common is the great crested grebe.

Seasonality was established by considering the ripening seasons of the plant species, the identification of seasonal migratory birds, and the analysis of enamel seasonal growth on gazelle teeth. All seasons are represented at the site, and thus the Ohalo II remains clearly indicate a year-round occupation of the camp. The broad range of consumed plants and animals rendered nomadism redundant for the Ohalo II group, and likely supported and enhanced the development of more complex social life and technological innovations.

Technology

A wide variety of remains pertain to past local technologies. These include the construction of the oldest known brush huts from identified local species and the oldest use of grass bedding on brush hut floors. Of particular importance is the flint assemblage, with more than 100,000 pieces retrieved and studied. The variety of raw materials, the general components of the assemblage, the technology of microlith production, and the refitting results all provide a comprehensive reconstruction of the manufacture and utilization of flint tools at the camp. Other aspects of technology comprise the production and use of ground stone implements, including some of the oldest cereal grinding stones, stone bowls, and weights for fishing nets. Wood implements were also preserved.

Ohalo II serves as a basis for many studies regarding the shift of human groups from hunting-gathering to sedentary lifeways based on agriculture. This is because of its geographical location at the heart of the earliest known shift, the year-round occupation of the site, evidence of relevant pre-Neolithic adaptations, and heavy reliance on cereals, later to be the pivot of the Neolithic economy.

See also ARCHAEOBOTANY; BROAD SPECTRUM REVOLUTION; FORAGING; HUNTER-GATHERER SUBSISTENCE; MACROREMAINS; PLANT PROCESSING; RESIDUE ANALYSIS, STARCH; SEDENTISM AND DOMESTICATION; TOOLS/UTENSILS, GROUND STONE; TOOLS/UTENSILS, ORGANIC MATERIALS; TOOLS/UTENSILS, STONE

Further Reading

Flannery, Kent V. 1969. Origins and Ecological Effects of Early Domestication in Iran and the Near East. In *The Domestication and Exploitation of Plants and Animals*, edited by Peter J. Ucko and G. W. Dimbleby, 73–100. London: Duckworth.

Nadel, Dani, ed. 2002. *Ohalo II: A 23,000-Year-Old Fisher-Hunter-Gatherers' Camp on the Shore of the Sea of Galilee*. Haifa: Hecht Museum.

Nadel, Dani, and Ella Werker. 1999. The Oldest Ever Brush Hut Plant Remains from Ohalo II, Jordan Valley, Israel (19,000 BP). *Antiquity* 73(282):755–64.

Piperno, Dolores R., Ehud Weiss, Irene Holst, and Dani Nadel. 2004. Processing of Wild Cereal Grains in the Upper Palaeolithic Revealed by Starch Grain Analysis. *Nature* 430(7000):670–73.

Rabinovich, Rivka, and Dani Nadel. 2005. Broken Mammal Bones: Taphonomy and Food Sharing at the Ohalo II Submerged Prehistoric Camp. In *Archaeozoology of the Near East VI, Proceedings of the Sixth International Symposium on the Archaeozoology of Southwestern Asia and Adjacent Areas*, edited by H. Buitenhuis, A. M. Choyke, L. Martin, et al., 34–50. Groningen: ARC.

Simmons, Tal, and Dani Nadel. 1998. The Avifauna of the Early Epipalaeolithic Site of Ohalo II (19,400 B.P.), Israel: Species Diversity, Habitat and Seasonality. *International Journal of Osteoarchaeology* 8(2):79–96.

Weiss, Ehud, Mordechai E. Kislev, Orit Simchoni, and Dani Nadel. 2004. Small-Grained Wild Grasses as Staple Food at the 23,000-Year-Old Site of Ohalo II, Israel. *Economic Botany* 58(1):S125–S134.

Weiss, Ehud, Mordechai E. Kislev, Orit Simchoni, et al. 2008. Plant-Food Preparation Area on an Upper Paleolithic Brush Hut Floor at Ohalo II, Israel. *Journal of Archaeological Science* 35(8):2400–2414.

■ DANI NADEL

OIL-BEARING SEED PLANTS

The use of plants for their oil-bearing parts, especially seeds and fruits, is of considerable antiquity. It is often the case, however, that plants with oil-bearing seeds also possess other properties, such as medicinal, aromatic, or psychoactive qualities, or they can be used as food per se (e.g., linseed, opium poppy). In most cases, therefore, their use for oil extraction can only be inferred from the archaeobotanical remains unless found in association with oil extraction installations. In addition to the olive, which may have been used for oil extraction by the fourth millennium BC in the Near East, other plants potentially used for oil extraction in the past include flax, opium poppy, the turpentine tree, mustard, *Lallemantia* or dragon's head (imported to Europe from central Asia in the Bronze Age), safflower, and sesame. In prehistoric times in the Near East, Egypt, Greece, and other parts of Europe, plant oils, in liquid form or as unguents mixed with other ingredients, usually circulated in small-sized containers, most likely intended for ritual uses (in religious, funerary, or healing contexts and for personal cleansing/purification) as indicated by pottery studies, residue analysis, and textual and archaeobotanical analyses. These uses continued in Greco-Roman times, during which the culinary use of oils, and of olive oil in particular, was restricted to wealthy families.

See also ARCHAEOBOTANY; FOOD AND RITUAL; FOODWAYS AND RELIGIOUS PRACTICES; FRUITS; OLIVE OIL; PLANT PROCESSING; PLANTS

Further Reading

Karg, Sabine. 2011. New Research on the Cultural History of the Useful Plant *Linum usitatissimum* L. (Flax), a Resource for Food and Textiles for 8000 Years. *Vegetation History and Archaeobotany* 20(6):507–8.

Melena, José L. 1983. Olive Oil and Other Sorts of Oil in the Mycenaean Tablets. *Minos* 18(1–2):89–123.

Serpico, Margaret, and Raymond White. 2000. Oil, Fat and Wax. In *Ancient Egyptian Materials and Technology*, edited by Paul T. Nicholson and Ian Shaw, 390–429. Cambridge: Cambridge University Press.

Valamoti, Soultana Maria. 2011. Flax in Neolithic and Bronze Age Greece: Archaeobotanical Evidence. *Vegetation History and Archaeobotany* 20:549–60.

■ SOULTANA MARIA VALAMOTI

OLD WORLD GLOBALIZATION AND FOOD EXCHANGES

As changes in subsistence, economy, and social organization during the Neolithic period spurred the growth of populations and social complexity, new urban formations and extensive trade networks began to emerge in parts of the Old World by the mid-Holocene. These trade networks, and the increasingly organized systems of exchange and commerce that emerged in concert with them, enabled the flow of a range of commodities across the Old World, as well as people, technologies, and ideas. Another key category of goods to move around the new routes of trade and travel was food.

Food moved along the networks of an increasingly globalized Old World in a variety of forms, ranging from containers of fully processed commodities like olive oil and wine to live crop plants and domesticated animals. While tracing food shipments is sometimes possible, it is the dispersal of domesticated species to new regions through trade that is the most archaeologically accessible feature of these food exchanges. Historical sources also provide insights.

Foods and agricultural species were moved for a variety of purposes. In many cases, food and new species were initially valued as exotic and often symbolically or ideologically meaningful entities. Diplomatic and other important visits in the ancient world often involved the transfer of rare and exotic plants and animals as gifts or tribute. But new crops also found uses as, for example, staple foods, condiments, beverages, medicines, dyes, perfumes, and fodder. Introduced domestic animals also were sources of food but additionally helped to improve local breeds, control pests, and provide traction.

While the geographic range of agricultural species expanded from the outset of the Neolithic, rates and distances of dispersal increased significantly under processes of proto-globalization. Species traveled along both terrestrial and maritime routes, moving via a range of forms of transit and often passing through several intermediaries before reaching their final destinations. But the agents who moved foods and agricultural species did not just include traders and political envoys. Many types of people traveled in the ancient world, for a wide variety of purposes, and the translocation of species and cuisines to new regions was aided by sailors, pilgrims, slaves, monks, colonists, and explorers. Species translocations might be deliberate, or the unintended consequence of food left over at the end of a journey.

States and other diverse types of societies were drawn into early processes of food globalization. More mobile groups assisted with transport and provided access to food and species from a wider range of ecological zones. For example, many of the prized spices of the ancient world initially had to be obtained from the forested regions of South and Southeast Asia, and ethnohistorical and ethnographic evidence suggests that foragers had a significant role to play. Pastoral nomads also helped transport foods and agricultural species—for example, across the arid regions of central Asia.

Bronze Age

The first long-distance plant and animal translocations that we can trace to processes of proto-globalization (as opposed to farming expansion) in the Old World currently date to the third millennium BC. They include a set of crop translocations along what has sometimes been referred to as the proto–Silk Road. East Asian domesticates like broomcorn millet and foxtail millet moved west, reaching Europe as early as the first half of the second millennium BC, while southwest Asian domesticates like wheat and barley traveled east, finding their way to East Asia by 2500–2000 BC. Central Asian evidence provides insights into both the agents and context of these movements. Pastoral nomadic sites in eastern Kazakhstan contain evidence of wheat and broomcorn millet in ritual contexts, suggesting that perhaps the use of these crops as symbolically meaningful prestige goods, especially among more nomadic peoples, motivated their spread across central Asia. Domesticated animals also were part of these early exchanges, including taurine cattle, which were introduced to East Asia during a similar timeframe.

Various new plants and animals also entered into South Asia in this time period. These included broomcorn millet, foxtail millet, apricots, peaches, and the *japonica* subspecies of rice from the east, as well as horses, camels, cannabis, almonds, and walnuts from central Asia. Flax, safflower, and several pulses (lentil, pea, chickpea, grass pea) also traveled from southwest to south Asia by the Harappan period, as did cultivated Mediterranean-zone fruits like grapes and hackberries. Donkeys arrived from Africa via Arabia. Many of these transfers probably flowed along emerging routes of trade and travel that began to link up the increasingly complex societies of Middle Asia and produced what some have referred to as a "Middle Asian Interaction Sphere." These routes extended into the sea, and maritime trade between the Bronze Age civilizations of the Indus Valley and Mesopotamia via the Persian Gulf is clearly attested by both archaeological and textual sources. Food and other organic products like wood also were among the goods that moved, along with species such as zebu cattle, a South Asian domesticate that appears on Gulf sites by the second millennium BC, and sesame, a South Asian crop that is in Mesopotamia by 2000 BC. Zebu, as well as chicken, may have traveled as far as Egypt by the second millennium BC, although more robust evidence is needed, and routes of movement remain unclear. Date palm, an eastern Arabian domesticate, reached Egypt and Nubia by the start of the second millennium BC.

There is some evidence to suggest maritime translocations along the northern Arabian Sea by the second millennium BC, perhaps as part of exploration or trade activities. Broomcorn millet seems to have traveled by maritime routes, from the northwestern part of the Indian subcontinent along the southern Arabian coast, reaching Yemen and Sudan by the third millennium BC. More remarkable, and still mysterious, is the eastward translocation of at least five African crops—sorghum, pearl millet, finger millet, cowpea, and hyacinth bean—that reached India by the second millennium BC and subsequently entered into small-scale cultivation in various regions of the subcontinent. The absence of these crops from Arabian peninsular archaeobotanical assemblages until millennia later suggests that they traveled by maritime routes. The mechanisms of these various maritime transfers remain obscure, however, since they appear to be unaccompanied by any other type of material evidence, such as ceramic sherds or precious trade goods, that might provide insights into how they moved such great distances.

Rare finds suggest that the beginnings of the spice trade may also be traced to the last millennia BC. Pepper, a South Asian plant, for example, has been identified in the mummy of the pharaoh Ramses II, which dates it to around 1200 BC. Possible cinnamon residues have also recently been identified from Phoenician flasks in Israel, dating to the 11th to mid-9th century BC. Farther east, sandalwood, an Island Southeast Asian tree and later spice route commodity, reached south India by the second millennium BC. Areca palm, whose betel nuts have traditionally been used in Asia as a stimulant, probably also arrived in south India more than 2,000 years ago from prehistoric origins in Island Southeast Asia. Other Southeast Asian tree crops that seem to have reached India in this period include citron (precursor of the lemon) and mango, both of which likely originated in the borderlands of northeastern India and mainland Southeast Asia. The movement of all of these plants at this stage was probably as high-value prestige goods, and foraging societies must have played some role in moving some of them from inaccessible forests into wider exchange networks.

Iron Age

Long-distance trade in the Old World began to intensify and expand into new regions in the mid- to late first millennium BC, leading to increasing globalization of foods and agricultural species. Trade and other links between South and Southeast Asia across the Bay of Bengal in the mid-first millennium BC, for example, resulted in the transfer of South Asian crops like mung and urd beans to Thailand, while the *indica* subspecies of rice spread this way somewhat later. New crops were perhaps established by diaspora communities of Indian merchants, craftsmen, and others, as suggested by some archaeological evidence. Figurative depictions potentially also place the arrival of zebu cattle from India in southern China in the mid- to late first millennium BC (though some argue for its arrival up to a millennium earlier). Genetic evidence indicates that these later migrated north and interbred with Mongolian taurine cattle (introduced from the Near East to northern China in the Bronze Age) in the plains of central China, creating new Chinese hybrid cattle.

In the mid- to late first millennium BC, a variety of new plants and animals also moved westward, initially primarily via terrestrial routes. Various new Southeast Asian spices and aromatics, for example, seem to have reached India, including nutmeg, mace, and aloeswood, although most were probably not cultivated for many more centuries or even millennia. Hellenistic trade with India meanwhile brought spices like pepper, cassia, cinnamon, and nard to Europe, with crops like South Asian rice, cucumber, and citrons possibly traveling along the same routes. Exotic birds like South Asian parakeet, peafowl, peacock, and crow are also attested in Hellenistic sources, and chicken seems to have reached Greece via Persia by the seventh century BC. Also probably traveling via Persia were coriander and cumin, native spices of the Mediterranean and the Near East that were introduced to India by the second half of the first millennium BC, when they are attested by Sanskrit names. Watermelons had also spread from early Egyptian origins to India by this time.

The consolidation of power across an enormous area of Eurasia by Rome, Parthia, and China in the last centuries BC, together with infrastructure and transport innovations, further intensified trade. Some of the best archaeobotanical and zooarchaeological evidence for the resulting increase in food transfers comes from European sites of the Roman period. This suggests both the arrival of new plants and animals as well as the increased commonness of previous arrivals, probably as a result of reintroductions. Chickens became much more common, for example, while new breeds were imported to diversify traditional herds of sheep, goats, cattle, asses, horses, and mules. A large number of crops, including fruits, nuts, and vegetables, also were imported, with many entering into cultivation. In the latter category were apple, pear, cherry, plum, medlar, walnut, peach, and Asian bottle gourd. The nut and fruit trees were particularly significant introductions in that they also indicate the arrival of new agricultural technologies (for example, grafting, possibly introduced from China or central Asia) and new kinds of agricultural spaces like orchards. Other plants that moved, but perhaps did not enter into cultivation, included rice, pistachio, date, and watermelon. Spices like black pepper, cinnamon, cardamom, and cassia also were imported.

Various crops also moved for the first time into north and even sub-Saharan Africa as part of the expansion of trade networks. Garamantian traders imported crops like cucumber (or melon, though the botanical evidence is not clear), pomegranate, olive, and almond, though the degree to which the latter three were grown locally is unclear. Further east, Egyptian sites of the Roman era, particularly port sites along the Red Sea, also saw the arrival of various new foods, reflecting in part the emergence of direct transoceanic trade links with south India. These included chicken and Asian plants like black pepper, rice, coconut, mung bean, and citron. Nonetheless, these foods mostly remained rare luxuries, and cuisine at these Roman-era port sites was strongly Mediterranean in flavor. Further south in Africa, the only other long-distance agricultural arrival is possibly banana, found in Iron Age pits in Cameroon dating to the mid-first millennium BC.

Numerous crop introductions to China during this phase are attested by textual evidence and occasionally archaeological finds from rich tombs. Most of these translocations occurred after the last centuries BC, when the Han Dynasty seized control of trade routes running along the northern and southern fringes of the Taklamakan Desert. In return for its silk and porcelain, China received such exotic foods as pomegranates, grapes, sesame, watermelon, fava beans, alfalfa, flax, and spices like cumin from the west, and galangal, long pepper, camphor, and cinnamon from the south. Various southern Chinese and northern Southeast Asian fruits and vegetables also became established in central China, some as local crops like aubergine, and others as valued imports, such as litchi fruits. Aromatic woods, resins, and exotic animals such as lions and peacocks also were brought to China during this period. The Chinese introduction to tea likely dates to this time; this species derives from hills of the southwestern periphery (Yunnan) and was one of the species encountered as Chinese influence and control spread southward. By the medieval period, tea was a well-established import from the south to the elites of central and northern China. Another important introduction was improved flour milling, probably derived ultimately from Mediterranean rotary querns, which in China transformed wheat from an uninspiring boiled grain into a valued staple for noodle production.

Medieval

A peak in the intensity of Indian Ocean trade led to an unprecedented scale of plant and animal translocations through maritime networks during the medieval period, causing major transformations in agricultural practices and foodways in regions around its rim. Some of the best evidence for the "Indian Oceanization" of agriculture comes from Egypt, where trading ports began receiving a new range of summer crops from South and Southeast Asia, including rice, aubergine, tree crops such as citrus, tropical vegecultural plants such as taro and banana, and cash crops such as sugarcane. The rise in importance of these crops correlates with the decline of Mediterranean crops such as lentils, wheat, and barley, which dominated subsistence in this region during the Roman period.

A similar suite of Indian Ocean crops also was adopted into foodways along the Swahili coast of eastern Africa at this time. This is seen initially in the arrival of small quantities of rice, mung bean, coconut, and possibly sesame, citrus, and Asian millets in the coastal region in the late first millennium AD, followed by a major shift to rice consumption at some trading sites in the early to mid-second millennium AD. This culinary change is linked to a broader set of social transformations in Swahili society, including increasing urbanism, cosmopolitanism, and Islamization, in which rice is likely to have taken on special significance as a prestige food. Zebu cattle also make their way to the East African coast in the medieval period, arriving around the mid- to late first millennium AD, most likely also through maritime trade connections. Direct trade links with Southeast Asia probably also brought plant and animal species such as *japonica* rice, taro, banana, Asian yam, coconut, and chicken to eastern Africa and Madagascar. Many of these species appear to have arrived as different varieties via diverse routes, and both a more circuitous northern Arabian Sea route and more direct transoceanic crossings are suggested. These multiple translocation pathways led to the development of novel crop varieties in their new regions, such as hybrids of *indica* and *japonica* rice that are unique to the highlands of Madagascar.

A wide range of new food crops also made their way into Europe during the medieval period, largely through Arab trade. During medieval times, Europeans further honed their taste for exotic spices, the demand for which drove a lucrative trade that saw large quantities shipped from Asia to European markets. Asian spices such as pepper, clove, cinnamon, cassia, and ginger, which were first introduced to European palates in Classical antiquity, continued to be popular. New arrivals include nutmeg from the Moluccas and melegueta pepper ("grains of paradise") from West Africa. Although likely present in Europe in previous eras, cardamom appears in the archaeobotanical record for the first time. The mysterious eastern origin of many spices and condiments was a large part of what made them so attractive, with this high consumer demand and sense of exoticism fueling later European expansion into Asia in direct search of their origins.

In addition to these spices, several cereals, fruits, and vegetables arrived in Europe for the first time in this period, including sorghum, buckwheat, aubergine, citrus, borage, Spanish vetchling, liquorice, sugarcane, and mango. Many that were available in previous periods also continued to be or became more common, including pear, peach, cucumber, fig, medlar, mulberry, parsley, and fennel. A number of foreign crops such as citrus, sorghum, and also rice (which had been traded into Europe since at least Roman times) began to be grown locally in this period, at least in southern Spain. In northern Europe, though, rice remained rare, with archaeobotanical evidence showing it was restricted largely to urban centers and thus likely a high-status luxury food rather than a staple. Differential access to exotic foods by social groups was a common theme of this period, with many imports functioning primarily in more affluent or privileged circles. Many foods that were prominent in Roman-era diets, such as olives, dates, bottle gourd, and pine nut, became much less common (and in some cases disappeared) from medieval archaeobotanical records. Other Asian crops, including southern crops like coconut, mung bean, cowpea, and tamarind, and eastern ones like soybean, Sichuan pepper, and star anise, did not arrive in Europe until sometime later in the postmedieval period.

New foods also moved east, of course, and an increase in long-distance commerce under the Tang Dynasty stimulated diffusions to China in particular. These flows were fueled by a newfound desire in Tang high culture for all things exotic, including foods, sourced from around the empire and beyond. Vegetables such as spinach as well as pistachios, dates, and figs arrived from the Middle East. Spices such as pepper and cloves, tropical fruits like bananas and mangoes, and stimulants such as areca nut and betel leaf came from South and Southeast Asia. Wine made from grapes rather than rice became fashionable and began to be locally produced. Many foods also doubled as medicines and were added to the repertoire of Chinese pharmacopoeia. This era also saw significant Chinese cultural influence on the Japanese archipelago, resulting in the introduction of traditions such as tea drinking as well as the Chinese writing system.

Conclusion

The traditional focus of archaeobotanical and zooarchaeological research on the subsistence patterns of less complex societies, and on such processes as domestication, has meant that the dietary patterns of later and, particularly, of urbanized societies are primarily known from textual sources. Yet it is increasingly clear that the application of archaeological science methods to later time periods holds much promise, not least in terms of the insights they can provide into long-distance species translocations and the extraordinary lengths that societies went to in order to obtain new and exotic foodstuffs. New methods like isotope and genetic analyses hold the potential to significantly extend our ability to explore these movements and food exchanges and the millennia of culinary and biological mixing that have preceded contemporary globalized food systems.

See also ARCHAEOBOTANY; BIOMOLECULAR ANALYSIS; COLUMBIAN EXCHANGE; DIASPORA FOODWAYS; FOOD AND COLONIALISM; FOOD AND STATUS; FOOD TECHNOLOGY AND IDEAS ABOUT FOOD, SPREAD OF; GLOBALIZATION; IMMIGRANT FOODWAYS; MARKETS/EXCHANGE; PACIFIC OCEANIC EXCHANGE; PRE–SILK ROAD AGRICULTURAL EXCHANGE; TRADE ROUTES; ZOOARCHAEOLOGY

Further Reading

Boivin, Nicole, Alison Crowther, Mary Prendergast, and Dorian Q Fuller. 2014. Indian Ocean Food Globalisation and Africa. *African Archaeological Review* 31:547–81.

Boivin, Nicole, and Dorian Q Fuller. 2009. Shell Middens, Ships and Seeds: Exploring Coastal Sub-sistence, Maritime Trade and the Dispersal of Domesticates in and Around the Ancient Arabian Peninsula. *Journal of World Prehistory* 22(2):113–80.

Boivin, Nicole, Dorian Q Fuller, and Alison Crowther. 2012. Old World Globalization and the Colum-bian Exchange: Comparison and Contrast. *World Archaeology* 44(3):452–69.

Foster, Karen Polinger. 1998. Gardens of Eden: Exotic Flora and Fauna in the Ancient Near East. *Yale Forestry and Environmental Studies Bulletin* 103:320–29.

Kiple, Kenneth F., and Kriemhild Concè Ornelas, eds. 2000. *The Cambridge World History of Food*. Cam-bridge: Cambridge University Press.

Laudan, Rachel. 2013. *Cuisine and Empire: Cooking in World History*. Berkeley: University of California Press.

Livarda, Alexandra. 2011. Spicing Up Life in Northwestern Europe: Exotic Food Plant Imports in the Roman and Medieval World. *Vegetation History and Archaeobotany* 20(2):143–64.

Miller, J. Innes. 1969. *The Spice Trade of the Roman Empire, 29 B.C. to A.D. 641*. Oxford: Oxford Uni-versity Press.

Pollard, Elizabeth Ann. 2009. Pliny's *Natural History* and the Flavian *Templum Pacis*: Botanical Imperial-ism in First-Century C.E. Rome. *Journal of World History* 20(3):309–38.

Schafer, Edward H. 1963. *The Golden Peaches of Samarkand: A Study of T'ang Exotics*. Berkeley: University of California Press.

Sidebotham, Steven E. 2011. *Berenike and the Ancient Maritime Spice Route*. Berkeley: University of Cal-ifornia Press.

Simoons, Frederick J. 1991. *Food in China: A Cultural and Historical Inquiry*. Baton Rouge, LA: CRC Press.

Turner, Jack. 2005. *Spice: The History of a Temptation*. London: HarperCollins.

Van der Veen, Marijke. 2011. *Consumption, Trade and Innovation: Exploring the Botanical Remains from the Roman and Islamic Ports at Quseir al-Qadim, Egypt*. Journal of African Archaeology Monograph 6. Frankfurt: Africa Magna Verlag.

Watson, Andrew M. 1983. *Agricultural Innovation in the Early Islamic World*. Cambridge Studies in Islamic Civilization. Cambridge: Cambridge University Press.

Zohary, Daniel, Maria Hopf, and Ehud Weiss. 2012. *Domestication of Plants in the Old World*. 4th edition. Oxford: Oxford University Press.

■ NICOLE BOIVIN, DORIAN Q FULLER, AND ALISON CROWTHER

OLDUVAI GORGE (TANZANIA)

Olduvai Gorge, commonly referred to as "The Cradle of Humankind," is renowned for Louis and Mary Leakey's remarkable discoveries of early human (hominin) fossils and concentrations of flaked stone artifacts in association with butchered animal bones, which Mary labeled "living floors." Olduvai lends its name to the Oldowan Industry, the earliest stone technology, and was the location where these primitive tools were first recognized. Its well-dated sedimentary deposits span the last two million years, coinciding with major events in human evolution such as the first appearance of *Homo erectus* and the extinction of *Homo habilis*. These deposits depict a fluctuating environment, dominated by a large lake that would have attracted the area's diverse wildlife. It is in the margin of this paleolake where the majority of the archaeological finds have been located, including the most significant discovery, the 1.8-million-year-old *Zinjanthropus* cranium, representing the type specimen of *Australopithecus boisei* and the first fossil hominin unearthed in East Africa.

Figure 44. Artist's reconstruction of feeding behavior by early *Homo* in Olduvai Gorge based on fossil evidence, butchery marks, and other archaeological data. The image depicts a *Homo habilis* group attempting to displace a *Dinofelis* individual from a kill in a grassland environment like those that dominated the landscape of Olduvai Gorge during Bed II times. Archaeologists continue to debate whether the evidence is demonstrative of hunting or scavenging behavior. Drawing by Gianfranco Mensi.

Olduvai has also become the foremost location for studying the carnivorous feeding behavior of early *Homo* because of its exceptionally preserved fossils that bear traces of hominin and carnivore carcass consumption. Butchery marks on fossils demonstrate that our ancestors consumed the flesh and bone marrow from mammals of all sizes, including giraffe and elephants, but whether they acquired these resources through hunting or scavenging remains a topic of debate (figure 44). Most recent evidence from Olduvai suggests *H. habilis* may have been a scavenger, while the larger and more technologically advanced *H. erectus* was likely a hunter. Regardless of how carcasses were obtained, they were likely an important resource in meeting the metabolic demands imposed by the increasing brain and body sizes seen in the fossil record of the genus *Homo*. Ongoing research in Olduvai Gorge will presumably help to determine the role of animal foods in the evolution of our own species.

See also BUTCHERY; DIGESTION AND HUMAN EVOLUTION; FORAGING; HUNTER-GATHERER SUBSISTENCE; LANDSCAPE AND ENVIRONMENTAL RECONSTRUCTION; MEAT; PALEODIETARY ANALYSIS; TEETH, DIET, AND HUMAN EVOLUTION; TOOLS/UTENSILS, STONE; WEAPONS, STONE; ZOOARCHAEOLOGY

Further Reading

Leakey, Mary. 1971. *Olduvai Gorge.* Vol. 3, *Excavations in Beds I and II, 1960–1963.* Cambridge: Cambridge University Press.

Pante, Michael C. 2013. The Larger Mammal Fossil Assemblage from JK2, Bed III, Olduvai Gorge, Tanzania: Implications for the Feeding Behavior of *Homo erectus. Journal of Human Evolution* 64(1):68–82.

■ MICHAEL C. PANTE

OLIVE OIL

The olive tree (*Olea europaea*) is considered to be the characteristic crop of Mediterranean regions, where oil largely replaces butter and other animal fats, and has been widely exported since prehistoric times. Its fruit, a drupe (a fruit with a stone or pit inside), is of major agricultural importance as a source of oil. Olives, on average, consist of 22 percent oil. Compared to oleasters (wild form), most cultivated olives are characterized by large fruits with a high oil content. The products generated by the pressing of olives are (1) the oil itself; (2) a solid residue employed as fuel, animal feed, or fertilizer; and (3) a sticky, black, liquid residue used as a fertilizer, insecticide, wood preservative, waterproofing substance, skin ointment, lubricant, and tonic for animals. Because of its importance as a cultivated species, archaeologists have studied extensively both the domestication of the olive tree and the prehistoric and historic-period uses of olive oil. Archaeobotanical, architectural, and material culture evidence from orchards, press and production sites, and trade-related sites, including shipwrecks, provides considerable insight into early cultivation and production (figure 45).

The first evidence of olive oil production, comprising thousands of crushed olive stones and olive pulp, was discovered in submerged sites (Kfar Samir, Kfar Galim, Tel Hreiz) south of Haifa, Israel. The prehistoric Kfar Samir settlement, located off the Carmel coast, provided evidence of an olive oil extraction technology dating from the Wadi Rabah period (Late Neolithic). Radiocarbon dates indicate that olive extraction/

Figure 45. Left: Oil press, Tel Hazor, Israel, eighth century BC. Right: Oil press, Tell Tweini, Syria, Iron Age II–III. Photographs by David Kaniewski.

oil production from wild forms started on the Carmel coast ~7,000 BP. Olive cultivation, based on the domesticated form, is thought to have begun during the Chalcolithic period. Archaeologists have recovered evidence for the development of techniques for oil extraction and the presence of cultivated olives at several sites in the Jordan Valley, in the Golan Heights, and throughout the Levant (Abu Hamid, el-Khawarij, Rasm Harbush, Samaria, Teleilat Ghassul, Tel Saf, Tell esh-Shuna).

During the Bronze Age, olives feature among the main Middle Eastern orchard crops, and evidence suggests intensive cultivation during this period. Olives were valued primarily as a source of oil for eating and cooking. Olive oil also was used as an ointment or as fuel for lamps. Olive oil could be stored for long periods and became a valued trade commodity for regional exchange in the eastern Mediterranean. The Uluburun shipwreck (~1316 BC), discovered off the southwestern coast of Turkey, carried trade goods and luxury products along the eastern Mediterranean coast toward Rhodes, including Canaanite jars with more than 2,500 olive pits. Despite the high density of olive trees during the Bronze Age, olive oil was considered a luxury product in ancient Mesopotamia and Egypt. Cuneiform tablets from Syria indicate that 4,000 years ago, the value of olive oil was five times that of wine and two and a half times that of seed oils.

In Egypt, iconographic and textual evidence from the New Kingdom shows that olive products were almost exclusively delivered to temples and to the royal house. Written sources indicate that olive goods were imported from the Levantine coastal areas and that olive oil was used only by elites. The profusion of olive oil in Canaan and Phoenicia (Land of Djahi) and its desirability as an elite good are demonstrated by the campaigns of the Pharaoh Thutmose III and documented upon the walls of the Temple of Karnak, in the Al-Amarna mural paintings, in the Harris Papyrus describing the gifts offered to Ramses III, and in the Anastasi Papyrus. By the time of Ramses II, olive oil was used in the royal house for perfumes, in illumination, and as a skin emollient for cracks and sunburn.

A major Iron Age oil production center with ~115 large olive oil presses (seventh century BC) was found at Ekron, suggesting that oil production was highly developed in ancient Israel and that trade with Egypt and Mesopotamia was considerable. Ekron had the potential to produce 1,000 tons of oil annually.

During the Greek and Roman periods, the collision and fusion of Greek and Roman notions of economic systems with those of the newly won lands of the Near and Middle East generated significant innovations with a remarkable variety of agricultural installations for oil extraction. The high demand for olive oil in the Greek and Roman Empires led to the construction of industrial-scale oil extraction facilities, and the Levant became a center for olive cultivation. Written sources from the Roman Empire indicate that the olive tree was exploited widely for its oil and edible fruit, but also for unguents, medicaments, perfumes, cosmetics and moisturizing skin oils, and lubricants, and as an energy source (lamp oil). Paleodietary reconstruction from nitrogen and carbon isotopic analyses of human remains dated from the early Roman period at the site of Natfieh (northern Jordan) indicates that olive oil was a main component of the Roman diet in the Middle East. At Sagalassos (Turkey), chemical residue analyses of late Roman amphorae and paleodietary reconstruction from botanical remains show that olive oil also was the main component of foodways in this area. Numerous olive presses were also found at the late Roman site of Akoris, Middle Egypt, providing evidence for large-scale olive oil production.

The increased importance of olive trees over the centuries has turned this species into an economic, sacred, and symbolic plant. Its economic value and sacred connotations have permeated the entire Mediterranean world.

See also AGRICULTURAL/HORTICULTURAL SITES; AMPHORAE; ARCHAEOBOTANY; FOOD AS A COMMODITY; FRUITS; INDUSTRIALIZATION OF FOOD AND FOOD PRODUCTION; INSECTICIDES/ REPELLENTS; SHIPWRECKS; TRADE ROUTES

Further Reading

Besnard, G., B. Khadari, M. Navasoués, et al. 2013. The Complex History of the Olive Tree: From Late Quaternary Diversification of Mediterranean Lineages to Primary Domestication in the Northern Levant. *Proceedings of the Royal Society B* 280(1756):20122833. doi:10.1098/rspb.2012.2833.

Kaniewski, David, Elise Van Campo, Tom Boiy, et al. 2012. Primary Domestication and Early Uses of the Emblematic Olive Tree: Palaeobotanical, Historical and Molecular Evidences from the Middle East. *Biological Reviews* 87(4):885–99.

Zohary, Daniel. 1982. *Plants of the Bible*. Cambridge: Cambridge University Press.

Zohary, Daniel, Maria Hopf, and Ehud Weiss. 2012. *Domestication of Plants in the Old World*. 4th edition. Oxford: Oxford University Press.

Zohary, Daniel, and Pinhas Speigel-Roy. 1975. Beginnings of Fruit Growing in the Old World. *Science* 187(4174):319–27.

■ DAVID KANIEWSKI AND ELISE VAN CAMPO

ORAL AND FOLK NARRATIVES

Foods and foodways have been shown to create powerful associations and memories in the human mind. This is in part linked to the sensorial aspects of food, whether smell, taste, or another characteristic, but food-related practices—whether ritualistic or everyday, whether involving physical hand gestures or aural, olfactory, or visual cues—also contribute to the formation of memory. Thus oral and folk narratives about food and foodways are a particularly fertile source for the archaeological study of food, providing information that allows us to contextualize the food choices and food practices of the past.

Oral history is broadly defined as the collection and preservation of oral narratives to record the remembered past based on firsthand experience; its practitioners use an integrated and often interdisciplinary approach that may combine methods of history and ethnography with interviewing techniques. Oral sources (including oral history interviews, oral narratives or recollections that have been written down, and oral traditions, i.e., knowledge that has been transmitted orally) may provide accounts of preparation methods and foods consumed, how implements were made or used, family structure and social hierarchy at the table, and so on. These sources are perhaps most useful to archaeologists when they reveal the communicative functions and symbolic content of foods and food practices. Oral narratives can reveal the perceptions of informants toward certain foods or food-related events, for example. Interviews with coal-mining families in western Pennsylvania (USA) documented the importance of subsistence gardening along with conflicting attitudes toward the coal company, which passed out candy on holidays but did not offer a living wage to most of its employees in the late 19th to early 20th century; this study also highlighted the commensal importance of "home brew" made in the crawl space of a company-owned miners' doublehouse.

Folk narratives, which recount beliefs, customs, or cultural practice that have been transmitted orally over one or more generations, also have applicability to the archaeological study of food practices. Archaeologists have turned to ancient lore, as recorded in classical texts or passed on as oral tradition, to glean details about the origins and meaning of certain foods and food practices. Amy Sherwood has argued the symbolic importance of cattle in Iron Age Ireland, for example, by combining traditional Irish folklore with archaeological, zooarchaeological, and textual evidence.

Oral and folk narratives can illuminate past foodways in a number of other ways. The study of the language of narrative may illuminate the way that events are perceived, understood, and remembered. These sources also highlight the overlap between practice, memory, artifacts, and foods. David Sutton has shown that specific memories and practices are embodied in food-related material culture—for example, utensils and cooking pots—thus aiding in the transmission of memory, history, and even genealogical information. Spaces associated with food rituals and food consumption often have folkloric associations—for example, hearths and wells. Food mapping using oral sources has been shown to be an effective method of connecting spaces in the landscape with multivalent events and practices. Folk and oral narratives may provide insight into different types of identity that are expressed through foodways by contextualizing certain behaviors—for example, food preparation methods—that are not only culturally significant but vary by gender, ethnicity, age, or other category. Folk narratives also convey traditional beliefs concerning foods, beverages, and medicinal substances. Studies in historical archaeology show that foods and food-related material culture are entangled with cultural beliefs about health and well-being. For example, the prevalence of soda water bottles in 19th-century deposits associated with Irish immigrants and Irish Americans in New York City (USA) has been linked to traditional Irish folklore and beliefs about the healing properties of water, but the bottles are also connected to themes of health, temperance, and nostalgia. There is also a considerable body of oral tradition and folk narrative in many cultures concerning the medicinal use of herbs or the economic roles of food plants that can potentially inform archaeological interpretation.

Folk and oral narratives also inform us about preferences, avoidances, and taboos—what is good to eat and what is not. Certain foods, like acorns, may take on associations with animal fodder after experiences of poverty or famine. Foods and foodways often are tied to beliefs about cultural "others," from urban legends, myths, and stereotypes about the foodways of immigrant groups to cultural beliefs about economic and social class (e.g., stigma associated with institutional food or handouts—"taking the soup" during the Great Famine in Ireland); about what is "wild" and what is tamed, domestic, or civilized; and about what is "authentic" (prepared in accordance with culturally defined methods and ingredients by group members). Thus folk and oral narratives connect foods and food practices to definitions of group membership, identity, and "otherness."

See also DOCUMENTARY ANALYSIS; FAMINE; FOOD AND IDENTITY; FOOD AS SENSORY EXPERI-
ENCE; GREENS/HERBS; IMMIGRANT FOODWAYS; MATERIAL CULTURE ANALYSIS; MULTI- AND
INTERDISCIPLINARY APPROACHES; NATIVE AMERICAN ETHNOBOTANY; OFFERINGS AND GRAVE
GOODS; SPATIAL ANALYSIS AND VISUALIZATION TECHNIQUES

Further Reading

Holzmann, Jon D. 2006. Food and Memory. *Annual Review of Anthropology* 35:361–78.
Krögel, Alison. 2009. Dangerous Repasts: Food and the Supernatural in the Quechua Oral Tradition.
   Food and Foodways 17(2):104–32.
Linn, Meredith B. 2010. Elixir of Emigration: Soda Water and the Making of Irish Americans in Nine-
   teenth-Century New York City. *Historical Archaeology* 44(4):69–109.
Metheny, Karen Bescherer. 2014. Modeling Communities through Food: Connecting the Daily Meal
   to the Construction of Place and Identity. *Northeast Historical Archaeology* 42:147–83.
Sherwood, Amy. 2009. An Bó Bheannaithe: Cattle Symbolism in Traditional Irish Folklore, Myth, and
   Archaeology. *PSU McNair Scholars Online Journal* 3(1), article 21. http://pdxscholar.library.pdx.edu/
   mcnair/vol3/iss1/21.
Silliman, Stephen W. 2009. Change and Continuity, Practice and Memory: Native American Persistence
   in Colonial New England. *American Antiquity* 74(2):211–30.
Sutton, David, and Michael Hernandez. 2007. Voices in the Kitchen: Cooking Tools as Inalienable
   Possessions. *Oral History* 35(2):67–76.

■ KAREN BESCHERER METHENY

ORGANIC RESIDUES

See BIOMOLECULAR ANALYSIS; RESIDUE ANALYSIS, BLOOD; RESIDUE ANALYSIS, DAIRY PROD-
UCTS; RESIDUE ANALYSIS, STARCH; RESIDUE ANALYSIS, TARTARIC ACID; RESIDUE ANALYSIS,
THEOBROMINE

ÖTZI
See ICEMAN

OVENS AND STOVES

Ovens and stoves are installations built to contain fire and allow its manipulation for
culinary purposes. Considered in the aggregate, these technologies have promoted the
development of culinary complexity in many cultures, as they offer a wide potential
range of cooking environments—from diffuse to intense, from dry to steamy, and from
extremely hot (near 1,000°F/530°C) to just above ambient temperature.

   For the archaeologist, a functional understanding of these tools is helpful in identifying their remains in the field. Each operates on a different essential principle: the stove
controls draft to a live fire, while the oven cooks using retained heat. (A technical understanding of draft and thermal mass underlies both kiln firing and metallurgy; by inference,
any cultural complex that includes ceramics or smelting implies the potential use of these
principles in cooking too.)

Live Fire/Draft

To intensify heat, an enclosure—usually masonry, often cylindrical—contains the fire; an opening at the base allows an ample supply of oxygen to be drawn through the fuel upon ignition. Cooking occurs toward the top of the enclosure, where heat is greatest. Such installations save fuel and are comparatively comfortable and responsive to use, quickly delivering intense heat when necessary. The *tannur* (var. *tandir*, *tandoor*, *tandur*) is such an installation intended primarily for baking flatbreads. Freestanding, or set into a retaining wall or patio, the tannur may be built in situ or may consist of a premade cylindrical core of tempered sun-dried or fired clay. Probably originating in northern Syria by at least the Late Neolithic, the *tannur* spread throughout the Levant into central and South Asia, North Africa, and the Arabian Peninsula. Fired as described above, the body of the *tannur* provides sufficient heat to bake bread adhering to its vertical inner surface; secondarily, other foods may be suspended within the cylinder for quick roasting.

The furnace begins with a similar masonry enclosure—a firebox with an inlet for draft from beneath—but is topped with a ceramic or metal pot. The technology seems to have developed independently in Mesopotamia, China, the Andes, Mexico, the Indus Valley, and sub-Saharan Africa. For millennia, the furnace and its variants have been deployed in both domestic and industrial settings across the globe. It is the ancestor of the charcoal-fired range or *potager* of early modern Europe. Topped with a stone, ceramic, or metal griddle, it becomes ideal for baking flatbreads, an arrangement found in the Middle East, Central America, and northwestern Europe.

Retained Heat

At an elemental level, retained heat roasts tubers in the ashes of a fire or parches seeds on a preheated rock. The retained-heat installation most prevalent globally in the last two millennia is the vaulted oven made of mud brick, fired brick, stone, or mud. The form and closure of this type of oven make it ideal for leavened breads made with high-gluten flours. This oven is often referred to generically as a Roman oven, surely since the technology followed the empire to its furthest reaches (and then accompanied its European adopters on their postmedieval colonial forays). The technology is more ancient, however: the remains of domed mud-brick ovens are found interspersed with those of *tannurs* on Bronze Age sites in northeastern Syria, such as Tell Brak and Tell Hamoukar. (The domed ovens appear to be more commercial/official, and the *tannurs* more domestic.) In use these ovens are fired from within until the masonry has absorbed sufficient heat. The oven's hearth is swept clean, the bread or other food introduced, and the oven's mouth closed up.

Generally, vaulted ovens are built on a solid or arched base so that they can be fired and loaded at waist height (although some Middle Eastern and North African versions are built flush with the ground and used while seated). The oven's hearth (floor) can be made of stone, tile, brick, mud brick, or raw clay; ideally, it is smooth, level, and reparable. Some brick or stone ovens are constructed by gradual vaulting, but most of these forms, and all "mud" (daub) ovens, are built up over a withy (a form made of osier or willow branches) or sand form (which is burned or dug out after construction).

Indoor ovens may be appended to chimneys or otherwise vented; in central Europe, Russia, and Scandinavia they have been incorporated into massive masonry heating stoves with highly reticulated flues. Kiln-fired oven cores (suitable for installation into a masonry mass) were used regionally (England and Portugal) and exported to support colonial ventures. Simplest of all, where soil type permits, a functional oven-shaped cavity may be dug into a hillside (or cellar wall); examples exist from the earliest English settlement at Jamestown, and as a type of field oven they are documented as recently as the American Civil War.

Variation and Interpretation

It is challenging to distinguish among the many permutations of ovens and stoves in the field. A familiarity with vernacular architecture and extant regional baking traditions may help clarify some of the confusion arising in these functional gray areas. For example, the *tabun*, a Neolithic oven type still extant in Palestine, consists of a very shallow dome with a central loading hole, built over a hearth of river pebbles. It is fired from within and cleaned out; coals are piled on the outside as foods bake inside. Indeed, beyond indicating a considerable degree of local variability in the construction and use of ovens in general, ethnographic studies are valuable in implementing and refining experimental models based on archaeological evidence. They also complement the archaeological record by documenting the social role of these installations; for example, ethnographic research has shown that in the Palestinian villages where the *tabun* is still used, it is the exclusive province of women and acts as a center for female social interchange, information that would be impossible to ascertain solely from excavated materials.

See also ARCHAEOLOGY OF COOKING; BREAD; COOKING VESSELS, CERAMIC; COOKING VESSELS, METAL; COOKING VESSELS, OTHER MATERIALS; ETHNOARCHAEOLOGY; ETHNOGRAPHIC SOURCES; EXPERIMENTAL ARCHAEOLOGY; FIRE AND THE DEVELOPMENT OF COOKING TECHNOLOGY; FIRE-BASED COOKING FEATURES; FOODWAYS AND GENDER ROLES; PHILISTINE FOODWAYS

Further Reading

Bottero, Jean. 2004. *The Oldest Cuisine in the World: Cooking in Mesopotamia.* Translated by Teresa Lavender Fagan. Chicago: University of Chicago Press.

Marcoux, Paula. 2013. Bread and Permanence. In *Exploring Atlantic Transitions: Archaeologies of Permanence and Transience in New Found Lands*, edited by Peter E. Pope and Shannon Lewis-Simpson, 48–56. Woodbridge, UK: Boydell and Brewer.

———. 2014. *Cooking with Fire*. North Adams, MA: Storey Publishing.

Parker, Bradley J. 2011. Bread Ovens, Social Networks and Gendered Space: An Ethnoarchaeological Study of Tandir Ovens in Southeastern Anatolia. *American Antiquity* 76(4):603–27.

■ PAULA MARCOUX

P

PACIFIC OCEANIC EXCHANGE

The archipelagos of the Pacific contain over 25,000 individual islands, most of which are, or have been, inhabited by people. The settlement history of the region is complex, with very ancient settlements in Near Oceania (New Guinea, the Bismarck Archipelago, and the Solomon Islands) dating to between 40,000 and 50,000 years ago. Much more recent settlements are found in Remote Oceania (east, north, and south of Near Oceania), which was settled after 4,000 years ago. The large islands of Near Oceania have yielded some of the earliest evidence for land management and were an independent center for agricultural development. Because of their isolated nature, islands also are excellent places to recognize archaeological evidence for both natural and human movement of flora and fauna. As a result, the islands of the Pacific have yielded some of the earliest and most widespread evidence for the intentional transport of plants and animals by humans.

Eastward of New Guinea, the plant and animal communities of islands become increasingly impoverished, compelling humans to introduce plants and animals of high utility in order to facilitate the successful colonization of new islands. These packages of resources are known as transported landscapes and re-create the familiar range of plants and animals that founding populations were accustomed to at home. These were necessary for long-term survival of humans in Oceanic island environments. Without the establishment of a dependable agricultural and food production system or external support networks, the settlements on remote islands would have failed. The archaeological record of several Pacific islands, such as Nihoa Island in Hawai'i, demonstrates that in some instances people were unable to sustain long-term populations as a result of the failure of the transported landscape in the face of extreme environmental constraints.

Archaeological sites that have revealed the early use of sophisticated land management techniques include the sites of Kosipe, in highland New Guinea, dated to between 40,000 and 50,000 BP. The recovery of waisted axes from archaeological excavations indicates the early settlers in this region intentionally cleared the trees. It is hypothesized that this land clearance was undertaken in order to encourage growth of plants that require more open environments and more sunlight in order to flourish. Remains of charred pandanus nuts (*Pandanus* sp.) and starch grains from *Dioscorea* yams at the same sites show humans were exploiting these species around 40,000 years ago. It is likely that early inhabitants were actively managing the landscape to encourage the growth of pandanus while heading into the lowlands or trading with lowland groups to obtain yams.

Excavations and subsequent analyses at the site of Kuk Swamp, also in New Guinea, have confirmed the independent development of agriculture in Near Oceania by 6,500 BP. Although there is clear modification of the landscape at Kuk to encourage the growth of specific plants by 10,000 BP, it is not yet clear if this activity can be defined as agriculture in its fullest sense. Later modifications to the site included purposeful development of mound and ditch networks. The ditches were used to direct water both to and away from the mounds. Evidence for taro, yam, and banana cultivation is associated with the long-term use of the site as a carefully maintained, cultivated landscape and attests to the human use of these resources for thousands of years in the highlands of New Guinea.

The people of New Guinea, the Bismarcks, and the Solomon Islands also exploited and translocated animals that they used as food resources at a very early date. The remains of a common cuscus (*Phalanger orientalis*) were recovered from a midden site in New Ireland dating to 20,000 years ago. The common cuscus is native to New Guinea, and its presence in rubbish pits demonstrates it was used as food. Its existence on an island to which it was not native provides strong evidence that this and probably other animals, including other phalangers, bandicoots, and several types of rats, were being moved by humans to provide future resources in new environments. Over the following millennia, the movement of animals and plants is increasingly evident in the archaeological record of Near Oceania, and these resources were widely dispersed to the islands east of their natural range in New Guinea.

While these internal agricultural developments were occurring in New Guinea and its neighboring archipelagos, domestication of many plant and animal species occurred also in Southeast Asia. As Austronesian-speaking groups moved eastward into the islands of Southeast Asia and the Pacific, they brought their own transported landscapes with them. These included pigs (*Sus scrofa*), dogs (*Canis lupus familiaris*), and chickens (*Gallus gallus*). Compelling arguments also have been made for the intentional transport of rats (*Rattus exulans, Rattus mordax, Rattus praetor*) for both food and other cultural reasons. It is likely that these resources were introduced to the islands of Near Oceania by different groups of people at different times and were incorporated into local agricultural systems. After 3,500 BP, a package of native and introduced flora and fauna was taken as part of the colonization package into the previously uninhabited islands of Remote Oceania. These same plants and animals also were introduced to inhabited islands in Micronesia, including the Mariana and Caroline Islands. It appears, however, that on most Micronesian islands the animals were not compatible with the existing subsistence regime and were not adopted by local populations.

The animal bones recovered from archaeological sites in the Pacific show that not all animals were taken to all islands, possibly a result of the size and agricultural potential of each individual island. Pigs typically are viewed as a storehouse for surplus and have been used as bridewealth, as a socioeconomic marker, and as ritual sacrifices. It has been shown, however, that it is very difficult to keep pigs on atolls and smaller islands because of the large agricultural surplus required to feed them. It also has been argued that dogs, like pigs, were not suited to life on smaller islands as they were predominantly fed with cultigens and therefore required an oversupply of crops to maintain sufficient populations. On smaller islands pigs and dogs may have been intentionally omitted from the transported landscape, or purposefully killed off and not replaced, likely because it was easier to obtain sustenance from fish and other marine protein than to try to grow enough plants to feed larger domestic animals as well as human populations.

Remote Oceanic plant species have more diverse origins than the animal resources, with 49 of the introduced plants in Oceania native to a wide range of continental domestication centers ranging from Indo-Malaysia to Africa. Of introduced Polynesian plants, 11 are believed to come from Melanesia, nine from Fiji, and two or three from South America. Twenty-one plant species were successfully translocated to West Polynesia but did not reach East Polynesia. Plants with seeded and pollinated varieties in Near Oceania may have been less suitable for long-distance transport; therefore, plants that could produce asexually may have been selected by humans, either intentionally or unintentionally, and represent the bulk of plants transported to central eastern Polynesia and beyond. Of those that were successfully carried to east Polynesia, most were seedless or vegetatively propagated, as from cuttings. These include ti (*Cordyline fruticosa*), pandanus (*Pandanus* sp.), breadfruit (*Artocarpus camansi, A. mariannensis*), taro (*Colocasia esculenta*), yams (*Dioscorea alata, Dioscorea esculenta*), and sweet potato (*Ipomoea batatas*).

The plants selected by ancient Pacific seafarers were also typically multipurpose plants. Banana leaves may be used for wrapping food and in medicine. Breadfruit is important in eastern Polynesia as a storable resource in the form of *ma* (a process in which the fruit is fermented in pits and stored for several years); the leaves were used to wrap food and to create rope. Timber from breadfruit trees was widely used for house and ship construction, bowls, coffins, and fishing floats. Breadfruit, paper mulberry, and banyan may all be used for the production of tapa cloth. Therefore, the utility of a plant, not only as food but also for building materials and culturally significant artifacts, certainly influenced its selection for transport by humans.

Because of the isolated nature of islands and their distance from continental landmasses, many of the plants and animals that are found on Pacific islands today could only have been introduced by people. The study of plants and animals imported to the islands provides another avenue for the study of human migration and interaction; this is known as a commensal model. The term *commensal* is used broadly by archaeologists and anthropologists to indicate any species, whether animals, plants, or microbial, that is closely associated with and transported by humans. Commensal models examine biological variation that reflects the movement of specific plants and animals to trace the routes by which individual species were moved in the past. This can include the use of comparative morphology and linguistics, DNA sequences, and stable isotopes.

The application of commensal models to understand the movement of plants and animals also has provided some of the strongest evidence for Pre-Columbian contacts between Polynesia and South America. Carbonized remains of sweet potato, a South American native, encountered during excavations of archaeological sites on the island of Mangaia in the Cook Islands were directly dated to between 800–1,000 years ago. Sweet potato remains that predate European contact with the Pacific or the Americas also have been recovered from several other archaeological sites on Polynesian islands.

The Polynesian words for sweet potato are all very similar and seem to be derived from native Quechuan terms for the same plant, indicating cultural contact that resulted in the dissemination of the plant as well as its name. Genetic studies also have revealed that the Pacific bottle gourd may have dual origins, owing some of its ancestry to South American varieties. The discovery and direct dating of chicken bones from the El Arenal site in Chile also suggests direct contacts between Polynesian voyagers and South American coastal groups before European contact with the Americas in AD 1492.

The movement of plants and animals did not cease with European contact, and in fact, the introduction of sweet potato to New Guinea, probably facilitated by Europeans, was incredibly important to later agricultural development in Near Oceania. In addition, the HMS *Bounty*, most famous for the mutiny that occurred on board, was initially sent to the Pacific in order to stock up on breadfruit to supply workers in the colonies of the East Indies. Cook's ships were regularly resupplied with produce and livestock from Pacific islands such as Tahiti. Ethnobotanists note that AD 1769, the year of Cook's first voyage, is the threshold for European domination of plant translocation in the Pacific.

See also AGRICULTURE, ORIGINS OF; ANIMAL DOMESTICATION; ARCHAEOBOTANY; BIOMOLEC-ULAR ANALYSIS; BOTTLE GOURD; CHICKEN; COLUMBIAN EXCHANGE; CULTIVATION; DNA ANALYSIS; LANDSCAPE AND ENVIRONMENTAL RECONSTRUCTION; OLD WORLD GLOBALIZA-TION AND FOOD EXCHANGES; PIG; PLANT DOMESTICATION; PLANT HUSBANDRY; RESIDUE ANALYSIS, STARCH; ROOT CROPS/TUBERS; STABLE ISOTOPE ANALYSIS; SWEET POTATO; TARO; YAM; ZOOARCHAEOLOGY

Further Reading

Denham, T. P., S. G. Haberle, C. Lentfer, et al. 2003. Origins of Agriculture at Kuk Swamp in the High-lands of New Guinea. *Science* 301(5630):189–93.

Giovas, Christina M. 2006. No Pig Atoll: Island Biogeography and the Extirpation of a Polynesian Domesticate. *Asian Perspectives* 45(1):69–95.

Jones, Terry L., Alice A. Storey, Elzabeth A. Matisoo-Smith, and José Miguel Ramirez-Aliaga, eds. 2011. *Polynesians in America: Pre-Columbian Contacts with the New World.* Lanham, MD: AltaMira Press/Rowman & Littlefield.

Kirch, Patrick Vinton. 2000. *On the Road of the Winds: An Archaeological History of the Pacific Islands before European Contact.* Berkeley: University of California Press.

Matisoo-Smith, Elizabeth. 2007. Animal Translocations, Genetic Variation and the Human Settlement of the Pacific. In *Genes, Language and Culture History in the Southwest Pacific,* edited by J. S. Friedlaender, 157–70. Oxford: Oxford University Press.

Storey, Alice A., Andrew C. Clarke, Thejn Ladefoged, et al. 2013. DNA and Pacific Commensal Models: Applications, Construction, Limitations, and Future Prospects. *Journal of Island and Coastal Archae-ology* 8(1):37–65.

Storey, Alice A., Daniel Quiroz, Nancy Beavan, and Elizabeth Matisoo-Smith. 2013. Polynesian Chick-ens in the New World: A Detailed Application of a Commensal Approach. *Archaeology in Oceania* 48(2):101–19.

Summerhayes, Glenn R., Matthew Leavesley, Andrew Fairbairn, et al. 2010. Human Adaptation and Plant Use in Highland New Guinea 49,000 to 44,000 Years Ago. *Science* 330(6000):78–81.

Whistler, W. Arthur. 1991. Polynesian Plant Introductions. In *Islands, Plants, and Polynesians: An Introduction to Polynesian Ethnobotany*, edited by Paul Alan Cox and Sandra Anne Banack, 41–66. Portland, OR: Dioscorides Press.

White, J. Peter. 2004. Where the Wild Things Are: Prehistoric Animal Translocation in the Circum New Guinea Archipelago. In *Voyages of Discovery: The Archaeology of Islands*, edited by Scott M. Fitzpatrick, 147–64. Westport, CT: Praeger.

■ ALICE STOREY

PAINTINGS
See WALL PAINTINGS/MURALS

PAISLEY CAVES, OREGON (UNITED STATES)

Human DNA recovered from 14,300-year-old coprolites (feces) has made the Paisley Caves the most widely accepted pre-Clovis site in North America. Coprolites contain pollen, phytoliths, plant starches, fibers, bone, hair, and identifiable chemical signatures. One 14,500-year-old specimen contained 9,000 Apiaceae (parsley family) pollen per cc, suggesting a meal of *Lomatium* roots, and one starch grain most likely representing grass seed. Chemical patterns identified by Fourier transform infrared analysis suggest that this person also consumed *Opuntia* (cactus) pads. Apiaceae, grass seed starches, and phytoliths also were extracted from the surface of a polished and battered grinding stone dated at 13,700 BP. The polished surface of this stone, and a utilized flake nearby, produced strong positive reactions to proboscidean (mammoth/mastodon) antibodies when the crossover immunoelectrophoresis method of protein residue analysis was applied. Horse protein residues were found on the surface of another polished hand stone. Soil recovered near these tools tested negative, indicating the positive results are not the product of natural contamination. A rectangular stone block in the same stratum produced grass seed starches and microscopic charcoal, possibly heat altered and folded (by grinding?). Plant remains recovered from these artifacts suggest that the site was occupied in the spring or early summer. The Pleistocene inhabitants of Paisley Caves were clearly broad-range foragers.

Pronghorn (*Antilocapra americana*), mountain sheep (*Ovis canadensis*), jackrabbit (*Lepus* sp.), marmot (*Marmota* sp.), and vole (*Microtus* sp.) were also on the menu. Pronghorn and hare are by far the dominant species exploited. Canines (*Canus latrans, C. lupus/ familiaris*), bison (*Bos bison*), fish, waterfowl, sage grouse (*Centrocercus urophasianus*), and Mormon crickets (*Anabrus simplex*) were consumed in smaller quantities. Food preparation on mats or hides on the cave floor made it impossible to keep dirt, hair, feathers, and rodent feces out of the food, and thus they are common in human coprolites. Lice and hookworms—in hair and coprolites, respectively—of Younger Dryas and early Holocene age were health hazards these broad-range foragers endured between 13,000 and 11,000 years ago (Clovis and younger).

See also BIOMOLECULAR ANALYSIS; DNA ANALYSIS; FORAGING; HUNTER-GATHERER SUBSISTENCE; INFRARED SPECTROSCOPY/FOURIER TRANSFORM INFRARED SPECTROSCOPY; PALEO-

DIETARY ANALYSIS; PALEOFECAL ANALYSIS; PALEOINDIAN DIET; PALYNOLOGY; PARASITOLOGI-
CAL ANALYSIS; PHYTOLITH ANALYSIS; RESIDUE ANALYSIS, STARCH; SOIL MICROTECHNIQUES

Further Reading

Gilbert, M. Thomas P., Dennis L. Jenkins, Anders Götherstrom, et al. 2008. DNA from Pre-Clovis Human Coprolites in Oregon, North America. *Science* 320(5877):786–89.

Jenkins, D. L. 2007. Distribution and Dating of Cultural and Paleontological Remains at the Paisley
Five Mile Point Caves in the Northern Great Basin. In *Paleoindian or Paleoarchaic: Great Basin Human
Ecology at the Pleistocene-Holocene Transition*, edited by K. E. Graf and D. Schmidt, 57–81. Salt Lake
City: University of Utah Press.

Jenkins, Dennis L., Loren G. Davis, Thomas W. Stafford Jr., et al. 2012. Clovis Age Western Stemmed
Projectile Points and Human Coprolites at the Paisley Caves. *Science* 337(6091):223–28.

Jenkins, Dennis L., Loren G. Davis, Thomas W. Stafford Jr., et al. 2013. Geochronology, Archaeological Context, and DNA at the Paisley Caves. In *The Paleoamerican Odyssey*, edited by K. E. Graf,
T. Goebel, and M. R. Waters, 485–510. College Station, TX: Center for the Study of First Americans.

■ DENNIS L. JENKINS

PALACE OF NESTOR (GREECE)

A Mycenaean (Late Bronze Age) building complex near Pylos in southwest mainland
Greece is popularly identified as the palace of legendary King Nestor. The site was destroyed about 1200 BC. In Homer's *Odyssey*, written down centuries later, Nestor sacrifices a heifer here, burning its thigh bones wrapped in fat for the gods. Deposits of cattle
bones excavated around the "palace" suggest similar Mycenaean sacrifices and enough
meat for substantial feasts. These deposits comprised selected body parts (lower jaw, upper
arm, and thigh) that had been stripped of meat (leaving diagonal or longitudinal knife
marks, characteristic of "filleting," on the bone shaft) and burned. The largest Mycenaean
event, involving at least 19 cattle and one deer and thus plentiful meat for hundreds or
thousands of guests, took place just before (and perhaps sought to avert) the palace's destruction. These events were also qualitatively distinctive: other bone fragments from the
palace, apparently representing more routine consumption and discard, are anatomically
mixed, mostly unburnt, and dominated by pigs and sheep, with few cattle.

Stores of plain ceramic tableware equipped the palace for large-scale hospitality, while
access routes suggest that some (presumably high-status) guests were entertained within
the building and others outside. Clay documents in Linear B script, from this and other
palaces, suggest that provision of wheat or barley signaled distinctions of gender and
status or context among participants. Feasts marked religious festivals and more secular
occasions, and some took place at outlying sanctuaries or in local communities. The palace probably contributed routine staples and sometimes wine or a grand venue for these
events, but loyal subjects provided fattened animals. Feasting apparently financed as well
as legitimized the social hierarchy.

See also BUTCHERY; FEASTING; FOOD AND GENDER; FOOD AND RITUAL; FOOD AND STA-
TUS; FOODWAYS AND RELIGIOUS PRACTICES; MEAT; OFFERINGS AND GRAVE GOODS; ZOO-
ARCHAEOLOGY

Further Reading

Isaakidou, Valasia, Paul Halstead, Jack Leonard Davis, and Sharon Stocker. 2002. Burnt Animal Sacrifice at the Mycenaean "Palace of Nestor," Pylos. *Antiquity* 76(291):86–92.

Shelmerdine, Cynthia W. 2008. Host and Guest at a Mycenaean Feast. In *DAIS: The Aegean Feast*, edited by Louise A. Hitchcock, Robert Laffineur, and Janice L. Crowley, 401–10. Aegaeum 29 (Annales d'archéologie égéenne de l'Université de Liège et UT-PASP). Leuven: Peeters Publishers.

■ PAUL HALSTEAD

PALEODEMOGRAPHY

Paleodemography involves the reconstruction of demographic patterns (such as age- and sex-specific mortality rates) in past populations using human skeletons from archaeological sites. Paleodemographic methods have been used to make inferences about health, nutrition, and dietary quality in ancient populations, the role of infectious diseases in population dynamics, long-term trends in health and longevity, and the impact of major changes in subsistence, such as the origins of agriculture, on human health. Paleodemography is closely related to paleopathology and paleoepidemiology. The current entry focuses on the possible insights that paleodemography may provide into the distribution of nutritional inadequacy and its implications for mortality patterns in past populations. There is considerable potential for this area of research, but important methodological advances must be made before its results can be considered credible.

Paleodemography is bedeviled by numerous technical problems, including biases in age estimation, the confounding effects of population growth ("demographic nonstationarity"), and our limited ability to deal with heterogeneous risks of death associated with factors other than simple age and sex (which can be reconstructed from skeletons, albeit often with considerable error). Biased aging primarily refers to the underestimation of ages at death in skeletons of older adults, that is, those over about 50 years of age. Discussions of the appropriateness of biostatistical methods (e.g., the Rostock Manifesto) are now commonplace, and although biased age estimation has yet to be fully eliminated, progress has been made. The confounding effects of demographic nonstationarity, which make it inherently difficult to separate patterns of fertility and mortality using skeletal samples, have proven harder to solve. The primary problem addressed here, the difficulty of linking nutritional status to population-level health and mortality, is a special case of the more general problem of heterogeneous risks of death and the selective mortality they inevitably give rise to. These problems are not confined to paleodemography but affect demography and epidemiology in general.

Many individual-level markers of nutritional status, some of them associated with specific nutritional deficiencies, have been identified by paleopathologists. As both demographic and epidemiological studies in the developing world suggest, however, the most informative markers of undernutrition may be less specific lesions associated with growth faltering—for example, short adult stature, macroscopic and microscopic enamel defects, and Harris lines in long bones. Growth faltering can have diverse causes, including psychological ones. But a huge literature on the demography and epidemiology of living populations highlights the near-universal influence of childhood

P A L E O D E M O G R A P H Y

undernutrition on the risk of growth faltering. Skeletal indicators of growth faltering may, therefore, be the most reliable (if nonspecific) pointers to the linkage between prehistoric nutrition and mortality.

Demography and epidemiology also suggest that there are two important effects of undernutrition on population processes, one short-term and the other much longer-term (and more subtle). The short-term effect has been well studied in the rural developing world: periods of undernutrition severe enough to cause growth faltering also impair various components of the immune system in affected children (mostly those under the age of five years), placing them at elevated risk of early childhood death from infectious diseases. (In addition, certain infectious diseases, especially diarrheal diseases, may initiate or exacerbate nutritional problems in children that in turn compromise their immunocompetence and growth.) This short-term effect, often acute and strong, should be detectable in juvenile skeletons by using appropriate statistical methods to estimate the selective relationship between age at death and skeletal markers of growth faltering. In this case, there should be little reason to suspect that lesions whose onset predated death by a fairly short period (e.g., less than a year) might be indicators of better health and survival, contra the so-called osteological paradox (the standard aggregate measures used by paleodemographers to interpret health from skeletal remains do not always have a direct relationship to *individual* experiences of illness and death). The analysis may, however, be complicated by poor preservation of juvenile skeletons. Accurate aging of children less than five should, however, be relatively easy.

The second, longer-term effect of undernutrition on mortality revealed by recent research on living populations has to do with possible effects of early childhood (even prenatal) exposures on later adult (even old-age) risks of death. In preindustrial communities, such exposure would certainly include the kinds of stresses associated with undernutrition, growth disruption, compromised immunocompetence, and infectious diseases. But in this context the difficulty of estimating the ages of older individuals will be a profound problem. And the potential here for the osteological paradox is real: people who recover from and then survive many decades following severe growth retardation may well be constitutionally less vulnerable (e.g., have more active immune systems) than those who die during or soon after such stress. Alternatively, people who die long after growth faltering might be victims of the long-term *negative* effects of childhood stress. Either is possible, as shown by research on the association between ages at death in adult skeletons from medieval Denmark and their dental ultrastructure, especially microscopic growth increments in enamel that provide reliable evidence of earlier growth faltering and the likely age during childhood when it occurred.

See also BIOARCHAEOLOGICAL ANALYSIS; PALEODIETARY ANALYSIS; PALEONUTRITION; PALEOPATHOLOGY

Further Reading

Chamberlain, Andrew. 2006. *Demography in Archaeology.* Cambridge: Cambridge University Press.
Hoppa, Robert D., and James W. Vaupel, eds. 2002. *Paleodemography: Age Distributions from Skeletal Samples.* Cambridge: Cambridge University Press.

Konigsberg, Lyle W., and Susan R. Frankenberg. 2012. Demography. In *Research Methods in Skeletal Biology*, edited by Elizabeth A. Digangi and Megan K. Moore, 293–323. Waltham, MA: Academic Press/Elsevier.

Milner, George R., and Jesper L. Boldsen. 2012. Transition Analysis: A Validation Study with Known-Age Modern American Skeletons. *American Journal of Physical Anthropology* 148(1):98–110.

Milner, George R., James W. Wood, and Jesper L. Boldsen. 2008. Advances in Paleodemography. In *Biological Anthropology of the Human Skeleton*, edited by M. Anne Katzenberg and Shelley R. Saunders, 561–600. 2nd edition. Hoboken, NJ: John Wiley & Sons.

Thomas, Rebecca Ferrell. 2003. Enamel Defects, Well-Being and Mortality in a Medieval Danish Village. Ph.D. dissertation, Department of Anthropology, Pennsylvania State University.

Wood, James W. 2014. *The Biodemography of Subsistence Farming: Population, Food and Family*. Cambridge: Cambridge University Press.

Wood, James W., George R. Milner, Henry C. Harpending, and Kenneth M. Weiss. 1992. The Osteological Paradox: Problems of Inferring Prehistoric Health from Skeletal Samples. *Current Anthropology* 33(4):343–70.

■ JIM WOOD

PALEODIETARY ANALYSIS

Paleodietary analysis, broadly and simply construed, is the study of past diet. In the archaeological literature, the term most frequently appears in association with stable-isotope-based approaches to reconstructing past human diet, but as this volume amply demonstrates, paleodietary analysis properly encompasses a wide and interdisciplinary range of techniques, including, for instance, analyses of botanical (e.g., archaeobotany or paleoethnobotany), faunal (e.g., archaeozoology or zooarchaeology), food residue (e.g., plant starch and phytolith), and human skeletal (e.g., dental) materials.

Different techniques for paleodietary analysis provide different but complementary types of information. For instance, whereas stable isotope and coprolite analyses can provide direct evidence for foods consumed by humans in the past, most other techniques focus on indirect evidence such as food refuse from past dietary events (i.e., materials left behind from acts of food production, processing, consumption, and disposal). While indirect forms of evidence cannot be used to directly quantify past human dietary intake, they are invaluable for interpreting broader trends in dietary practices and contextualizing food-related economic, social, spiritual, and sensual activities within their broader cultural and environmental framework.

Paleodietary analyses are carried out at a range of temporal, spatial, biological, and cultural scales. For instance, stable isotope analyses of different human tissues can provide a record of certain kinds of dietary intake during discrete times of an individual's youth as well as a lifetime dietary average. Botanical and residue analyses of food remains adhering to a potsherd or preserved in a coprolite may provide evidence for foods consumed at the scale of a single individual or small group and over a very short time interval. At the other end of the continuum, analyses of faunal and other food remains from a midden deposit may inform upon the dietary activities of larger groups occurring at the scale of weeks, months, years, and even generations. Thus, by employing techniques from a variety of specialties on different analytes, paleodietary studies are able to reconstruct richer, multifocal understandings of past diet.

Diet in the past, as now, is a highly integrated part of the human experience, and, as such, paleodietary studies lend themselves to diverse theoretical approaches. More specifically, this stems from the fact that diet is the product of an articulation between human biology and culture, reflecting the diachronic interaction of social norms and ideas as well as environmental constraints and opportunities. For instance, some researchers approach paleodietary studies from the perspective of nutritional adequacy or optimal foraging theory, while others may focus on the importance of social functions and meanings that are projected onto different aspects of diet and associated practices. Most often, however, paleodietary studies are informed by a broader theoretical cognizance of diet in terms of both its biological and symbolic implications.

While paleodietary analyses are integral to a wide variety of archaeological research programs, they are particularly germane to investigations of the role played by diet and associated subsistence activities in human biological and cultural adaptations and related processes. For example, a number of hypotheses about key developments in hominin and specifically human evolution have focused on the important roles played by food and subsistence activities. In the same vein, dietary adaptations have featured in some explanations of why Neanderthals disappeared from Europe whereas anatomically modern humans persisted. Paleodietary analyses also continue to make invaluable contributions to studies of the transition from hunting and gathering to farming and pastoral lifeways around the globe. Key questions in this area have been directed toward identifying the origins and progenitors of domesticated plant and animal species, the social and environmental processes that led to their domestication, and the means, timing, and routes by which a dependence upon plant cultivation and animal husbandry spread across much of the Old and New World continents. Other key research questions focus on the role that food and food production have played in the appearance and development of hierarchical social organization and processes of social inequality.

There is a growing recognition that answers to these and many other questions about past human diet and subsistence practices are not only inherently interesting and important in and of themselves but can also help to contextualize some of the diet- and health-related issues facing societies today. For this and many other reasons, paleodietary analyses, and the diverse and multiscalar sets of tools they encompass, are an invaluable part of archaeological efforts to understand the human past.

See also ARCHAEOBOTANY; BIOARCHAEOLOGIAL ANALYSIS; BIOMOLECULAR ANALYSIS; DENTAL ANALYSIS; DNA ANALYSIS; GUT ANALYSIS; MULTI- AND INTERDISCIPLINARY APPROACHES; PALEOFECAL ANALYSIS; PALEONUTRITION; PALEOPATHOLOGY; STABLE ISOTOPE ANALYSIS; ZOOARCHAEOLOGY

Further Reading

Ambrose, Stanley H., and M. Anne Katzenberg, eds. 2000. *Biogeochemical Approaches to Paleodietary Analysis*. New York: Kluwer Academic/Plenum Publishers.

Gerritsen, Fokke. 2000. Of Calories and Culture: Introduction to an Archaeological Dialogues Special Section on Food and Foodways. *Archaeological Dialogues* 72(2):169–72.

Hublin, Jean-Jacques, and Michael P. Richards, eds. 2009. *The Evolution of Hominin Diets: Integrating Approaches to the Study of Palaeolithic Subsistence.* Berlin: Springer.

Pearsall, Deborah M. 2001. *Paleoethnobotany: A Handbook of Procedures.* 2nd edition. San Diego, CA: Academic Press.

Reitz, Elizabeth J., and Elizabeth S. Wing. 2008. *Zooarchaeology.* 2nd edition. Cambridge: Cambridge University Press.

Staller, John E., Robert H. Tykot, and Bruce F. Benz, eds. 2006. *Histories of Maize: Multidisciplinary Approaches to the Prehistory, Linguistics, Biogeography, Domestication, and Evolution of Maize.* Walnut Creek, CA: Left Coast Press.

Twiss, Katheryn. 2012. The Archaeology of Food and Social Diversity. *Journal of Archaeological Research* 20(4):357–95.

■ ERIC GUIRY

PALEOENVIRONMENTAL RECONSTRUCTION

See Landscape and Environmental Reconstruction

PALEOETHNOBOTANY

See Archaeobotany

PALEOFECAL ANALYSIS

Paleofeces, or desiccated human fecal matter, take one of three major forms: cess (commingled feces from multiple individuals), coprolites (individual specimens excreted by a once-living person), and gut contents (materials still within the body of a preserved person, but also from soils taken from the abdomen areas of burials). Identification of a specimen as human is generally done during laboratory processing based on morphology (size and shape), color, context, and smell.

The analysis of paleofeces involves the rehydration of the specimens using a 0.5 percent solution of trisodium phosphate and the gentle washing of the specimens through 850- and 250-micrometer mesh to separate visible botanical and faunal specimens. The remaining sediment is then examined for pollen, phytolith, and endoparasite material. Next, the recovered material must be separated, identified, and quantified.

Quantification is an issue since the visible constituents represent only a portion of the diet, quantification methods for faunal and botanical remains are often different, and estimating dietary contribution is tied to the first two issues. Quantification approaches include a general estimate of abundance per specimen, an actual count of macrofossils per specimen, and simple weight. Once quantified, a cluster analysis of constituents by sample also can be used to model both diet (general constituents) and cuisine (combinations of constituents representing meals).

In addition to visible remains (macroremains, such as seeds, and microremains, such as pollen), chemical methods (e.g., protein residue analysis) can also be used to detect the presence of plants and animal remains that are not visible to the human eye. DNA analysis also may be applicable for the identification of invisible materials. These identified materials are then added to the constituent list and provide a more complete view of the foods and other materials (e.g., medicines) consumed. In addition, the analysis of DNA can be used to confirm species (e.g., human) of origin and, with coprolites, the sex of the individual. Hormone analysis can also be used to identify the sex of an individual. Finally, the recovery and identification of endoparasites from samples can be used to gauge the health of individuals and populations.

See also ARCHAEOBOTANY; BIOARCHAEOLOGIAL ANALYSIS; BIOMOLECULAR ANALYSIS; DNA ANALYSIS; GUT ANALYSIS; PALEODIETARY ANALYSIS; PALEONUTRITION; PALEOPATHOLOGY; PARASITOLOGICAL ANALYSIS; ZOOARCHAEOLOGY

Further Reading

Sutton, Mark Q., Kristin D. Sobolik, and Jill K. Gardner. 2010. *Paleonutrition.* Tucson: University of Arizona Press.

■ MARK Q. SUTTON

PALEOINDIAN DIET

Paleoindian diet refers to the resources exploited for consumption by hunter-gatherers who produced the oldest archaeological cultures of North America, ca. 12,000–9,000 BP. Although traditionally inferred to have focused on the exploitation of large, now-extinct terrestrial prey, including mammoth, horse, camel, and long-horned bison, current research emphasizes vertebrate taphonomy and geographic variation in prey choice, while drawing on human behavioral ecology (HBE) as a theoretical construct for understanding foraging decisions. Key variables and research considerations in elucidating diet and subsistence activities include taxonomic structure, skeletal part representation, age-frequency data, bone modifications, and season of procurement.

Exceptional faunal preservation on the Great Plains provides the most complete extant record of Paleoindian diet. Here, long-horned bison were focal prey, with animals procured singly and in small herds throughout the year. Occasional, fortuitous circumstances allowed hunters to kill large numbers en masse, primarily in arroyos or gullies serving as natural traps. Carcass butchery ranges from highly selective removal of choice segments (e.g., tongue) to extensive muscle stripping and processing of long bones for marrow.

Recent research on the Channel Islands, California, reveals exploitation of coastal resources, including marine mammals, shellfish and other invertebrates, as well as seabirds, waterfowl, and fish. Unfortunately, the character of Paleoindian diet in other regions is more ambiguous because of insufficient data. In the Eastern Woodlands, evidence exists for use of caribou, arctic hare, white-tailed deer, beaver, muskrat, waterfowl, turtle, fish, and some gathered plant foods. In the Far West and Rocky Mountains, the diet also included pronghorn, mountain sheep, bison, and wapiti.

Fresh primary evidence coupled with reanalysis of extant material has the potential to fill current gaps in baseline data sets. Questions abound concerning the foraging activities of women and children, the fitness benefits of male large-game hunting, and the effect of changes in food-resource structure on foraging patterns, residential mobility, and demography. Research on gathered plant foods is also necessary to develop a more complete dietary picture. This will involve the identification of sites with preserved botanical remains and the adoption of appropriate frames of reference and recovery methods.

See also BONE FAT EXTRACTION; BUTCHERY; COOPERATIVE HUNTING; FISH/SHELLFISH; FOOD SHARING; FORAGING; HUNTER-GATHERER SUBSISTENCE; MARINE MAMMALS; MEAT; PALEO-DEMOGRAPHY; PALEODIETARY ANALYSIS; ZOOARCHAEOLOGY

Further Reading

Meltzer, David J. 2010. *First Peoples in a New World: Colonizing Ice Age America*. Berkeley: University of California Press.
Walker, Renee B., and Boyce N. Driskell, eds. 2007. *Foragers of the Terminal Pleistocene in North America*. Lincoln: University of Nebraska Press.

■ MATTHEW G. HILL

PALEOLITHIC DIET

The history of hominin diet in the Paleolithic is basically the 2.5-million-year-old story of game consumption. The heavy dietary focus on animal food resources apparent from the archaeological record may be the result of a preservation bias against organic material, but this focus is also emphasized by interpretations based on results of biochemical isotope analyses. The manner and intensity in which game products were consumed throughout the Paleolithic (2.6 MYA–11,600 BP) and Mesolithic (11,600–7,500 BP) depended on the energy requirements of the various hominin species that existed during this enormous time span, as well as on the flexibility of group structure and organization when key resources became scarce or failed.

Australopithecines subsisted on a diet of C_3 and C_4 plants, and evidence for meat eating is only inferential. Direct evidence of game exploitation appears around 1.8 MYA. At around this time we witness a remarkable expansion in brain size in early *Homo*. A shift toward a higher-quality diet (i.e., the systematic exploitation of animal resources) was required to compensate for the high energetic costs of larger brains. In this context, the African Olduvai Bed I (FLK *Zinj*) and the site of 'Ubeidiya (Israel) demonstrate that regular hunting of medium-sized mammals formed part of the hominin behavioral repertoire. From then on, accumulations of butchered animal remains form a regular part of Pleistocene archaeological cave and open-air sites in Eurasia and bear witness to this hunting way of life.

For much of the Paleolithic, subsistence focused on the exploitation of large herd animals and territorial game killed in large cooperative hunts as well as by ambush and confrontational hunting. Especially during the Middle Paleolithic, animal exploitation tactics focused on obtaining the best nutritional resources, often targeting only the strongest and well-nourished individuals of an animal population.

During the Middle Paleolithic in southern Europe and the Levant, but especially during the Upper Paleolithic, the dietary spectrum broadened, and small game and birds regularly enlarged the diet. Especially toward the end of the Upper Paleolithic and during the Mesolithic, fish and marine resources became an important dietary component. The huge variety of fishing equipment known especially from the Mesolithic is indicative of differing fishing techniques, mass kills, and hunting of large marine fishes. Again, interpretations of results of biochemical isotope analyses underline the archaeological evidence.

Meat seems to have been the most important nutritional source throughout the Paleolithic. This has been demonstrated by analyses of cut-marked bone surfaces from numerous Pleistocene sites. Nutritional deficiencies caused by lean ungulate meat, providing a high-protein but low-energy diet during late winter and spring, could have been compensated for with carbohydrate-rich tubers or by rendering grease from bones. The archaeological evidence indicates that bones were systematically broken to exploit grease resources. Impressive early examples come from the 800,000-year-old site of Gesher Benot Ya'aqov, Israel, where even the tiniest phalanges of fallow deer were split to extract marrow.

Measured by the wealth of evidence for meat eating, consumption of plant foods is only rarely visible in the archaeological record. Studies of phytoliths, starch grains, and human dental calculus show that plants played a role in the diet of Neanderthals during the Middle Paleolithic. Upper Paleolithic sites provide evidence for the systematic exploitation and processing of plants in the form of grinding stones. The Upper Paleolithic site of Ohalo II, Israel, is characterized by outstanding preservation of plant remains, and even the processing of dough made of grain flour is identifiable. Our modern plant-food-based nutrition is rooted in the Mesolithic, however. During this epoch, we see the costly provisioning of grains and fruits at specialized task camps that were operated over generations. Evidence for sustainable subsistence practices is apparent with the pruning and thinning out of hazel groves, the intentional setting of bushfires, and the management of mussel banks.

Food preparation using fire was already employed during the Lower Paleolithic to increase the digestibility of protein and starch. A skewer with a charred tip from the 300,000-year-old site of Schöningen, Germany, attests to the roasting of meat over an open fire, as do burned bones from numerous Eurasian Middle Paleolithic cave and open-air sites (e.g., the site of Kebara, Israel). The rendering of grease from bones by stone boiling can be traced back to the late Middle Paleolithic and becomes common practice during the Upper Paleolithic. At numerous sites, smashed bone fragments and fragments of heat-cracked boiling stones were found associated in pits (e.g., the late Upper Paleolithic site of Gönnersdorf, Germany).

Paleolithic Diet is also the term for a modern diet program that focuses on lean meat, fish, vegetables, fruit, roots, and nuts. Foods that are considered to have come into focus with the onset of the Neolithic, such as cereal grains, milk, salt, refined fat, and sugar, are avoided as they are suspected of causing serious diseases in affluent Western societies.

See also ARCHAEOBOTANY; BIOMOLECULAR ANALYSIS; BONE FAT EXTRACTION; BROAD SPECTRUM REVOLUTION; BUTCHERY; COOPERATIVE HUNTING; DENTAL ANALYSIS; FIRE AND THE DEVELOPMENT OF COOKING; FIRE AND THE DEVELOPMENT OF COOKING TECHNOLOGY; FOOD SHARING; FORAGING; GESHER BENOT YA'AQOV; HUNTER-GATHERER SUBSISTENCE; MESOLITHIC DIET; NEANDERTHAL DIET; OHALO II; OLDUVAI GORGE; PALEODIETARY ANALYSIS;

PHYTOLITH ANALYSIS; RESIDUE ANALYSIS, STARCH; STABLE ISOTOPE ANALYSIS; SUBSISTENCE MODELS; TOOLS/UTENSILS, GROUND STONE; WEAPONS, STONE; ZOOARCHAEOLOGY

Further Reading

Domínguez-Rodrigo, Manuel, Rebeca Barba, and Charles P. Egeland. 2007. *Deconstructing Olduvai: A Taphonomic Study of the Bed I Sites.* Dordrecht: Springer.

Gaudzinski, Sabine. 2005. Monospecific or Species-Dominated Faunal Assemblages during the Middle Palaeolithic in Europe. In *Transitions before the Transition: Evolution and Stability in the Middle Paleolithic and Middle Stone Age,* edited by Erella Hovers and Stephen L. Kuhn, 137–47. New York: Springer.

Holst, Daniela. 2010. Hazelnut Economy of Early Holocene Hunter-Gatherers: A Case Study from Mesolithic Duvensee, Northern Germany. *Journal of Archaeological Science* 37(11):2871–80.

Leonard, William R., J. Josh Snodgrass, and Marcia L. Robertson. 2007. Effects of Brain Evolution on Human Nutrition and Metabolism. *Annual Review of Nutrition* 27:311–27.

Piperno, Dolores R., Ehud Weiss, Irene Holst, and Dani Nadel. 2004. Processing of Wild Cereal Grains in the Upper Palaeolithic Revealed by Starch Grain Analysis. *Nature* 430(7000):670–73.

Rabinovich, Rivka, Sabine Gaudzinski-Windheuser, Lutz Kindler, and Naama Goren-Inbar. 2011. *The Acheulian Site of Gesher Benot Ya'aqov.* Vol. 3, *Mammalian Taphonomy: The Assemblages of Layers V-5 and V-6.* Dordrecht: Springer.

Stiner, Mary C. 2005. *The Faunas of Hayonim Cave, Israel: A 200,000-Year Record of Paleolithic Diet, Demography and Society.* American School of Prehistoric Research Bulletin 48. Cambridge, MA: Peabody Museum of Archaeology and Ethnology, Harvard University.

■ SABINE GAUDZINSKI-WINDHEUSER

PALEONUTRITION

Paleonutrition is the study of prehistoric human diet in relation to health and nutrition for both individuals and populations (the field of nutritional anthropology deals with much the same thing in extant populations and can serve as a source of models of past adaptations). The field of paleonutrition is not confined only to foods and other consumed materials but encompasses the methods, technologies, and organizations used by prehistoric peoples to obtain, process, and ingest such materials. It also includes the study of food choice (no culture eats all of the possible foods present in their habitat); the natural, social, and political influences on diet (e.g., drought or war-related famine); and how these factors influence human adaptations through time.

Current studies related to paleonutrition are overwhelmingly concerned with diet and how diet affects health. To understand how diet and health are related, however, it is necessary to understand the entire subsistence system. Diet can be seen as what is eaten, nutrition as how the diet provides the necessary materials to maintain the body, and subsistence as the entire system (strategies, tactics, settlement, and technology) of procurement, processing, and consumption of foodstuffs. Health is a reflection of nutrition plus other stress experiences. These components are intertwined, and an understanding of all of the components is necessary for an understanding of both individuals and populations.

Although "diet" is generally thought of as foods that were consumed, it also includes any other materials ingested into the body, such as condiments, medicines, ritual substances, recreational substances, and things accidentally ingested. Thus, when diet is analyzed, some or all of the other nonfood materials consumed may be present in the data and so require analytical consideration. Even the diet of certain domesticated animals may be of interest in that they may mirror human diet (e.g., dogs) or relate to other cultural practices (e.g., growing certain crops as feed).

Paleonutritional data are derived from many diverse sources, including plant and animal remains, skeletal materials, procurement and processing technology, and even settlement patterns, and can be characterized as either direct or indirect. Direct data are those where no inference is necessary; the remains are directly linked to human paleonutrition (such as constituents in paleofeces or nutritional pathologies in bone). Indirect data require an inference to link them to human paleonutrition, however, and constitute the vast majority of paleonutritional data from archaeological sites. For example, burned seeds found in a hearth may allow archaeologists to infer the consumption of a particular plant. Burned animal bone found in a site midden may allow archaeologists to infer the consumption of that particular animal. In both cases, however, consumption is not directly demonstrated. While it is likely that many of these materials are human dietary debris, it remains possible that some remains may be debris from other human activities, such as the manufacture of clothing, the use of firewood, the construction of shelter, and the manufacture and use of tools. It is also possible that such remains originated from the activities of nonhumans, such as rodents and carnivores.

Other aspects of culture may also constitute indirect paleonutritional data. We may deduce the procurement, processing, and consumption of animals and plants from the presence of hunting technology and seed-grinding implements, but again, those data do not directly demonstrate consumption. The existence of an "antelope shaman" in certain Great Basin societies may suggest the hunting of pronghorn antelope but does not constitute direct evidence that pronghorn were consumed. The same arguments can be made of the presence of fishing camps, agricultural fields, and the like. This is not to say that the inferences made using indirect data are weak; not at all. Many of the inferences are very, very strong, but they are still inferences and not direct data.

Data relating to prehistoric diet, nutrition, and health are present in the archaeological record in five basic types: paleobotanical, zooarchaeological (faunal), bioarchaeological, paleofecal, and biomolecular. Most data also come in one or two forms, macro- and microremains. Macroremains are those that are large enough to be seen and identified with no or low magnification, such as bones and seeds. Microremains are those that must be recovered and identified with the use of specialized microscopy equipment or techniques, such as pollen and phytoliths. Biomolecular remains are those substances that are not visible, or visibly identifiable, and so must be identified through chemical analyses.

Paleobotanical Data

Paleobotanical remains include macroseeds, nuts, fruits, fiber, wood, and charcoal, plus microscopic pollen, phytoliths, and fibers. The preservation, recognition, and recovery of botanical specimens is always an issue since most botanical specimens are fragile and only preserve under certain circumstances, such as carbonization. Some botanical remains are collected during routine (coarse) screening of site soils, but most are collected as specialized samples, such as carbonized posts, charcoal samples from hearths, soil samples from hearths or other features, soil samples from the general midden, and pollen and phytolith samples from site soils or even from artifacts.

Paleobotanical remains are visually identified with the aid of comparative collections of seeds, pollen, phytoliths, and wood morphology by species (for charcoal). In addition, plant remains can be identified on tools and other materials using protein residue analysis and even aDNA analysis. Pollen and phytoliths represent different parts of a plant that may be differentially used or preserved. Pollen and phytolith analyses can also complement each other; in many situations, phytoliths preserve where pollen does not, and phytoliths can identify some plants to a higher taxonomic level than pollen.

Quantification of paleobotanical remains is a significant problem as many researchers use different methods. For all methods, absolute counts of the specimens are necessary. Following that, the ubiquity (presence/absence) method is nearly universal. In addition, many researchers use other methods that detail ranking or diversity. One is the percentage weight method, another is the percentage count method, and still another is the percentage volume method. While it is recognized that many botanical remains naturally occur in sites, it is assumed that most remains recovered from features are cultural in origin, used either for food, fuel, shelter, or manufacturing.

Paleobotanical remains are a significant component of paleonutritional studies because plants often represent the dietary staples for many populations. As such, the analysis of botanical remains from archaeological sites is necessary to recognize the importance of plants to the diet and nutrition of a given population. If such remains are preserved at a site and consistent sampling of all levels and areas is provided, a wide array of dietary information can be ascertained. The information can then be compared with other botanical data from nearby sites to reveal the entire botanical diet of a population, changes in dietary practices through time, possible differences in status areas of a site or a region, and differential environmental selection procedures of a population in a specific area. The analysis of seed, nut, fruit, and fiber remains also can determine dietary plant selectivity, seasonality of site occupation, and possible storage practices that could influence nutrition during seasons that provide little plant variety to the diet.

Zooarchaeological Data

Zooarchaeology is the study and interpretation of animal remains from archaeological sites, materials that are generally called faunal remains. Faunal remains include a variety of materials, primarily bone, but also shell, chitin (e.g., insect exoskeletons), soft tissues (e.g., skin, muscle, hair, feathers), blood, proteins, aDNA, and even impressions in a matrix.

Faunal remains are from either vertebrates or invertebrates, and the individual parts (e.g., bones) are called elements. The primary categories of vertebrates are fish, amphibians, reptiles, birds, and mammals. Fish have either a full bony skeleton or a skeleton of cartilage reinforced by calcium in heavy load areas. Amphibians and reptiles generally have the same basic skeletal elements as mammals. However, turtles and tortoises have bony shells that, if fragmented, may appear to be large mammal cranial parts. Birds tend to have relatively thin bones, and while they share some skeletal elements in common with mammals, many elements are unique (including eggshells).

Mammals (flying, marine, and terrestrial) share a generally similar limb structure with common elements. Many mammals were used for food and other purposes in antiquity; among terrestrial mammals, artiodactyls (i.e,. hoofed mammals), lagomorphs (e.g., rabbits, hares), and rodents were the most widely used and are common constituents in site assemblages in many parts of the world.

Invertebrates include insects, mollusks (e.g., shellfish), crabs, lobsters, shrimp, spiders, scorpions, and worms. Archaeologists typically recognize and collect the remains of mollusks at sites, but few consider insect remains to be important. Virtually all peoples ate or used insects, however, and their remains are present in sites, although problems exist in their analysis, including taxon identification (there are few comparative collections) and quantification (such remains tend to be highly fragmented).

Most faunal remains recovered from sites consist of bones from vertebrates. Bone is a material that generally preserves fairly well, although shell can be abundant at some sites. Most bone is recovered during routine excavation and (coarse) screening (screen size will impact the taxa recovered since many animals are quite small), with fewer specimens being recovered from specialized samples. It is generally assumed that most faunal remains were cultural in origin, with food residue the most common interpretation. Animals were used for purposes other than as food, however, such as for raw materials (e.g., dung, hides, and fibers), as pets, as labor (transport and traction), and in ceremonies. Animal remains also can enter site soils through natural processes (e.g., rodent burrow deaths).

Faunal remains are identified first to element and then to taxon as closely as possible with the aid of comparative collections. If possible, the age and sex of the animals is also noted. Burned or modified elements are separated, counted, and weighed. Quantification of faunal remains has been conducted with more precision and frequency than in paleobotanical studies. The most frequently used techniques are number of identified specimens (NISP), ubiquity, and minimum number of individuals (MNI). Other quantification techniques that have been used include minimum number of elements (MNE), meat weight, and various taxonomic diversity and richness indices.

Simple quantification figures do not necessarily reflect economic importance, and so it may be useful to adjust the numbers for meat weight. The calculation of age profiles, mortality profiles, and sex differences can help to understand prey populations, the human impact on these populations, and human adaptations. For example, the sex and age profiles in domesticated animal populations should show many young males, a few old males, a few young females, and many old females.

Bioarchaeological Data

Bioarchaeology, defined here as the analysis of human skeletal remains, is an important aspect of paleonutrition studies. Human remains are found in one of three major forms: preserved bodies (naturally or purposefully mummified), inhumations (primary or secondary), and cremated remains (primary or secondary). Once material has been determined to be human (and after the appropriate legal requirements are fulfilled), it is identified by element, metrics are recorded, and if possible, determinations of age, sex, stature, and race are made. Any nonmetric traits, such as skull deformation, are noted. The skeletons of subadults (adolescents, children, and infants) are morphologically different than those adults and present their own analytical challenges. On preserved bodies, any evidence of soft-tissue paleopathology, trauma, or parasites is recorded. Long bones are often radiographed for evidence of nutritional deficiencies, and preserved bodies are scanned (by CT or MRI).

While there are a variety of analytical avenues, much of the information obtained from human remains is derived through the study of paleopathology, the analysis of disease that manifests itself on bone. Dietary stress and health issues are the source of much paleopathology and form a core data set for paleonutritional analyses. The most frequently used paleopathological assessments involve growth arrest lines, such as linear enamel hypoplasia on teeth and Harris lines on long bones, evidence of anemia through porotic hyperostosis and cribra orbitalia, and evidence of infections through periostitis and osteomyelitis. Other paleopathologies that can be observed in the skeleton include bone loss (osteoporosis), disease such as syphilis and yaws, tuberculosis, and leprosy, and vitamin-related nutritional deficiencies such as scurvy and rickets. Tooth wear can be indicative of some dietary issues, such as the consumption of grit from food processing. The analysis of soft tissues of preserved bodies has revealed the presence of lung and heart diseases, high cholesterol, parasitic infections, degenerative joint disease, anthracosis (a common affliction due to the use of indoor fires), cancers, and various tumors. These discoveries not only shed light on past health but also show these afflictions are not new in contemporary society.

Paleofecal Remains

Paleofeces (desiccated human fecal matter) are a unique resource for analyzing paleonutrition because they offer direct insight into prehistoric diet and, in some cases, health. The constituents of paleofeces are mostly the remains of intentionally consumed food items, with the possible exception of wind-blown pollen contaminants and feces-thriving insects. Parasites also may be found in paleofeces and reflect the parasitic load of the individual, and potentially the load of the population, therefore providing direct data on health. Proteins and aDNA also have been identified from paleofeces, providing the identification of a broader range of ingested plants and animals.

Biomolecular Remains

Biomolecular remains include aDNA, proteins, stable isotopes, and trace elements. Much of the material subjected to these analyses is human bone, but other materials can also be studied. Analysis of aDNA is now becoming less expensive and more commonplace. Ancient proteins also can be recovered and analyzed using a variety of techniques, most commonly crossover immunoelectrophoresis (CIEP). Protein residue (not to be confused with blood residue analysis) can be used to identify proteins from any living thing: animals, plants, and even pathogens.

Stable isotopes are differentially absorbed by different types of plants. Animals that eat the plants will absorb those isotopes in the same ratios as contained in the plants. In theory, humans who eat plants and animals will then reflect the basic isotopic ratios of those foods. The stable isotopes within a tissue sample can be measured, plotted, and so used to deduce the diet of the animal (including humans) from which the sample was taken. Isotopic ratios can originate in a number of ways unrelated to diet, however, such as biogenesis (changes resulting from post-depositional biological activity, such as bacterial action), which can distort the analytical results. Isotopes of carbon, nitrogen, and strontium appear to be the most useful in paleonutrition studies, although sulphur, hydrogen, and calcium also have potential.

The majority of stable isotope work has been conducted on bone, usually collagen, although other materials (such as seeds) can be used. Carbon isotopes in the food chain are the best known, and three pathways have been identified: the Calvin (C_3), the Hatch-Slack (C_4), and the crassulacean acid metabolism (CAM), via either the C_3 or C_4 path. One of the major research directions using isotopic data has been to understand the role of maize (a C_4 plant) in the diet.

Isotopic analysis also has been used to ascertain the ratios of terrestrial to marine foods, types of animals eaten, whether animals were raised locally or imported, whether animals were foddered, the role of dairy resources, the identification of faunal remains, general categories of foods, issues of group mobility, general residence location, migration and mobility, social and economic status, population variation, diets based on age (e.g., breastfeeding and weaning), the transition to agriculture, intensification among hunter-gatherers, the use of fertilizer on ancient fields, crop management, and crop yields. Using isotopic data on human bone from two separate Mesolithic cemeteries in coastal France, for example, researchers detected differences in the consumption of marine foods between the two populations. It was determined that young women had consumed fewer marine foods and so it was hypothesized that these women had come to the coast later in life, possibly reflecting an exogamous, patrilocal marriage pattern. Another possible explanation may be differential access to certain foods based on sex or status.

Trace elements in the body originate from food or from environmental exposure. Only a few trace elements are potentially useful, and there is considerable concern that trace elements may not be very useful as a consequence of post-depositional changes in concentrations. Some trace elements are essential while others are toxic.

The majority of archaeological work on trace element analysis has been performed on bone. Hair and nails contain short-term records, while tooth enamel, which develops during childhood, may contain a record that reflects childhood diet. As it does not re-model during adulthood, tooth enamel is the material of choice. Strontium, barium, zinc, and lead are the primary trace elements examined, with strontium being the most useful.

Interest in trace elements centers on issues of diet, health, and behavioral correlates and may be employed to investigate a variety of ecological, dietary, and social questions. These include relative contribution of plant and animal foods (trophic levels) in the diet, the similarity of diet by sex, social status, the contributions of marine resources, migration and mobility, identification of group affinity, whether a woman might have been pregnant or lactating, weaning patterns, and perhaps seasonality. Trace element analysis also has been employed to deduce dietary deficiencies since levels of various elements that are too high or too low may have serious health consequences. In addition, some aspects of pollution (e.g., lead concentrations) can be measured. Measurement methods include electroanalysis, mass spectrometry (MS), neutron activation analysis (NAA), spectrographic analyses (emission, absorption, plasma analysis), atomic absorption, various X-ray methods, and inductively coupled plasma–mass spectrometric analysis (ICP–MS).

Problems in using trace elements in dietary analyses include the role of post-depositional changes and sampling procedures. Other issues include incomplete data on trace element contents for certain resources, the shifting percentages of consumed resources, the consumption of some resources high in trace elements (e.g., nuts and berries) that overwhelm the signature of other resources, and the usually small archaeological sample size.

Soil chemistry analysis may also provide clues to past diet. As people and animals alter site soils, concentrations of some chemicals, including calcium, magnesium, nitrogen, phosphates, and potassium, can occur, along with an alteration of soil pH. Soil chemistry can be used to detect anthropogenic activities, such as midden concentrations, activity areas, latrine areas (e.g., an increase in nitrogen), cemeteries, and even plow soils or agricultural fields.

See also ARCHAEOBOTANY; BIOARCHAEOLOGIAL ANALYSIS; BIOMOLECULAR ANALYSIS; DENTAL ANALYSIS; DNA ANALYSIS; FLOTATION; INSECTS; MACROREMAINS; MUMMIES; PALEODEMOGRAPHY; PALEODIETARY ANALYSIS; PALEOFECAL ANALYSIS; PALEOPATHOLOGY; PALYNOLOGY; PHYTOLITH ANALYSIS; SOIL MICROTECHNIQUES; STABLE ISOTOPE ANALYSIS; TRACE ELEMENT ANALYSIS IN HUMAN DIET; ZOOARCHAEOLOGY

Further Reading

Gilbert, Robert I., Jr., and James H. Mielke, eds. 1985. *The Analysis of Prehistoric Diets*. Orlando: Academic Press.

Schulting, Rick J., and Michael P. Richards. 2001. Dating Women and Becoming Farmers: New Paleodietary and AMS Dating Evidence from the Breton Mesolithic Cemeteries of Téviec and Hoëdic. *Journal of Anthropological Archaeology* 20(3):314–44.

Sutton, Mark Q. 1995. Archaeological Aspects of Insect Use. *Journal of Archaeological Method and Theory* 2(3):253–98.

Sutton, Mark Q., Kristin D. Sobolik, and Jill K. Gardner. 2010. *Paleonutrition*. Tucson: University of Arizona Press.

Wing, Elizabeth S., and Antoinette B. Brown. 1979. *Paleonutrition: Method and Theory in Prehistoric Foodways*. New York: Academic Press.

■ MARK Q. SUTTON

PALEOPATHOLOGY

Paleopathology is a subdiscipline of human bioarchaeology, the study of human remains from archaeological sites, interpreted with reference to archaeological and historical context. Paleopathologists examine evidence for disease in human remains, whether they are cremated remains, skeletons, preserved bodies, or even the gut contents of mummies, and coprolites, both of which may preserve parasites and food residues. Understanding when, why, and where diseases originated, evolved, and flourished allows us to understand better those health problems people experience today in different parts of the world. Archaeological human remains provide deep-time evidence for disease over hundreds and even thousands of years.

Paleopathology is multi- and interdisciplinary in scope and combines different forms of data to reconstruct the history of our ancestors' disease experience. This includes material culture, environmental data, and evidence of structures in which people lived or worked, alongside relevant documentary or even artistic representations of how people lived their lives. Analysis focuses chiefly on macroscopic or visual examination of human remains, but also involves radiographic, histological, and biomolecular methods. Characteristic pathological changes (bone formation and destruction) on bones and teeth are recorded, their skeletal distribution noted, and various possible diagnoses suggested, based mainly on data from clinical medicine.

Paleopathology can provide direct and indirect data about what subsistence economy people practiced, what diet they ate, and whether they were malnourished or too well fed. If there is no evidence of dietary deficiency or excess, one can only suggest that people had a well-balanced diet. Human remains provide only a limited view of health problems related to what people ate (or did not) in the past for a number of reasons. Many remains are not examined using all methods available, limiting the data for study. Not all skeletons are well preserved, so vital bones that would help to diagnose specific disease may be missing (e.g., the skull for vitamin C deficiency). It is often the case that only skeletons are preserved for study, but only a small percentage of diseases affect the bones or teeth. Acute diseases also kill quickly, leaving no imprint on the skeleton, so paleopathologists only see evidence of chronic disease.

Stable isotope studies of carbon and nitrogen from samples of preserved bones and teeth have revolutionized the archaeological study of past diets. Isotopes are elements with the same number of protons but different numbers of neutrons. Stable isotopes are those that do not undergo radioactive decay. The isotopic ratios of carbon ($^{12}C/^{13}C$) and nitrogen ($^{14}N/^{15}N$) recovered from bones and teeth will reflect the food and water consumed. Nitrogen isotope ratios can provide information concerning marine versus terrestrial exploitation of food sources, the trophic level (the position that the organism, in this case, a human, occupies in the food chain) of food sources (e.g., meat versus vegetable diet), and infant-feeding practices. Carbon isotopes can provide complementary information concerning the types of plants consumed (temperate or tropical), differentiating between maize and wheat, for example. When examined in conjunction with the archaeological and paleopathological evidence, isotopes provide an invaluable source of data for examining past nutrition.

Paleopathological study inevitably includes the study of age at death and biological sex (demography) because it is understood that males and females in different age groups are differentially predisposed to contracting certain diseases. Equally important are ancestral background and social status because these two variables can also affect what diseases people suffered, and what they ate. Age, sex, ancestry, and social status all potentially impact diet and ultimately health.

Past subsistence patterns and dietary health also were affected by key epidemiological transitions. The *first* transition occurred when people began to domesticate animals and plants and to practice agriculture, moving away from hunting and foraging. A *second* transition began when people started to live in industrialized communities, with an eventual decline in mortality caused by infections, along with improved living conditions and the discovery of antibiotics, and an increase in diseases associated with old age (e.g., cancer and heart disease). We are currently living in the *third* transition as "old" infectious diseases reemerge and new ones appear, with increasing resistance to antibiotics. Different foods and their production characterize these transitions. Agriculture led to a poorer, less varied diet that caused nutrient deficiencies, and settled communities that led to accumulations of refuse, higher population numbers, poor hygiene, a reliance on crops that might fail, and more person-to-person contact as surpluses were traded. With industrialized communities, food production intensified, industries became mechanized, and large urban centers emerged.

As a result of these transitions, diet changed and health problems developed. Dietary deficiencies may be seen in the skeleton as problems with growth and final attained stature (height), cribra orbitalia, linear enamel hypoplasia, and vitamin C and D deficiencies, while dental caries, gout, and diffuse idiopathic skeletal hyperostosis (DISH) may be associated with dietary excess. Indirectly, entheseal changes (bone formation or destruction at sites of tendon and ligament attachments) and biomechanical changes to bones, specific fractures, and degenerative joint disease may be related to subsistence practices (work).

Diet and health are closely interrelated. Malnutrition will exacerbate the likelihood of contracting infectious disease, which in turn leads to greater risk of malnourishment. We may infer a variety of both nonspecific and specific dietary deficiencies from the presence of pathological lesions on the human skeleton. The prevalence and distribution of these lesions when interpreted in conjunction with the archaeological evidence may shed light on the effects of differing subsistence regimes on the human body.

Dietary Deficiencies and Diseases Identified through Paleopathological Analysis

Compromised Growth and Stature

Adult height (stature) is widely recognized as an important indicator of socioeconomic well-being in past and present societies. Attained stature reflects the interaction between genetics, health, and the living environment. A compromised diet or poor health will inhibit the growth of individuals who ultimately may not reach their full stature potential.

It is not possible to determine stature during childhood because the long-bone shafts (diaphyses) and bone ends (epiphyses) are separated by the growth plate (cartilage), the thickness of which varies throughout development. Skeletal growth profiles can be produced from long-bone length measurements, however, using dental age as a proxy for known age. Children who are properly nourished tend to be larger than children of low socioeconomic status with poor nutrition. If disparities in health and nutrition continue throughout childhood, final adult stature is likely to be compromised. If not, a period of catch-up growth could obliterate previous growth differentials. Studies of archaeological populations have shown that appositional growth (i.e., the thickness of the bone cortex) is more sensitive to nutritional and health insults than longitudinal growth.

Harris lines indicate arrested growth that can be observed on radiographs as lines of increased opacity and have frequently been interpreted as representing periods of growth arrest resulting from poor nutrition. This interpretation is now considered unreliable, however, as such lines can occur as a consequence of normal healthy growth processes that often include periods of stasis followed by rapid growth.

Cribra Orbitalia

Cribra orbitalia is one of the most commonly reported conditions in the paleopathological literature and describes small holes or perforations in the orbits of the skull. These lesions form in response to hyperplasia (marrow expansion) of the middle spongy layer of the skull and the thinning of the outer bone cortex. This occurs in response to anemia, which is a red blood cell disorder. The body attempts to counteract anemia through expansion of the red-blood-cell-producing marrow. A similar form of porosity, known as porotic hyperostosis, can manifest itself on the cranial vault. Archaeologically, it has been observed that cranial lesions may be present without orbital lesions and vice versa; the relationship between these different manifestations is not clear.

While associated with anemia, the precise cause (etiology) of cribra orbitalia is debated. Most archaeological interpretations have been based on the premise that it occurs as a consequence of acquired iron-deficiency anemia (the most common anemia today) because of factors such as poor diet, blood loss, parasitism, or exposure to environments with a high pathogen load. Most interpretations invoke a synergistic combination of these factors. More recently, the dietary deficiencies of vitamin B_9 (folic acid), vitamin B_{12}, and megaloblastic anemia have been implicated as a likely cause.

Orbital and vault lesions most often develop in children aged between six months to two years, hence their presence is often interpreted as the consequence of a nutritionally inadequate weaning diet. For example, the high prevalence of this condition in children's skeletons from Italian sites dating to the first and second centuries AD was thought to result from poor sanitation and a cereal-based weaning diet. A correlation with other anemia-inducing conditions such as malaria, however, is another possible complication in these contexts, and care must be taken when inferring a purely dietary cause. While such lesions are observed in adults, the changing loci of red-blood-cell-producing bone marrow with age suggests that they represent healed childhood episodes of anemia.

Other conditions that produce similar lesions to cribra orbitalia or porotic hyperostosis are vitamin D or C deficiencies and infectious processes, and care must be taken to distinguish these, particularly in the absence of marrow hyperplasia. While the multiple etiologies of cribra orbitalia may cause interpretational difficulties, it is generally accepted as a robust (though nonspecific) index of health stress that, in some instances at least, has a nutritional cause.

Linear Enamel Hypoplasia

Linear enamel hypoplasias (LEH) are bands of decreased enamel thickness on the external surface of the tooth crown, most commonly observed on the anterior dentition. These bands result from a temporary disruption in enamel formation. No specific etiology has been implicated in LEH, but when multiple defects are found on several teeth within an individual, severe childhood illnesses or malnutrition are the most likely causes.

Examination of enamel hypoplasia has an advantage over other stress indicators in that the teeth once formed do not remodel during adulthood as bone does, and so a permanent chronological record (barring extensive dental wear) of episodes of stress is retained. By measuring the location of the defect on the crown surface in relation to the cemento-enamel junction and taking into account mean crown height for the tooth type within the population, the age at which the defect formed can be estimated. It has been shown, however, that the relationship between LEH location and chronological age is not as straightforward as previously assumed; teeth do not grow in a simple linear manner, and enamel formation continues after initial mineralization. Studies of LEH in relation to diet have been inconclusive, and it seems that the range of possible causes of these defects renders the interpretation of these lesions problematic.

Vitamin D Deficiency

Vitamin D plays an important role in calcium metabolism and is essential for the adequate mineralization of the organic bone matrix (osteoid). Vitamin D synthesis is partly dependent on dietary intake (e.g., oily fish, eggs, liver) but is mostly produced in the skin on contact with sunlight. Vitamin D deficiency in children results in a condition known as rickets, which is most classically expressed through bowed limbs because of their soft, poorly mineralized condition. Other observable skeletal changes include the flaring of the ends of the bones (metaphyses), nodules on the ribs, and porosity on the cranial vault. Rickets is most commonly observed in children between the ages of six months to two years today and is seen with increasing frequency in paleopathology because diagnostic signs have been better defined in the literature over the last 20 years. It is observed most frequently in populations experiencing the second epidemiological transition. The presence of the condition in infants only a few months in age also has been noted archaeologically, for example, at sites in Roman Britain, and this would suggest that the mothers also were deficient. If breastfeeding mothers are deficient in vitamin D, then their milk will not be plentiful. The substitution of animal milk for breast milk during the first six months of life may also increase an infant's risk of rickets as the former is lower in vitamin D. This practice also would expose the infant to a greater risk of pathogens and parasites, particularly in unsanitary conditions, and the infant would be deprived of the passive immunity inherent in breast milk. As humans metabolize the majority of the vitamin D they need from contact with sunlight, childcare practices such as swaddling and keeping children indoors also would significantly increase susceptibility to this condition.

Vitamin D deficiency in adults is known as osteomalacia and also results in bones that are insufficiently mineralized. Bioarchaeologists must take care to ensure that healed childhood episodes of the condition, known as residual rickets, in which bowed limbs are retained into adulthood, are not confused with adult-onset deficiencies. The characteristic skeletal lesions of osteomalacia more frequently affect the axial skeleton, including "folding" deformities in the vertebrae and pelvis. In women the deformation of the pelvis may pose the additional danger of obstetrical problems. The nondietary component to vitamin D deficiency means that care must be taken when interpreting its presence in the skeletal record because it more likely represents lack of exposure to sunlight. Examples of osteomalacia have been noted from urban industrial sites in England (e.g., St. Martin's-in-the-Bull Ring, Birmingham) and in these contexts is likely related to air pollution as well as indoor work in poorly lit factories.

Vitamin C Deficiency

Vitamin C (ascorbic acid) deficiency results in the condition known as scurvy. Vitamin C is important in the formation of the connective tissues, including collagen. A deficiency causes (among other problems) weak blood vessels that are liable to hemorrhage easily, even during normal movement. Vitamin C is also vital for bone formation as it is necessary for the formation of the organic bone matrix (osteoid). Scurvy is a condition that manifests most obviously in soft tissues, resulting in swollen and bleeding gums, red blotches on the skin, and bleeding into the joints. The skeletal manifestations are more readily diagnosed in children than adults, in part because of the greater demand for bone growth during this period. Infantile scurvy is identified by the presence of new bone formation and porosity along the long bone shafts of the upper and lower limbs and symmetrical new bone formation on the cranium and in the orbits. These changes are linked to hemorrhages that occur adjacent to the bone and subsequent inflammation. Scurvy has been identified at a variety of sites, including the Roman site of Poundbury in Dorset, England, where its presence has been interpreted as a result of the early cessation of breastfeeding. Infants who are breastfed should not exhibit signs of scurvy, as breast milk is a good source of vitamin C.

Once growth has ceased, the skeletal changes indicative of scurvy may be much more subtle and less readily identifiable; as a consequence, scurvy has only rarely been documented in adults. The recent analysis of skeletons from a mid-19th-century workhouse in Kilkenny, Ireland, believed to have been victims of the Great Famine, revealed signs of scurvy in both the children and adults. The adults exhibited porosity on the facial bones, new bone formation bilaterally on the lower limb bones, and periodontal disease. These changes, though nonspecific, are similar to skeletal changes interpreted by researchers as scurvy in skeletons of South African miners and Arctic whalers. Scurvy is not common in modern Western populations, though recent concerns have been expressed regarding its increasing prevalence among children and adults who are reluctant to eat fresh fruit or vegetables. In the absence of appropriate nutrition, vitamin supplements may readily circumvent the risk of this condition in the present.

Dental Caries

Dental caries (*caries* is Latin for "rottenness") are destructive lesions of the teeth (cavities) that today are filled by dentists. They result from the action of bacteria in dental plaque on carbohydrates in the diet. The bacteria ferment the carbohydrates (sugars), leading to acid production and the demineralization of the tooth structure. Caries is therefore related to diet, but also to low levels of fluoride in drinking water and poor oral hygiene. It could be argued that caries in past populations is more likely to have developed in people of high status because of their access to sugary foods such as dates and figs. Linear enamel hypoplasia can predispose teeth to caries too. Today caries is still common although, certainly in the Western world, oral hygiene is better and many countries have added fluoride to water to prevent caries. Caries can be recognized on any part of the tooth but most commonly affects the enamel or crown. In paleopathological studies, the different types of teeth affected and the position of the lesion on the teeth are important to record. For example, if not worn down, the molar teeth have surface fissures that can attract food debris that may stagnate and lead to caries, and the same trapping of food debris can occur between the teeth. Teeth survive burial better and for longer periods than bones, and caries is commonly recorded by paleopathologists. It has been seen to increase through time, as people have eaten more carbohydrates, especially at the transition to agriculture and as more people had access to sugars in their diet. In Britain, for example, caries increased from about the 12th century AD when sugar was first imported, again increasing with industrialization as individuals were exposed to higher levels of sugar and as refined flours became the norm. It is important to note, however, that this pattern is not universally expressed; in Thailand, for example, the transition to rice agriculture did not result in increased caries frequency because of this crop's low cariogenicity.

Gout

Gout is a joint disease, or inflammatory arthritis, that is related to diet. It is caused by a high level of uric acid in the blood, as a result of the production of excess uric acid or a decline in excretion by the kidneys. This causes an accumulation of uric acid crystals in the joint cavities that causes destruction of bone. The big toe joints tend to be most affected, and the condition is very painful. These crystals also accumulate in the soft tissues associated with the joint (tendons and ligaments). It is a condition that is associated with excessive and frequent alcohol consumption, especially beer and spirits, which are all high in purines (chemical compounds in foods that are broken down by the body into uric acid), and immoderate levels of protein and fat in the diet; there is also evidence of a correlation between specific foods such as offal, some fish and shellfish, and spinach—all high in purines—with heart disease, high blood pressure, obesity, and diabetes. Today gout appears to be much more of a problem for people than in the past, is increasing particularly in Western countries, and affects men ten times more than women. It is recognized in the skeleton by characteristic destructive lesions in relevant joints, especially the big toe, and has been identified in mummies; urate crystals have also been identified. Gout seems to have been associated first with Roman populations, although Hippocrates (fifth century BC) writes about it in Greece. Paleopathologists have attributed the prevalence of gout in the Roman period to the consumption of alcohol in lead vessels or from the use of lead containers in the alcohol distillation process. Both added lead to the alcoholic product, resulting in kidney failure and an increase in uric acid.

DISH

Defined as diffuse idiopathic skeletal hyperostosis (Forestier's disease), this may also be a health condition linked to a particular type of diet. DISH is classed as a degenerative disease. It affects the spine and some of the bones in the skeleton in areas where tendons and ligaments attach. The spine in particular is affected with the formation of new bone with a "candlewax appearance" that fuses the vertebrae. People affected are "bone formers" because much new bone is formed on the skeleton. It affects males more than females and is more commonly found among older age groups, probably because it takes time to develop the bone changes. Northern Europeans seem to be more commonly affected, and Type II diabetes and obesity are associated with it today. A genetic predisposition also has been suggested. In the past a Neanderthal skeleton has been recorded with DISH, but this condition appears to be more prevalent in medieval monastic and high-status communities. It could be that individuals in these communities were affected because they were more likely to eat a rich, high-protein diet and become obese. Increasingly, however, nonmonastic archaeological populations are reported as affected.

Other Factors Relating to Diet Affecting Skeletal Remains

Subsistence strategies can impact the demography of a population and are an important consideration when interpreting sex- and age-specific mortality at a site. For example, research shows that the pattern of age-specific fertility among hunter-gatherer populations is later in females than among sedentary agricultural populations that exhibit overall higher female fertility. Agricultural populations are also more likely to undergo population growth than are hunter-gatherer populations, though this depends on available resources and there are exceptions to this rule. Demographic changes have been observed during other economic transitions. For example, during the period of industrialization, the mean age of weaning dropped from eighteen months to approximately seven months because mothers from lower-class families had to work. This had an impact on birth-spacing (because of the contraceptive effect of breastfeeding) and infant mortality.

Diet also may be reflected indirectly in changes to the skeletons of people who performed specific physical activities associated with food production and processing. Although not without controversy in their interpretation, a number of bone changes have been identified, including entheseal and biomechanical changes, specific fractures, and degenerative joint disease, with the latter two classed as pathological (disease). Entheseal changes refer to bone formation or destruction on bones into which ligaments and tendons insert, reflecting the movement of the limbs. While these changes can be activity related, they can also be caused by disease (e.g., DISH) and increasing age (i.e., older people get them more). Biomechanical changes are seen as differences in shape and cross section in bones that are subject to standard radiography and computed tomography (computer-processed X-rays to produce slices of specific areas of the body, in this case usually long bones). It has been noted that biomechanical changes do occur in people's limb bones with the economic transition from hunting and gathering to agriculture, but the shape and cross sections of bones also can vary between populations negotiating different terrains.

Fractures are classified as a break in the bone as a result of acute injury, an underlying disease weakening the bone, or repeated stress. These injuries may be related to subsistence practice (e.g., working rough ground), but two specific fractures of the spine may be related to activity. A condition in the back of the fifth lumbar vertebra, known as spondylolysis, is likely caused by an inherited weakness; the vertebra can then fracture because of bending and lifting. A spinous-process fracture of the seventh cervical or first thoracic vertebra also has been linked to physical activity such as shoveling heavy soils (or similar activities). In some studies, fractures of the bones of the skeleton increase overall with the transition to agriculture, and in some they do not. Degenerative joint disease is identified as bone formation (osteophytes) and destruction (porosity and eburnation) in joints, with osteoarthritis affecting only the synovial joints (e.g., major joints of the skeleton such as the hip and knee) and the minor joints of the spine (e.g., the apophyseal joints at the back of the spinal column). While some studies of the physical impact of the agricultural transition have found an increase in osteoarthritis in the past, other studies have noted a decline. Many factors cause degenerative joint disease, including increasing age, obesity, an inherited inclination, various diseases that predispose to joint degeneration, and underlying badly healed trauma. It is debatable, then, whether it is possible to assign joint disease to occupation. Ideally, when using skeletal data to attribute workload to individuals and populations, it is preferable to use a suite of markers, although each one can be caused by many factors other than activity.

Agriculture (The First Epidemiological Transition)

The change from hunter-gatherer subsistence to agriculture signaled a major change in people's way of life. The transition to agriculture occurred independently in Africa, Asia, the western Pacific, and the Americas between 10,000 and 5,000 years ago. Previously, hunting, fishing, and gathering wild foods provided small groups of mobile people a varied seasonal diet. When resources were exhausted, groups could move on because they did not have permanent settlements. Thus the hazards to health associated with permanent settlements (refuse, vermin, zoonoses, high population density, air and water pollution) were avoided. Humans also were fitter and leaner because they were more active, and they had a varied diet with low amounts of fat. While population densities were lower in a hunting and gathering environment, there were some advantages to settling down to an agricultural way of life, including having an economy that could support more people and sustain people who were ill and needed care, and trade with others to generate a wider variety of foodstuffs.

It seems these communities developed poorer health, nevertheless, although the picture is inconsistent and thus complex. Archaeologists continue to debate whether a population increase enabled farming or farming led to an increase in population. Clearly, though, fertility increased, contributing to population increase. It should be noted, however, that populations did not, and do not, "change" their subsistence patterns overnight, and often they may practice farming, pastoralism, and hunting and gathering, according to preference, season, and availability of resources. Transitions can be long-term processes. For example, the adoption of maize agriculture in North America varied regionally in extent and by temporal period.

While studies around the world have shown a decline in health with the development of agriculture, health further declines when agriculture is intensified. Most "poor health" indicators increased in skeletons from sites in South Asia at the agricultural transition, and this tended to also correlate with reduced longevity. The pattern can vary considerably around the world, however. In Southeast Asia (e.g., Thailand), health did not decline with the introduction of agriculture, its intensification, or increasing sedentism over a period of several thousand years. One possible explanation is that rice, the staple crop, is highly nutritious (unlike other cereals such as wheat), thus preventing poor health.

This overall decline in health has been linked to the increasing complexity of society, and especially to the foods people were consuming and the work they were carrying out. Diet became less varied, and harvests could fail. Increasingly, it has been recognized that the abandonment of a hunter-gatherer diet led to a "mismatch" between how humans evolved and their diet and health. Studies of health in hunter-gatherer and agricultural populations have focused on a number of indicators, and especially those related specifically to diet (e.g., dental caries, wear on the teeth, and scurvy, but also changes to the shape of the skull and tooth size), living conditions (e.g., infections, work-related bone changes such as trauma and joint degeneration), and skeletal data relevant to both diet and living conditions (e.g., demographic profiles, problems with growth and attained stature, LEH, and cribra orbitalia).

Generally, dental disease, especially caries, tends to increase with the transition to agriculture; this has been interpreted as the result of the carbohydrate content of cereals. For example, studies of sites in Mesolithic and Neolithic western Europe have found an increase in caries. It must be noted, however, that the causative mechanisms are complex and that dental attrition could be a predisposing factor. In prehistoric Africa (Lower Nubia), caries increased from 1 percent (Mesolithic hunter-gatherers) to 18 percent (intensive agriculture) of archaeological populations. Some studies have shown no change in frequency at the agricultural transition, however. For example, in Southeast Asia where rice was/is the mainstay crop, other cereals were deemed more likely to cause an increase in caries, and rice has low cariogenicity. Dental wear also changes in character, with hunter-gatherers having flat wear compared to angled wear in agriculturists, but attrition overall declines with the softer agricultural diet. The softer diet also leads to more dental plaque, gum inflammation, and underlying bone changes (periodontal disease).

The consumption of a softer diet also led to changes in the shape of skulls and to shorter jaws with smaller tooth sizes. In general, people who hunted and gathered had long and narrow skulls compared to farmers, who had shorter and wider skulls. In a study in central Europe from the early Upper Paleolithic to the Late Neolithic, tooth size of individuals also declined. In prehistoric Africa, a robust skull was noted in hunter-gatherer Mesolithic groups (12000–6400 BC) that changed in a later agricultural phase to a less robust skull, accompanied by shorter jaws and smaller teeth because of reduced dental wear (softer, more cariogenic diet). Changes in diet will ultimately affect growth, and some studies have found a decline in stature associated with agriculture (e.g., on the central Peruvian coast) and some an increase (e.g., in western Europe and in Tennessee, USA), while enamel hypoplasia is also seen to increase overall at the transition to agriculture. For example, in the Levant, Natufian hunter-gatherers had lower rates of enamel hypoplasia compared to Neolithic agricultural populations. In southern Scandinavia, however, there was a high frequency of hypoplasia in Late Mesolithic and Early Neolithic populations, with a decline in the Middle and Late Neolithic periods.

Cribra orbitalia also rises in agricultural populations. Long associated with iron-deficiency anemia (a result of low iron levels in cereal crops along with phytates that prevent iron absorption), its interpretation is still subject to debate. It is likely that this condition is related to increased parasite load and infectious disease as a result of living in permanent settlements with the transition to agriculture. It also has been associated with a marine diet and fish parasites, however, as suggested by the high frequency of cribra orbitalia in Ecuadorian skeletal remains, particularly at coastal sites where marine exploitation occurred. It is also interesting to note the association of cribra orbitalia with infections in skeletal remains, as seen in skeletons from the late medieval leprosy hospital cemetery of Naestved, Denmark. Tuberculosis, a bacterial disease that is related to leprosy through cross immunity, increases through time in general, in both the New and Old Worlds, but is rarely, like leprosy, seen in hunter-gatherer groups and becomes an increasing problem with settled groups. A combination of factors for its occurrence in sedentary populations was possibly at play—for example, higher population densities (allowing bacteria-laden droplets to spread by coughing and sneezing), poorer diets that compromised people's immune systems, interaction with domesticated animals (droplet spread), and ingestion of infected animal meat and milk. Evidence of respiratory infections occurs with greater frequency in urban, agriculturally based populations in comparative studies of the maxillary sinuses of skeletons from agricultural, hunter-gatherer, and urban populations. Overall, data from sites in North America, England, and Sudan suggest that hunter-gatherers lived with better air quality. Work and its intensity also have been the subject of comparative study of hunter-gatherer and farmer health. It has been observed in many studies that hunter-gatherers have much more robust bones and obvious muscle markings than farmers, suggesting greater physical activity, although, as noted, the potential causes of such bone changes are complex. Osteoarthritis and muscle markings together tended to decline with settled communities and agricultural practice (less strenuous activity), for example, in Alabama, Florida, and Georgia (USA). In Florida and Georgia, however, the arrival of 16th-century European groups reversed the trend, showing that populations were exploited for their labor.

As can be seen from this brief overview, the work of paleopathologists to relate diet to health in the past, and to explore questions about health at the transition from hunting and foraging to farming in human skeletal remains, is highly complex. Diet is just one factor that contributes to health and well-being, with many other variables at play to create the picture observed in the skeletons of our ancestors. In some parts of the world this transition resulted in a decline in health overall, but some indicators suggest that farming provided some advantages to people's lives.

Industrial Revolution (Second Epidemiological Transition)

Industrialization in Britain was a major economic transition during the 18th and 19th centuries. The rapid development of large urban centers and a shift toward factory-based modes of production resulted in significant socioeconomic changes that had repercussions for most of the population. The seismic shift from a rural, domestic workforce to one that was primarily urban and factory/mining-oriented resulted in increased population density, inadequate housing and sanitation, air pollution, poor work conditions, and long working hours. Women and children were also employed, and this led to subsequent changes to family structures. All of these factors ultimately had consequences for nutrition and overall well-being. The impact of these changes has been observed in the skeletal health of those living at the time.

With industrialization, people who relocated to urban centers were removed from direct involvement in food production and instead became consumers. As a consequence, for those on the lower rungs of the social ladder, diet became less varied and was deficient in protein and fresh vegetables (with the possible exception of potatoes). Instead, there was a high dependency on food low in nutrition, such as white bread, tea, and sugar. Adulteration of food products such as flour with products such as alum during this period was rife and also had detrimental consequences for health. A reliance on sugar, which became less expensive, is illustrated in the increase in caries prevalence during this period, in particular the presence of occlusal caries in children. Diet at this time also was softer and more processed, and consequently wear patterns are no longer useful as an indicator of age at death in skeletons from the postmedieval period in Britain. Related to this change in diet, malocclusion (misalignment of the teeth of the upper and lower jaws) and dental crowding become more common.

Studies in economic history have indicated that a rural/urban divide in health was present during this time; those living in rural areas generally were taller and of better health. Regional variations in diet and living environment, together with greater population mobility, mean that this pattern is not always so apparent in the osteological record, however. For example, at the rural site of Fewston in Yorkshire, England, infectious and respiratory diseases, dental caries, rickets, and scurvy were all present and in comparable numbers to those at some contemporary urban sites. This pattern could indicate the presence of migrant children brought into the area to work in the nearby mill, and hence some of the pathological conditions might relate to their living environment prior to being at Fewston. Even so, the fact remains that these children did not survive to adulthood in this rural locale, and so there are likely to have been detrimental health factors here as well as in nearby towns. Documentary sources indicate that infectious diseases were rife in rural areas as well as in densely populated towns, with cholera and typhus decimating families. Differences in growth and stature between urban and rural centers do not appear to relate simply to the process of urbanization then, as it has been shown that medieval urban health was not as poor as that of the later period. Instead, it seems that the specific factors associated with industrialization had a more profoundly detrimental effect.

The vast majority of skeletal evidence for this period relates to urban areas, and a number of contemporary reports discuss the abysmal living and working conditions of the poorer urban workers, with a high prevalence of infectious diseases such as tuberculosis, as well as deficiency diseases such as scurvy and rickets. At the site of St. Martin's-in-the-Bull Ring, Birmingham, a number of children with infantile scurvy were noted, as well as high levels with rickets caused by poor diet, dark living and working conditions, and air pollution. The association between rickets and urban areas during this period is well documented from contemporary accounts. High levels of cribra orbitalia also were recorded in people buried at St. Martin's as well as at other urban postmedieval sites in England such as Newcastle Royal Infirmary. Historical evidence from this period indicates that women and children were even less likely to have access to meat, milk, and butter than males, who were the primary breadwinners. Pregnant females who were nutrient deficient would give birth to nutrient-deprived infants, and we might see skeletal indicators of deficiencies in infants under six months of age, as observed in infant remains from the site of Coach Lane, near Newcastle. The fact that poorer mothers had to return to work shortly after giving birth also led to improper care and nutrition for the developing infant.

Interestingly, it is not just the skeletons of the poor that show evidence of nutritional deficiencies. The skeletons of middle-class and higher-status individuals from this period have been excavated from sites such as Christ Church Spitalfields and St Marylebone, both in London. Among these children, rickets, cribra orbitalia, and scurvy were found to be similarly high. Again, this has been interpreted in terms of "fashionable" but not very healthy childcare practices, an inadequate weaning diet, and the high numbers of pregnancies expected for higher-status women. These dietary deficiencies are also reflected in "lags" in growth profiles for both the Marylebone and Spitalfields children. In the poorer London parish of Broadgate, dental enamel defects and more severe growth stunting in infants again point to the possible influence of poor maternal nutrition on the health of offspring in these industrialized environments. The skeletal data for this period demonstrate the extent and impact of dietary deficiency diseases that, when examined in conjunction with the historical data, can provide a rich source of evidence.

Conclusion

Paleopathology can help to explore the diets of our ancestors by revealing evidence of dietary deficiency and excess diseases and, indirectly, how diet can affect mortality and degeneration of the skeleton through workload. It has also shown how the data can be limited and complex to interpret. As discussed, a balanced diet promotes a healthy immune system, while an unhealthy diet places populations at risk from disease. Changing diets associated with the first and second epidemiological transitions have had demonstrable effects on populations. Paleopathology has shown both the benefits and risks of such behavior, and has posed complex questions for future research.

See also AGRICULTURE, ORIGINS OF; BIOARCHAEOLOGICAL ANALYSIS; BIOMOLECULAR ANALYSIS; FAMINE; FORAGING; GUT ANALYSIS; HUNTER-GATHERER SUBSISTENCE; INDUSTRIALIZATION OF FOOD AND FOOD PRODUCTION; MUMMIES; PALEODEMOGRAPHY; PALEODIETARY ANALYSIS; PALEOFECAL ANALYSIS; PALEONUTRITION; STABLE ISOTOPE ANALYSIS; SUBSISTENCE MODELS

Further Reading

Brickley, Megan, and Rachel Ives. 2008. *The Bioarchaeology of Metabolic Bone Disease*. Oxford: Elsevier/ Academic Press.

Chamberlain, Andrew T. 2006. *Demography in Archaeology*. Cambridge: Cambridge University Press.

Cohen, Mark Nathan. 1989. *Health and the Rise of Civilization*. New Haven, CT: Yale University Press.

Cohen, Mark Nathan, and George J. Armelagos, eds. 1984. *Paleopathology at the Origins of Agriculture*. Orlando, FL: Academic Press.

Cohen, Mark Nathan, and Gillian M. M. Crane-Kramer, eds. 2007. *Ancient Health: Skeletal Indicators of Agricultural and Economic Intensification*. Gainesville: University Press of Florida.

Gowland, Rebecca, and Peter Garnsey. 2010. Skeletal Evidence for Health, Nutritional Status and Malaria in Rome and the Empire. In *Roman Diasporas: Archaeological Approaches to Mobility and Diversity
in the Roman Empire*, edited by Hella Eckardt. *Journal of Roman Archaeology* 78:S131–S156.

Harper, Kristen, and George Armelagos. 2010. The Changing Disease-Scape in the Third Epidemiological Transition. *International Journal of Environmental Research and Public Health* 7(2):675–97.

Hillson, Simon. 1996. *Dental Anthropology*. Cambridge: Cambridge University Press.

Jurmain, Robert. 1999. *Stories from the Skeleton: Behavioral Reconstruction in Human Osteology*. Williston,
VT: Gordon and Breach.

Katzenberg, M. Anne, and Shelley R. Saunders, eds. 2008. *Biological Anthropology of the Human Skeleton*.
2nd edition. Hoboken, NJ: John Wiley & Sons.

Larsen, Clark S. 2008. *Our Origins: Discovering Physical Anthropology*. London: W. W. Norton.

Lewis, Mary E. 2002. Impact of Industrialization: Comparative Study of Child Health in Four Sites
from Medieval and Postmedieval England (A.D. 850–1859). *American Journal of Physical Anthropology*
119(3):211–23.

———. 2007. *The Bioarchaeology of Children: Perspectives from Biological and Forensic Anthropology*. Cambridge: Cambridge University Press.

Miles, Adrian, Don Walker, Natasha Powers, and Robin Wroe-Brown. 2008. *St Marylebone Church and
Burial Ground in the 18th to 19th Centuries*. MOLAS Monograph 46. London: Museum of London
Archaeology Service.

Ortner, Donald J. 2003. *Identification of Pathological Conditions in Human Skeletal Remains*. 2nd edition.
New York: Academic Press.

Pinhasi, Ron, P. Shaw, B. White, and A. R. Ogden. 2006. Morbidity, Rickets and Long-Bone Growth
in Post-Medieval Britain—A Cross-Population Analysis. *Annals of Human Biology* 33(3):372–89.

Pinhasi, Ron, and Jay T. Stock, eds. 2011. *Human Bioarchaeology of the Transition to Agriculture*. Chichester,
UK: Wiley-Blackwell.

Roberts, Charlotte A. 2009. *Human Remains in Archaeology: A Handbook*. York: Council for British Archaeology.

Roberts, Charlotte, and Margaret Cox. 2003. *Health and Disease in Britain: From Prehistory to the Present
Day*. Stroud, UK: Sutton.

Tayles, N., K. Dommett, and K. Nelsen. 2000. Agriculture and Dental Caries? The Case of Rice in
Prehistoric Southeast Asia. *World Archaeology* 32(1):68–83.

Wood, James W., George R. Miller, Henry C. Harpending, and Kenneth M. Weiss. 1992. The Osteological Paradox: Problems of Inferring Health from Skeletal Samples. *Current Anthropology* 33(4):343–70.

■ CHARLOTTE A. ROBERTS AND REBECCA L. GOWLAND

PALYNOLOGY

The primary sources contributing to pollen spectra in an archaeological site can be separated into a natural background component derived from the native vegetation, a land-use
component contributed by plants colonizing soils disturbed by human activities, and an
ethnobotanical component composed of the pollen of plants cultivated or selected for
exploitation by members of a given society from among the plants yielding the other two
components. About half of the pollen grains found in archaeological sites can be identified
to the genus level and about half only to the family. A few pollen types can be attributed
to species on the basis of morphology (maize [*Zea mays*], for instance), or because there
is only one species growing in the subject area.

Pollen spectra reflecting the consumption of plants are identified by comparing the
measures of pollen types found within cultural settings with those that are characteristic

of the natural background and land-use components in the vicinity of the archaeological site. The ethnobotanical histories of areas under investigation and analogs created by comparing the pollen spectra found inside and outside modern farmed areas also have been important in interpreting pollen deposits as originating with food plants. Pollen grains of nominally noncultivated plants often are interpreted as those of food plants because they are accompanied by macrofossils of the parent plants or are found in the same deposits as the pollen grains and macrofossils of cultigens.

Pollen adheres to cultivated and gathered produce and waste products. It is deposited in distinctive quantities where the plants were used and is not significantly diffused by subsequent human activity. Wind-pollinated (anemophilous) plants produce large quantities of pollen and disperse it widely, while the pollen of insect-pollinated (entomophilous) plants is produced in much smaller quantities and is retained in the flower by sticky oils. It will fall in large clumps with, or near, the flower. The pollen of self-pollinated (autogamous) plants is woven through with pollen tubes and is not liberated when the flower opens. In extreme cases (cleistogamous plants), the flower never opens. Analysts have greater confidence in interpreting concentrations of the more meagerly produced and less widely dispersed pollen from entomophilous plants in cultural settings as economic deposits than those from anemophilous plants, while the pollen of autogamous/cleistogamous plants is rare, except where seed heads, produce, or produce waste were deposited.

Food pollen preservation varies by geographic area and deposition site environment. Pollen is generally well preserved in situ in arid lands. Palynologists working in such environments have been able to distinguish storage rooms from habitation rooms on the basis of food plant pollen concentrations in the storage spaces and have found that large percentages of such pollen grains are characteristic of task-specific areas involving plants. The pollen of cultivated plants has been recovered from prehistoric agricultural areas, along with pollen of native perennials that appear to have been protected as food sources, as well as evidence of native soil disturbance favoring annuals (i.e., weeds) that are thought to have been encouraged as ethnobotanical resources. Coprolites provide the most direct pollen evidence of food consumption. Experimental data indicate, however, that the human gastrointestinal system disperses pollen through feces, complicating interpretation of individual counts. Attempts to recover food pollen from buried ceramic vessels and milling stones have not proven successful, but it has been found in vessels in sealed tombs.

The pollen that is deposited on the surface of soil in moist environments is carried down through the soil by percolating rainwater and is attacked and destroyed by aerobic fungi, groundwater oxygen, and repeated hydration and dehydration. Pollen sequences yielding food pollen data from the tropics and temperate zones have been largely limited to samples from bodies of water near agricultural field locations, and the stratigraphy of such deposits is modified to some extent by burrowing metazoans. Palynologists working in China appear to prefer river deltas, where rapid sedimentation and permanent moist deposits favor pollen preservation.

Food pollen has also been recovered from singular matrices: from the inside surface of a human sacrum and from floors and textiles in graves, under flat rocks and artifacts in archaeological sites, under peat, from soil fertilized with manure, under the floors of historical-era kitchens, under volcanic ash, from latrines, wells, pasture deposits, runoff from cattle feedlots, historical-era marine docks, and under structures subsequently built around docks. The presence of herbivore dung spores in or near sites registers the presence of food-yielding livestock. Other environments that protect environmental and background pollen and should eventually yield food pollen data are deposits from under slopewash, earthworks, the concave side of mollusk shells, and in cave speleotherms (mineral deposits) and the oxides around buried copper and iron artifacts. The land-use component—a pollen sequence of native taxa followed by weeds that are succeeded in turn by a modified native flora after site abandonment—is itself evidence of agricultural, horticultural, or pastoral food production and is the most frequently cited evidence of human subsistence activities in areas where pollen preservation in archaeological sites is inadequate.

See also AGRICULTURAL FEATURES, IDENTIFICATION AND ANALYSIS; ARCHAEOBOTANY; EXPERIMENTAL ARCHAEOLOGY; LANDSCAPE AND ENVIRONMENTAL RECONSTRUCTION; MIDDENS AND OTHER TRASH DEPOSITS; PALEODIETARY ANALYSIS; PALEOFECAL ANALYSIS

Further Reading

Dimbleby, Geoffrey W. 1985. *The Palynology of Archaeological Sites*. New York: Academic Press.

Hill, James N., and Richard H. Hevly. 1968. Pollen at Broken K. Pueblo: Some New Interpretations. *American Antiquity* 33(2):200–210.

Iversen, Johannes. 1956. Forest Clearance in the Stone Age. *Scientific American* 194(3):36–41.

Kelso, Gerald K., and Allen M. Solomon. 2006. Applying Modern Analogs to Understand the Pollen Content of Coprolites. *Palaeogeography, Palaeoclimatology, Palaeoecology* 237(1):80–91.

Minnis, Paul E., ed. 2004. *People and Plants in Ancient Western North America*. Washington, DC: Smithsonian Books.

Reinhard, Karl J., Sherrian Edwards, Teyona R. Damon, et al. 2006. Pollen Concentration Analysis of Ancestral Pueblo Dietary Variation. *Palaeogeography, Palaeoclimatology, Palaeoecology* 237(1):92–109.

Vuorela, Irmeli. 1973. Relative Pollen Rain around Cultivated Fields. *Acta Botanica Fennica* 1032:1–27.

■ GERALD K. KELSO

PARASITOLOGICAL ANALYSIS

Food-borne parasites come from a variety of archaeological materials. The evidence ranges from infections of single individuals to infections of entire communities. Individually, the analysis of a single mummy reveals evidence of parasites that were present in the environment while the individual was alive. On a population scale, parasites have much to reveal about general patterns and distributions through time and space. Specifically, subsistence transitions involving both wild and domestic food animals are evident in parasites.

Some food-borne parasites reveal geographic and temporal depths of otherwise unknown food practices. In the Americas, hunter-gatherers were more commonly infected with food-borne parasites than agricultural peoples. Consumption of insects was a common behavior in the Great Basin and its margins in North America. Several studies of coprolites documented human infection with acanthocephalans in the Great Basin from Oregon through Utah. Acanthocephalans are a small group of parasites that mainly infect animals. However, they can be found in humans after insect consumption. Symptoms include abdominal pain, edema, dizziness, and constipation or diarrhea.

Other parasites reveal trade. The fish tapeworm, *Diphyllobothrium pacificum*, is a food-borne parasite with great antiquity associated with coastal fishing in marine environments at the base of the Andes. The normal host for *D. pacificum* is the sea lion, but it also infects dogs and humans. The most ancient Chilean culture, the Chinchorro, hosted *D. pacificum* over 4,800 years ago. Further north at Huaca Prieta, Peru, *D. pacificum* was a human parasite by 4,500 years ago. Later agricultural peoples of the Chiribaya and Inca cultures also were infected. The discovery of *D. pacificum* eggs in coprolites 40 kilometers inland from the Chilean coast dated to between 6,060 and 3,900 BP indicates that trade in fish led to the infection of people far from the coast in preagriculture times. Martinson and her colleagues have demonstrated that the fish trade diversified subsistence in agricultural times. Inland food trade between the villages resulted in infection.

Kristjánsdóttir and Collins focused on evidence recovered from skeletonized burials. They recovered calcified cysts from *Echinococcus granulosus* (tapeworm) infection in burials from medieval Iceland. This pathology is called hydatid disease. The tapeworms live in the intestine of the dogs, and the eggs are passed in dog feces. When eaten by sheep, the worms encyst. When dogs eat infected sheep organs, the cysts release the infective tapeworm stages. Humans are an alternative host. The cysts develop one to five centimeters in diameter per year. Secondary cysts, called brood capsules, develop within the main cyst. If the cysts rupture, brood capsules start new cysts in the host tissues. Cysts can form in the liver, lungs, or other organs, including the spleen, brain, heart, and kidneys, and cause serious complications. This infection was probably quite common and was clearly related to a sheep-based economy in the area. Kristjánsdóttir and Collins suggest that the parasite was introduced into Iceland during the ninth-century settlement period and became endemic in Iceland by AD 1200 following the introduction of dogs from Germany. The normal dog–sheep life cycle was thereby established, and humans became involved as dead-end hosts. Thus subsistence and economy based on sheep created a web of infection for the human population.

Fascinating work has emerged from Korea during the past decade as interdisciplinary research focuses on cultural and human remains discovered in Joseon Dynasty tombs dating from the 15th to 19th centuries AD. Some of the wealthy individuals buried in tombs during this dynasty (AD 1392 to 1897) were occasionally mummified. Seo and his colleagues, who analyzed 18 Joseon mummies, found four species of food-borne parasites, all of which are trematodes, or flukes. Flukes are parasitic flatworms. Two species are similar in that they are transferred to humans by the consumption of fish. These are *Clonorchis sinensis* (Chinese liver fluke) and *Metagonimus yokogawai*, an intestinal fluke. Six mummies were infected with one or both of these flukes, five with *C. sinensis*, and three with *M. yokogawai*. Consumption of noncooked fish causes these infections. Another parasite in the mummies shows that the elite also ate uncooked crab. *Paragonimus westermani*, a lung fluke in humans, was found in four of the mummies. Its final intermediate hosts include species of freshwater crabs. *Gymnophalloides seoi* is an intestinal fluke transferred by eating raw oysters. Two mummies were found to be positive for eggs of this parasite. In total, 11 of 18 Joseon mummies were infected with one or more species of fluke, underscoring the importance of sushi-style foods from several sources in ancient Korean diet.

More broadly, the evidence of food-borne parasites on a global scale falls into three patterns. In the Americas, food-borne disease was long associated with hunter-gatherer subsistence, and the pattern did not change with agricultural times. In contrast, animal domestication in Europe resulted in infection with sheep liver flukes, lancet flukes, pork tapeworm, beef tapeworm (*E. granulosus*), and other parasites of domestic animals. As noted above, the Korean evidence shows that dietary practices specific to Asia resulted in seafood-related fluke infections.

The study of parasites from archaeological sites has implications beyond food procurement, preparation, and animal association. Many parasite infections result in pathology. Thus parasitological studies are an important nexus of paleonutrition and paleopathology.

See also ANIMAL HUSBANDRY AND HERDING; FISH/SHELLFISH; GUT ANALYSIS; HUNTER-GATHERER SUBSISTENCE; INSECTS; LATRINES AND SEWER SYSTEMS; MANURING AND SOIL ENRICHMENT PRACTICES; MUMMIES; PALEOFECAL ANALYSIS; PALEONUTRITION; PALEOPATHOLOGY; TRADE ROUTES

Further Reading

Kristjánsdóttir, S., and C. Collins. 2011. Cases of Hydatid Disease in Medieval Iceland. *International Journal of Osteoarchaeology* 21(4):479–86.

Reinhard, Karl J. 1990. Archaeoparasitology in North America. *American Journal of Physical Anthropology* 82(2):145–63.

———. 1992. Parasitology as an Interpretive Tool in Archaeology. *American Antiquity* 57(2):231–45.

Reinhard, Karl J., L. F. Ferreira, F. Bouchet, et al. 2013. Food, Parasites, and Epidemiological Transitions: A Broad Perspective. *International Journal of Paleopathology* 3(3):150–57.

Seo, Min, Chang Seok Oh, Jong-Yil Chai, et al. 2014. The Changing Pattern of Parasitic Infection among Korean Populations by Paleoparasitological Study of Joseon Dynasty Mummies. *Journal of Parasitology* 100(1):147–50.

■KARL J. REINHARD AND ADAUTO ARAÚJO

PASTORALISM
See ANIMAL HUSBANDRY AND HERDING

PATHOLOGY
See PALEOPATHOLOGY

PHILISTINE FOODWAYS
The Philistines are an ethnic/cultural group that appeared in the Southern Coastal Plain of the Levant at the beginning of the Iron Age (ca. 1200 BC), and continued to inhabit this area until the late seventh century BC. This culture comprised foreign, non-Levantine elements with connections to the Aegean, Cyprus, and the central

Mediterranean who intermingled with local populations to form a unique, "entangled" culture that, although developing and becoming more locally oriented throughout the Iron Age, retained a distinct cultural identity.

Evidence from the main Philistine sites (Ashdod, Ashkelon, Ekron, and Gath) shows that with their arrival, nonlocal elements appeared in the material culture, including architecture, pottery, and cultic paraphernalia, and in their foodways. New foods that were not overly popular beforehand in the Levant are seen, including pig and dog meat (at most Philistine sites), and new types of plant food (such as *Lathyrus sativus* [grass pea]). These foods are more typical of the Aegean and most probably were the food preferences of the foreigners among the Philistines. New methods of food preparation also are seen at Ashkelon, Ekron, and Gath, including Cypriote-style pebbled hearths (figure 21), Aegean-style cooking jugs (figure 46), and various non-Levantine serving vessels. Evidence of continued usage of Canaanite-style cooking pots indicates that local Canaanites retained their foodways as well (figure 46).

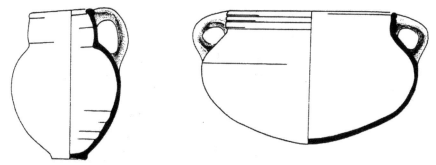

Figure 46. Changes to foodways practices among the Philistines through population movement and cultural exchange include adoption of different styles of ceramics. Left: Iron Age IIA Aegean-style cooking jug from Tell es-Safi/Gath. Right: Iron Age IIA Canaanite-style cooking pot from Tell es-Safi/Gath. Courtesy of the Tell es-Safi/Gath Archaeological Project, Aren M. Maeir, Director.

An interplay of foodways can be seen between the Philistines and other Levantine cultures. While the Judahites chose to abstain from pork, perhaps to differentiate themselves from the Philistines, the appearance of the Philistine cooking jug in cultures throughout the Levant indicates that while some of the Philistine foodways were purposefully not adopted, others were. As the Iron Age progressed, nonlocal foodways stop appearing in Philistia; there is a decline in the consumption of pork at some sites, and the pebbled hearth disappears. The unique, but entangled foodways of the Philistines illustrate both the complex nature of Philistine society and the cultural negotiations between them and neighboring cultures.

See also EXPERIMENTAL ARCHAEOLOGY; FIRE-BASED COOKING FEATURES; FOOD AND IDENTITY; FOOD TECHNOLOGY AND IDEAS ABOUT FOOD, SPREAD OF; FOODWAYS; IMMIGRANT FOODWAYS; MATERIAL CULTURE ANALYSIS; PREFERENCES, AVOIDANCES, PROHIBITIONS, TABOOS

Further Reading

Ben-Shlomo, David, Itzhaq Shai, Alexander Zuckerman, and Aren M. Maeir. 2008. Cooking Identities: Aegean-Style and Philistine Cooking Jugs and Cultural Interaction in the Southern Levant during the Iron Age. *American Journal of Archaeology* 112(2):225–46.

Maeir, Aren M., and Louise A. Hitchcock. 2011. Absence Makes the *Hearth* Grow Fonder: Searching for the Origins of the Philistine Hearth. *Eretz Israel (Amnon Ben-Tor Volume)* 30:46★–64★.

Maier, Aren M., Louise A. Hitchcock, and Liora Kolska Horwitz. 2013. On the Constitution and Transformation of Philistine Identity. *Oxford Journal of Archaeology* 32(1):1–38.

■ AREN M. MAEIR

PHYTOLITH ANALYSIS

Phytoliths are part of a suite of microfossil remains used to identify foods in the archaeological record. They remain inextricably linked to pollen and starch, providing a trio of proxies at the microscopic level that join macrofloral remains to provide visual evidence of plant/vegetable food. Whether influenced by the part of the plant processed and consumed or by preservation concerns, the archaeobotanical record of food requires study of these four proxies to understand prehistoric diet more fully.

Opal phytoliths are silica casts of the inside of plant cells. Silica dissolved in groundwater enters through plant roots and is deposited in cells. Not all plants accumulate silica, however. The grass family accumulates silica in various parts of the plant, but not in the seeds. Each plant family either has or has not developed a mechanism for sequestering silica. For some, silica is deposited in cells covering structures that transport vital fluids. In others, silica accumulation provides rigidity. Opal phytoliths survive fire but are dissolved by water when deposited in alkaline (basic) sediments. They sometimes survive when pollen and macrofloral remains do not, but this is not true universally.

Calcium oxalate crystals are included as phytoliths. They are formed in spaces between cells and include various shapes: raphids (long rods), styloids (thick long rods with blunt ends), druses (mace head shape), or polyhedral (three-dimensional with sharp angles). Hairs visible on stems and leaves of some plants are silicified and identifiable.

Long thought to be the proxy of choice for identifying grasses on the landscape, phytoliths also contribute to dietary reconstructions using the archaeological record. Research questions concerning the beginnings of cereal use and agriculture in the Old World may be addressed with phytoliths. The earliest records of threshing cereals, using phytoliths as the proxy record, derive from the Middle East. For example, early evidence for processing cereals in northern Iraq comes from the phytolith and starch records. Silica sheets (neighboring phytoliths still joined together) bearing straight-line or curved cuts across cells, particularly when not at exactly 90 degrees to the long axis of the cells, indicate threshing. Experimental work by Patricia Anderson indicates that threshing sledges produce these "cut" phytoliths. This contribution enhances our understanding of prehistoric and historic-period food processing and economy, and also sheds light on both crop diffusion and technology. Study of an adobe brick sample from Santa Inez Mission in California (USA) yielded several cut phytoliths, indicating use of a threshing sledge at the mission and documenting transport of this technology from Europe.

Phytolith morphometrics have been an important tool for identifying Old World cultigens such as cereals and bananas. Arlene Miller Rosen provided phytolith analysts with a system for identifying specific Old World crops using the pattern of the gap between dendritic long cells on silica sheets to distinguish between wheat, barley, rye, or weed grasses. Further, experimental work with emmer wheat by Rosen and Stephen Weiner suggested a method using opaline phytoliths as indicators of irrigation. Pioneering work by Deborah Pearsall and Dolores Piperno inaugurated the use of phytoliths from maize (*Zea mays*) leaves in the study of the primary New World grass domesticate. Linda Scott Cummings applied morphometric techniques to maize cob phytoliths to identify races of *Zea mays* in the American Southwest and to examine relationships among people and movement of those people across the landscape.

Identification of phytoliths in food residues and coprolites also has contributed to our understanding of food processing and consumption. Food residue adhering to ceramic vessels often contains identifiable phytoliths that can indicate foods that were cooked; work on ceramics from formative sites in the Americas, for example, has yielded *Zea mays* phytoliths. In the Old World, date consumption in northern Africa, a tradition attested by the presence of large "date jars" in villages today, can be observed in coprolites from the early and late Christian eras along the Nile. There the phytolith record was co-dominated by date spiny spheroids and cereal dendritic elongates. Identification of sorghum seeds in coprolites and a child's stomach aided association of the dendritic elongates with this cereal. At the time, morphometric analysis, a viable tool today, had not been applied to phytoliths. Steven Bozarth described *Cucurbita* rind phytoliths and bean phytoliths (silicified pod hairs) in the American Southwest. In coprolites from Step House (Mesa Verde National Park, Colorado, USA), recovery of silicified hook-shaped hairs from bean pods (the fuzzy part) and macrofloral bean hila (the hard part of the side of the beans) contributed primary evidence of *Phaseolus* bean consumption. Because the coprolites were recovered in a room near the back of Step House, they likely represent deposition during inclement weather (winter) rather than during the warmer days and nights of summer, suggesting both storage and consumption of dried beans, including the pods.

Phytolith evidence for native foods in the diet has been more elusive in both the Old and New Worlds. Although several foods, both cultivated and native (including wild, tolerated, encouraged, and tended or husbanded plants), produce calcium oxalate druses, raphids, or styloids, they do not preserve well in sediments, although recovery from coprolites has been excellent. Druses from goosefoot or saltbush leaves or fruits are common. Recovery of raphids typical of *Yucca* confirms yucca leaf chewing. Yucca quids are common in the archaeological record in Anasazi dry shelters (American Southwest).

Phytolith studies also contribute to our understanding of local vegetation and animal populations—a valuable source of food for people living in or moving through the area. Identification of dayflower seed phytoliths documents growth of weedy dayflower plants in abandoned fire features in southeastern New Mexico (USA). Their presence suggests hunter-gatherer use of the landscape (building hearths for cooking or heating) also helped to extend or maintain the range of Montezuma's quail, a species that subsists on dayflower seeds in the winter. This would have increased the local population of quail, making quail hunting easier for people who crossed this landscape.

See also AGRICULTURAL FEATURES, IDENTIFICATION AND ANALYSIS; AGRICULTURE, PRO-CUREMENT, PROCESSING, AND STORAGE; ARCHAEOBOTANY; CULTIVATION; EXPERIMENTAL ARCHAEOLOGY; FOOD STORAGE; FOOD TECHNOLOGY AND IDEAS ABOUT FOOD, SPREAD OF; GUT ANALYSIS; IRRIGATION/HYDRAULIC ENGINEERING; LANDSCAPE AND ENVIRONMENTAL RECONSTRUCTION; MAIZE; MULTI- AND INTERDISCIPLINARY APPROACHES; PALEOFECAL ANALYSIS; PLANT HUSBANDRY; QUIDS; WEEDS

Further Reading

Anderson, Patricia C., ed. 1999. *The Prehistory of Agriculture: New Experimental and Ethnographic Approaches.* Institute of Archaeology Monograph 40. Los Angeles: University of California, Los Angeles.

Anderson, Patricia C., Linda S. Cummings, Thomas K. Schippers, and Bernard Simonel, eds. 2003. *Le traitement des récoltes: Un regard sur la diversité, du Néolithique au présent.* Centre d'Études Préhistoire, Antiquité, Moyen Âge. Antibes: APDCA.

Ball, T., L. Vrydaghs, I. Van Den Hauwe, et al. 2006. Differentiating Banana Phytoliths: Wild and Edible *Musa acuminata* and *Musa balbisiana. Journal of Archaeological Science* 33(9):1228–36.

Bozarth, Steven R. 1990. Diagnostic Opal Phytoliths from Pods of Selected Varieties of Common Beans (*Phaseolus vulgaris*). *American Antiquity* 55(1):98–103.

Cummings, Linda Scott. 1994. Anasazi Diet: Variety in the Hoy House and Lion House Coprolite Record and Nutritional Analysis. In *Paleonutrition: The Diet and Health of Prehistoric Americans,* edited by Kristin D. Sobolik, 134–50. Center for Archaeological Investigations, Occasional Paper 22. Carbondale: Southern Illinois University.

Madella, Marco, and Débora Zurro, eds. 2007. *Plants, People and Places: Recent Studies in Phytolith Analysis.* Oxford: Oxbow.

Piperno, Dolores R. 2006. *Phytoliths: A Comprehensive Guide for Archaeologists and Paleoecologists.* Lanham, MD: AltaMira Press.

Rosen, Arlene Miller, and Stephen Weiner. 1994. Identifying Ancient Irrigation: A New Method Using Opaline Phytoliths from Emmer Wheat. *Journal of Archaeological Science* 21(1):125–32.

■ LINDA SCOTT CUMMINGS

PIG

The pig (*Sus domesticus*) is the quintessential meat-producing animal, as it is fast growing, prolific, and is not kept for secondary products such as milk or wool. The pig was domesticated from the wild boar (*Sus scrofa*), a widespread species that also represented an important food resource for human populations of the Paleoarctic. The original date of pig domestication is debated, but evidence from sites such as Hallan Çemi and Çayönü in Turkey points toward a gradual process stretching between the eighth and seventh millennia BC. Archaeological and paleogenetic evidence indicates that the pig was independently domesticated in different areas, including Europe, the Near East, the Far East, and possibly central and south Asia. Pork consumption is particularly widespread in the Far East and Southeast Asia, where pigs have been a key food resource for millennia. In Muslim and Jewish traditions, however, pork consumption is avoided for a combination of religious, social, and ecological reasons.

It is likely that for most of the Neolithic, pigs were allowed to browse freely and to mix with wild boar populations. By the end of the Neolithic, there is evidence that the animals were enclosed, which led to a genetic separation between wild and domestic populations. Free-range keeping is, however, not labor intensive and has, in some areas, remained a popular way to raise pigs. In such regimes, pigs can feed independently, particularly in woodland areas and during the autumn and early winter. These pigs would be relatively small and slow growing. In late medieval and early modern times, pigs were often confined to house backyards and small enclosures. This provided the opportunity for people to closely monitor their reproductive behavior and to develop improved breeds that are fast growing and often of a very large size. The large, fat, pink pig we are familiar with today is a product of such development but was unknown to premodern societies.

See also ANIMAL DOMESTICATION; BUTCHERY; FOODWAYS AND RELIGIOUS PRACTICES; MEAT; PREFERENCES, AVOIDANCES, PROHIBITIONS, TABOOS; ZOOARCHAEOLOGY

Further Reading

Albarella, Umberto, Keith Dobney, Anton Ervynyk, and Peter Rowley-Conwy, eds. 2007. *Pigs and Humans: 10,000 Years of Interaction*. Oxford: Oxford University Press.

Nelson, Sarah M., ed. 1998. *Ancestors for the Pigs: Pigs in Prehistory*. MASCA Research Papers in Science and Archaeology 15. Philadelphia: University of Pennsylvania Museum of Archaeology and Anthropology.

■ UMBERTO ALBARELLA

PLANT DOMESTICATION

Plant domestication represents a process of evolutionary change involving the genetics and biogeography of plant populations through human and natural selection. Such evolutionary processes create to varying degrees an interdependent relationship between human populations and certain kinds of plants, and their continued reproduction and modification by humans and the natural environment. Domesticated plants are ultimately cultural artifacts in that they could not exist in nature without human assistance. While the reproduction and dispersal of domesticated plants is totally dependent upon humans, this is not necessarily the case among wild plant species. Changes in the natural environment related to domestication, cultivation, and cultural and economic dependence upon certain plants have broad implications for the surrounding ecology.

The process of plant domestication begins with the deliberate or unintentional selection of plants through gathering, management or husbandry, and cultivation. Cultivation represents the modification of natural environments through human action involving the management of the natural ecology. Cultivation is characterized by conscious selection for certain favorable traits or characteristics, as well as unconscious selection, that is, genetic and phenotypic changes through plant management. Cultivation is generally focused on the production of seasonal plant supplements to broad-based vegetable diets as a guarantee to a bountiful harvest, and may eventually eliminate further need for wide-ranging searches for additional food crops. Intensive gathering or the selection of larger seeds versus smaller ones also can have unexpected genetic consequences, selecting against less desirable traits. The very act of gathering vegetable foods and plants can lead to unintentional or unconscious tending of plants, and thus to accidental seed dispersal and trampling, causing intended and unintended change to the surrounding landscape. In many regions of the world, archaic hunters and gatherers used fire to induce the regeneration of grasses and edible plants. Such factors may benefit certain wild resources as well. Cultivation may or may not include wild plant species, while domestication is characterized by a mutual interdependence of particular domesticated plants upon humans for their reproduction. Cultivation does not imply full domestication, but allows us to infer that the life cycle of a plant has in some way been disrupted by human selection.

Archaeological evidence for plant domestication and cultivation recovered by Jeffrey Parsons in central Mexico, Richard MacNeish and Kent Flannery at various cave and rockshelter sites in Mexico and the Andes, as well as ethnobotanical and genetic research by Jack Harlan, John Doebley, Jane Dorweiler, Christine Hastorf, Bruce Smith, and others indicates such changes in adaptation represent a long, gradual process with both intended and unintended consequences for humankind, the surrounding biota, and sociocultural development. The gradual interdependence and changes in adaptation associated with plant domestication involve a shift from mobile campsites governed by the seasonality and availability of resources to sedentary populations in permanent settlements associated with rivers and streams or other permanent sources of water. Archaeological evidence of ceramic technology and grinding stones has been considered a strong indication of an adaptive shift to an agricultural economy (e.g., maize and beans require soaking in ceramic containers). Archaeologists have traditionally analyzed the spread of agriculture and primary food crops in terms of transitions along an adaptive continuum, from seasonally mobile hunters and gatherers to a fully developed agricultural economy. The transition from food gathering to food production is central to archaeological debates surrounding the development of civilization. Food production or cultivation begins with the deliberate care afforded the propagation of a species. The genetic responses of plants to human modification of the environment through direct or indirect management vary depending upon the ecology, the plant, and what traits are being selected.

Recent advances in ethnobotanical, biological, and molecular approaches emphasize the role of Darwinian natural selection in the process of domestication and cultivation. Conscious or unconscious modification of the natural environment and ecology will to varying degrees affect all plant and animal species. The setting of controlled fires that select for certain species is not generally considered an example of deliberate plant production, but it does show how cultures can have dramatic effects upon the plant and animal species in an ecology. When humans began to consciously domesticate the landscape, they created plant communities that were essentially the dominant component in their ancient diets. Some of these plants became totally dependent upon humans for their reproduction; others did not and either became extinct or reverted, sometimes in modified form, to a wild state. The domestication process varies with the plant species, its dietary role or use, and where, when, and why it is being selected. Ethnobotanists and DNA researchers are documenting domestication with increasing detail. Plant and molecular biologists perceive the domestication process as involving the gradual and fortuitous accumulation of genetic mutations that create a form of mutualism and interdependence that develops between human populations and certain target plant species or populations. Humans select for these interrelationships because they provide strong selective advantages for both the plant(s) and the human populations dependent upon them.

See also AGRICULTURE, ORIGINS OF; ARCHAEOBOTANY; BIOMOLECULAR ANALYSIS; CULTIVATION; DNA ANALYSIS; PLANT HUSBANDRY; SEDENTISM AND DOMESTICATION; WEEDS; WILD PROGENITORS OF DOMESTICATED PLANTS

Further Reading

Bellwood, Peter. 2005. *First Farmers: The Origins of Agricultural Societies*. Malden, MA: Blackwell.

Darwin, Charles. [1868] 1905. *The Variation of Animals and Plants under Domestication*. London: John Murray.

Ford, Richard I., ed. 1985. *Prehistoric Food Production in North America*. Anthropological Papers 75. Ann Arbor: Museum of Anthropology, University of Michigan.

Harlan, Jack R., and J. M. J. de Wet. 1973. On the Quality of Evidence for Origin and Dispersal of Cultivated Plants. *Current Anthropology* 14(1–2):51–62.

Smith, Bruce D. 1998. *The Emergence of Agriculture*. Scientific American Library Publication. New York: W. H. Freeman.

Staller, John E. 2010. *Maize Cobs and Cultures: History of Zea mays L.* Heidelberg: Springer.

Zeder, Melinda A., Daniel G. Bradley, Eve Ernshwiller, and Bruce D. Smith, eds. 2006. *Documenting Domestication: New Genetic and Archaeological Paradigms*. Berkeley: University of California Press.

Zohary, Daniel, Maria Hopf, and Ehud Weiss. 2012. *Domestication of Plants in the Old World*. 4th edition. Oxford: Oxford University Press.

■ JOHN E. STALLER

PLANT HUSBANDRY

In a broad sense, plant husbandry is the relationship between plants and humans. In more specific terms, it is the care and management of wild plants or crops. Gathering, tending, burning vegetation, weeding, grafting, budding, land clearing, tilling, transplanting, planting, sowing, plant breeding, conservation, and landscape transformation (such as terracing, drainage, and irrigation) are all examples of plant husbandry practices that require different degrees of human intervention.

The concept of plant husbandry plays an important role in the study of the origins of agriculture, especially in models that explain the transition from gathering to farming in ecological and evolutionary terms. *Husbandry* is a term used to describe exploitation practices that fall between hunting-gathering and agriculture. They can lead to agriculture, or may not. The term *husbandry* is preferred to *domestication*, in order to emphasize the whole spectrum of human interventions and their induced transformation of the natural environment. This, in turn, has formalized the definition of domestication as the morphological transformation that results from selective breeding.

Archaeologists have proposed numerous models to conceptualize the range of subsistence strategies involving plant use. One model from the 1980s suggests five categories of human–plant relationships: casual gathering, systematic gathering, limited cultivation, developed cultivation, and intensive cultivation. In the late 1980s, Harris suggested an evolutionary continuum of people–plant interaction; this model describes plant-exploitative activities and their associated ecological impact along a continuum gradient that translates into progressively closer people–plant interactions and an increasing input of human energy per unit of land, along with the modification of natural ecosystems and their gradual replacement by agrosystems.

See also AGRICULTURE, ORIGINS OF; CULTIVATION; FORAGING; HUNTER-GATHERER SUBSISTENCE; PLANT DOMESTICATION

Further Reading

Chomko, Stephen A., and Gary W. Crawford. 1978. Plant Husbandry in Prehistoric Eastern North America: New Evidence for Its Development. *American Antiquity* 43(3):405–8.

Harris, David. 2007. An Evolutionary Continuum of People-Plant Interaction (1989). With an update by Tim Denham. In *The Emergence of Agriculture: A Global View*, edited by Tim Denham and Peter White, 26–44. New York: Routledge.

Matsui, Akira, and Masaaki Kanehara. 2006. The Question of Prehistoric Plant Husbandry during the Jomon Period in Japan. *World Archaeology* 38(2):259–73.

■ MANON SAVARD

PLANT PROCESSING

Plant processing refers to a variety of practices people use to transform vegetal matter into foodstuffs. People process plants to improve taste and to change the physical structure and biochemistry of plants, making them palatable, less toxic, and more stable. They also process plant foods to follow culturally derived recipes. These technological and cultural developments influence (both positively and negatively) the bioavailability of minerals, vitamins, and phytonutrients by breaking down and transforming physiological and phytochemical structures into digestible forms. The five general processing strategies include mechanical processing, thermal alteration, soaking (leaching), fermentation, and absorption. More often than not, these approaches are used in combination, which tends to increase efficacy. Processing strategies extend beyond mere subsistence, however; these activities also have deeper socioeconomic and political implications related to access to resources as well as issues involving class- and gender-based social stratification.

Mechanical techniques physically reduce the size of plant matter via pounding, grinding, or slicing. Tools commonly used include knives, graters, mortars, pestles, *manos*, *metates*, and millstones. These instruments break up seeds, nuts, underground storage organs, and grains into smaller sizes, aiding in the separation of inedible or exceptionally fibrous portions from the nutrient-rich components. Mechanical processing techniques increase the area over which chemical processes occur. For this reason, mechanical techniques ordinarily precede other preparations, as greater surface area tends to improve their efficacy. Early Holocene deposits at Kuk Swamp, Papua New Guinea, revealed stone tool assemblages used to process taro (*Colocasia esculenta*) and yams (*Dioscorea* sp.).

Thermal processes, also known as cooking, change the physical structure of plant tissue and trigger biochemical reactions. These changes range from the rupturing of cell walls to the neutralization of toxins and antinutrients. People perform these activities using a variety of apparatus, including ceramics, hot rocks, earthen ovens, and steaming pits. Archaeological evidence of ceramic-based thermal processing includes the recovery of maize (*Zea mays*) and squash (*Cucurbita* sp.) phytoliths in food residues adhering to early ceramics in central New York (USA) and the recovery of garlic mustard seed (*Alliaria petiolata*) phytoliths from 6,000-year-old ceramics in the western Baltics. Archaeological and ethnographic accounts show that prehistoric populations used thermal processing to effectively break down resilient carbohydrates and phytochemicals present within underground storage organs. For example, at the Wilson-Leonard site in central Texas (USA), researchers identified charred camas bulbs in an 8,200-year-old earthen oven. Further distinctions can be made between cooking techniques that use water (e.g., steaming and boiling) and those that do not (e.g., roasting). None of these types of cooking necessitate nonperishable container technology; for example, stone boiling can be carried out using bags or baskets.

Soaking and leeching involve the use of water to alter plant phytochemistry. When vegetal material is soaked for an extended period of time, the water can trigger biological responses within germplasm. For instance, all grains and many legumes contain phytic acid, a potent inhibitor of mineral and trace element absorption in the body. Soaking/germination activates phytase, a co-occurring compound that breaks down phytic acid. In addition, the immersion of plant matter into flowing water enables unpalatable soluble compounds such as tannins to be leached. At the Sunken Village Wetsite in Oregon (USA), researchers identified approximately 100 leaching pits used to process acorns.

Fermentation refers to the introduction of beneficial microorganisms into food as part of its preparation. Studies show this ancient tradition increases the preservation potential of perishable foods in the absence of refrigeration, enhances flavor, aids in digestibility, and increases nutritional and pharmacological value. Agents commonly responsible for fermentation included lactic acid bacteria (LAB) and yeasts. As LAB and yeasts feed upon sugar, they alter the chemical composition of the base, creating a deleterious environment for pathogenic bacteria. Chemical analyses of jars used to hold fermented beverages have been recovered from the seventh millennia BC site of Jiahu, Henan Province, China. At Puerto Escondido, Honduras, chemical signatures of a fermented cacao beverage extend the date of this plant's usage back to 3,000 BP. Ethnohistoric and ethnographic accounts describe the purposeful burial of plants in the mud to encourage microbial colonization, as well as traditional food preparations that capture wild, airborne microbiota.

The intentional addition of substances to plant matter creates a chemical reaction through which the added substance absorbs or detoxifies phytochemicals from the processed plant matter. Geophagy, for instance, involves the addition of clay to detoxify a foodstuff by binding with organic compounds such as alkaloids and tannins. Researchers working in Kalambo Falls, Zambia, uncovered clay samples that may have been used to detoxify tree nuts recovered from the same Paleolithic living floors. Substances also are added during processing to impart plants with additional minerals. In nixtamalization, maize kernels are boiled in an alkali-rich solution to loosen the pericarp, facilitate the uptake of potassium or calcium (depending upon the alkaline additive) by the kernel, and render niacin accessible for absorption by the body. Evidence from the Basketmaker

II period (Utah, USA) indicates that people likely used limestone to stone boil maize ca. 1,650 BP. Experimental studies also demonstrate the efficacy of boiling bitter plant tissues, such as *Cucurbita* gourd seeds, with wood ash to neutralize the plant's astringent alkaloids.

Processing activities are deeply entwined in the relationships between people and plants and ultimately contribute to larger sociocultural structures. For instance, plant processing takes time and energy to complete, often during a busy season of the year when many plants require harvesting and processing to prevent spoilage or infestation. Harvest schedules and an established rhythm of food processing contribute to food security and provide insight into economic or cost-benefit decisions within societies. Gender and socioeconomic status also figure into these relationships as specific members or groups within a society carry the knowledge and perhaps bear the responsibility for processing plants.

With the exception of those species eaten raw, processing is needed to physically, chemically, and culturally change plants into food. Processing detoxifies, preserves, and improves taste or access to nutrition. Processing may also follow culturally derived recipes and reflect broader socioeconomic aspects of food production. These strategies are thus a testament to the complex plant-based knowledge systems at work within societies.

See also ARCHAEOLOGY OF COOKING; EXPERIMENTAL ARCHAEOLOGY; FERMENTATION; FIRE AND THE DEVELOPMENT OF COOKING TECHNOLOGY; FOOD PRESERVATION; FOODWAYS AND GENDER ROLES; MILLING; NIXTAMALIZATION; RESIDUE ANALYSIS, STARCH; SUBSISTENCE MODELS; TOOLS/UTENSILS, GROUND STONE; TOOLS/UTENSILS, METAL; TOOLS/UTENSILS, ORGANIC MATERIALS; TOOLS/UTENSILS, STONE; YEAST

Further Reading

Gremillion, Kristen J. 2004. Seed Processing and the Origins of Food Production in Eastern North America. *American Antiquity* 69(2):215–33.

Hotz, Christine, and Rosalind S. Gibson. 2007. Traditional Food-Processing and Preparation Practices to Enhance the Bioavailability of Micronutrients in Plant-Based Diets. *Journal of Nutrition* 137(4):1097–1100.

Johns, Timothy, and Isao Kubo. 1988. A Survey of Traditional Methods Employed for the Detoxification of Plant Foods. *Journal of Ethnobiology* 8(1):81–129.

Stahl, Ann B. 1989. Plant-Food Processing: Implications for Dietary Quality. In *Foraging and Farming: The Evolution of Plant Exploitation*, edited by D. R. Harris and G. C. Hillman, 171–94. London: Unwin Hyman.

Watson, Patty Jo, and Mary C. Kennedy. 1991. The Development of Horticulture in the Eastern Woodlands of North America: Women's Role. In *Engendering Archaeology: Women and Prehistory*, edited by Joan M. Gero and Margaret W. Conkey, 255–75. Oxford: Basil Blackwell.

■ TIMOTHY C. MESSNER

PLANTS

Plants are the base of all food chains and global primary production. Energy from the sun, in combination with carbon dioxide and water, is fixed or captured and converted into sugars. Thus plants provide the basic energy for all organic systems on earth, as they are then fed upon by animals (including humans), and the hydrocarbons they provide also offer high energy fuels that can be burned for heat, most notably wood but also the fossilized and transformed wood that is coal. Modern taxonomy defines true plants as land plants, separate from the photosynthetic algae that dominate the seas, photosynthetic single-cell blue-green algae (cyanobacteria), and fungi (which are nonphotosynthetic decomposers and recyclers at the far end of the food chain). Humans utilize plants directly for a wide range of purposes, from fuel for fires to raw materials for tools, clothes, and shelter and, of course, as food and sources of medicine. The total number of modern plant species is estimated to be around 400,000 (about 300,000 have accepted scientific names), of which around 250,000 are flowering plants (angiosperms) that evolved around 135 million years ago and came to dominate most terrestrial ecosystems over the past 65 million years.

Out of this vast number of species, the number that have played major roles in human history and that have been subjected to archaeological study (through archaeobotany or paleoethnobotany) are surprisingly few. While the potential uses of plants are highly diverse, as well, archaeobotanical research has tended to focus on the use of major food plants, the circumstances of their production, and the evidence for wood fuel use. A great many species are used by people, however, and probably the majority have been used as materials or fuels at one time or another. Estimates of numbers of economic plants often range up to about 10,000 species. The number of species that are regarded as domesticated is also not settled. Depending on definitions, estimates range up to 2,500 cultivated species, excluding garden ornamentals, but there are probably only several hundred that have been domesticated as food crops. When considered in terms of the origins of agriculture and crop domestication, the roster of early domesticates in each center of origin was remarkably small. Thus, for example, in the Yangtze region of China it is only rice and bottle gourd that can be regarded as domesticated initially, while in northern China there were two species of millets with soybeans, hemp, probably *Chenopodium*, and a few trees and vegetables. In Mesoamerica, the classic trio maize-squash-beans includes beans that were domesticated millennia later, while chili peppers and trees like avocado were added to cultivation sometime after the early Holocene origins of maize and squash. Even in the Fertile Crescent of western Asia, which involved the greatest number of early crop domestications, the number of species involved may be only 15. Current archaeobotanical inferences support perhaps 20 independent centers of crop domestication globally, but in each of these, the number of early domestications was only a few. This means that the vast majority of domesticated crops were brought into cultivation over the course of the Holocene, mainly during the middle Holocene (broadly speaking, the Neolithic or early Metal Ages), as historical evidence suggests relatively few have been brought into cultivation in the past 2,000 years.

Plants provide a wide spectrum of elements of the human diet as well as nondietary uses. Plants are a major source of necessary macronutrients (carbohydrates, proteins, lipids) as well as micronutrients required by the human diet (vitamins, minerals, rare lipids like omega-3 fatty acid ALA [α-linolenic acid]). The spectrum and quantity of these compounds in any given species or plant part are highly variable, however, and tend to promote dietary diversity among humans. Plants also produce a diverse range of secondary metabolite chemicals, some of which are highly restricted taxonomically. These are important, as many are toxic and require processing of the plant prior to their consumption by humans. The development of varied techniques of post-harvest processing of plant products is a key aspect of human technological and cultural evolution. In addition, plant secondary metabolites include many substances (from caffeine to codeine to capsaicin to the phellandrenes in many incense species) actively sought by humans or used culturally for their aroma, taste, or neurophysiological effects. Secondary metabolites include the key active ingredients in stimulants, spices, drugs, and medicines.

See also AGRICULTURE, ORIGINS OF; ARCHAEOBOTANY; CEREALS; COLUMBIAN EXCHANGE; FORAGING; FRUITS; FUNGI; GREENS/HERBS; HUNTER-GATHERER SUBSISTENCE; LEGUMES AND PULSES; NATIVE AMERICAN ETHNOBOTANY; NUTS; OIL-BEARING SEED PLANTS; OLD WORLD GLOBALIZATION AND FOOD EXCHANGES; PACIFIC OCEANIC EXCHANGE; PLANT HUSBANDRY; PLANT PROCESSING; PSYCHOACTIVE PLANTS; ROOT CROPS/TUBERS; SPICES; VEGETABLES; WEEDS

Further Reading

Harlan, Jack. 1992. *Crops and Man*. 2nd edition. Madison, WI: American Society of Agronomy.

Mabberley, John. 2008. *Mabberley's Plant-Book: A Portable Dictionary of Plants, Their Classifications, and Uses*. 3rd edition. Cambridge: Cambridge University Press.

Meyer, R. S., A. E. DuVal, and H. R. Jensen. 2012. Patterns and Processes in Crop Domestication: An Historical Review and Quantitative Analysis of 203 Global Food Crops. *New Phytologist* 196:29–48.

Usher, George. 1974. *A Dictionary of Plants Used by Man*. London: Constable.

Wiersema, John H., and Blanca León. 1999. *World Economic Plants: A Standard Reference*. Boca Raton, FL: CRC Press.

Zeven, A. C., and J. M. J. de Wet. 1982. *Dictionary of Cultivated Plants and Their Regions of Diversity Excluding Most Ornamentals, Forest Trees and Lower Plants*. Wageningen, the Netherlands: Center for Agricultural Publishing and Documentation.

■ DORIAN Q FULLER

POLITICS
See FOOD AND POLITICS

POLLEN
See PALYNOLOGY

POMPEII
See HERCULANEUM AND POMPEII

POPLAR FOREST, VIRGINIA (UNITED STATES)

Archaeologists have studied four slave quartering sites dating from ca. 1770–1860 at Poplar Forest as part of a multiyear research program. Up to 100 enslaved laborers lived and labored at this tobacco and wheat plantation in the western Virginia piedmont. A succession of owners, including John Wayles, Thomas Jefferson, and William Cobbs, managed the property. The analysis of diverse data sets, including artifacts, macro- and microbotanical evidence, faunal remains, and plantation and local records, reveals contrasting stories. Provisioning systems for slaves were characterized by monotony, nutritional limitations, and poor quality. By contrast, slaves' strategies for finding alternative food sources, and the outcomes of their efforts through gardening, poultry raising, foraging, hunting, fishing, and shopping built social alliances, and resulted in a diverse diet of meat, fish, eggs, fruits, vegetables, grains, herbs, nuts, and varied beverages that promoted better health and allowed for dietary choice. Over time, plantation management practices, and the environmental degradation and land sales that resulted, negatively impacted the ability of enslaved people to acquire and share food. Conversely, improvements to transportation infrastructure and the availability of consumer goods in the first half of the 19th century positively affected access to food. Despite these significant changes, proportions of provisioned, gardened, and foraged plants within slave diet remained relatively constant on this plantation, suggesting that 18th-century foodways practices and preferences were coalescing into tradition by the time of emancipation.

See also DIASPORA FOODWAYS; INFORMAL ECONOMIC EXCHANGE; SLAVE DIET, ON SLAVE SHIPS; SLAVE DIET, ON SOUTHERN PLANTATIONS; SLAVE DIET, ON WEST INDIAN PLANTATIONS

Further Reading

Heath, Barbara J. 2001. Bounded Yards and Fluid Borders: Landscapes of Slavery at Poplar Forest. In *Places of Cultural Memory: African Reflections on the American Landscape Conference Proceedings*, 69–81. U.S. Department of the Interior, National Park Service. http://www.cr.nps.gov/crdi/conferences/AFR_69-82_Heath.pdf.

Heath, Barbara J., and Jack Gary, eds. 2012. *Jefferson's Poplar Forest: Unearthing a Virginia Plantation*. Gainesville: University Press of Florida.

Klippel, Walter E., Jennifer A. Systelien, and Barbara J. Heath. 2011. Taphonomy and Fish Bones from an Enslaved African American Context at Poplar Forest, Virginia, USA. *Archaeofauna* 20:27–47.

Lamzik, Kathryn E. 2012. The Identification and Analysis of the Bird Eggshell Fragments Recovered from Thomas Jefferson's Poplar Forest, Site A, the Southeast Terrace. *Archeological Society of Virginia Quarterly Bulletin* 67(2):63–71.

■ BARBARA J. HEATH

POTATO

Potato (*Solanum tuberosum L.*, Solanaceae) is the world's fourth most important food crop, producing high yields of underground tubers. Indigenous populations in the Bolivian-Peruvian Andes were the first to cultivate potato around 7,000 to 10,000 years ago. After centuries of selection and breeding, there are now over 5,000 potato varieties worldwide. In addition to seven cultivated potato species, there are around 200 wild potato species. Potato production has spread from its origin in the high-altitude environment of the Andes to all elevation zones on all the continents, including the tropics. The rise of the potato as a staple food is the result of many factors, not least of which are its high yields and nutritional value. The potato is full of complex carbohydrates, is low in fat, and contains high-quality protein with balanced essential amino acids. Potatoes provide the most affordable source of potassium and are a very good source of vitamin B6 and vitamin C. Potatoes also contain a variety of important health-promoting compounds or phytonutrients, such as carotenoids in yellow-fleshed potato, and anthocyanins with antioxidant activity in purple-fleshed potato.

Evidence of wild potato consumption (skins and starch grains of *Solanum maglia*) has been found with other processed vegetal remains at the archaeological site of Monte Verde in Chile in a layer dated to 14,800–14,500 cal BP, suggesting that ancient populations were foraging for wild potatoes at this early date. Potatoes were widely cultivated and likely first domesticated in the Peruvian and Bolivian highlands. Several fossilized remains of possibly cultivated tubers recovered from the Tres Ventanas Cave at the Chilca Canyon in Peru have been dated to 8000–6000 BC. Evidence of domesticated potato is more widespread after 2000 BC. The remains of 20 potato tubers dating between 2000 BC and 1200 BC were identified through their starch grains from four archaeological sites in the Casma Valley of Peru, for example. Over the course of the next few millennia, the indigenous peoples developed sophisticated potato agriculture in Pre-Columbian times.

The Spanish explorers were the first Europeans to come into contact with potatoes when they conquered Peru. Carried back to Spain in the 1570s, potatoes slowly spread to Italy and other European countries. Eventually, agriculturalists in Europe found potatoes easier to grow and cultivate than other staple crops. In the 1840s a major outbreak of potato blight, a plant disease, was introduced and swept through Europe and Ireland, wiping out the initial introduction of potatoes and causing famine among the poor. Since that time, scholars have debated the origin of the European potato. DNA analysis has become a powerful tool in the study of the origin, domestication, and global dispersal of potatoes. By analyzing the DNA of historical potato specimens, scientists found that Canary Islands potatoes, thought to be the source of the modern European potato, possessed DNA from both the Andean and Chilean types, and possibly from hybrids of the two. Potatoes were originally believed to have been brought to North America from Europe. The Ozette potato from the Makah Indians on the Pacific Northwest coast exhibited unusual characteristics, however, and was shown, based on DNA fingerprinting, to originate from a different source than the old European cultivated potatoes.

Historically, the potato has been a significant food source in many cultures because of its productivity, adaptability to a range of climates, and suitability for both short- and long-term storage. In the Andes, the Quechua and other indigenous groups developed methods to detoxify, process, prepare, and preserve the potato harvest. A process used to freeze-dry potatoes (the process is known as *chunoficación*, and the product is known as *chuño*) is still practiced today. The potato has been credited with fueling the rise of the West and the Industrial Revolution. It has become a component of European diets and has found its way into Asian diets as well because of its versatility and adaptability for many different cuisines. Production and consumption of potatoes have increased rapidly in developing countries in recent decades. Simultaneously, the potato has come under criticism both for its high carbohydrate content, contributing to declining health in developed countries where it is often fried in cooking oils, and for its role in globalization,

Figure 47. Native potato harvest in Chopcca, Huancavelica, Peru. Farmer selecting tuber seed from his mixed landrace stock. Photograph by Stef de Haan, International Potato Center.

industrial agriculture, and loss of biodiversity in some countries. In its Andean birthplace, however, on-farm or in situ conservation is an ongoing process driven by farmers to preserve the genetic diversity, agrobiodiversity, and heritage of the native potato (figure 47). To feed rapidly growing populations and address global climate change, the humble potato may be the best hope for securing the world's food future for billions of people.

See also COLUMBIAN EXCHANGE; DNA ANALYSIS; FOOD PRESERVATION; FOOD STORAGE; PLANT PROCESSING; RESIDUE ANALYSIS, STARCH; ROOT CROPS/TUBERS

Further Reading

De Haan, Stef. 2009. Potato Diversity at Height: Multiple Dimensions of Farmer-Driven *In-Situ* Conservation in the Andes. Ph.D. thesis, Wageningen University, Netherlands. Reprinted by the International Potato Center (CIP), Peru.

Pearsall, Deborah. 2008. Plant Domestication and the Shift to Agriculture in the Andes. In *Handbook of South American Archaeology*, edited by Helaine Silverman and William H. Isbell, 105–20. New York: Springer.

Ríos, Domingo, Marc Ghislain, Flor Rodriguez, and David M. Spooner. 2007. What Is the Origin of the European Potato? Evidence from Canary Island Landraces. *Crop Science* 47(3):1271–80.

Salaman, Redcliffe N., with W. G. Burton. 1985. *The History and Social Influence of the Potato*. Revised and updated by J. G. Hawkes. Cambridge: Cambridge University Press.

Ugent, Donald, Tom Dillehay, and Carlos Ramirez. 1987. Potato Remains from a Late Pleistocene Settlement in Southcentral Chile. *Economic Botany* 41(1):17–27.

Ugent, Donald, Sheila Pozoroski, and Thomas Pozoroski. 1982. Archaeological Potato Tuber Remains from the Casma Valley of Peru. *Economic Botany* 36(2):182–92.

Zhang, Linhai, Charles R. Brown, David Culley, et al. 2010. Inferred Origin of Several Native American Potatoes from the Pacific Northwest and Southeast Alaska Using SSR Markers. *Euphytica* 174(1):15–29.

■ LINHAI ZHANG AND FLOR RODRÍGUEZ

POTTERY

See COOKING VESSELS, CERAMIC; MATERIAL CULTURE ANALYSIS; USE-WEAR OR USE-ALTERATION ANALYSIS, POTTERY

POWER

See FOOD AND POWER

PREFERENCES, AVOIDANCES, PROHIBITIONS, TABOOS

Every ancient society had foods they preferred and foods they avoided. Preferred foods typically consisted of foodstuffs that were eaten on a daily basis and those eaten on special occasions. The preferences of certain foods for ordinary meals and those for extraordinary meals differed. For instance, meat was a preferred food but was seldom prepared for ordinary meals since most ancient societies were dependent upon their herds for their secondary products, such as milk, wool, and dung for fuel. Meat might be eaten for several reasons: because of a successful hunt; as part of a hospitality norm such as a celebratory, cultic, or agricultural feast; if an animal was sick, injured, or dying; or the family needed ready cash. Foods that were preferred for everyday meals varied according to the society's geographical and topographical location but typically were dependent upon cereals, maize, or rice. Some foods and meals were viewed as sacred, and their consumption was set apart in certain locations and conducted at certain times. For example, sacrifices were often viewed as a way to share a meal with the divine, with the altar serving as the table and the sacrifice (usually of meat) as the meal. Sharing a meal with the divine was one way of giving thanks, atoning for sins, appeasing the deities, and maintaining a sense of spiritual balance.

Food avoidances and taboos also differ as a result of a society's geographical and topographical location, but also their cultic and social regulations. A society's worldview on food pollutions often became part of their cultic regulations, even if that taboo was already part of their community code for practical reasons. The circumstances of how the avoidance of certain foods developed into an official, culturally, or religiously acceptable prohibition of those same foods can usually be tied to physical or social protection. Societies value social and moral standards, and by connecting specific foods to danger or to group acceptance, the organized society may persuade and pressure its members into conformity. Certain foods are permanently forbidden (e.g., Hindus view the cow as sacred and therefore do not eat it), while others are only prohibited for specific physical reasons (e.g., pregnancy or lactation), during religious periods (e.g., Lent), or for particular classes of people (e.g., priests).

A society's rules and categories of the natural world often mirror that society's dominant anxieties, such as chaos/order and sexual norms. Claude Lévi-Strauss described cooking as a cultural transformation that differentiates where nature ends and culture begins. Mary Douglas argued that the many food taboos from ancient Israel, as listed in the book of Leviticus (Lev. 11), reflect social and religious beliefs, and that forbidden foods were seen as ambiguous and therefore threatening. Avoidance of these threatening foods reduced chaos and disorder by placing them into the sacred category. Islam has similar laws separating foods into ones that are permitted and others that are prohibited.

Prohibitions against certain foods may develop from more practical considerations. Marvin Harris states that food prohibitions can be explained by nutritional, ecological, or financial choices. Harris argues there were basic ecological reasons for the food prohibition against pork in ancient Israel, Egypt, Babylon, and Phoenicia: pigs are not ruminants and are unable to thrive on grass and other high-cellulose plants commonly found in the Levant; and pigs do not adapt well to the climate and ecology of the Middle East. He concludes that the food prohibitions in Leviticus were mostly preexisting traditional food prejudices that were systematized.

Given the perishable nature of food remains and the blending or immersion of raw ingredients into a meal, most of the evidence regarding a society's food preferences or prejudices is found in textual references. Archaeologically, one might document the presence or absence of zoological and botanical remains on a given archaeological excavation. The analysis of plant and animal remains and their spatial relationship to buildings (e.g., a home, a temple), installations (e.g., cooking ovens or grinding stones), and other artifacts (e.g., cooking pots, altars or shrines) is key to inferring the context of their use and consumption and possible preferences. Food prohibitions are most difficult to observe archaeologically. Prescriptive and proscriptive rules have different effects and leave behind different traces, if any, within the material record. The absence of zoological and botanical remains may provide evidence for a culture's food prohibition, but it must be shown that this behavior was intentional. Questions to be asked regarding the archaeological evidence for food taboos include: When is the absence of food a conspicuous absence? When is the absence of food an unexpected absence? When does the absence of food indicate a culture's conscious ideological practices? Severin M. Fowles's "criteria of conspicuousness" may be a way to help determine the presence of food taboos in the archaeological record: Is the disappearance of an ingredient or practice gradual or rapid? When analyzed spatially, are there sudden gaps or holes in the distribution?

It must also be kept in mind that textual resources are often written from limited or ideological perspectives. For instance, the Greek historian Herodotus wrote that pork was prohibited in ancient Egypt; yet the abundance of pig bones from archaeological contexts indicates that pork was consumed as a cheap, low-status food. The lack of pig bones in elite tombs also suggests that if there was a prohibition against pork, it was limited to the upper priestly class. Ancient Near Eastern sites with evidence of pig bones include the Neolithic site of Çatalhöyük in Turkey and the Iron Age Philistine sites of Ashkelon and Ekron. These excavations suggest that the prohibition against pork was not as common as previously thought.

See also ÇATALHÖYÜK; CONSUMPTION; FOOD AND IDENTITY; FOOD AND RITUAL; FOODWAYS AND RELIGIOUS PRACTICES; MEAT; PHILISTINE FOODWAYS; PIG

Further Reading

Douglas, Mary. 1966. *Purity and Danger: The Analysis of Concepts of Pollution and Taboo.* London: Routledge.

———. 1972. Deciphering a Meal. *Daedalus* 101:61–81.

Fowles, Severin M. 2008. Steps toward an Archaeology of Taboo. In *Religion, Archaeology, and the Material World*, edited by Lars Fogelin, 15–37. Center for Archaeological Investigations, Occasional Paper 36. Carbondale: Southern Illinois University.

Harris, Marvin. 1986. *Good to Eat: Riddles of Food and Culture.* London: Allen and Unwin.

Hesse, Brian. 1990. Pig Lovers and Pig Haters: Patterns of Palestinian Pork Production. *Journal of Ethnobiology* 10(2):195–225.

Ikram, Salima. 1995. *Choice Cuts: Meat Production in Ancient Egypt.* Orientalia Lovaniensia Analecta 69. Leuven: Peeters.

■ CYNTHIA SHAFER-ELLIOTT

PRESERVATION
See FOOD PRESERVATION

PRE-SILK ROAD AGRICULTURAL EXCHANGE (CENTRAL ASIA)

Recent discoveries of ancient grains and legumes at third- and second-millennia BC archaeological sites from across central Asia, from Kazakhstan (in the north) to Turkmenistan (south), are allowing researchers to map the spread of agriculture. While mobile pastoralism has clearly been a significant aspect of economic life in central Asia for millennia, new data now show that agriculture was important in the past as well (figure 48). Irrigation technology, glume wheats, and barley spread into southern central Asia from the Iranian Plateau by 6000 cal BC. The northern spread of this technology did not occur for another three millennia, however, during which time the long-distance exchange of goods is evident in the archaeological record. During the third and second millennia BC, pastoralists facilitated the spread of a variety of goods and ideas through the mountain valleys of central Asia; these valleys provided an arable corridor of land linking east and southwest Asia. The later intensification of this exchange corridor is colloquially referred to as the Silk Road.

The earliest remains of domesticated grains from northern central Asia come from the sites of Tasbas (Phase 1: 2800–2300 cal BC) and Begash (2450–2100 cal BC), both

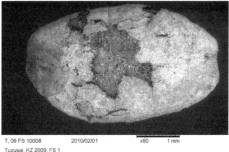

T, 09 FS 10008   2010/02/01   x60   1 mm
Tuzusai, KZ 2009, FS 1

Figure 48. Left: A modern Kazakh herder's yurt near the town of Taldy Kurgan in 2008. Archaeobotanical analyses of material from five millennia ago link agricultural activities to herders in this same region of eastern Kazakhstan. Bronze Age herders were responsible for spreading crops and technology across Eurasia. Right: Barley grain from Tuzusai, Kazakhstan, ca. 410–150 BC, photographed using scanning electron microscopy. Discoveries of ancient grains and legumes at archaeological sites from across central Asia, from Kazakhstan (in the north) to Turkmenistan (south), are allowing researchers to map the spread of agriculture in this region. Photographs by Robert N. Spengler.

in Kazakhstan. Broomcorn millet grains at the pastoral seasonal camp of Begash provide a central point in the spread of this crop out of China and into southwest Asia; likewise, free-threshing wheat at both sites illustrates the reverse spread of southwest Asian crops into China. By Phase 2a at Tasbas (1450–1250 cal BC), a distinct package of crops had spread throughout central Asia, including a highly compact form of free-threshing wheat, naked six-rowed barley, broomcorn millet, and peas. The introduction of new crops continued through the Iron Age. At the site of Tuzusai (410–150 cal BC), also in Kazakhstan, we see the adoption of foxtail millet, new varieties of wheat, and grapes. Mobile pastoralists in the mid-third millennium BC brought agricultural knowledge into the same mountain valleys that would later support the historic Silk Road; by the second millennium BC they directly influenced the globalization of foodways by intermingling crops of east and southwest Asian origin and spreading them across Eurasia.

See also Animal Husbandry and Herding; Barley; Food Technology and Ideas about Food, Spread of; Legumes and Pulses; Millets; Old World Globalization and Food Exchanges; Wheat

Further Reading

Spengler, Robert, Michael Frachetti, Paula Doumani, et al. 2014. Early Agriculture and Crop Transmission among Bronze Age Mobile Pastoralists of Central Eurasia. *Proceedings of the Royal Society B* 281(1783):20133382. doi:10.1098/rspb.2013.3382.

Spengler, Robert N., III, and George Willcox. 2013. Archaeobotanical Results from Sarazm, Tajikistan, an Early Bronze Age Village on the Edge: Agriculture and Exchange. *Journal of Environmental Archaeology* 18(3):211–21.

■ ROBERT N. SPENGLER

PRIVIES

See LATRINES AND SEWER SYSTEMS

PROHIBITIONS

See PREFERENCES, AVOIDANCES, PROHIBITIONS, TABOOS

PROJECTILE POINTS

See WEAPONS, BONE/ANTLER/IVORY; WEAPONS, METAL; WEAPONS, STONE

PROTEINS

See BIOMOLECULAR ANALYSIS

PSYCHOACTIVE PLANTS

Psychoactive plants feature in many traditional cultures, but their prehistoric use is poorly understood, largely because of poor preservation. Much evidence comes from the Americas because of uneven species distribution. Peyote (*Lophophora williamsii*), which contains mescaline and is similar in effect to LSD, is known primarily from botanical remains found in ritual caves. Sites from Texas yield peyote dating between 3700 and 3000 BC. The deliriant Jimsonweed (*Datura stramonium*) is found throughout North America and contains scopolamine. Southwestern vessels with spiked exteriors that are evocative of the plant indicate prehistoric use. Jimsonweed evidence is typically botanical and associated with ritual structures, but Jimsonweed seeds also have been identified among prehistoric farmers in the Southwest and Midwest. Tobacco (*Nicotiana rustica*) is the most prevalent psychoactive in the Americas. Much of the earliest evidence for tobacco is from smoking pipes, most often recovered from burials. South America contains numerous psychoactive plants, notably San Pedro cactus (*Trichocereus pachanoi*) and Yopo (*Anadenanthera peregrina*). San Pedro cactus contains mescaline and is native to the north Andean highlands. Botanical evidence is rare in comparison to iconographic representations. Such evidence indicates use of San Pedro cactus as early as 1200 BC. Yopo is a South American perennial containing bufotenin and dimethyltryptamine. Evidence is based on ethnography and material culture. Probable Yopo snuff tubes have been recovered from tombs in San Pedro de Atacama dating to as early as AD 320. Opium poppy (*Papaver somniferum*) is the most notable Old World psychoactive. The earliest known seeds are from southern Europe, 5700 BC. Poppies feature in Egyptian iconography, and seeds have been found in 18th Dynasty pottery (1540–1307 BC). While trade in opium in the Old World is assumed, data are limited to iconography, historical references, and vessel morphology. Marijuana (*Cannabis sativa*), the preeminent psychoactive plant of Asia, is often found in botanical deposits in burials. There is early documented use of cannabis from Bactria, in central Asia, by 2200 BC.

See also ARCHAEOBOTANY; COCA; FOOD AND RITUAL; MATERIAL CULTURE ANALYSIS; OFFERINGS AND GRAVE GOODS; PLANTS; QUIDS; TOBACCO

Further Reading

Furst, Peter T., ed. 1990. *Flesh of the Gods: The Ritual Use of Hallucinogens.* Prospect Heights, IL: Waveland Press.

Rudgely, Richard. 1993. *The Alchemy of Culture: Intoxicants in Society.* London: British Museum Press.

Schulters, Richard Evans, Albert Hofmann, and Christian Ratsch. 1998. *Plants of the Gods: Their Sacred, Healing and Hallucinogenic Powers.* Rochester, VT: Healing Arts Press.

■ SEAN M. RAFFERTY

PULQUE

Pulque, originally called *ochtli* by the Aztecs, was one of the most important beverages in ancient Mesoamerica. It is produced by the fermentation of *aguamiel*, the sap extracted from the maguey plant. Every few years, a flower sprouts in the plant. This is cut and the "heart" of the plant is scraped; the *aguamiel* is then suctioned twice a day using a long gourd and is left to ferment several hours. *Pulque* can be consumed in a pure form ("white") or "cured" with different flavors.

The brewing and consumption of *pulque* dates to at least the Classic Period (first centuries AD). Some evidence for its consumption in pre-Hispanic times comes from codices and mural paintings, and evidence from the contact period is abundant. The chemical markers of *pulque* have been identified in some ceramic wares from Teotihuacán, confirming their interpretation as vessels for *pulque* consumption. Conversely, the chemical analysis of some Aztec *copas pulqueras* (*pulque* cups), with spot tests to identify the presence of phosphates, fatty acids, protein residues, and carbohydrates, suggests some more likely contained fatty liquids (possibly blood) rather than *pulque*, which is rich in carbohydrates and not in fats.

In Mesoamerica *pulque* was often associated with mother's milk because of its whitish color and was consumed mostly in ritual ceremonies where it was offered to the gods. There were many Aztec *pulque* deities, known collectively as the "400 rabbits," because, following Sahagún, there were "many different ways of getting drunk." When the gods gave *pulque* to humans, they warned them never to drink more than four cups. Written sources from the contact period indicate, however, that there were laws intended to discourage drunkenness and only the elderly were allowed to drink *pulque* without restriction. In general *pulque* was consumed only on special occasions, like religious festivals, baptisms, and weddings. Young commoners found drunk were beaten in public as an example to others. Public drunkenness could lead to the confiscation of personal goods or even to public execution. The consumption of *pulque* in Mexico as a secular beverage was common in the Colonial era and after independence. It is still consumed today, but this traditional drink is at risk of disappearing, despite its valuable nutritional qualities.

See also Agave Distillation; Biomolecular Analysis; Distillation; Distilled Spirits; Ethnoarchaeology; Experimental Archaeology; Food and Ritual; Plant Processing

Further Reading

Barba, Luis, Agustin Ortiz, and Alessandra Pecci. 2014. Los residuos químicos: Indicadores arqueológicos para entender la producción, preparación, consumo y almacenamiento de alimentos en Meso-américa. *Anales de Antropologia* 48(1):201–39.

Casillas, Leticia E., and Luis Alberto Vargas. 1984. La alimentación entre los Mexicas. In *Historia general de la medicina en México*, vol. 1, *Mexico Antiguo*, edited by Fernando Martínez Cortés, 133–56. Mexico City: Facultad de Medicina y Academia Nacional de Medicina, Universidad Nacional Autónoma de México.

Correa-Ascencio, Marisol, Ian G. Robertson, Oralia Cabrera-Cortés, et al. 2014. Pulque Production from Fermented Agave Sap as a Dietary Supplement in Prehispanic Mesoamerica. *Proceedings of the National Academy of Sciences USA* 111(39):14223–28.

Godoy, Augusto, Teófilo Herrera, and Miguel Ulloa. 2003. *Más allá del pulque y el tepache: Las bebidas alcoholicas no destiladas indígenas de México.* Mexico City: Instituto de Investigaciones Antropológicas, Universidad Nacional Autónoma de México.

Parsons, Jeffrey R., and Mary H. Parsons. 1990. *Maguey Utilization in Highland Central Mexico: An Ethnoarchaeological Ethnography.* Museum of Anthropology, Anthropological Papers 82. Ann Arbor: University of Michigan.

■ ALESSANDRA PECCI

PULSES

See LEGUMES AND PULSES

Q

QUERNS
See Tools/Utensils, Ground Stone

QUIDS
Chewing but not swallowing plant products is an ancient technique and is widely practiced throughout the world. The most well-known plants that were chewed are tobacco leaves, betel leaves/areca nut, and coca leaves, but yucca leaves were chewed in the American Southwest, and chewing gum is quite similar to what is more commonly thought of as quid chewing. In each situation, the goal is to chew the plant parts to extract chemicals or juices and not to swallow the parts. A quid is the remaining masticated plant material.

Chewing is an ancient method in the Americas for consuming tobacco, and the tobacco was often combined with lime. The quid chewing method of tobacco consumption spread to the rest of the world with tobacco. Coca leaves were chewed prehistorically in South America where they were also combined with lime. Chewing the mixture of areca nut and betel leaf has a long tradition in much of South and Southeast Asia, and there too lime is often added.

Less well known are prehistoric quids from the American Southwest and parts of the Great Basin (USA) and Mesoamerica (figure 49). Here yucca, juniper, and other plant leaves were shredded and then chewed or sucked. There is the possibility that lime was also added in some cases. There does not seem to be any ethnographic continuity to the present for this type of quid chewing, and there is little consensus on why these plants were chewed. They are found in dry caves, and some have clear, deep tooth impressions in them. In some instances, several hundred have been found in a single cave, so it must have been a common practice. It has been possible to extract human DNA from ancient (yucca) quids, so they represent an important investigative resource. (Modern betel quids also yield DNA.)

Chewing various "gums" or sap or other tree parts was also widely practiced in prehistory, from Finland to Greece to Mesoamerica. Our modern chewing gum derives from the practice of chewing tree sap, which was converted to chewing chicle, the tropical plant chewed prehistorically in Mesoamerica.

In all these cases, quid chewing was medicinal; provided pain relief; served as a mild narcotic; or was chewed for recreational purposes, as a stimulant, or for other nonnutritional purposes.

See also Coca; DNA Analysis; Psychoactive Plants; Tobacco

Figure 49. Quids, or plant materials that have been chewed but not swallowed, are common finds in the archaeological record. Quid chewing is an ancient practice. The examples here, from the American Southwest, are of yucca leaves and date to ~1,000–2,000 BP. Tobacco leaves, betel leaves/areca nut, agave, corn stalks, and coca leaves were also chewed. Quids are a source of mtDNA evidence that may be used to trace population movements (LeBlanc et al. 2007). Photograph by Steven A. LeBlanc.

Further Reading

LeBlanc, Steven A., Lori S. Cobb Kreisman, Brian M. Kemp, et al. 2007. Quids and Aprons: Ancient DNA from Artifacts from the American Southwest. *Journal of Field Archaeology* 32(2):161–75.

Plowman, Timothy. 1984. The Origin, Evolution and Diffusion of Coca, *Erythroxylum* spp., in South and Central America. In *Pre-Columbian Plant Migration*, edited by Doris Stone, 125–64. Papers of the Peabody Museum of Archaeology and Ethnology 76. Cambridge, MA: Peabody Museum Press.

Winter, Joseph C. 2000. *Tobacco Use by Native North Americans: Sacred Smoke and Silent Killer.* Norman: University of Oklahoma Press.

■ STEVEN A. LEBLANC

QUSEIR AL-QADIM (EGYPT)

The food remains discovered at the ancient port of Quseir al-Qadim have revealed important new information about the ancient spice trade and about the food practices of those engaged in this trade. The site acted as a transshipment port in the Indian Ocean spice trade during both the Roman and medieval Islamic periods. It is located on the Red Sea coast of Egypt and was active between ca. AD 1–250 (Myos Hormos) and again during ca. AD 1050–1500 (Kusayr).

Excavations revealed a spectacular array of foodstuffs: some 20 faunal species and 85 food plants (mostly preserved through desiccation), including several never previously found (cardamom, ginger, banana, taro). Marked differences between the two chronological periods are in evidence, including a significant temporal increase in the range of foodstuffs coming from India and beyond. Black pepper was the key spice in Roman trade, but by the Islamic period this had been augmented by cardamom, ginger, turmeric, and betel nut (figure

50). Additionally, by the latter period sugarcane, aubergine, banana, lime, taro, and rice had become part of the diet. These are so-called introduced crops, that is, they originated from South/Southeast Asia but became incorporated into local agriculture in Egypt and other parts of the Middle East, unlike the spices, which always remained imported trade items.

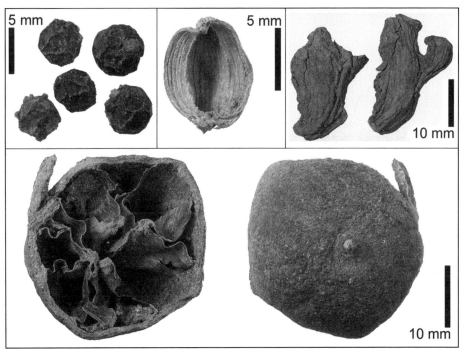

Figure 50. Plant remains preserved through desiccation at Quseir al-Qadim, an important Roman and medieval port of trade on the Red Sea coast, Egypt. Top row, left to right: black pepper (*Piper nigrum*, Roman); cardamom (*Elettaria cardamomum*, medieval); ginger (*Zingiber officinalis*, medieval). Bottom row: lime (*Citrus* cf. x *aurantifolia*, medieval). Photographs by Jacob Morales. After Van der Veen 2011, figs. 2.3, 2.10, 2.12, and 3.6.

The food remains clearly highlight changes in the nature and scale of the Indian Ocean trade between the Roman and medieval Islamic periods, as well as a major shift in the way the inhabitants of the ports saw themselves and located themselves in the wider world. For example, during the Roman period the diet of the inhabitants of the port reflected strong ties with the Mediterranean region, while during the medieval period the focus shifted east.

See also FOOD AS A COMMODITY; FOOD TECHNOLOGY AND IDEAS ABOUT FOOD, SPREAD OF; FRUITS; INNOVATION AND RISK; MARKETS/EXCHANGE; OLD WORLD GLOBALIZATION AND FOOD EXCHANGES; RICE; SPICES; SUCROSE; TARO; TRADE ROUTES

Further Reading

Hamilton-Dyer, S. 2011. Faunal Remains. In *Myos Hormos—Quseir al-Qadim: Roman and Islamic Ports on the Red Sea*, vol. 2, *Finds from the Excavations 1999–2003*, edited by David Peacock and Lucy Blue, 245–88. Oxford: Archaeopress.

Van der Veen, Marijke. 2011. *Consumption, Trade and Innovation: Exploring the Botanical Remains from the Roman and Islamic Ports at Quseir al-Qadim, Egypt*. Journal of African Archaeology Monograph 6. Frankfurt: Africa Magna Verlag.

■ MARIJKE VAN DER VEEN

R

RADIOCARBON DATING

Radiocarbon dating is the most widely used absolute dating technique in archaeology. It can be applied to a variety of organic materials and is effective over approximately the last 50,000 years. The technique has been instrumental in understanding the archaeology of food, from tracing the domestication of plant and animal species to pinpointing innovations in food processing technology.

Radiocarbon (^{14}C) is one of three naturally occurring forms of carbon, called isotopes. Unlike the two stable isotopes (^{12}C and ^{13}C), it is comparatively short-lived: it is continually created in the upper atmosphere and continually lost through nuclear decay. Radiocarbon is taken up by plants during photosynthesis and then transmitted throughout the food chain. When a plant or animal dies, however, its uptake of radiocarbon ceases, and the $^{14}C/^{12}C$ ratio of the tissue decreases exponentially through nuclear decay. The dating process involves determining the $^{14}C/^{12}C$ ratio of the sample and then comparing it with a reference set of measurements for past years, built up mainly from measurements on known-age tree rings.

In most cases, tissue grown within one year is best for radiocarbon dating, as this ensures the date relates to a precise point in time. It is also important that the sample comes from a defined archaeological context. Food remains often meet both criteria. Stores of grain, fruits, and even the residues of food on ceramics are all materials that have produced excellent results. In fact, demonstrating that a substance was consumed as food can increase its suitability for dating. Shells from middens, for example, are inherently more accurate than shell ornaments, because the latter could have been fashioned a long time after the shellfish died.

As knowledge of the origins and culture of food is furthered, it is likely that radiocarbon dating will continue to provide the chronological framework within which new developments are understood.

See also ANIMAL DOMESTICATION; BIOMOLECULAR ANALYSIS; COOKING VESSELS, CERAMIC; FOOD TECHNOLOGY AND IDEAS ABOUT FOOD, SPREAD OF; PLANT DOMESTICATION; SHELL MIDDENS

Further Reading

Ramsey, C. Bronk. 2008. Radiocarbon Dating: Revolutions in Understanding. *Archaeometry* 50(2): 249–75.

Stott, A. W., R. Berstan, P. Evershed, et al. 2001. Radiocarbon Dating of Single Compounds Isolated from Pottery Cooking Vessel Residues. *Radiocarbon* 43(2A):191–97.

■ MICHAEL W. DEE

RECIPES

A recipe is a set of instructions, including a list of ingredients, for preparing, cooking, or preserving food. It was known in the 19th century as a receipt. The etymological differences between the two are significant. A recipe frequently indicated a formula, especially one for medicine, and was found in pharmaceutical and medical texts. The word *recipe* was derived from the Latin imperative *recipere*, which meant "take." A modern remnant—Rx—is found on doctor's prescriptions. *Receipt* is also derived from Latin but carries with it the notion of written proof of purchase, affirmation of money received, or, in the case of food, directions and ingredients. The use of *receipt* predates that of *recipe*; the words are of 17th- and 18th-century origin. Today *receipt* is the archaic English form. Recipes, however, are universally used, and given different names among different cultures. Thus it is more appropriate to ask what a recipe does.

Synonyms express the broader sense of the term: formulas, methods, directions, ingredients, instructions, procedures, and techniques. When humans began preparing food, one learned by experience. Verbal instructions and transfer of knowledge probably took place within small groups: grandmother to daughter or granddaughter; or individuals of older age teaching younger ones within the community (i.e., from one age set to another). High mortality rates and short individual lives until the late modern era suggest knowledge loss was inevitable. In such situations, one would not expect much standardization in the subtle nuances of food preparation.

The first known recipes are from Mesopotamia ca. 1800 BC and show that elites were preoccupied with fine cuisine. A song honoring a Sumerian goddess describes making beer. Dough, including sweet aromatics, mixed in a pit, produces beer-bread, which is oven baked; malt is soaked in jars, mash spread to cool on reed mats; finally, the goddess holds the beverage until it rushes out of its vat. Jean Bottéro recently translated three Akkadian tablets from 1700 BC that include partial recipes for meat-based and vegetable-based stews, meat pies, sauces, and grain side dishes. The recipes summarize essential ingredients and steps, are missing quantities and cooking times, and presume considerable knowledge on the part of the cook. The same might be said for many 19th- and early-20th-century instructions. Archaeologists have looked to recipes for insights into past material culture and foodways; more recent efforts seek to correlate food remains (e.g., faunal evidence, butchery marks) with food preparation techniques described in period recipes.

See also BUTCHERY; COOKBOOKS; DOCUMENTARY ANALYSIS; FOOD PRODUCTION AND THE ORIGINS OF WRITING IN MESOPOTAMIA; MATERIAL CULTURE ANALYSIS; ZOOARCHAEOLOGY

Further Reading

Bottéro, Jean. 1995. *Textes Culinaires Mésopotamiens/Mesopotamian Culinary Texts*. Winona Lake, IN: Eisenbrauns.

Carroll, Ruth. 2010. The Visual Language of the Recipe: A Brief Historical Survey. In *Food and Language: Proceedings of the Oxford Symposium on Food and Cooking, 2009*, edited by Richard Hosking, 62–72. Totnes, UK: Prospect Books.

Goody, Jack. 1977. The Recipe, the Prescription, and the Experiment. In *The Domestication of the Savage Mind*, 129–45. Cambridge: Cambridge University Press.

■ ANNE E. YENTSCH

RELIGIOUS PRACTICES

See FOODWAYS AND RELIGIOUS PRACTICES

REPRESENTATIONAL MODELS OF FOOD AND FOOD PRODUCTION

Many ancient cultures made models of food and food production, but it is the models from ancient Egypt that are the most extensive and varied. By the Pyramid Age (Old Kingdom, ca. 2649–2100 BC) and particularly at Giza and Saqqara, models of foods including various breads, fowl, and meat were placed in burial chambers to magically supply the deceased with food in eternity. Often these were accompanied by a variety of plates, drinking vessels, and even miniature tables. At the same time, relatives of the dead person were depicted in small-scale statuary in activities associated with food production, such as grinding grain, baking bread, and butchering meat. All of the models were made of stone.

The Egyptian Middle Kingdom (ca. 2040–1640 BC) was a high point for models of food production, which were most often made of local woods. Some of the finest come from the tomb of Meketre at Thebes and include models of granaries, baking and brewing, and the force-feeding and subsequent slaughter of animals (figure 51). No individual had more such models than the Provincial Governor Djehutynakht from Bersha, who had nine models depicting the force-feeding of cattle, eight granaries, and three scenes combining the making of bread and brewing of beer. Food models of the Middle Kingdom tombs were greater in variety and finer in detail than those of the Old Kingdom. These were most often made of wood or cartonnage (linen stiffened with plaster covering a core of mud or clay). Taken together, these presented an idealized view of life on wealthy estates and the hope for continuity in the afterlife.

Actual foods were more likely to replace models in tombs of the New Kingdom (ca. 1550–1070 BC) and later, but vessels might be fancifully formed in the shape of foods such as vegetables, fowl, and fruit. For example, the tomb of Tutankhamen included a small silver vessel in the shape of a pomegranate, a treasured import from Syria.

Tombs in Beotia, Greece, from the sixth century BC also occasionally include terracotta models showing food and drink production, and food models are occasionally found in Chinese tombs of the Han Dynasty (206 BC–AD 220) but become more popular by the Ming Dynasty (AD 1348–1644).

Figure 51. Model bakery and brewery from the tomb of Meketre, Middle Kingdom, 12th Dynasty, reign of Amenemhat I, ca. 1981–1975 BC. Meketre was royal chief steward for several kings during the 11th and 12th Dynasties. Bakery processes depicted here include crushing and grinding the grain, working the dough, and baking. In the adjacent brewery, dough is mixed with water; workers tread the mash, then set it into jars to ferment. From the necropolis at Thebes in Upper Egypt. Medium: Wood, gesso, paint, linen. Courtesy of Rogers Fund and Edward S. Harkness Gift, 1920. © The Metropolitan Museum of Art. Image source: Art Resource, NY.

See also CARVINGS/CARVED REPRESENTATIONS OF FOOD; FOOD AND RITUAL; FOOD AND STATUS; FOODWAYS AND RELIGIOUS PRACTICES; OFFERINGS AND GRAVE GOODS

Further Reading

Darby, William J., Paul Ghalioungui, and Louis Grivetti. 1977. *Food: The Gift of Osiris.* London: Academic Press.

Winlock, H. E. 1955. *Models of Daily Life in Ancient Egypt.* Published for the Metropolitan Museum of Art. Cambridge, MA: Harvard University Press.

■ RITA E. FREED

RESIDUE ANALYSIS, BLOOD

In archaeological science, blood residues are the dry remnants of blood left on the surface of lithic, ceramic, bone, or metal objects or are intermixed with other materials used as a binding agent of rock art paintings. Blood residues preserve best under dry and desiccated circumstances, frozen, in clay-rich soils, and in cave and rockshelter sites. The most frequently found blood residues are red blood cells (erythrocytes), which contain hemoglobin, an iron-containing protein. The blood cells of mammalian vertebrates also have platelets but no nucleus, while nonmammalian vertebrates contain a nucleus. Even so, it has been debated whether species identification through very small amounts of blood residues is feasible.

The challenge for residue specialists consists in the microscopic differentiation and identification of blood residue, especially if there are only minute remnants of residue present. Biochemical reaction methods such as the Hemastix test help in the identification of blood residue, although supplementary techniques are sometimes needed as other residues can cause false positives. Direct radiocarbon dating of stone tools by accelerator mass spectrometry (AMS) has been carried out successfully on artifacts that contained sufficient blood residues.

Blood residues help archaeologists to understand the use and function of an artifact. On lithic artifacts blood residues are generally related to hunting, butchering, and meat-processing activities. Residues have been found preserved on 90,000-year-old stone tools from Tabun Cave, Israel, and there are suggestions for blood residue conservation on 2-million-year-old lithics from the Sterkfontein Caves in South Africa. Blood residues found inside surfaces of four ceramic vessels from the Maya site of Copán, Honduras, support inferences that the vessel type was used for ritual purposes.

See also BIOMOLECULAR ANALYSIS; BUTCHERY; COOKING VESSELS, CERAMIC; HUNTER-GATHERER SUBSISTENCE; RADIOCARBON DATING; ROCK ART; TOOLS/UTENSILS, METAL; TOOLS/UTENSILS, STONE; WEAPONS, METAL; WEAPONS, STONE

Further Reading

Haslam, Michael, Gail Robertson, Alison Crowther-Smith, et al., eds. 2009. *Archaeological Science under a Microscope: Studies in Residue and Ancient DNA Analysis in Honour of Thomas H. Loy*. Canberra: Australian National University E Press.

Loy, T. H. 1990. Prehistoric Organic Residues: Recent Advances in Identification, Dating, and Their Antiquity. In *Archaeometry '90*, edited by Ernst Pernicka and Günther A. Wagner, 645–56. Basel: Birkhäuser Verlag.

Loy, T. H., and B. L. Hardy. 1992. Blood Residue Analysis of 90,000-Year-Old Stone Tools from Tabun Cave, Israel. *Antiquity* 66(250):24–35.

■ ANDREA BETTINA YATES

RESIDUE ANALYSIS, DAIRY PRODUCTS

Dairy products contain distinctive fats and proteins that are amenable to organic residue analysis using a range of techniques. Arrays of triacylglycerides (lipids) can be extracted from archaeological pottery and identified using gas or liquid chromatography combined with mass spectrometry. This approach has been used to tentatively distinguish goat, ewe, and cow milk associated with Middle/Late Neolithic pottery from the French Jura. These complex lipids only tend to maintain their original profiles in very well-preserved contexts, however. Carbon isotopic analysis of individual fatty acids by gas chromatography–combustion–isotope ratio mass spectrometry (GC/C/IRMS) is an alternative method that has been much more widely applied, mainly because fatty acids are the most abundant compounds encountered in archaeological food residues. Fatty acids are present in most foodstuffs but vary by their isotopic composition, allowing dairy products to be distinguished from other animal fats. Using this approach, it has been possible to demonstrate the processing of dairy products in Anatolian pottery dating to 9,000 BP, shortly after the arrival of domesticated animals. Dairy products also have been identified in later European prehistoric pottery and in distinctive Neolithic ceramic sieves that have been interpreted as cheese strainers. Proteins from dairy foods offer much greater resolution into the species and even breeds of animal but are much more susceptible to degradation in the burial environment. New approaches using soft-ionization mass spectrometry are being developed to identify these molecules in archaeological contexts.

See also ANIMAL HUSBANDRY AND HERDING; BIOMOLECULAR ANALYSIS; GAS CHROMATOGRAPHY/GAS CHROMATOGRAPHY–MASS SPECTROMETRY; MILK AND DAIRY PRODUCTS; SECONDARY PRODUCTS REVOLUTION; STABLE ISOTOPE ANALYSIS

Further Reading

Regert, Martine. 2011. Analytical Strategies for Discriminating Archeological Fatty Substances from Animal Origin. *Mass Spectrometry Reviews* 30(2):177–220.

■ OLIVER CRAIG

RESIDUE ANALYSIS, LIPIDS

See BIOMOLECULAR ANALYSIS

RESIDUE ANALYSIS, PROTEINS

See BIOMOLECULAR ANALYSIS; RESIDUE ANALYSIS, BLOOD

RESIDUE ANALYSIS, STARCH

Starch granules are the primary means of carbohydrate storage and transport in higher plants. Large numbers of starch granules are formed and stored in roots, rhizomes, corms, tubers, seeds, and fruits. Individual granules (1–100+ micrometers) are composed of two kinds of glucose chains with a regular structure that is responsible for their durability and taxonomically significant morphologies, sometimes permitting identifications of specific plant parts at the genus and species levels.

Archaeological starch research has focused on the humid tropics of the New World and Australasia, where materials traditionally used to reconstruct ancient diets and food practices (e.g., macrobotanical remains and animal bone) tend to decompose rapidly; this technique is applicable worldwide, however. Moreover, studies reveal that starch granules can be preserved for long periods of time. For instance, Thomas Loy and colleagues reported ca. 28,000-year-old taro starch on stone tools from the Solomon Islands, and Amanda Henry and colleagues employed starch and phytolith analyses to explore the vegetal component of Neanderthal diets up to ca. 46,000 years ago. Starch granules have been recovered from surface residues and within microcrevices of stone and ceramic objects, dental calculus, coprolites, and, less frequently, sediments (where exposure to low pH and microbial activity can destroy them rapidly). They provide direct evidence of human behaviors associated with plant foods. Experimental studies reveal that patterns of damage to starch granules can index specific food preparation and processing techniques, such as grinding, various forms of cooking, and even sprouting and brewing. A variety of published protocols outline methods of sampling for starch, as well as how to control for contamination. The basic method for recovering artifact residues involves placing the artifact in an ultrasonic water bath to dislodge starch granules (and phytoliths) embedded in microcrevices, or using a pipette to agitate a few drops of water on a used surface of the artifact. The residues are then concentrated in a centrifuge, mounted on a microscope slide, and identified based on comparison with modern reference specimens.

See also ARCHAEOBOTANY; BIOMOLECULAR ANALYSIS; DENTAL ANALYSIS; EXPERIMENTAL ARCHAEOLOGY; NEANDERTHAL DIET; PALEOFECAL ANALYSIS; PHYTOLITH ANALYSIS; PLANT DOMESTICATION; PLANT PROCESSING; ROOT CROPS/TUBERS; STARCHES, ROLE OF; TOOLS/UTENSILS, GROUND STONE; TOOLS/UTENSILS, STONE; USE-WEAR ANALYSIS, LITHICS; USE-WEAR OR USE-ALTERATION ANALYSIS, POTTERY

Further Reading

Henry, Amanda G. 2015. Formation and Taphonomic Processes Affecting Starch Grains. In *Method and Theory in Paleoethnobotany*, edited by John M. Marston, Jade D'Alpoim Guedes, and Christina Warinner, 35–50. Boulder: University of Colorado Press.

Torrence, Robin, and Huw Barton, eds. 2006. *Ancient Starch Research*. Walnut Creek, CA: Left Coast Press.

■ STEPHANIE R. SIMMS

RESIDUE ANALYSIS, TARTARIC ACID

Tartaric acid is considered a primary biomarker of wine. Since the 1970s, with the development of the chemical analysis of organic residues preserved in archaeological ceramics, the search for wine residues has focused on this acid or its salts. Analysis has focused mainly on amphorae but also on storage jars and other vessels (e.g., jugs, drinking vessels, and cooking pots) from a variety of contexts, including storage rooms and warehouses, shipwrecks, houses, wine-making installations, and burials. Different extraction methods and chemical analysis techniques have been used for the identification of this acid, although the validity of some methods is still disputed.

Some problems have been highlighted regarding the reliability of this biomarker. Tartaric acid is in fact associated not only with wine but also with grape juice, syrup, or wine derivatives. In addition, it is present not only in grapes but also in other fruits (e.g., tamarind, star fruit, and yellow plum). These plants did not play an important role in the production of fermented beverages, especially in the Mediterranean area. It is important, however, to take into account the archaeological context of the findings when interpreting the results of the chemical analyses. Moreover, tartaric acid is soluble in water. Therefore, it is possible that some archaeological materials that were in contact with wine will not preserve the traces of this acid. In the search for chemical residues in ancient materials, it is therefore important to also look for other compounds that are characteristic of wine.

Despite these issues, tartaric acid still plays a key role in the identification of wine and its derivatives in archaeological materials. Its identification has allowed archaeologists to understand the early production of wine in the Near East, the offering of wine in the pharaohs' tombs, the trade of wine in amphorae, and its production in ancient installations.

See also AMPHORAE; ARENI; GAS CHROMATOGRAPHY/GAS CHROMATOGRAPHY–MASS SPECTROMETRY; OFFERINGS AND GRAVE GOODS; TRADE ROUTES; WINE; WINERIES

Further Reading

Barnard, Hans, Alek N. Dooley, Gregory Areshian, et al. 2011. Chemical Evidence for Wine Production around 4000 BCE in the Late Chalcolithic Near Eastern Highlands. *Journal of Archaeological Science* 38(5):977–84.

Pecci, Alessandra, Gianluca Giorgi, Laura Salivini, and Miguel Ángel Cau Ontiveros. 2013. Identifying Wine Markers in Ceramics and Plasters with Gas Chromatography–Mass Spectrometry: Experimental and Archaeological Materials. *Journal of Archaeological Science* 40(1):109–15.

■ ALESSANDRA PECCI

RESIDUE ANALYSIS, THEOBROMINE

Absorbed organic chemical analysis on archaeological ceramics provides information on the identity, origin, and circumstances of the consumption of foodstuffs. Residues absorbed onto porous unglazed ceramics can be preserved in the interior pores of the ceramic vessel. Theobromine is a biomarker for cacao and can be used in the differentiation of caffeinated drinks from plants, such as *Ilex vomitoria*, *Ilex cassine*, or *Theobroma cacao*, by determining the ratio of theobromine to other methylxanthines such as caffeine or theophylline. For example, detection of theobromine ratios with caffeine and theophylline provided evidence of prehispanic use of *Ilex* in ritual black drink activity at Cahokia and surrounding smaller sites in Illinois.

Theobromine is detected using liquid chromatography–mass spectrometry/mass spectrometry (LC-MS/MS). Samples of ceramics approximately one square centimeter in size are prepared for analysis by burring their exterior surfaces using a tungsten-carbide bit, removing any surface contamination before the sample is subsequently ground into a powder. Approximately 500 milligrams of the ground sample is weighed, three milliliters of hot deionized water is added, and the sample is heated at 85°C for 20 minutes. The sample is cooled to room temperature and centrifuged for ten minutes at a speed of at least 1,000 RPM. The supernatant (the sediment-free liquid remaining above the solid) is decanted and reduced at 90°C until 1.5 milliliters remains. This sample is then transferred to an autosampler vial for LC-MS/MS analysis. A Varian 325 LC-MS/MS is used for the analysis. The drying gas temperature is 400°C and the detector voltage is 1,400 volts. LC separations are performed on a Grace 50 x 4.6 millimeter C18 reverse phase column with a mobile phase of 85 percent, 0.1 percent ammonium acetate buffer at pH 4.2 and 15 percent acetonitrile at a flow rate of 200 microliters/minute.

See also BLACK DRINK (CASSINA); CACAO/CHOCOLATE; HIGH PERFORMANCE LIQUID CHROMATOGRAPHY; USE-WEAR OR USE-ALTERATION ANALYSIS, POTTERY

Further Reading

Crown, Patricia L., Thomas E. Emerson, Jiyan Gu, et al. 2012. Ritual Black Drink Consumption at Cahokia. *Proceedings of the National Academy of Sciences USA* 109(35):13944–49.
Evershed, Richard P. 2008. Organic Residue Analysis in Archeology: The Archaeological Biomarker Revolution. *Archaeometry* 50(6):895–924.
Hurst, W. Jeffrey, Stanley M. Tarka Jr., Terry G. Powis, et al. 2002. Archaeology: Cacao Usage by the Earliest Maya Civilization. *Nature* 418(6895):289–90.

■ TIMOTHY J. WARD

RICE

Rice is the world's most important staple crop, feeding nearly half the population and forming one fifth of the world's annual caloric intake. Rice forms the basis of many of the highly elaborated cuisines of East, Southeast, and South Asia and is important in parts of central Asia, Europe, and Africa. In places where it is widespread, rice often plays a major ritual role, as well, and is fed to gods or even deified itself. Indeed, rice is often seen as a critical part of human identity. *Oryza sativa* is one of the earliest domesticated grasses in the world, with a history reaching back as far as wheat or barley. In spite of this, rice has been understudied in archaeology, with most research focused on establishing the time and place of its initial domestication. Among the areas needing further research are the timing, causes, and consequences of the expansion of rice agriculture and its intensification, especially in the form of "wet rice" or paddy rice, the labor- and water-intensive farming of transplanted seedlings into seasonally flooded fields. The use of rice as food, too, which has been addressed by historians and ethnographers, has not been intensively examined by archaeologists even though in many regions rice has significant status associations and its adoption may have had long-term implications for human health, culture, and even climate change.

Domesticated rice consists of two major species, *Oryza glaberrima*, independently domesticated in Africa before 1500 BC and transported to the New World as part of the Atlantic slave trade, and *Oryza sativa*, which has two major variants, *japonica* and *indica*. The recent decipherment of the rice genome has shown that *japonica* and *indica* forms had differentiated even prior to domestication; since then, rice has undergone a complex evolutionary history leading to the staggering diversity of rice today: more than 100,000 known varieties that exhibit a range of qualities from color (white, red, black), to size, shape, stickiness, starch content, and aroma.

Given its varietal diversity, it is not surprising that rice can be grown in a variety of contexts. Nonirrigated or "dry" rice is sometimes also called "hill rice" in recognition of its occurrence in swidden or slash-and-burn farming, often practiced in hilly tropical and semitropical locations. Here grains are broadcast as a part of garden-like intercrops, and the degree of labor expended is modest. In stark contrast, "wet" rice requires intensive water management and a high degree of labor input. Over its long history, this type of cultivation has transformed entire landscapes through irrigation, terracing, and modification of soils. In the semiarid interior of southern India, for example, the desire to grow culturally and ritually valorized rice led to massive investments in irrigation features and led, as elsewhere, to the formation of "paddy soils," with water-resistant hard pans that can be difficult to turn to other kinds of farming. Forms of "floating" or swamp rice suited to flooded environments have even been developed, making rice perhaps the most diverse of all domesticates.

Most archaeological attention to rice has been focused on establishing the time and place of its initial domestication. While this is a complex and still contested topic, most scholars agree that *O. sativa* was initially domesticated between 10,000 and 8,000 years ago in southern China, a process that continued in multiple locations from South to East Asia until around 6,000 years ago. By 2,000 years ago, rice farming was firmly established across much of Asia and rice had, in many places, come to be so highly regarded that words for food and rice were the same.

Rice is not only a highly productive and calorically dense food, but it also stores very well, making it an ideal grain for the sustenance of dense urban populations. Because wet rice receives most of its nutrients from water rather than soil, crops can be grown over and over on the same fields without loss of productivity, making irrigated rice highly sustainable. Flooded fields also may support commensal algae, weeds, fish, and water birds that both provide food and add nutrients to the crop, creating viable mixed farming systems that are nutritionally complete. The expansion of rice agriculture did not always follow a "least-cost" logic, however. In Island Southeast Asia, it replaced more cost-effective sago cultivation. In semiarid parts of south India, its production was clearly a consequence of status associations and cultural desire for rice, a grain, unlike dry-farmed millets, fit for both gods and kings. In many parts of Asia, these status associations continue today.

See also Agricultural Features, Identification and Analysis; Agricultural/Horticultural Sites; DNA Analysis; Food and Identity; Food and Ritual; Food and Status; Foodways and Religious Practices; Irrigation/Hydraulic Engineering; Plant Domestication

Further Reading

Bray, Francesca. 1986. *The Rice Economies: Technology and Development in Asian Societies*. Berkeley: University of California Press.

Carney, Judith A. 2001. *Black Rice: The African Origins of Rice Cultivation in the Americas*. Cambridge, MA: Harvard University Press.

Fuller, Dorian Q. 2012. Pathways to Asian Civilizations: Tracing the Origins and Spread of Rice and Rice Cultures. *Rice* 4(3–4):78–92.

Grist, D. H. 1986. *Rice*. 6th edition. New York: John Wiley & Sons.

Hamilton, Roy W., ed. 2003. *The Art of Rice: Spirit and Sustenance in Asia*. Los Angeles: Fowler Museum of Cultural History at UCLA.

Londo, Jason P., Yu-Chung Chiang, Kuo-Hsiang Hung, et al. 2006. Phylogeography of Asian Wild Rice, *Oryza Rufipogon*, Reveals Multiple Independent Domestications of Cultivated Rice, *Oryza Sativa*. *Proceedings of the National Academy of Sciences USA* 103(25):9578–83.

Morrison, Kathleen D. 2001. Coercion, Resistance, and Hierarchy: Local Processes and Imperial Strategies in the Vijayanagara Empire. In *Empires: Perspectives from Archaeology and History*, edited by Susan E. Alcock, Terence N. D'Altroy, Kathleen D. Morrison, and Carla M. Sinopoli, 252–78. Cambridge: Cambridge University Press.

Zhao, Zhijun. 2011. New Archaeobotanic Data for the Study of the Origins of Agriculture in China. *Current Anthropology* 52(S4):S295–S306.

■ KATHLEEN D. MORRISON

RISK
See INNOVATION AND RISK

RITUAL
See FOOD AND RITUAL

RNA ANALYSIS

RNA molecules, which make up the transcriptome (the complete set of RNA transcripts expressed by an organism), offer a snapshot of the activity of a cell, indicating which genes are being expressed and to what extent at a given time. Some of the most investigated effects of transcriptomic changes concern crops such as maize (*Zea mays* spp. *mays*) that have undergone extensive morphological and nutritional changes over the past 10,000 years as a result of domestication. Transcriptomic research using modern plant material has revealed some of the genes responsible for these agricultural changes. Additionally, the characterization of transcriptomes from archaeological specimens might offer some insight into the process of domestication, although it is unclear whether transcripts appearing in archaeological samples would reflect the true content of transcripts from the living tissue.

There are three main steps for analyzing RNA: extracting RNA from the sample, generating complementary DNA (cDNA) strands, and quantifying the transcripts. Extracting and quantifying RNA from archaeological materials can be challenging since the nucleic acids are often impure and degraded. When extracting RNA from a sample, it is also important to note that gene expression levels are tissue specific. Several methods can be used to extract RNA from samples, including various commercial extraction kits or organic (phenol-chloroform) extraction. Next, the RNA needs to be reverse-transcribed to make cDNA, using reverse-transcription polymerase chain reaction (RT-PCR). Quantitative PCR (qPCR) can then be utilized for the quantification of genes being expressed in the tissue and is generally considered the most sensitive method. Additionally, microarray technology has been used to measure the relative concentration of transcripts, including methods such as serial analysis of gene expression (SAGE). More recently, next-generation sequencing (NGS) technology has been applied for quantifying and characterizing transcriptomes at the nucleotide level, in a method referred to as RNA-Seq or whole transcriptome shotgun sequencing (WTSS). The latter approach has been utilized for the RNA analysis of ancient maize kernels, dated to 723 ± 23 ^{14}C years BP, collected from Turkey House Ruin, Arizona (USA).

See also Biomolecular Analysis; DNA Analysis; Maize; Plant Domestication

Further Reading

Fordyce, Sarah L., Maria C. Avila-Arcos, Morten Rasmussen, et al. 2013. Deep Sequencing of RNA from Ancient Maize Kernels. *PLoS ONE* 8(1):e50961. doi:10.1371/journal.pone.0050961.

■ SARAH L. FORDYCE

ROCK ART

Rock art consists of human-made marks on natural rock. Paintings, drawings, stencils, prints, engravings, bas-relief, and figures made of beeswax are found all over the world in rockshelters and caves, on boulders and platforms. These are special, often spectacular places that reflect ancient experience, identity, history, spirituality, and relationships to land. Rock art also provides us with unique insights into human cultural evolution, settlement patterns, what long-extinct animals looked like, and contact between different cultures. Furthermore, it allows us to see what creatures ancient peoples viewed as both good to eat and good to think about.

Rock art was made from at least 40,000 years ago to as recently as 40 years ago. The oldest surviving figurative art of Europe, Asia, Africa, and Australia consists almost exclusively of animals. Although some dangerous creatures, such as bears, lions, or crocodiles, were depicted, it was most often food animals that were painted, drawn, or engraved on rock. Deer and goats (including ibex) are particularly common in the Magdalenian rock art of Europe as well as the oldest rock art of China. Deer are common in the oldest art of India and Southeast Asia, and we know from archaeological excavations that they were a very important food source in all of these regions. The earliest rock art of northern Australia is dominated by depictions of macropods (e.g., wallabies and kangaroos) that people depended on for survival. Later depictions in rockshelters of the Kakadu/Arnhem Land region indicate that fish were most important to paint (figure 52), while in the Keep River region to the west it was reptiles. These creatures were very important as food but they also could be used as symbols and to express relationships.

It was long believed that rock art was related to hunting magic—that by depicting a creature a person would be more successful in the hunt. But ethnographic research in northern Australia suggests most paintings of animals, especially fish, were made after the catch. Stories would be told and memories of other hunting expeditions recalled after paintings were made. The rock art could also be used to illustrate how to butcher the catch and what portions were to be given to certain individuals.

Figure 52. Rock painting of a barramundi, northwest Arnhem Land, located in the Northern Territory of Australia. Fish have been an important source of food in Kakadu/Arnhem Land for millennia and feature prominently in the rock art of this region. Photograph by Paul S. C. Taçon with permission of traditional owner Ronald Lamilami.

See also CARVINGS/CARVED REPRESENTATIONS OF FOOD; ETHNOGRAPHIC SOURCES; FOOD AND IDENTITY; FOOD AND RITUAL; HUNTER–GATHERER SUBSISTENCE; WALL PAINTINGS/MURALS

Further Reading

Chippindale, Christopher, and Paul S. C. Taçon, eds. 1998. *The Archaeology of Rock-Art.* Cambridge: Cambridge University Press.

McDonald, Jo, and Peter Veth, eds. 2012. *A Companion to Rock Art.* Chichester, UK: Wiley-Blackwell.

Smith, Benjamin, Knut Helskog, and David Morris, eds. 2012. *Working with Rock Art: Recording, Presenting and Understanding Rock Art Using Indigenous Knowledge.* Johannesburg: Wits University Press.

■ PAUL S. C. TAÇON

ROCKSHELTERS/CAVES

Sheltered sites were attractive to humans as protected places of residence and were also used intermittently for storage, ritual, or other special purposes. Many rockshelters and caves throughout the world have environments that promote the long-term preservation of organic remains. Consequently, sites of this type have an importance in the archaeology of food that is greater than their proportion of the archaeological record might suggest. Rockshelters are relatively shallow overhangs created by differential erosion of sedimentary rocks, frequently limestone or sandstone. True caves are solution cavities that typically occur in karst (eroded limestone) landscapes and often include lengthy passages that are completely dark. Decay is retarded in both types of sites by various combinations of constant temperature and humidity; absence of water; and chemical constituents of sediments, such as nitrates.

Not all rockshelters and caves facilitate preservation of organic materials such as seeds and wood, textiles, skin, and bone. Nonetheless, rockshelters and caves have made major contributions to our understanding of the origins of agriculture. For example, the Mammoth Cave system in Kentucky (USA) is known for its early evidence of domesticated native seed crops. There, upper passages have extremely dry sediments and a constant temperature of 56°F. In eastern Kentucky, remains of these same plants have survived for thousands of years beneath sandstone overhangs protected from rainfall and streamflow. The well-preserved seeds and fruits of domesticates such as sunflower, squash, and goosefoot from both types of sites continue to provide metric data useful for documenting the domestication process. This material is of particular value for such studies because it has not been modified by charring, which is responsible for the preservation of most collections of prehistoric seeds. More recently, ancient DNA has been extracted from these seeds and studied to reconstruct genetic changes under domestication. Sheltered sites of Kentucky have also preserved human fecal material, providing direct evidence of diet during the transition to food production.

Other sheltered sites that have made major contributions to the documentation of early plant food production are located in Arkansas, in the southeastern United States, and in Tamaulipas, Oaxaca, and Tehuacán, Mexico.

See also AGRICULTURE, ORIGINS OF; ARCHAEOBOTANY; DNA ANALYSIS; FRANCHTHI CAVE; GRAN DOLINA; GUILÁ NAQUITZ; HILAZON TACHTIT; MACROREMAINS; NIAH CAVES; PAISLEY CAVES; PALEODIETARY ANALYSIS; PALEOFECAL ANALYSIS; PLANT DOMESTICATION; TEHUACÁN VALLEY; WONDERWERK CAVE

Further Reading

Gremillion, Kristen J. 2008. From Dripline to Deep Cave: On Sheltered Sites as Archaeobotanical Contexts. In *Cave Archaeology of the Eastern Woodlands: Essays in Honor of Patty Jo Watson*, edited by David H. Dye, 117–26. Knoxville: University of Tennessee Press.

Lev, Efraim, Mordecai E. Kislev, and Ofer Bar-Yosef. 2005. Mousterian Vegetal Food in Kebara Cave, Mt. Carmel. *Journal of Archaeological Science* 32(3):475–84.

Watson, Patty Jo, ed. 1974. *Archaeology of the Mammoth Cave Area*. New York: Academic Press.

■ KRISTEN J. GREMILLION

ROOT CROPS/TUBERS

Several of the world's most important food plants are cultivated for edible starch-rich underground storage organs (USOs). These staple crops include cassava/manioc (*Manihot esculenta*), potato (*Solanum tuberosum*), sweet potato (*Ipomoea batatas*), taro (*Colocasia esculenta*), and yams (*Dioscorea* spp.). Numerous other plants are also cultivated for USOs in traditional agricultural societies around the world, although most are only locally or regionally significant, such as kudzu (*Pueraria lobata*) in the highlands of New Guinea and alocasias (*Alocasia* spp.) in Southeast Asia. Additionally, numerous USOs serve important roles as colorings, condiments, drugs, medicines, and restoratives in local and regional cuisines and customs around the world, for example, turmeric (*Curcuma longa*), ginger (*Zingiber officinale*), kava (*Piper methysticum*), liquorice (*Glycyrrhiza glabra*), and burdock (*Arctium* spp.), and many of these have multiple uses. The remainder of this entry will focus on USOs that are staple crops.

USO staple crops were primarily domesticated through selection for the accumulation of carbohydrate in roots, corms, rhizomes, tubers, and other subterranean plant parts. Other factors—rather than size or carbohydrate yield alone—are likely to have been significant in the early and later domestication and dispersal of plants for USOs, however, including acridity, color, shape, taste, texture, and toxicity. For instance, although cultivated taro varieties have been selected for lower acridity, it seems that the early domestication of manioc focused upon a more toxic variety. Certainly, numerous phenotypic attributes have been important in the generation of hundreds or thousands of cultivated varieties (cultivars) for some plants, although much variation among varietals arose once the initial stages of domestication were complete. Additional phenotypic attributes would have been important during selection under cultivation, including resistance to disease, drought, frost, and pests; edaphic requirements (e.g., soil moisture, nutrients, and structure); and altitudinal and climatic tolerances.

The majority of the globally important plants domesticated for USOs are vegetatively propagated; that is to say, rather than cultivating plants from fertilized seed—as with cereals and legumes—they are cultivated through the removal and replanting of a plant part, usually part of the underground storage organ, such as a seed potato. Consequently, these plants are clonally reproduced, and reproduction does not require fertilization or seed production. Indeed, most plants are harvested before seed set to maximize yields of stored carbohydrate. Arguably, the vegetative reproduction of plants enables greater control over phenotype (namely, a plant's observable characteristics, such as morphology, behavior, properties, etc.); people directly select a favored phenotype without genetic dilution from another parent, as occurs in sexual reproduction. However, many USOs exhibit considerable phenotypic variability through a multitude of factors, including phenotypic plasticity and gene expression, somaclonal variation (genetic variation as a result of chromosomal rearrangements and changes in ploidy levels, or changes to the number of sets of chromosomes within a plant), and incorporation of new genetic material.

The phenotypes of the subterranean storage organs for many species change considerably with environment of growth; for instance, larger USOs occur in tilled and friable soils. Consequently, phenotype may not be a reliable indicator of domestication status for such plants, because they may revert to a "wild type" once feral. Although vegetative propagation ensures clonal reproduction, genetic variation among the resultant cultivated populations may emerge as a result of somaclonal variation. Additionally, few clonally reproduced crops are completely sterile, that is, unable to flower, be fertilized, and produce viable seed. Most can be reproduced by seed, and new genetic material can be introduced into cultivated stock where adventitious sexual reproduction occurs and resultant offspring are vegetatively propagated. However, for reasons not fully understood, some plants that are subject to prolonged clonal reproduction can lose the ability to sexually reproduce. These sterile plants become increasingly dependent upon people for reproduction and dispersal.

For reasons that are not entirely clear, plant exploitation in wet tropical environments tends to be predominantly vegetative, as opposed to predominantly seed-based in semiarid and temperate environments. Potential biological reasons for harnessing the vegetative aspects of USO reproduction may have arisen from the more aseasonal tropical climates, as opposed to the sexual, often more seasonal, reproduction of grasses. Furthermore, many USOs arguably provide higher return rates than cereals in terms of carbohydrate returns per expenditure of effort for cultivation and processing prior to consumption. Most starch-rich staples originally cultivated for USOs were domesticated in the tropics. Although the precise loci of domestication for most of these plants are not well known, cassava/manioc, potato, and sweet potato are thought to have originated in the tropical lowlands or highlands of South America and taro and yams in Southeast Asia and New Guinea.

Under cultivation, USO staple crops are harvested before pollination and seed set. Furthermore, they have been domesticated for starch-rich storage organs that are effectively soft plant tissues that readily decay following death or discard in wet tropical environments. Consequently, the archaeology of cultivation and domestication for these plants has been harder to establish than for staple crops in other parts of the world. Other than a handful of charred, desiccated, or waterlogged finds for each species, the archaeobotany of most USOs has had to await the application of two new techniques: starch grain/granule analysis (especially starch granules from the surface of tools, but also from the surrounding soil) and parenchyma research (primarily of plant tissues that have been charred or desiccated), although these are still not routinely applied during archaeological investigations. In contrast, cereals and legumes, as well as many fruits and nuts, readily preserve hardier plant parts—such as seeds, nutshells, and fruit stones—when charred, desiccated, or waterlogged. As a result, the antiquity, locus, and character of early cultivation and domestication for most USOs are relatively poorly understood in comparison to other staple crops.

There is considerable debate about the sociopolitical implications of societies reliant upon vegetatively propagated USOs vis-à-vis those reliant on seed-based cultivation. USO-based societies are often assumed to be smaller, less hierarchical, and less liable to expand. Oft-cited reasons for these social characteristics are the inability to control the long-term production, harvesting, storage, and redistribution of USO staples, in contrast to cereals and legumes. The veracity of this argument is unclear because hierarchical societies based on yam storage are known in West Africa, and this hypothesis is considered by some to have Eurocentric, evolutionary, and teleological underpinnings.

See also AGRICULTURE, ORIGINS OF; AGRICULTURE, PROCUREMENT, PROCESSING, AND STORAGE; ARCHAEOBOTANY; CULTIVATION; FOOD PRODUCTION AND THE FORMATION OF COMPLEX SOCIETIES; MANIOC/CASSAVA; PLANT DOMESTICATION; PLANT HUSBANDRY; PLANT PROCESSING; PLANTS; POTATO; RESIDUE ANALYSIS, STARCH; SOIL MICROTECHNIQUES; STARCHES, ROLE OF; SWEET POTATO; TARO; YAM

Further Reading

Barton, Huw, and Tim Denham. 2011. Prehistoric Vegeculture and Social Life in Island Southeast Asia and Melanesia. In *Why Cultivate? Anthropological and Archaeological Approaches to Foraging-Farming Transitions in Southeast Asia*, edited by Graeme Barker and Monica Janowski, 17–25. McDonald Institute Monographs. Cambridge: McDonald Institute for Archaeological Research.

Denham, T. P., S. G. Haberle, C. Lentfer, et al. 2003. Origins of Agriculture at Kuk Swamp in the Highlands of New Guinea. *Science* 301(5630):189–93.

Denham, Tim, José Iriarte, and Luc Vrydaghs, eds. 2007. *Rethinking Agriculture: Archaeological and Ethnoarchaeological Perspectives.* Walnut Creek, CA: Left Coast Press.

Eckert, Christopher G. 2002. The Loss of Sex in Clonal Plants. *Evolutionary Ecology* 15:501–20.

Fuller, Dorian Q, Tim Denham, Manuel Arroyo-Kalin, et al. 2014. Convergent Evolution and Parallelism in Plant Domestication Revealed by an Expanding Archaeological Record. *Proceedings of the National Academy of Sciences USA* 111(17):6147–52.

Harris, D. R. 1973. The Prehistory of Tropical Agriculture: An Ethnoecological Model. In *The Explanation of Culture Change: Models in Prehistory*, edited by Colin Renfrew, 391–417. London: Duckworth.

Hather, Jon G. 1994. *Tropical Archaeobotany: Applications and New Developments.* London: Routledge.

Piperno, Dolores R., and Deborah M. Pearsall. 1998. *The Origins of Agriculture in the Lowland Neotropics.* San Diego, CA: Academic Press.

■ TIM DENHAM

RYE

Rye is a cereal with outstanding tolerance to cold, drought, and acidity, thriving in poor and sandy soils unsuitable for other cereals. It has been part of resilient farming systems and remains a staple in central/north Europe and Russia. In the south of Europe and Morocco, it is cultivated in temperate mountain areas. Its nutrient efficiency and tolerance of diseases make it an attractive choice toward reduction of fertilizers and pesticides. In the 20th century, the man-made crop triticale was produced by artificially crossing rye with wheat.

Rye has a high nutritional value and is rich in fiber, vitamins (B and E), and minerals. It is poor in gluten, and upon rising produces a heavy, dark bread with a characteristic flavor and texture. Rye can also be consumed as pumpernickel, porridge, or pudding and is used to produce whiskey and vodka. In Scandinavia rye is used to produce the crisp bread *knäckebröd*, which preserves under storage for long periods of time. Grains and green plants can be used as fodder. Traditionally, rye was also valued for its long and strong straw, used for thatching, bedding, basketry, and rain-proof clothing. It was cultivated as a winter or spring cereal and in Scandinavia was the main crop in slash-and-burn farming systems.

Cultivated rye is a diploid (the majority—somatic—cells have two sets of chromosomes, represented as $2n=14$, where n represents the basic number of chromosomes; in the case of rye, there are 7, so each rye cell has a total of 14 chromosomes) annual grass unique among Old World cereals as an outbreeder (wind cross-pollinated). It belongs to the species *Secale cereale* ssp. *cereale*, which also includes weedy and wild forms (e.g., ssp. *segetale, dighoricum, afghanicum,* and *ancestrale*). The latter occur as weeds in cereal fields and have differential geographic distributions, mostly in the Near East and central Asia. Wild rye species include *S. vavilovii*, distributed throughout southwest Asia, and *S. strictum* (=*S.*

montanum), occurring throughout the Mediterranean basin, southwest Asia, the Caucasus, and central Asia. It is still unclear whether rye was domesticated from one or both of these wild species. Other wild rye species that are assumed not to be involved in rye's domestication include *S. sylvestre*, *S. africanum*, and *S. iranicum*.

Compared with other cereals, little is known about rye's history. Rye domestication has been studied using a combination of archaeobotany, genetics, pollen analysis, and biology. The earliest evidence of wild rye use comes from Epipaleolithic layers in the Syrian Tell sites of Mureybit (11,800–11,300 cal BP) and Abu Hureyra (12,700–11,100 cal BP). Seeds of domesticated rye appear in small quantities in the Turkish sites of Can Hassan III (9,450–8,450 cal BP) and are rare anywhere else in the Near East. The first evidence of the cultivation of rye as a dedicated crop comes from Alaca Höyük (ca. 4,000 BP). Turkey, Transcaucasia, Iran, and central Asia are assumed to be centers of domestication of rye, and it is likely that domesticated forms evolved more than once in these different areas.

It is still unclear which route rye followed as it was introduced into Europe: north of the Black and Caspian Seas into central Europe (and from here to the Balkans and Turkey), or along the Mediterranean route followed by the other Neolithic cereals. Most researchers agree that rye is a secondary crop that spread as a tolerated weed of wheat and barley. Wild ryes with a mutation conferring a tough rachis (the spine of the ear holding the spikelets) would have been picked up in small amounts with other grain. Rye's resemblance to wheat and the inability to separate rye from other cereal grains through traditional winnowing allowed rye to be harvested and sown each growing season. The first European rye remains appear in Neolithic contexts in Italy (Sammardenchia, 7,550–6,450 cal BP), Slovakia (Šarišské Michal'any, 6,950–6,650 cal BP), and in Bronze Age settlements in central Europe. The "tolerated weed" status of rye is attested by the low percentage of grains found in European sites up to the Iron Age and by the frequent contamination of wheat/barley assemblages.

During the pre-Roman Iron Age, the distribution of rye expanded, and in many places farmers cultivated it exclusively. Researchers hypothesize that climate cooling in Europe in the first millennium BC favored rye's survival over the cereals it was initially infesting, leading farmers to adopt it as a full crop as a result of its superior performance in cold years. Alternatively, the introduction of iron tools (e.g., machines or scythes) permitted harvesting near the ground instead of ear-picking by hand or sickle, making it more difficult to weed out rye, and leading to its increase in the fields over time.

Although rare in the Mediterranean region, as sprouting requires hard frost and cold, rye was part of Roman farming, especially in the cooler northern provinces. Classical authors Pliny and Galen wrote of it but advised against its taste. It is known that Germanic tribes of the Migration Period cultivated rye, and it is likely they were responsible for rye's expansion everywhere in Europe during the Middle Ages. During this period, rye was cultivated even in rich soils, becoming the predominant cereal in many north/central European regions, although it remained marginal in the south. European settlers brought rye with them to America during the 16th and 17th centuries.

Ergot (*Claviceps purpurea*) is a common fungal disease of rye. Ingestion of ergot-contaminated rye flour can lead to ergotism, a severe and potentially fatal neurological disorder. The disease, known as St. Anthony's Fire, became common in the Middle Ages (most likely associated with rye's increase in the diet). Ergotism and the hallucinogenic properties of ergot were probably already known in ancient Greece.

Further research is necessary to elucidate the history of rye cultivation. In the near future, the predicted loss of quality of arable soils and climate change are likely to increase rye cultivation.

See also AGRICULTURE, ORIGINS OF; ARCHAEOBOTANY; BREAD; CEREALS; PLANT DOMESTICATION; WEEDS; WILD PROGENITORS OF DOMESTICATED PLANTS

Further Reading

Behre, Karl-Ernst. 1992. The History of Rye Cultivation in Europe. *Vegetation History and Archaeobotany* 1:141–56.

Lee, M. R. 2009. The History of Ergot of Rye (*Claviceps purpurea*) I: From Antiquity to 1900. *Journal of the Royal College of Physicians Edinburgh* 39(2):179–84.

Zohary Daniel, Maria Hopf, and Ehud Weiss. 2012. *Domestication of Plants in the Old World*. 4th edition. Oxford: Oxford University Press.

■ HUGO R. OLIVEIRA

S

SALT

Salts (sodium and potassium) are essential to human and animal diets. Sufficient salt for physiological regulation frequently is obtained through other foods, particularly meat and salty plants. Salt, however, can also be crucial for medicinal purposes, mining, dyeing cloth, flavor enhancement, food preservation, and other uses. Surplus salt was critical to the development of all complex societies and many smaller-scale communities. Salt archaeology began among scholars studying native North American salt making, particularly in the Mississippi Valley. As the field developed, a comparative archaeology of salt emerged starting in the 1970s.

Salt is available from five primary sources: rock salt, seawater, salt lakes, brine springs, and salty plants. All can be used directly, but more often they are processed to remove impurities and obtain salt crystals. Salt archaeology examines the contexts where salt was produced to supplement normal food consumption, and the salt trade. Rock salt can be mined directly. Archaeological research on rock salt (e.g., at Hallstatt, Austria) focuses on mine technology and associated artifacts. Processing other forms of salt required solar evaporation or the intentional heating of brine acquired from lakes, springs, or the sea, or from combining ashes of burned salty plants with water. In solar evaporation, fields of evaporation facilities may remain for archaeological investigation. These exist in highland Peru as terraces, in East Africa as lakeside facilities, and in many coastal locations, such as coastal Maya sites. Most archaeologically visible are locations where brine was collected and then artificially heated. Remains include brine-collection facilities, such as troughs and pits at sites in Romania, Mexico, England, China, and elsewhere, and vessels used for heating brine and forming salt cakes. Ceramic vessels and terra-cotta objects used to prop them up are collectively known as briquetage and are the most common category of salt-related archaeological artifact. Briquetage has been used to understand salt production techniques and organization in contexts as diverse as inland and coastal China, central Europe, England, West Africa, the Philippines, the Mississippi River Valley (USA), central Anatolia, Japan, and elsewhere.

See also ARCHAEOLOGY OF HOUSEHOLD FOOD PRODUCTION; FERMENTATION; FOOD PRESERVATION; FOOD STORAGE; MATERIAL CULTURE ANALYSIS

Further Reading

Flad, Rowan K. 2011. *Salt Production and Social Hierarchy in Ancient China.* Cambridge: Cambridge University Press.

Kern, Anton, Jacqueline Thomas, Timothy Taylor, et al., eds. 2009. *Kingdom of Salt: 7000 Years of Hallstatt.* Vienna: Natural History Museum.

Li, Shuicheng 李水城, and Lothar von Falkenhausen, eds. 2010. *Salt Archaeology in China.* Vol. 2, *International Research on Salt Archaeology.* Beijing: Kexue chubanshe.

McKillop, Heather. 2002. *Salt: White Gold of the Ancient Maya.* Gainesville: University Press of Florida.

■ROWAN K. FLAD

SAN GENESIO, MEDIEVAL TAVERN SITE
(SAN MINIATO, PISA, ITALY)

The village of San Genesio (San Miniato, Pisa, in central Italy) was an important site on the Via Francigena, the famous medieval road connecting north and south Europe to the Holy Land. It was inhabited from Etruscan to medieval times until it was destroyed by fire in AD 1248. While the site has significant archaeological remains, this entry focuses on the case study of a medieval tavern site. Among the buildings destroyed by the fire was a structure characterized by the presence of several fireplaces and broken ceramic vessels preserved in situ. To better understand the function of the structure, chemical analyses of floor samples were conducted with spot tests aimed at identifying the presence of phosphates related to the decomposition of organic matter, fatty acids that are present in fat materials (e.g., oils, broths, meat, incense), and protein residues related to vegetal and animal proteins (e.g., blood, meat, beans). These residues are often related to domestic food preparation and consumption activities and were found in abundance on the floor of the structure and around the fireplaces in particular. The residue concentrations, multiple fireplaces, and abundant ceramics indicated an intense level of food preparation that is not consistent with domestic activities, however, but rather with those carried out in a tavern, where food preparation and consumption are abundant. The recovery of coins, gaming pieces, dice, and fragments of glasses during excavations further supported the interpretation of this structure as a tavern that would have served pilgrims traveling along the Via Francigena. The data allowed archaeologists to identify specific activity areas. The abundant residues identified in association with the fireplaces in the main room and the recovery of in situ remains of cooking vessels suggest that this room was the kitchen. The absence of fireplaces and the recovery of ceramics used primarily for food storage suggests a second room served as a storeroom, although the huge quantity of residues on the floor suggests it also was used for the preparation of food before cooking.

See also ARCHAEOLOGY OF COOKING; ARCHITECTURAL ANALYSIS; BIOMOLECULAR ANALYSIS; RESIDUE ANALYSIS, BLOOD; RESIDUE ANALYSIS, STARCH; SOIL MICROTECHNIQUES; TAVERNS/INNS

Further Reading

Barba, Luis. 2007. Chemical Residues in Lime-Plastered Archaeological Floors. *Geoarchaeology* 22(4): 439–52.

Cantini, Federico, ed. 2015. *Vicus Wallari-burgus sancti Genesii: Campagne di scavo 2001–2012*. Firenze: All'Insegna del Giglio. In press.

Inserra F., and A. Pecci. 2011. Chemical Analyses of Floors at San Genesio (San Miniato, Pisa): A Medieval Tavern. In *Proceedings of the 37th International Symposium on Archaeometry, 12th–16th May 2008, Siena, Italy*, edited by Isabella Turbanti-Memmi, 459–64. Berlin: Springer.

■ ALESSANDRA PECCI

SARDIS, RITUAL EGG DEPOSIT (TURKEY)

At Sardis, eggs were used in ritual purification offerings or foundation deposits. In 2013, two nearly identical ritual offerings were found buried beneath the floor of a first-century AD house or workshop (figure 53). Each deposit contained a coin, a bronze needle and pin, an iron stylus point or pin, and a whole egg, one of which was preserved intact and pierced on one side. One deposit was inside of a thin-walled mug sealed by an Eastern Sigillata B dish, and the other deposit was sealed between two plainware bowls, one serving as the lid for the other. Both coins date to the reign of Nero: one minted at Sardis with an image of Zeus Lydios, and the other minted at Smyrna with an image of a lion engraved over a rasura—the lion was a symbol of Lydian royalty and the local goddess Cybele.

Figure 53. Ritual egg deposits from Sardis, Turkey, dating to the Roman period (AD 70–80). The deposits were found buried beneath the floor of a first-century AD house or workshop. One bowl, covered by a second, inverted bowl, contained a coin, a number of small, sharp metal objects, and an intact egg with a hole that was pierced before its burial. A second offering, found in a lidded ceramic vessel, contained similar objects though the egg was not intact. Literary sources suggest such ritualistic food offerings were common during this period. F49 13.1 votive deposit with small objects-SD2013.2355. Photograph by Richard Francis Taylor. © Archaeological Exploration of Sardis/Harvard University.

According to Juvenal (*Sat.* 6.518), eggs were used in purification rituals associated with the goddess Cybele. In the Greek Magical Papyri (*PGM* XII. 96–106), we have evidence for the burial of bird eggs below floors in workshops to ensure prosperity in business. Pliny (*N.H.* 28.4) also suggests that the breaking or piercing of eggs was practiced to protect against curses. Below the same floor, a deposit of cooking and dining vessels was also found, and an ashy pit containing the bones of a piglet below the floor of an adjacent room may also be related.

Similar deposits were found at Sardis in 1913 during excavations of the Artemis temple. H. C. Butler, who directed the excavations, noted that more than a dozen ovoid cups were recovered at the base of walls, usually outside of buildings, with each containing a coin, the shell of an egg, and a small bronze instrument. Further, one eggshell was deposited whole with the exception of a small hole pierced in one end. Of the three identifiable coins from these excavations, one was locally minted in the second century BC, the second minted in Smyrna during the first century BC, and the third, minted in Germe, dates to the reign of Trajan. Thus, such rituals may have been practiced for centuries. Thus far, these archaeological finds seem to be unique to Sardis. According to literary accounts, however, similar rituals may have been practiced elsewhere in the Roman east.

See also FOOD AND RITUAL; OFFERINGS AND GRAVE GOODS

Further Reading

Adkins, L., and R. A. Adkins. 1998. Vows and Votive Offerings. In *Handbook to Life in Ancient Rome*, 299–300. Oxford: Oxford University Press.

Butler, H. C. 1922. *Sardis I; The Excavations, Part 1: 1910–1914*. Leiden: Brill.

Greenewalt, Crawford H., Jr. 1976. *Ritual Dinners in Early Historic Sardis*. Berkeley: University of California Press.

■ WILLIAM BRUCE AND ELIZABETH DERIDDER RAUBOLT

SCANNING ELECTRON MICROSCOPY (SEM)

Scanning electron microscopy has been broadly used in archaeology for five decades (the acronym SEM describes the instrument and technique). Its two principal functions are imaging and providing chemical information. Consequently, it has been used for nearly every application in which archaeologists wish to observe magnified images of a specimen or establish composition on microscopic scales, including investigation of dietary and subsistence practices.

SEM permits one to acquire highly magnified images. The magnification range is much greater than visible-light microscopy (VLM). Depending on the instrument, magnification can range six orders of magnitude, from 5X (equivalent to a hand lens) to 500,000X (hundreds of times higher than a powerful VLM). Additionally, SEM offers a greater depth of field than VLM (about 300 times better), so more of a specimen appears in focus.

SEMs are commonly equipped to identify composition based on X-rays emitted under the electron beam. Because the beam can be focused to a spot, composition can be measured for a small area of a specimen. This permits one to obtain localized compositional data and measure specimens so small that they cannot be analyzed by other techniques. Imaging occurs under vacuum to avoid scattering by air and other effects, and often nonmetals must be coated with an ultrathin layer of a conductive material, usually gold or carbon. Some instruments, called environmental SEMs, operate at lower vacuums (closer to atmosphere), so coatings and other preparations (which may alter biological specimens) are unnecessary.

Providing both imaging and chemical analyses, SEM is a versatile tool for reconstructing foodways. Pollen species identification, one of the first archaeological applications, is often combined with species identification of charcoal and other botanical evidence (e.g., seed fragments) to reconstruct vegetation histories. Other SEM uses include identifying eggshell species and other microfaunal evidence, investigating dental microwear as a dietary proxy, and studying residues on ceramics, such as starches from cereals used in Egyptian brewing.

See also ARCHAEOBOTANY; BREWING/MALTING; DENTAL ANALYSIS; MACROREMAINS; PALYNOLOGY; RESIDUE ANALYSIS, STARCH; ZOOARCHAEOLOGY

Further Reading

Grine, F. E., P. S. Ungar, and M. F. Teaford. 2002. Error Rates in Dental Microwear Quantification Using Scanning Electron Microscopy. *Scanning* 24(3):144–53.

Pilcher, J. R. 1968. Some Applications of Scanning Electron Microscopy to the Study of Modern and Fossil Pollen. *Ulster Journal of Archaeology* 31:87–91.

Ponting, Matthew. 2004. The Scanning Electron Microscope and the Archaeologist. *Physics Education* 39(2):166–70.

Samuel, Delwen. 1996. Archaeology of Ancient Egyptian Beer. *Journal of American Society of Brewing Chemists* 54(1):3–12.

■ ELLERY FRAHM

SECONDARY PRODUCTS REVOLUTION

The Secondary Products Revolution model was formulated by Andrew Sherratt in 1981 to explain the dramatic changes in economic organization (subsistence, settlement, and trade) in the Near East and Europe between the end of the Neolithic and beginning of the Bronze Age. He hypothesized that these changes were the result of innovations in domestic animal production and related technologies, namely, a shift from an emphasis upon the exploitation of domestic livestock for their primary products to include both primary and secondary products. Primary products can be extracted from animals only once in their lifetime (i.e., meat, bone, and hide), while secondary products can be repeatedly extracted from an animal (i.e., milk, wool, and traction).

Sherratt proposed that sheep, goats, and cattle were originally domesticated for their primary product exploitation. Primitive breeds of cattle, sheep, and goats would not yield large quantities of milk, wild sheep do not have woolly coats, and there is no evidence for plows or wagons in the archaeological record until the Chalcolithic period. He argued that it would take several millennia of genetic manipulation to breed milking cows and woolly sheep. As a result, the origins of the large-scale and intensive use of domestic live-stock for their secondary products in Europe and the Near East would not begin with the earliest Neolithic cultures, but would appear much later in time during the Chalcolithic and Bronze Age. This model has now been extended as far east as China.

This entry discusses food-related secondary product exploitation. Some secondary products are not directly subsistence-related (e.g., wool). Some species were probably domesticated for their secondary products only. For example, dogs and cats were domesticated for protection (from predators and rodents) and companionship. While there are examples of dogs being consumed in some cultures, there is little evidence for widespread consumption. Dung is another type of secondary product that would be used for fuel and to fertilize the fields.

Milk Production

While all mammals produce milk, most wild forms only produce sufficient milk for their offspring. Among wild mammals and most primitive domesticates, if the infant offspring is removed from the immediate proximity of the mother and the mother cannot see or sense it, she will cease lactating. Herders of unimproved breeds keep the infant nearby in order to milk the mother for human consumption. Many of the major mammal species that have been domesticated in the Old World can be exploited for their milk, such as cattle (and their various local forms), sheep, goats, camels, and horses. No New World species were milked since the teats of llamas and alpacas are small and difficult to milk. Of all the early domestics of large and medium mammals, only pigs and dogs were never exploited for their milk (although the quality of their milk is very high and most similar to that of a human mother's milk). Only those herd animals that stand up while lactating were eventually improved to the point where they could be intensively milked. Secondary product exploitation has clear economic implications. Milking adds new forms of animal protein, vitamins, and minerals to the diet without slaughtering the animals. Milking also yields byproducts such as butter and cheese.

Evidence for early secondary product exploitation in the Near East and Europe consists of artifacts, iconographic and textual sources, zooarchaeological data, and lipid analysis. There are depictions from Mesopotamia of animals pulling plows and cattle and sheep being milked that date to the beginning of the Chalcolithic (ca. 4000 BC); figurines and bas-reliefs of sheep with what appear to be woolly coats from a slightly earlier period (ca. 5000 BC); cuneiform tablets documenting the exploitation of animals for their wool and milk from the Near East (ca. 3500 BC); models of carts and yoked cattle from the Near East and Europe (ca. 3500 BC); and preserved wool textiles, cattle yokes, wooden ards (a simple form of plow), wooden vehicles, and plow marks in waterlogged or buried contexts from eastern, central, and northern Europe (ca. 3000 BC). There is no unambiguous large-scale archaeological evidence for secondary product exploitation in any region of the Old World before the Chalcolithic.

Zooarchaeological studies of harvest (age at death) profiles for goats suggest that goats were milked from the beginning of the Neolithic. Most goats were culled as older adults, in contrast with sheep, who were more intensively exploited while young. This pattern does not change over time. In contrast, cattle and sheep harvest profiles indicate a shift in exploitation practices toward a more diversified pattern that would include both primary and secondary products at the beginning of the Chalcolithic (ca. 5000 BC) in the Near East. This shift entailed keeping more animals alive for longer periods of time. X-ray analysis of sheep and goat metapodials (Israel) demonstrates cortical bone thinning in older females associated with the introduction of larger-scale milking activities during the Chalcolithic. These changes happen progressively later to the west and east (southeastern Europe, ca. 3500 BC; northwestern Europe, ca. 2500 BC; China, ca. 3000 BC).

The study of lipids (animal fats) recovered from ceramics has yielded evidence for early milking, with the earliest Neolithic ceramics from the Near East (northwestern Anatolian Pottery Neolithic, ca. 6000 BC) and Europe (ranging from early sixth millennium Hungary to late fifth millennium England). This implies that milking was already in existence when pottery was invented in the Near East and accompanied the spread of early farming cultures from the Near East across Europe. It is not possible to use this method to determine if milking began immediately upon the domestication of sheep, goats (ca. 8000 BC) or cattle (ca. 7000 BC) since this process occurred during the Pre-Pottery Neolithic. That few ceramic sherds from the beginning of the Neolithic have yielded evidence for fatty animal acids suggests, however, that dairying was practiced on a small scale only, as part of a broad mixed economy and as a minor component of the diet. Intensive milking only developed much later. Zooarchaeological data suggest that the lipids in European Neolithic ceramics probably belonged primarily to goats.

Traction

The plow and wagon enabled intensification of production agriculture (i.e., higher yields per labor unit), expansion of the range of environments in which agriculture can be practiced (i.e., heavier soils can be more easily and effectively cultivated), and improved efficiency in transportation across the landscape. The same task can be performed with greater energy savings and with increased return since fewer people are needed to till a field or carry a load more efficiently across a variety of terrains.

The earliest evidence for the plow comes in the form of plow marks (ca. 5000 BC, southwestern Iran). During the later Chalcolithic (late Uruk), the first cuneiform and pictorial evidence (cylinder seals) for well-developed plows appears in Mesopotamia. The plow appears later in Europe (after 3500 BC) in the form of ard marks under barrows in Denmark, Germany, and Poland in association with the Corded Ware and related cultures.

Domestic cattle were probably used to transport goods prior to the advent of the wagon during the Neolithic. The Indo-European etymology for wheeled-vehicle terminology suggests an eastern European steppe origin, and most of the earliest evidence for their origin points to the late fourth millennium BC, with cattle as the heavy draft animal. These early vehicles would have been large, heavy, slow moving, and awkward. The zooarchaeological data show a clear increase in traction-related pathologies from the Near East during the Chalcolithic (late fifth–early fourth millennia BC) and from England to India during the Early Bronze Age (late fourth–early third millennia BC), and harvest profiles of cattle indicate that the vast majority (around 80 percent) were culled as adults. These changes are contemporaneous with the appearance of wheeled vehicle figurines. The spread of the plow and wheeled vehicles in Europe (during the Chalco-lithic) coincides with dramatic shifts in cattle harvest profiles that indicate a preference for more adults in cattle herds. This suggests that cattle were more intensively exploited for traction from this point in time.

See also Agriculture, Procurement, Processing, and Storage; Animal Husbandry and Herding; Lactase Persistence and Dairying; Manuring and Soil Enrichment Practices; Milk and Dairy Products; Representational Models of Food and Food Production; Residue Analysis, Dairy Products; Zooarchaeology

Further Reading

Anthony, David W. 2007. *The Horse, the Wheel, and Language: How Bronze-Age Riders from the Eurasian Steppes Shaped the Modern World.* Princeton, NJ: Princeton University Press.

Craig, Oliver E., John Chapman, Carl Heron, et al. 2005. Did the First Farmers of Central and Eastern Europe Produce Dairy Foods? *Antiquity* 79(306):882–94.

Evershed, Richard P., Sebastian Payne, Andrew G. Sherratt, et al. 2008. Earliest Date for Milk Use in the Near East and Southeastern Europe Linked to Cattle Herding. *Nature* 455(7212):528–31.

Greenfield, Haskel J. 2010. The Secondary Products Revolution: The Past, the Present and the Future. *World Archaeology* 42(1):29–54.

———, ed. 2014. *Animal Secondary Products: Archaeological Perspectives on Domestic Animal Exploitation in the Neolithic and Bronze Age.* Oxford: Oxbow.

Sherratt, Andrew. 1981. Plough and Pastoralism: Aspects of the Secondary Products Revolution. In *Pattern of the Past*, edited by Ian Hodder, Glynn Isaac, and Norman Hammond, 261–306. Cambridge: Cambridge University Press.

———. 1983. The Secondary Exploitation of Animals in the Old World. *World Archaeology* 15(1):90–104.

■ HASKEL J. GREENFIELD

SEDENTISM AND DOMESTICATION

Sedentism is the process by which groups of mobile hunter-gatherers have settled down. Archaeological evidence indicates that this process occurred earlier than food production in the primary centers of domestication. Though the concept has evolved, sedentism is still considered a prerequisite for food production, and it plays an important role in theoretical models on the origins of agriculture.

Domestication, the process leading to morphological and physiological changes in wild plants and animals, was induced by human management associated with food production. It occurred independently in more than 20 regions of the world. Many of the first plants and animals domesticated are still the staple food of their traditional cuisine. The earliest center of domestication known thus far is the Fertile Crescent, where cereals and pulses were domesticated between 13,000 and 10,000 BP, shortly followed by sheep and goat.

By collecting, processing, and planting seeds gathered from the wild, humans have favored, consciously or not, specimens that were lacking features essential to the plants' survival on their own. These ultimately dominated the crops, making human intervention essential. The main archaeologically attested features found on domesticated plants are stronger attachment points preventing or delaying the fruits or seeds from falling or shattering when ripe, and larger fruits and seeds. By keeping and breeding wild animals and selecting features that facilitated their management, humans have favored a reduction of body size along with a reduction of tusks and horns. In theory, domestication could have been a short process, just a few years in the case of plants, but archaeological data suggest that it was a long one: the earliest unequivocal evidence of domestication was found at the Turkish site of Nevalı Çori, dated to ca. 9,200 BP, while predomestic cultivation, early cultivation prior to any morphological change, is attested by indirect evidence such as weeds from ca. 11,500 BP.

The settling of hunter-gatherers is a common trait of most theoretical models that set the scenarios leading to domestication. Sedentism is most often seen as an opportunity made possible by a rich and diversified environment. This is supported by archaeological and ethnographic evidence, such as the fish- and nut-based diets of the Jōmon people of Japan and of the California Indians (USA). The growing biodiversity associated with the Pleistocene–Holocene transition, the climatic warming that followed the last Ice Age, is often seen as a new opportunity that made sedentism possible. Alternatively, sedentism and food production are sometimes considered the results of an imbalance between the needs of a population and the carrying capacity of its natural environment. Population growth or climatic deterioration, such as the Younger Dryas, a short but sharp return to glacial conditions, are the most common culprits evoked, although evidence for demographic expansion and the actual impact of the Younger Dryas are both debated. In this type of model, competition forced human groups to settle in areas that were less affected by the Younger Dryas, or they strategically chose to occupy favorable territories by settling down. Another three-phase scenario mixes both positive and negative perspectives: sedentism was made possible by the postglacial warming, demographic growth was favored by sedentism, and the needs of this growing population, perhaps aggravated by climatic deterioration, were met by food production and domestication. Though archaeologists continue to debate the mechanism for change, they agree that by settling down, hunter-gatherers developed knowledge of the wild resources of their territory, allowing them to invest it by producing food. Domestication is thus seen as a result of human–plant co-evolution. With ethnographic evidence of food plant production by mobile populations, and with an increase in archaeological data that do not quite fit the existing models, the link between sedentism, food production, and domestication is now seen as more nuanced, and sedentism itself is viewed with a less rigid approach.

The labor investment required for building long-term structures, and the presence of several of these structures, has long been considered satisfactory evidence of sedentism. Archaeological sites from the Early Natufian (ca. 14,500–12,800 BP) in the Levant, with their round stone structures, are the earliest permanent settlements known. With the wider development of environmental archaeology in the 1980s and 1990s, claims for sedentism had to be supported by evidence of multi-seasonality of hunting and gathering. Multi-seasonality became the focus of a set of evidence that, in addition to permanent structures, included storage facilities, abundant immovable goods such as large querns, commensal fauna, weeds, evidence of rebuilding, and dense archaeological deposits. With multi-seasonality, the notion of sedentism necessarily applied to the hunter-gatherers themselves, not only to their settlements. Notions of semi-sedentism or semi-mobility depended on the number of seasons or months represented by the bioarchaeological data. Most archaeological data lack the resolution that could attest multi-seasonality over a one-year span, however. Asouti and Fuller recently suggested that evidence of multi-seasonality might simply reflect periodic returns to the same site at different moments of the year rather than continued occupation. This opened new perspectives on sedentism: a permanent settlement may not necessarily be occupied year-round but may be visited periodically by one or several groups, as a meeting point or as part of a cycle of mobility. Nonetheless, the considerable human investment in a specific geographic location that transforms it into a permanent, man-made *locus* undoubtedly reveals a change of perception and engagement toward space.

See also AGRICULTURE, ORIGINS OF; ANIMAL DOMESTICATION; BEDROCK FEATURES; CULTIVATION; DHRA'; OHALO II; PLANT DOMESTICATION; PLANT HUSBANDRY; STORAGE FACILITIES; SUBSISTENCE MODELS

Further Reading

Asouti, Eleni, and Dorian Q Fuller. 2013. A Contextual Approach to the Emergence of Agriculture in Southwest Asia: Reconstructing Early Neolithic Plant-Food Production. *Current Anthropology* 54(3):299–345.

Boyd, Brian. 2006. On "Sedentism" in the Later Epipalaeolithic (Natufian) Levant. *World Archeology* 38(2):164–78.

Nesbitt, Mark. 2002. When and Where Did Domesticated Cereals First Occur in Southwest Asia? In *The Dawn of Farming in the Near East*, edited by René T. J. Capper and Sytze Bottema, 113–32. Berlin: Ex Oriente.

Purugganan, Michael D., and Dorian Q Fuller. 2009. The Nature of Selection during Plant Domestication. *Nature* 457(12):843–48.

Savard, Manon, Mark Nesbitt, and Martin K. Jones. 2006. The Role of Wild Grasses in Subsistence and Sedentism: New Evidence from the Northern Fertile Crescent. *World Archaeology* 38(2):179–96.

Willcox, George. 2012. Searching for the Origins of Arable Weeds in the Near East. *Vegetation History and Archaeobotany* 21(2):163–67.

Zeder, Melinda A. 2011. The Origins of Agriculture in the Near East. *Current Anthropology* 52(S4): S221–S235.

■ MANON SAVARD

SEEDS
See MACROREMAINS

SENSORIALITY
See FOOD AS SENSORY EXPERIENCE

SEWER SYSTEMS
See LATRINES AND SEWER SYSTEMS

SHEEP/GOAT

Caprini are the earliest domesticated herbivores. The process of domestication took place in the Near East around 12,000 years ago. The earliest evidence for domestication of goats (*Capra hircus*) and sheep (*Ovis aries*) comes from the region of eastern Taurus, in Turkey, where the wild ancestors of these species, *Capra aegagrus* and *Ovis orientalis*, respectively, were present. According to zooarchaeological data, goats and sheep do not have the same history and timing of domestication. For goats, in addition to the Anatolian region, an independent center of domestication outside the Pre-Pottery Neolithic (PPNB) cultural sphere has been identified in western Iran, in Ganj Dareh in the Zagros Mountains. By contrast, the domestic sheep was introduced several centuries later from more western regions, while its wild ancestor was widespread on the Iranian Plateau.

Before their domestication, caprini were widely hunted in the Near and Middle East, and at Paleolithic sites (e.g., Yafteh Cave in Iran; Shanidar in Iraq; Dederiyeh in Syria) in these regions, faunal evidence indicates that they constituted one of the most important components of the food economy of mobile hunter-gatherers. Zooarchaeological techniques and the analysis of demographic profiles and kill-off patterns for goat and sheep have shown, however, that very soon after their initial domestication, human communities exploited goats and sheep for products other than meat, as demonstrated at Early Neolithic sites in the western Mediterranean basin like Baume d'Oulin in France. It is now believed that one of the stimuli for the domestication of herbivores (caprini and cattle) was milk and, subsequently, dairy products. Sheep and goats have been and continue to be utilized as the main domestic animal resources in the Near East and southern central Asia because of their ability to adapt to the arid and mountainous or steppic environment of this region. The nomadic populations of this area base their economies on pastoralism with a mobile or semi-mobile way of life. Intra-tooth isotopic analysis on sheep and goats has provided evidence of the cyclic mobility of prehistoric herders seeking grass to ensure herd survival. Nonpermanent residency necessitated the development of food conservation techniques and, in particular, dairy products. In pastoral communities today, a wide range of dairy products is produced in addition to the butter and cheese that are derived from yogurt.

The environmental impact of the pastoral economy is overgrazing and aridification of exploited territories. One example of the anthropogenic impact of nomadic practices on the environment is the production of dairy products like *kashk*, a dried paste of casein that is used as a food condiment by Bakhtiari nomads or other tribes and is very popular in Iran and central Asia, among rural and even urban populations. To make *kashk*, significant quantities of wood are used by nomads for fuel to heat and evaporate the yogurt liquid residue.

Besides the economic importance of goats and sheep in prehistoric and historic-period economies, these animals also had great symbolic value and are depicted on a range of forms, including reliefs, paintings, carvings, and pottery, from a variety of domestic and ritual contexts—for example, Tepe Zaghe in Iran, where goat skulls were exposed in a communal building. The male wild goat is also the most represented animal on ancient Iranian pottery, with particular emphasis on its horn cores.

See also Animal Domestication; Animal Husbandry and Herding; Butchery; Carvings/Carved Representations of Food; Food Preservation; Food Storage; Meat; Milk and Dairy Products; Representational Models of Food and Food Production; Residue Analysis, Dairy Products; Secondary Products Revolution; Stable Isotope Analysis; Sustainability; Zooarchaeology

Further Reading

Cribb, Roger. 1991. *Nomads in Archaeology*. Cambridge: Cambridge University Press.

Harris, David R., ed. 1996. *The Origins and Spread of Agriculture and Pastoralism in Eurasia*. London: UCL Press/Routledge.

Mashkour, Marjan, Hervé Bocherens, and Issam Moussa. 2005. Long Distance Movement of Sheep and Goats of Bakhtiari Nomads Tracked with Intra-Tooth Variations of Stable Isotopes (13C and 18O). In *Diet and Health in Past Animal Populations: Current Research and Future Directions*, edited by J. Davies, M. Fabis, I. Mainland, et al., 113–24. Proceedings of the Ninth ICAZ Conference, Durham, 2002. Oxford: Oxbow.

Naderi, Saeid, Hamid-Reza Rezaei, François Pompanon, et al. 2008. The Goat Domestication Process Inferred from Large-Scale Mitochondrial DNA Analysis of Wild and Domestic Individuals. *Proceedings of the National Academy of Sciences USA* 105(46):17659–64.

Vigne, Jean-Denis. 2011. The Origins of Animal Domestication and Husbandry: A Major Change in the History of Humanity and the Biosphere. *Comptes Rendus Biologies* 334(3):171–81.

Vigne, Jean-Denis, and D. Helmer. 2007. Was Milk a "Secondary Product" in the Old World Neolithisation Process? Its Role in the Domestication of Cattle, Sheep and Goats. *Anthropozoologica* 42(2):9–40.

Zeder, Melinda A., and Brian Hesse. 2000. The Initial Domestication of Goats (*Capra hircus*) in the Zagros Mountains 10,000 Years Ago. *Science* 287(5461):2254–57.

■ MARJAN MASHKOUR

SHELL MIDDENS

Shell middens are dense deposits of the shells left over after people eat, dry, or discard the oyster or clam inside. Because archaeologists do not know why the shell has been concentrated, the use of the word *midden*, which means "garbage," may be misleading. Shellfish can be food for people or, indirectly, food for people via their use as bait for fish and birds. The 300,000-year-old site of Terra Amata in France has the earliest evidence of shell collecting. Several South African sites have a shell matrix 130,000 to 30,000 years old. There are numerous deflated sites with freshwater shells in southern Egypt as early as 22,000 BC. The majority of shell-bearing sites were created in the last 10,000 years, in part the result of stabilizing sea levels and in part because human ritual life took a dramatic turn with the incorporation of feasting in rites, creating very large heaps in the process. Shellfish are an excellent feasting food, as they are easy to harvest, plentiful, and rapidly replenishing. Thus we see not just shell matrix sites but mounds of shells, often with burials incorporated. The feasting remains become the burial place and (perhaps) food for the gods. Feasting mounds of shells with burials can be seen in the Jōmon culture of Japan (7,000–3,000 BP), in the southeastern United States (where they consist of freshwater bivalves) (8,000–3,000 BP), along the Pacific coast of

California (USA) (3,000–500 BP), and in Brazil (5,250 BP). Nonburial shell feasting sites have also been recognized, particularly along the Atlantic coast of the southeastern United States. Shell works—ramps, mounds, rings, arcs, and ridges—were created with shells generated through feasting, and through work parties who added to site layout during their gatherings. The height of shells in these works has been used to suggest social differences among guests and between guests and hosts.

See also FEASTING; FISH/SHELLFISH; FOOD AND STATUS; MIDDENS AND OTHER TRASH DEPOSITS; OFFERINGS AND GRAVE GOODS

Further Reading

Claassen, Cheryl. 1998. *Shells*. Cambridge: Cambridge University Press.
———. 2010. *Feasting with Shellfish in the Southern Ohio Valley*. Knoxville: University of Tennessee Press.
Luby, Edward M., and Mark F. Gruber. 1999. The Dead Must Be Fed: Symbolic Meanings of the Shell Mounds of the San Francisco Bay Area. *Cambridge Archaeological Journal* 9(1):95–108.

■ CHERYL CLAASSEN

SHELLFISH
See FISH/SHELLFISH

SHIPWRECKS

There are two categories of food found on shipwrecks: victuals for the use of the vessel's crew and passengers, and foodstuffs transported as the ship's cargo. Utensils and small containers provide clues about shipboard life. A well-known example comes from excavations of the *Mary Rose*, Henry VIII's flagship, which sank in 1545. Evidence of provisioning for the crew, facilities for food preparation, and the material culture of dining (e.g., wooden tankards, plates, and bowls, pewter and wooden utensils, even a pepper mill) was preserved. Isotopic analysis of skeletal remains for some of the crew contributed to a larger study of the British Navy's dietary regime and showed that the sailor's diet remained largely unchanged from the 16th to the 18th centuries.

Evidence of food transported as cargo may be preserved in the original shipping containers. For ancient Mediterranean shipwrecks, this information is most commonly derived from the ubiquitous amphora. This ceramic jar was designed specifically for maritime transport of bulk liquid and semiliquid commodities. Mediterranean traders employed amphorae throughout the region for at least fifteen centuries, so the potential database for archaeologists is enormous. In most cases, the amphorae recovered from shipwrecks are empty of contents. Hints about what they once contained can be divined from preserved macroremains such as olive pits or grape pips. Organic residues can sometimes be identified using chemical analytical techniques such as gas chromatography and gas chromatography–mass spectrometry. In rare cases, archaeologists have recovered food remains such as beef bones. Until recently, however, archaeologists usually had to guess at the contents of empty amphorae based upon the few ancient written sources that described amphora contents, or the fame of goods associated with the amphora's place of origin. Though some scholars have suggested that amphorae may have contained fish products, it was commonly assumed that the amphorae contained wine or sometimes olive oil.

Advances in molecular biology have changed our understanding of ancient trade in food, however. Using techniques revised from police forensics, nondestructive swabs of the interiors of ostensibly empty amphorae can capture trace ancient DNA of the original contents. The picture emerging from these studies is entirely new: instead of wine, ancient DNA shows wide varieties of foodstuffs inside fifth- to third-century BC Greek amphorae (figure 54). A recent study detected olive DNA in 66 percent of the analyzed jars, with grape DNA appearing in 55 percent. More tellingly, both grape and olive products were

Figure 54. Analysis of amphorae recovered from shipwrecks has identified the presence of ancient DNA (aDNA) trapped in the porous ceramic bodies of many containers. Though commonly described as wine jars, amphorae aDNA studies now indicate that they were used to transport a wide variety of foodstuffs. Amphora BE 94-27, shown in this figure, comes from Corcyra on the island of Corfu and dates to the third century BC. Photograph by P. Vezirtis, Ephorate of Underwater Antiquities. Drawing by E. Paul Oberlander, Woods Hole Oceanographic Institution. Reprinted from Foley et al. 2012 (fig. 1.9, fig. 2) with permission from Elsevier.

mixed with several different herbs, spices, and flavorings: rosemary, sage, thyme, oregano, mint, juniper, and terebinth. DNA of legumes, ginger, pine, and walnut also appeared in those amphorae. DNA studies of ceramic containers will continue to provide hard data for the trade in ancient foods, the primary goods traded in the earliest economies.

See also AMPHORAE; BIOMOLECULAR ANALYSIS; DNA ANALYSIS; GAS CHROMATOGRAPHY/ GAS CHROMATOGRAPHY–MASS SPECTROMETRY; MACROREMAINS; RESIDUE ANALYSIS, TARTARIC ACID; TRADE ROUTES

Further Reading

Badura, Monika, Beata Możejko, and Waldemar Ossowski, 2013. Bulbs of Onion (*Allium cepa* L.) and Garlic (*Allium sativum* L.) from the 15th-Century Copper Wreck in Gdańsk (Baltic Sea): A Part of Victualling? *Journal of Archaeological Science* 40(11):4066–72.

Carlson, Deborah N. 2003. The Classical Greek Shipwreck at Tektaş Burnu, Turkey. *American Journal of Archaeology* 107(4):581–600.

Foley, Brendan P., Maria C. Hansson, Dimitris P. Kourkoumelis, et al. 2012. Aspects of Ancient Greek Trade Re-Evaluated with Amphora DNA Evidence. *Journal of Archaeological Science* 39(2):389–98.

Lund, John, and Vincent Gabrielsen. 2004. A Fishy Business: Transport Amphorae of the Black Sea Region as a Source for the Trade in Fish and Fish Products in the Classical and Hellenistic Periods. In *Ancient Fishing and Fish Processing in the Black Sea Region*, edited by Tonnes Bekker-Nielsen, 161–69. Black Sea Studies 2. Aarhus: Aarhus University Press.

Roberts, Patrick, Sam Weston, Bastien Wild, et al. 2012. The Men of Nelson's Navy: A Comparative Stable Isotope Dietary Study of Late 18th Century and Early 19th Century Servicemen from Royal Naval Hospital Burial Grounds at Plymouth and Gosport, England. *American Journal of Physical Anthropology* 148(1):1–10.

■ BRENDAN P. FOLEY

SLAVE DIET, ON SLAVE SHIPS

European ships forcibly transported more than ten million Africans to the Americas between 1514 and 1866, and many African captives encountered European foods and foodways for the first time on their voyage into slavery. The round trip for a slave ship took a year. A typical vessel carried a crew of 20–30 men and, for several months, some 300 captive Africans. The provisioning of slave ships was therefore an expensive and logistically demanding enterprise. Flour, grains, dried beans and peas, and salted meat and fish were purchased before the voyage began. English ships carried large supplies of peas and beans, French vessels favored oats, while manioc (cassava) was preferred by the Portuguese. Yams, rice, maize, malagueta (chili) pepper, and palm oil from the West African coast were sourced in enormous quantities to sustain the captives during the Atlantic crossing. Ships were restocked in the Americas before the return journey to Europe. Slave ships also carried large quantities of alcohol—principally rum, brandy, and wine—and fresh water. Tobacco and clay tobacco pipes also were taken aboard: tobacco was regularly issued to captives at mealtimes because smoking was perceived to have a calming influence.

The Portuguese established precise regulations regarding the provisioning of slave ships as early as 1519, but the documentary evidence for British slave ships is particularly rich. Voyage logbooks, diaries, and data collated from 1788 to 1792 during the Parliamentary Inquiries into the trade point to a remarkably consistent dietary regime that was well established before 1700 and persisted until the abolition of the British trade in 1807. Long-distance merchant ships were invariably reliant on dried and salted foods, but slave ships also made extensive use of West African produce. Ships leaving Upper Guinea were laden with rice, while those leaving Angola acquired maize. Yams were purchased in huge quantities by ships visiting the Niger Delta. Rice, maize, and yams were central to the diets of these African regions, and slave ship captains were not only aware of this but recognized that captives were more likely to remain healthy if their diet was based on familiar foods. In 1693 Thomas Phillips, captain of the British ship *Hannibal*, described a dietary regime based on West African dietary preferences and chiefly comprising boiled beans and *dabbadabb*. The latter was a maize-based porridge made from finely ground grain boiled with water, and served with a relish of salt, malagueta pepper, and palm oil. Alexander Falconbridge noted in 1788 that the diet of the African captives on Bristol ships of this period chiefly comprised boiled horse beans, yams, and rice. "Slabber sauce" (a corruption of *dabbadabb*), made from palm oil, flour, water, and pepper, was still eaten in this period.

According to Phillips, *dabbadabb* was prepared in a copper furnace. Two copper cooking kettles were recovered from the wreck of the *Henrietta Marie* (1700). The smaller of these riveted sheet copper containers was divided internally to make two small chambers. It was used in cooking for the crew, whose diet included a far higher proportion of salted beef and pork than was fed to captive Africans. The larger kettle comprised a vast single chamber, ideally suited to preparing one-pot, glutinous meals like *dabbadabb*. The capacity of this cauldron was calculated to be about 321.71 liters, large enough to feed at least 300 captives.

Food onboard slave ships also was prepared in African ways. Some ships, though by no means all, employed African cooks specifically for this purpose. The wreck of the Danish ship *Fredensborg* (1768) produced a sandstone mortar of a type regularly employed in West Africa (and also by plantation slaves in South Carolina) to pound rice or millet. The log of the *Fredensborg* reveals that three such mortars were carried on the ship, facilitating the preparation of one-pot meals based almost entirely on beans and millet.

The dehydrating effect of a diet based on dried, starchy, and salty foods contributed directly to the poor physical and mental health of African captives. Sickness and depression led in turn to a loss of appetite. The refusal to eat was also one of the few forms of active resistance open to captives. For precisely that reason, those who refused food faced severe punishments from the cat (whip) or thumbscrews. Many British ships carried a speculum oris, a device shaped like a pair of scissors that was inserted into the mouth and employed to force apart the jaws; captives were then force-fed.

Despite these brutalities, slave ships were a locus of culinary interchange on a number of levels. African captives ate largely familiar meals, but did so using wooden bowls, platters, and spoons fashioned by the ships' carpenters. At the same time, European sailors developed a nuanced understanding of African dietary preferences, while consuming many African-grown foodstuffs themselves and flavoring their meals with the same pepper and oil consumed by their captives. Bioarchaeological studies of the skeletal remains of African-born slaves who died in the United States, the Caribbean, and South Africa demonstrate that the diet of most captives changed both rapidly and radically once they were enslaved. Those changes began on the slave ship itself. Only a handful of wrecks from the slave trade have been excavated by maritime archaeologists, but as the finds from the *Henrietta Marie* and *Fredensborg* suggest, wrecks offer important new insights into many aspects of life onboard slave ships.

See also BIOARCHAEOLOGICAL ANALYSIS; FOOD AND IDENTITY; FOOD AND INEQUALITY; FOOD AND POWER; MAIZE; MANIOC/CASSAVA; RICE; SHIPWRECKS; SLAVE DIET, ON SOUTHERN PLANTATIONS; SLAVE DIET, ON WEST INDIAN PLANTATIONS; STABLE ISOTOPE ANALYSIS; YAM

Further Reading

Christopher, Emma. 2006. *Slave Ship Sailors and Their Captive Cargoes, 1730–1807*. Cambridge: Cambridge University Press.

Covey Herbert C., and Dwight Eisnach. 2009. *What the Slaves Ate: Recollections of African American Foods and Foodways from the Slave Narratives*. Santa Barbara, CA: Greenwood Press.

Cox, Glenda, and Judith Sealy. 1997. Investigating Identity and Life Histories: Isotopic Analysis and Historical Documentation of Slave Skeletons Found on the Cape Town Foreshore, South Africa. *International Journal of Historical Archaeology* 1(3):207–24.

Svalesen, Leif. 2000. *The Slave Ship* Fredensborg. Kingston, Jamaica: Ian Randle.

Voyages: The Transatlantic Slave Trade Database. 2009. http://slavevoyages.org.

Webster, Jane, ed. 2008. The Archaeology of Slave Ships. *International Journal of Historical Archaeology*, special issue, 12(1).

■ JANE WEBSTER

SLAVE DIET, ON SOUTHERN PLANTATIONS

Did enslaved African Americans on plantations in the southeastern United States get enough to eat? Was the diet nutritionally adequate? How did slaves supplement the rations provided to them by their owners? Did African culinary traditions remain a strong influence on foodways in New World settings? What was the role of food in plantation social life? Archaeologists seek to answer these questions using direct evidence for slave diet. This work generally takes a broad anthropological approach to diet, focusing on the cultural and social context as well as on nutrition and physiology.

Broad historical scholarship has long looked to diet as a key marker in questions about the physical treatment of slaves. Using documentary sources, historians have come to the consensus that typical weekly rations to slaves consisted of about 1.25 pecks (about ten dry quarts) of corn meal and 3.5 pounds of cured or salt pork. There is also common recognition that rations were only one side of the plantation subsistence triangle, with garden produce and livestock raised by slaves as the second, and hunting, fishing, and foraging in the wild as the third food source. (For slaves living within or near urban centers, bartering for or purchasing foods from market sources served as another possible way to supplement rations.) One important study concluded that slaves on southeastern plantations must have had a nutritionally adequate food supply in order to maintain their capacity for hard labor and to maintain the high birth rate in the region. Plantation diet may have been physiologically adequate while being dreadfully unsatisfactory, an attitude constantly expressed in writings and oral narratives from the slaves themselves. Archaeological research has focused on using excavated evidence and contextual analysis to explore these ideas and to fill in gaps in the historical record.

Excavations at slave dwellings yield a variety of artifacts related to food preparation and consumption, including animal bones, floral remains, ceramics, and cooking tools. Archaeological research has focused largely on faunal remains in seeking direct information on slave diet. Bones commonly survive well in the ground and are usually readily identifiable in terms of species and body parts. Floral remains, because of preservation issues, are much less common sources of direct information on slave diet.

Bones and other categories of archaeological data cannot be easily linked to fine-grained details of diet as a result of differential preservation, post-depositional disturbance, and other transformations of the archaeological record. Animal bones from slave contexts do serve as reliable sources on the range of represented species. Bones of wild species as well as domestic animals are commonly found on slave sites, providing strong confirmation of hunting, fishing, and foraging to supplement diet. Faunal studies are less reliable in identifying the relative amounts of meat from different animals within the slave diet. For example, the number of recovered pig bones from archaeological contexts seriously underrepresents the amount of pork typically eaten by slaves, since boneless salt pork usually dominated the rations distributed to the plantation community.

Archaeological studies of slave diet typically seek to understand food within its broader social context. A common focus is on the use of food by slave owners not just as sustenance for their labor force but also in systems of reward, punishment, and subordination. A complementary approach attempts to reconstruct how enslaved African Americans bent and circumvented these efforts. An effective way to study this issue is to consider the sources and flow of food into the slave community. The distribution of rations, slave-directed gardening and livestock raising, foraging for plants and animals from the wild, and "gleaning" and theft of food each involved complicated social decisions and interaction between masters and slaves. Were rations given out as raw ingredients on a weekly basis, or was there a central kitchen serving meals on a daily basis? Were variations in the amount of rationed food used as incentive and punishment? Were slave gardens allowed, and how much control did owners exert over what was grown and how the produce was used? Was hunting allowed, or did slaves undertake it surreptitiously? What risks were slaves willing to take in stealing to supplement their food supply? To answer these questions, archaeologists need to see slave and owner as each having an active role in determining the details of slave diet. From this perspective, food reveals the tensions over what planters sought to control and how slaves, often thought of as passively accepting domination, took effective action in determining the details of their diet. Understanding diet in this way points to the active role of the slave community in shaping other aspects of plantation life.

Archaeological studies of slave diet also have wrestled with questions about the survival of African culinary traditions in plantation settings. Results of this search have been mixed, largely as a result of the limitations of the archaeological record. The West African emphasis on one-pot meals or stewing survived as a key cooking technique within slave communities, and researchers have linked this to bone breakage patterns and the types of ceramic vessels recovered from slave dwelling sites. Along with the millions caught in the slave trade, a variety of food plants crossed to the New World. Yams, sorghum, okra, watermelon, pumpkins, sesame seeds, certain strains of rice, legumes like black-eyed peas, and leafy greens like collards all had an established place in West African cuisine and became important in American cooking as well. African culinary traditions continue to inspire African American and broader American foodways, filtered through the brutal setting and limitations of plantation slavery.

See also COLUMBIAN EXCHANGE; CREOLE CUISINES/FOODWAYS; CREOLIZATION; DIASPORA FOODWAYS; FOOD AND IDENTITY; FOOD AND INEQUALITY; FOOD AND POWER; OLD WORLD GLOBALIZATION AND FOOD EXCHANGES; ORAL AND FOLK NARRATIVES; POPLAR FOREST; SLAVE DIET, ON SLAVE SHIPS; SLAVE DIET, ON WEST INDIAN PLANTATIONS

Further Reading

Covey, Herbert C., and Dwight Esnach. 2009. *What the Slaves Ate: Recollections of African American Foods and Foodways from the Slave Narratives.* Santa Barbara, CA: Greenwood Press.

Gibbs, Tyson, Kathleen Cargill, Leslie Sue Lieberman, and Elizabeth Reitz. 1980. Nutrition in a Slave Population: An Anthropological Examination. *Medical Anthropology* 4(2):175–262.

McKee, Larry. 1999. Food Supply and Plantation Social Order: An Archaeological Perspective. In *"I, Too, Am America": Archaeological Studies of African-American Life,* edited by Theresa A. Singleton, 218–39. Charlottesville: University Press of Virginia.

■ LARRY MCKEE

SLAVE DIET, ON WEST INDIAN PLANTATIONS

By the close of the 17th century, the subset of Caribbean Islands known generally as the British West Indies was on a social and historical trajectory dominated by plantation agriculture. While indentured servitude provided labor for several of the islands first settled by the British, including Barbados, Jamaica, Nevis, and Montserrat, by the 18th century most of the West Indian planters had turned to African slavery as a source of labor. The size of the enslaved workforce varied greatly depending on the crop produced, the island in question, and the relative wealth of the planter. Small-scale planters may have had as few as a dozen slaves while the largest estates employed hundreds, with individual planters on the larger islands owning multiple plantations and thousands of slaves. Feeding a large enslaved workforce was a central concern of plantation managers.

Archaeologists working on the question of West Indian slavery tend to analyze diet from several perspectives, including reference to primary documentary sources describing diet and available food sources, direct archaeological evidence of foodways based on the recovery of food remains and the analysis of ceramic vessels related to food preparation and consumption, and the analysis of human remains recovered from slave burial ground contexts.

Plantation owners and managers developed an economic system that relied on multiple sources of food. It was customary for planters to provide some staple foods to their enslaved populations, including imported rice, wheat flour, salted beef, and a variety of salted fishes, the most important of which were cod and herring. These staples were joined with a variety of locally grown vegetable foods that were produced on small swidden farms known as provision grounds and in kitchen gardens attached to slave houses in the plantation villages. Primary sources from the 18th and 19th centuries indicate that slaves produced a variety of tubers in the provision grounds (to this day known as "ground provisions" in Jamaica), including potatoes, sweet potatoes, yams, and cassava. Plantains and cooked (fried or boiled) bananas provided additional carbohydrates. A diversity of New World fruits were consumed, including chayote or cho-cho (*Sechium edule*), avocado (*Persea americana*), and star apple (*Chrysophyllum cainito*). A variety of plants introduced from South Asia and Oceania were also central to the diet, including breadfruit (*Artocarpus altilis*, famously introduced from Tahiti by Captain Bligh of the *Bounty*), jack fruit (*Artocarpus heterophyllus*), and mango (genus *Mangifera*). Ackee (*Blighia sapida*) was an important component of the slave diet on several islands, notably Jamaica. Other important plant foods include a variety of beans and leafy greens, such as cabbage, amaranth, and taro leaves (taro is often referred to as *dasheen* in the West Indies). Flavoring was added through onions, peppers, and a variety of locally produced spices. On many estates, the enslaved kept poultry and hogs to provide additional protein sources for their diet.

Because enslaved plantation workers in the West Indies seldom used privies, a common source of archaeological data on diet, most of the direct archaeological evidence for diet comes from midden contexts and tends to be biased toward faunal remains. Archaeological evidence of meat consumption has been recovered in several midden contexts, notably at Clifton Plantation in the Bahamas and at Drax Hall and Montpelier Plantation in Jamaica. At Clifton, domestic mammals and land crabs dominated the assemblage. In the assemblage from Drax, fewer wild food sources were recovered, and pig, cow, goat, and chicken were predominant. Similar results were obtained at Montpelier Plantation in Jamaica, where domestic mammals and chicken were predominant, with only a small percentage of recovered food remains coming from nondomesticated animals. In each case, relatively little faunal material was recovered. This can be partially explained by the common practice of stewing meat; food preparation thus resulted in the fragmentation of bone material into pieces so small that few survive in the archaeological record.

For most of the 18th century, enslaved populations throughout the Caribbean used locally produced earthenwares for food preparation. The majority of these are hollow-bodied forms used for cooking stews over an open flame. Such earthenwares have been found in archaeological contexts throughout both the Greater and Lesser Antilles. In most cases, they appear to have been produced by local ceramic experts and traded either across the larger islands or between the smaller. Although these ceramics continued to be used into the 20th century, by the early 19th century locally produced ceramic cooking pots were largely replaced with more durable imported iron pots, though these would be used to prepare foods in much the same way.

Human remains have been recovered from several archaeological contexts and have been analyzed for evidence of nutritional stress and other indicators of diet. Pathological signatures, particularly enamel hypoplasia and porotic hyperostosis, on skeletal remains recovered from Montserrat and Jamaica reveal nutritional stresses brought on by chronic malnutrition and anemia. Although the plantation diet encompassed protein and salt from imported meat and fish, and carbohydrates and vitamins from locally produced foodstuffs, many of the enslaved suffered from nutritional diseases. As Dr. David Collins, a West India planter, noted in the early 1800s, "the most frequent error" in the management of the diet of the enslaved "is not giving them enough."

See also AGRICULTURAL/HORTICULTURAL SITES; BIOARCHAEOLOGICAL ANALYSIS; BUTCHERY; COLUMBIAN EXCHANGE; DIASPORA FOODWAYS; FOOD AND INEQUALITY; FOOD AND POWER; MIDDENS AND OTHER TRASH DEPOSITS; OLD WORLD GLOBALIZATION AND FOOD EXCHANGES; PACIFIC OCEANIC EXCHANGE; PALEODIETARY ANALYSIS; PALEONUTRITION; PALEOPATHOLOGY; SLAVE DIET, ON SLAVE SHIPS; SLAVE DIET, ON SOUTHERN PLANTATIONS

Further Reading

Armstrong, Douglas V. 1990. *The Old Village and the Great House: An Archaeological and Historical Examination of Drax Hall Plantation, St. Ann's Bay, Jamaica.* Urbana: University of Illinois Press.

Higman, Barry W. 1998. *Montpelier, Jamaica: A Plantation Community in Slavery and Freedom, 1739–1912.* Mona, Jamaica: University of the West Indies Press.

Watters, David R. 1994. Mortuary Patterns at the Harney Site Slave Cemetery, Montserrat, in Caribbean Perspective. *Historical Archaeology* 28(3):56–73.

Wilkie, Laurie A., and Paul Farnsworth. 2005. *Sampling Many Pots: An Archaeology of Memory and Tradition at a Bahamian Plantation.* Gainesville: University Press of Florida.

■ JAMES A. DELLE

SOIL CHEMISTRY
See SOIL MICROTECHNIQUES

SOIL MICROTECHNIQUES

Soil microtechniques encompass a wide range of methods that researchers use to investigate nonvisible aspects of archaeological sediments and soils. Although macroscopic remains constitute the majority of evidence used to reconstruct past subsistence strategies and foodways, the ephemeral nature of food means that much information is lost as a result of taphonomic destruction. Soil microtechniques provide archaeologists with information that would otherwise not be recovered through standard macroscopic analyses. Researchers have successfully applied the methods described here to interpret the use of space within residential and ritual structures, stabling and animal husbandry practices, the processing and storage of plant foods, food waste disposal, manuring and other agricultural practices, and the use and control of fire.

Soil microtechniques generally rely on two different types of sampling methods: loose samples and block samples. Loose samples are the most common type of sediment samples collected at archaeological sites and can be used for the recovery of macroscopic and microscopic fossil remains. Soil microtechniques employed on loose samples can include elemental, mineralogical, molecular, and biomarker analyses.

Archaeologists often employ chemical analysis of archaeological deposits to investigate lateral variations in the concentration of elements across a site. The concept behind these analyses is that certain activities, such as waste disposal, food processing, or craft production, leave behind specific elemental signatures. Multi-elemental concentrations can be readily measured using a variety of techniques, including inductively coupled plasma–atomic emission spectroscopy (ICP-AES), inductively coupled plasma–mass spectroscopy (ICP-MS), and X-ray fluorescence (XRF). In theory, any element's concentration can be mapped across a site. Some elements that have been used in past studies include calcium (Ca), barium (Ba), mercury (Hg), lead (Pb), potassium (K), rubidium (Rb), zinc (Zn), copper (Cu), strontium (Sr), magnesium (Mg), and, most frequently, phosphorus (P). The elemental data produced in these studies are often statistically manipulated (e.g., discriminant analysis, principle component analysis) to determine the significance of patterns of distribution.

Phosphorus (P) analysis has been widely used since the 1970s for archaeological prospection and also the reconstruction of past human activities. At archaeological sites, phosphorus is usually associated with biological input, and it has been linked with several anthropic sources, including human waste, refuse disposal, burials, and ash. Agricultural practices associated with fertilization and penning of animals can also lead to the enrichment of phosphorus in archaeological deposits.

Parnell and colleagues, in a chemical study of deposits associated with a structure at the Late Classic Maya site of Piedras Negras (Guatemala), identified spatial variation in the distribution of phosphorus and heavy metals. They argued that areas exhibiting concentrations of heavy metals were likely used for craft production, whereas areas rich in phosphate but poor in heavy metals were likely used for food processing.

Loose samples can also be analyzed using molecular techniques. For example, Fourier transform infrared (FTIR) spectroscopy has a wide range of applications. It has been successfully applied in the analysis of chemical alteration of archaeological deposits, which can be useful when determining the preservation potential of bones, phytoliths, and other fossils that potentially contain information about past foodways. Organic chemicals, in the form of biomarkers, are also a rich source of information preserved in archaeological sediments and soils. For example, the identification of coprastanol—an organic molecule formed in the gut of higher mammals—can be used to identify the presence of human waste and also to interpret manuring practices.

Although chemical analyses of archaeological deposits have proven useful, these methods have their limitations. A major problem is that there are a large number of nonhuman variables that can influence the concentration of elements within an archaeological site. Practitioners must factor in natural sources for these elements and compounds, and they must rule out the possibility of taphonomic mixing or destruction. Therefore, it is generally advisable to use loose-sample methods in concert with techniques that rely on block samples, namely, micromorphology.

Micromorphology is the study of oriented, intact blocks of archaeological soil or sediment that are indurated, or hardened, with a resin, sliced, and made into thin sections. Practitioners analyze the thin section using a range of magnifications, normally employing a petrographic microscope to identify sedimentary components, structures, and pedogenic (soil-forming) and anthropogenic features. Because the spatial integrity of the sample is preserved, micromorphologists can determine the relative spatial and temporal relationship between materials and processes. Micromorphology is a useful method in the analysis of past subsistence strategies and foodways. For example, Shahack-Gross, among others, has shown that micromorphology can be used in the identification of in situ accumulations of herbivore dung. Micromorphology also has been useful in the study of midden deposits and in the identification of past agricultural, fertilization, and irrigation practices. This method also has proven successful in the investigation of fire and its role in human evolution.

Soil microtechniques, when conducted together with more traditional macroscopic methods, provide the archaeologist with information about past foodways that would otherwise remain invisible. The methods described here can be applied in almost any archaeological setting and are essential for a more holistic approach to the archaeology of food.

See also AGRICULTURAL FEATURES, IDENTIFICATION AND ANALYSIS; ANIMAL HUSBANDRY AND HERDING; ARCHAEOLOGY OF HOUSEHOLD FOOD PRODUCTION; BIOMOLECULAR ANALYSIS; EXPERIMENTAL ARCHAEOLOGY; FIRE-BASED COOKING FEATURES; INFRARED SPECTROSCOPY/ FOURIER TRANSFORM INFRARED SPECTROSCOPY; LANDSCAPE AND ENVIRONMENTAL RECONSTRUCTION; MANURES AND OTHER FERTILIZERS, IDENTIFICATION AND ANALYSIS; MIDDENS AND OTHER TRASH DEPOSITS; SAN GENESIO, MEDIEVAL TAVERN SITE (SAN MINIATO, PISA); STORAGE FACILITIES; WONDERWERK CAVE

Further Reading

Bookidis, Nancy, Julie Hansen, Lynn Snyder, and Paul Goldberg. 1999. Dining in the Sanctuary of Demeter and Kore at Corinth. *Hesperia* 68(1):1–54.

Courty, Marie-Agnés, Paul Goldberg, and Richard Macphail. 1989. *Soils and Micromorphology in Archaeology.* New York: Cambridge University Press.

Holliday, Vance T., and William G. Gartner. 2007. Methods of Soil P Analysis in Archaeology. *Journal of Archaeological Science* 34(2):301–33.

Parnell, J. Jacob, Richard E. Terry, and Zachary Nelson. 2002. Soil Chemical Analysis Applied as an Interpretive Tool for Ancient Human Activities in Piedras Negras, Guatemala. *Journal of Archaeological Science* 29(4):379–404.

Shahack-Gross, Ruth. 2011. Herbivorous Livestock Dung: Formation, Taphonomy, Methods for Identification, and Archaeological Significance. *Journal of Archaeological Science* 38(2):205–18.

Wilson, Clare A., Donald A. Davidson, and Malcolm S. Cresser. 2008. Multi-Element Soil Analysis: An Assessment of Its Potential as an Aid to Archaeological Interpretation. *Journal of Archaeological Science* 35(2):412–24.

■ CHRISTOPHER MILLER

SORGHUM

At an ancient archaeological site in southern Egypt called the Nabta Playa, charred Sorghum (*Sorghum bicolor* L. Moench) was dated to 8,000 BP. It was hypothesized that this important cereal was collected and stored for unknown rituals and food uses. Today, sorghum is used worldwide as an important gluten-free cereal and in traditional dishes.

Its origin is the rich savannas of ancient Ethiopia and Sudan, from whence it dispersed throughout Africa along human migratory paths and was domesticated into five major races based on various climates and food uses. Africans make the thick porridge *tô* and fermented *kisra* bread with sorghum, couscous in West Africa, and fermented beverages in southern Africa.

From ports along the eastern African shore, sorghum traveled to India and China. It was clearly described by Chinese authors of the Yuan Dynasty in the 14th century AD and is known in modern China as "wine." Because of its inherent drought tolerance and its low susceptibility to insects and disease, it became a mainstay in India for rain-fed farmers, where it was and continues to be used for both unfermented and fermented breads, thick and thin porridges, boiled whole grain, and alcoholic beverages.

Sorghum's path to Europe and the Americas is less clear, though it must have been cultivated in Italy by the late 1600s to early 1700s AD as evidenced by its use in festoons (wall decorations) in the Villa Farnesina. From slave ports in West Africa, it is surmised that sorghum traveled to the Americas, where some of the oldest sorghums are thought to be located on the island of Haiti. Specialty sweet sorghums may have traveled from the Caribbean to the southeast United States, where production of sorghum molasses or syrup continues to fill niche markets for sweeteners. Its path to Central America is unknown, but sorghum's importance as an alternative cereal for tortilla production is growing throughout the region. More research is needed to understand the introduction and movement of sorghum into the Americas and its impact on various ethnic cultures and food systems.

See also AGRICULTURE, ORIGINS OF; CEREALS; COLUMBIAN EXCHANGE; OLD WORLD GLOBALIZATION AND FOOD EXCHANGES; SLAVE DIET, ON SOUTHERN PLANTATIONS

Further Reading

Smith, C. Wayne, and Richard A. Frederiksen, eds. 2000. *Sorghum: Origin, History, Technology, and Production.* New York: John Wiley & Sons.

■ JEFF A. DAHLBERG

SPATIAL ANALYSIS AND VISUALIZATION TECHNIQUES

Archaeologists use a number of multiscalar techniques to reconstruct and visualize ancient landscapes and spaces associated with past subsistence practices. Applications include broad landscape analyses using satellite, airborne, and ground imagery (e.g., LiDAR) to reveal field systems, irrigation networks, farm and mill structures, and even the road systems across which goods and foodstuffs were moved. More focused spatial analysis within individual sites may include the study of architectural or spatial configurations, as well as identification of discrete activity areas using soil chemistry and microarchaeological techniques in combination with architectural and other types of analyses.

Increasingly sophisticated, computer-based spatial modeling programs (e.g., GIS) have made it possible to reconstruct and visualize a variety of past landscapes, sites, and features using 2D- and 3D-mapping techniques. Integrated approaches are increasingly important—for example, laser scanning with soil chemistry to reconstruct farming practices and create 3D images of historical settlement patterns in Scotland, or the use of ROVs (remotely operated vehicles) and sonar to map ancient water storage systems. These techniques can produce highly accurate, detailed maps of past landscapes.

It is more difficult to visualize past human behaviors within specific landscapes, particularly those with social or symbolic dimensions. Archaeologists have developed or borrowed a number of tools to conceptualize such interaction. To date, most applications have been directed toward the study of ancient trade networks. Spatial models are increasingly used to hypothesize not only the flow of goods but also communication networks and a range of socioeconomic relationships associated with exchange and reciprocity. Network analysis has been combined with techniques such as portable X-ray fluorescence technology (pXRF) and instrumental neutron activation analysis (INAA) to source material goods (e.g., pottery) and natural resources (e.g., obsidian) to reconstruct trade networks. By mapping the distribution of physical objects, archaeologists may chart the transmission of information, technology, and new ideas about food. With advances in residue analysis and other techniques, it is possible to chart the exchange and distribution of new or specialized foods (e.g., the contents of Roman amphorae, or the spread of cacao into the southwestern United States) and the contexts of their use (e.g., ceremonial or trade based). Other applications of network analysis include a study of the vast Inca road system and locations of the state's production and storage sites (including those associated with the production and storage of maize and *chicha*) and administrative sites. Through an analysis of centrality, two distinct types of economic exchange were discerned, involving different sets of socioeconomic relationships and different spatial relationships.

Alternate visualization techniques draw upon the concept of spatial syntax (how space is connected to society). Archaeologists have used the theory and methods of this approach to examine commercial spaces in Pompeii, including bakeries, taverns, and inns. Using a computer reconstruction of the street network, specific features of the built environment, including doors, windows, and lines of sight, as well as spatial characteristics such as access and density, were examined to investigate the impact of architectural or spatial relationships upon social and economic interaction. Reconstructions of urban landscapes such as Pompeii and Ostia have focused not only on identifying the distinctions between commercial and domestic spaces, but on how space is experienced differently (e.g., by gender), how access and space affect proxemics, and how spatial relationships may involve an archaeology of the senses.

Domestic spaces are also subject to a range of spatial analyses and visualization techniques. Soil chemistry and microarchaeology have helped to identify household food production areas at Xaltocan, Mexico, for example. Flotation samples from the earthen and adobe floors of domestic structures were combined with trace element analysis of soil samples to detect fish-processing activities (characterized by high levels of the sodium used as a preservative, fish scales, and fishing-related artifacts) and tortilla production (e.g., the chemical signatures of *nixtamal*), and to distinguish between household and market production based on the intensity of the activities. Chemical testing of floors at a medieval tavern site at San Genesio, Italy, and at the Maya Royal Kitchens at Kabah identified the functions of specific rooms within these structures. Mapping of in situ hearths, storage caches and pits, furnishings, and artifacts associated with food processing (e.g., ground stone tools or bedrock features) and consumption at Natufian base camps and Pre-Pottery Neolithic village sites was used to discern the locations of these activities, but also to examine the spatial and social implications of food production, including the sexual division of labor and changing social relations within household and community. Food mapping, a technique borrowed from anthropology, has been proposed as a tool to connect the physical spaces, food remains, and material culture associated with food production and consumption with individuals and families in historic-period communities. Mapping of food-related activities in a Pennsylvania coal mining community using archival sources, oral history, family reconstruction, and archaeological data showed that relationships enacted through food sharing and shared food tasks varied by age, gender, ethnicity, religion, and other identities and were integral to the negotiation of place and identity, as well as network and community formation. This approach mirrors techniques used by anthropologists, ethnographers, and geographers who use mapping to study cognitive landscapes, proxemics, spatial tactics, and phenomenology.

See also AGRICULTURAL FEATURES, IDENTIFICATION AND ANALYSIS; AMPHORAE; ARCHAEOLOGY OF HOUSEHOLD FOOD PRODUCTION; ARCHITECTURAL ANALYSIS; CACAO/CHOCOLATE; *CHICHA*; FOOD AS SENSORY EXPERIENCE; FOOD TECHNOLOGY AND IDEAS ABOUT FOOD, SPREAD OF; HERCULANEUM AND POMPEII; HOUSEHOLD ARCHAEOLOGY; IRRIGATION/HYDRAULIC ENGINEERING; KABAH, MAYA ROYAL KITCHEN; MARKETS/EXCHANGE; SAN GENESIO, MEDIEVAL TAVERN SITE (SAN MINIATO, PISA); SOIL MICROTECHNIQUES; STAR CARR; TRADE ROUTES

Further Reading

Brughmans, Tom. 2010. Connecting the Dots: Towards Archaeological Network Analysis. *Oxford Journal of Archaeology* 29(3):277–303.

De Lucia, Kristin. 2013. Domestic Economies and Regional Transition: Household Multicrafting and Lake Exploitation in Pre-Aztec Central Mexico. *Journal of Anthropological Archaeology* 32(4):353–67.

Entwistle, J. A., K. J. W. McCaffrey, and P. W. Abrahams. 2009. Three-Dimensional (3D) Visualisation: The Application of Terrestrial Laser Scanning in the Investigation of Historical Scottish Farming Townships. *Journal of Archaeological Science* 36(3):860–66.

Jenkins, David. 2001. A Network Analysis of Inka Roads, Administrative Centers, and Storage Facilities. *Ethnohistory* 48(4):655–87.

Ossa, Alanna. 2013. Using Network Expectations to Identify Multiple Exchange Systems: A Case Study from Postclassic Sauce and Its Hinterland in Veracruz, Mexico. *Journal of Anthropological Archaeology* 32(4):415–32.

Paliou, Eleftheria, Undine Lieberwirth, and Silvia Polla, eds. 2014. *Spatial Analysis and Social Spaces: Interdisciplinary Approaches to the Interpretation of Prehistoric and Historic Built Environments.* Berlin Studies of the Ancient World 18. Berlin: De Gruyter.

Wright, Katherine I. 2000. The Social Origins of Cooking and Dining in Early Villages of Western Asia. *Proceedings of the Prehistoric Society* 66:89–121.

■ KAREN BESCHERER METHENY

SPECTROSCOPY

See INFRARED SPECTROSCOPY/FOURIER TRANSFORM INFRARED SPECTROSCOPY

SPENT GRAIN AS ANIMAL FEED

Spent grain is a byproduct of brewing and distilling. Throughout history and prehistory, it has been an important and nutritious source of food for domesticated animals. Today, it is common practice for breweries and distilleries to sell or give their spent grain to local farmers. Also known as draff or brewer's grains, the spent grain left in the mash tun after lautering and sparging is excellent animal fodder. Spent grain leaves no trace in the archaeological record.

In both brewing and distilling, fermentable sugars are made in a mash tun. Hot water is added to crushed malt, which is heated to 65°C for up to an hour. We now understand that, at these temperatures, enzymes within the malt reactivate and convert grain starch into sugars. This has been scientifically understood only within the last sixty years.

After the mash is lautered and sparged to extract the sweet liquid for brewing, what is left in the mash tun is the spent grain. It is not alcoholic. It consists of grain husks, residual sugars, proteins, and lipids. It does not keep well and spoils within five to seven days, depending upon ambient temperature. Older strains of barley, such as bere, provide three times as much spent grain as modern barley.

Archaeological evidence is limited. At Durrington Walls, a Neolithic henge and large settlement situated a few miles from Stonehenge, England, the teeth of slaughtered pigs had dental caries. This is probably the result of eating spent grain as fodder.

See also ANIMAL HUSBANDRY AND HERDING; BARLEY; BREWING/MALTING; CATTLE; DISTILLATION

Further Reading

Dineley, Merryn. 2006. The Use of Spent Grain as Cattle Feed in the Neolithic. In *Animals in the Neolithic of Britain and Europe*, edited by Dale Serjeantson and David Field, 56–62. Neolithic Studies Group Seminar Papers 7. Oxford: Oxbow.

■ MERRYN DINELEY

SPICES

Spices are first and foremost articles of trade; most derive from South/Southeast Asia (notable exceptions are vanilla, chili pepper, and allspice) and represent the aromatic parts (bark, root, flower, or seed) of tropical plants, unlike herbs, which are mostly used for their leaves and are usually not of tropical origin. In reality, the situation is more complicated, as the seeds of many herbs are viewed as spices (e.g., coriander seeds), while their leaves are used as herbs (e.g., cilantro). Today, most spices are employed primarily in cuisine and medicine, but in classical antiquity they also played an important role in perfumery and ritual. Archaeologically, they are often found in burials, in temples, and at hospital sites during the Roman period, as well as in elite domestic contexts, the latter increasingly so during the medieval and later periods. Their seeds and other macroremains are mostly found in waterlogged deposits but also charred, the latter especially on burial and temple sites, and desiccated in arid zone regions.

The attraction of spices lies in their strong flavors and scents, which are derived from phytochemicals that either facilitate the plant's reproductive process by attracting pollinators or defend the plant against predators and disease. Certain plant families are particularly rich in these substances, hence the concentration of spices within certain families (e.g., cardamom, ginger, turmeric, and grains of paradise in Zingiberaceae; allspice, clove, and myrtle in Myrtaceae; coriander, cumin, anise, dill, fennel, and caraway in Apiaceae).

Their strong flavors mean that only small quantities are needed, which, considering their restricted geographical origin, facilitated the trade. Recent excavations at ports involved with the ancient spice trade have greatly improved our understanding of the nature and scale of this trade prior to the 16th century. Their exotic origin meant that many spices (black pepper, cinnamon, ginger, cardamom, cloves, and nutmeg) were difficult to obtain and expensive, and thus available only to the elite until relatively recently.

Whether spices were utilized in medieval Europe to preserve meat or mask food spoilage has been much debated. What is clear from recent scientific research is that the phytochemicals in spices (and herbs) have antimicrobial (antibacterial and antifungal) properties as well as a host of other medicinal applications, making them far more than just food flavorings.

See also FOOD AS A COMMODITY; GREENS/HERBS; MACROREMAINS; OLD WORLD GLOBALIZATION AND FOOD EXCHANGES; QUSEIR AL-QADIM; TRADE ROUTES

Further Reading

Dalby, Andrew. 2000. *Dangerous Tastes: The Story of Spices*. London: British Museum Press.
Freedman, Paul. 2008. *Out of the East: Spices and the Medieval Imagination*. New Haven, CT: Yale University Press.
Turner, Jack. 2004. *Spice: The History of a Temptation*. London: HarperCollins.

■ MARIJKE VAN DER VEEN

SQUASH/GOURDS

The genus *Cucurbita* is native to the Americas and comprises 20–27 species, five of which are Pre-Columbian domesticates and were economically important for prehistoric populations. Considered one of the founder crops of the New World, *Cucurbita* are among the earliest species identified in the transition to food production. Among the most important are *C. pepo* (summer and winter squashes found in Mexico and North America, e.g., pumpkin, zucchini, acorn, scallop, neck and crookneck varieties), *C. moschata* (winter squashes from Mesoamerica and South America), *C. maxima* (winter squashes and pumpkins from South America), and *C. argyrosperma* (e.g., cushaw, from the southwestern United States and Mesoamerica). Squashes and gourds are members of the Cucurbitaceae family and thus are related to the bottle gourd (*Lagenaria siceraria*), also an early New World domesticate.

Evidence for the domestication and economic role of *Cucurbita* in the Americas is drawn from multiple sources. Early research was based on the identification of macrobotanical remains, including seeds and rind and stem (peduncle) fragments. Phytolith studies have advanced this research, providing evidence of plant use in areas where plant preservation is poor. In addition, *Cucurbita* rinds produce phytoliths that can be identified by genus and sometimes by species. Residue analysis has revealed *Cucurbita* phytolith residues on the surfaces of stone tools used for plant processing. More rarely, phytoliths have been recovered from sediments. Additional contributions have come from starch grain analysis, providing insight into methods of food processing and cooking. Squash starch grains have been identified on the surfaces of fired clay balls from Escalera al Cielo in the Yucatán (Mexico), for example, providing evidence not only for the role of squash in Maya cuisine but also for its likely preparation through steaming or baking. The discovery of starch grains in the calculus of human teeth also has been significant, providing direct evidence for the consumption of *Cucurbita* flesh. Recent efforts have focused on the identification of protein and DNA-based molecular markers. Supported by genetic studies, the growing body of evidence now suggests multiple, independent domestication events in the Americas, rather than a single event in Mesoamerica. The wild progenitors of these early domesticates likely colonized disturbed soils associated with both human activity and annual flooding of river valleys, providing a ready food source, and one easily brought into cultivation.

Unquestionably, *Cucurbita* was an early and important domesticate in Mesoamerica. Some of the earliest archaeobotanical evidence for the exploitation of *Cucurbita* comes from the site of Guilá Naquitz (Mexico). AMS (accelerator mass spectrometry) dates of 10,000 BP for domesticated *C. pepo* were obtained from rind, seed, and stem fragments. Archaeobotanical data show that *Cucurbita* domestication preceded that of maize and beans, and that squashes (*C. argyrosperma*, *C. moschata*, and *C. pepo*) were an important component of *milpa* agriculture during the Archaic period (7000–2400 BC). The importance of squashes to the foodways of the Aztec, Maya, and other Mesoamerican cultures has been documented through archaeological and ethnohistorical sources.

Despite the antiquity of squash domestication in Mesoamerica, phytolith and starch grain analyses now show that multiple domestication events occurred in the Americas. Recent work by Piperno suggests that in South America *Cucurbita* were domesticated from multiple local varieties by 12,000 to 10,000 BP, at the same time as, if not earlier than, the domestication of *Cucurbita* in Mesoamerica. Domesticated squash (possibly *C. ecuadorensis*) was present in southwestern Ecuador by 10,000 BP, while squash phytoliths from central Panama date as early as 8,600 BP. Macrobotanical, starch grain, and phytolith evidence from northern Peru, southern coastal Peru, southeastern Uruguay, Ecuador, and the eastern Amazon in Colombia suggests fairly rapid dispersal of these cultivars from their points of origin. Charred seeds from domestic sites (hearths, pits, floors) indicate the use of *C. moschata* as part of an emerging agricultural economy in the Ñanchoc Valley between 6,000 and 8,000 BP, for example. Notably, starch grains extracted from dental calculus provided direct evidence for the consumption of the flesh of cultivated *C. moschata* by these farmers.

Squashes also were domesticated independently in eastern North America from native wild gourds. *C. pepo* was an important part of the Eastern Horticultural Complex by 3,800 BP, and squash remains and seeds have been found at sites ranging from Illinois to Florida. Seeds and rind and stem fragments have been recovered from hearths, paleofecal remains, storage pits, and cultural deposits in rockshelters and caves, as well as from waterlogged contexts.

Cucurbita were transported across the globe following European contact and are today a major food source in many cultures. Squashes and gourds have been cultivated primarily for their fruits and seeds and provide a range of vitamins and nutrients. The fruit are generally baked, steamed, boiled, dried, or eaten raw. The oil- and protein-rich seeds can be eaten raw, roasted, and processed into flour. Squash flowers and leaves are also edible. As a food source, *Cucurbita* are particularly useful because certain varieties mature at different times of the year (e.g., spring and winter squash) and some are eaten when immature. Many squashes with harder rinds can be stored for long periods. Gourds also have been used as containers and tools associated with domestic food production and consumption. Such practice is not limited to utilitarian contexts. Serving vessels of squash (*Cucurbita* sp.) and bottle gourd (*Lagenaria siceraria*) were recovered from a small ceremonial center at Buena Vista in the Chillón River Valley, Peru (~2200 BC), for example. Residue analysis revealed the presence of starch grains from manioc (*Manihot esculenta*), arrowroot (*Maranta arundinacea*), algarrobo (*Prosopis* sp.), chili pepper (*Capsicum* sp.), and potato (*Solanum* sp.) adhering to the surface of the vessel fragments. The context from which these artifacts were recovered suggests their role in serving ritual foods or beverages. Representational forms also suggest the importance of *Cucurbita* as a food source among Pre-Columbian cultures. Among the many decorated ceramic vessels created by the Moche in the shape of food plants and animals are stirrup bottles in the shape of a squash (figure 55). Such effigy vessels have been recovered from mortuary contexts, but their use in high-status households is also indicated. Squash seeds and rinds are frequently present in Maya ritual offerings. The Late Pre-Classic mural from San Bartolo (Guatemala) depicts a birth scene in which a supernatural being watches five infants emerging from a broken gourd.

See also ARCHAEOBOTANY; BOTTLE GOURD; CLAY COOKING BALLS; DENTAL ANALYSIS; FEASTING; GUILÁ NAQUITZ; ÑANCHOC VALLEY; PHYTOLITH ANALYSIS; RESIDUE ANALYSIS, STARCH; REPRESENTATIONAL MODELS OF FOOD AND FOOD PRODUCTION; ROCKSHELTERS/CAVES; WALL PAINTINGS/MURALS

Further Reading

Dillehay Tom D., Jack Rossen, Thomas C. Andres, and David E. Williams. 2007. Preceramic Adoption of Peanut, Squash, and Cotton in Northern Peru. *Science* 316:1890–92.

Duncan, Neil A., Deborah M. Pearsall, and Robert A. Benfer Jr. 2009. Gourd and Squash Artifacts Yield Starch Grains of Feasting Foods from Preceramic Peru. *Proceedings of the National Academy of Sciences USA* 106(32):13202–6.

Piperno, Dolores R. 2009. Identifying Crop Plants with Phytoliths (and Starch Grains) in Central and South America: A Review and an Update of the Evidence. *Quaternary International* 193:146–59.

———. 2011. The Origins of Plant Cultivation and Domestication in the New World Tropics. *Current Anthropology* 52(S4). Online supplement. doi:10.1086/659998.

Piperno, Dolores R., and Tom D. Dillehay. 2008. Starch Grains on Human Teeth Reveal Early Broad Crop Diet in Northern Peru. *Proceedings of the National Academy of Sciences USA* 105(50):19622–27.

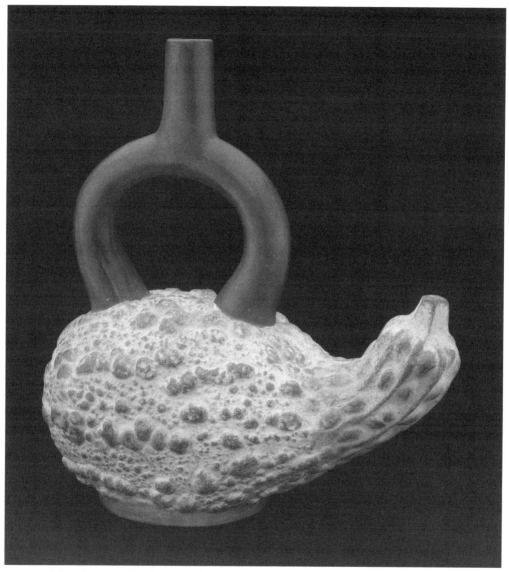

Figure 55. Moche ceramic stirrup bottle in the form of a squash. North coast of Peru, AD 100–800. © Photograph courtesy of the Fowler Museum at UCLA.

Smith, Bruce D. 1997. The Initial Domestication of *Cucurbita pepo* in the Americas 10,000 Years Ago. *Science* 276:932–34.

———. 2006. Eastern North America as an Independent Center of Plant Domestication. *Proceedings of the National Academy of Sciences USA* 103:12223–28.

Smith, Bruce D., and Richard A. Yarnell. 2009. Initial Formation of an Indigenous Crop Complex in Eastern North America at 3800 B.P. *Proceedings of the National Academy of Sciences USA* 106(16): 6561–66.

■ KAREN BESCHERER METHENY

STABLE ISOTOPE ANALYSIS

Isotopes of an element are atoms with the same number of protons but different numbers of neutrons. Stable isotopes do not undergo radioactive decay and are suitable for archaeological investigations. Commonly analyzed elements are carbon (C), nitrogen (N), and sulfur (S), used to identify the protein fraction of ancient diet. Strontium, oxygen, and hydrogen (H) are helpful to reconstruct past interactions with the environment.

For paleodietary studies, the ratio between different stable isotopes of carbon ($^{12}C/^{13}C$), nitrogen ($^{14}N/^{15}N$), and, to a lesser extent, sulfur ($^{32}S/^{34}S$) is measured in the bone collagen of human and animal skeletons. Values are expressed as reference to a standard in the d-notation, with units of parts per thousand (‰). Early works demonstrated that carbon isotope ratios of consumers reflected that of species consumed, whereas an enrichment of nitrogen was observed between predator and prey. Because plants and animals intake carbon and nitrogen according to different processes, the measurement of isotope ratios in the tissues of their consumers may be used to identify foods eaten. $d^{13}C$ can help discriminate between groups of plants according to their photosynthetic pathway (C_3 vs. C_4), so that consumers of C_3 as opposed to C_4 species will have nonoverlapping $d^{13}C$. Early work on carbon isotope ratios focused on the introduction of maize (a C_4 plant) in North America. Marine organisms have less negative $d^{13}C$, so that their consumers will have values that partially overlap with those of C_4 plant eaters.

The nitrogen isotopic ratio is typically enriched by 3‰ at each trophic level (i.e., the position that an organism occupies in the food chain) so that each species will have increasing $d^{15}N$ along the food chain. Nitrogen is used to determine the relative contribution of animal proteins to the human diet, as well as to detect consumption of marine resources, given that aquatic species have increased N values. Strontium isotope ratios ($^{87}Sr/^{86}Sr$) are used to investigate residence and mobility. The concentration of strontium in the inorganic fraction of human tissues is directly connected to the geology of the place of residence, as it is passed unaltered from the soil to the plants and their consumers. Similarly, oxygen isotope abundance ratios are linked to local climate and water availability; they can also vary with latitude, altitude, and distance from the coast. Oxygen ratios analysis can be used to reconstruct climate variation/seasonality or mobility throughout an individual's life. As an example, $d^{18}O$ in animal teeth has been used to detect seasonal mobility of prehistoric herders in South Africa.

See also BIOARCHAEOLOGICAL ANALYSIS; BIOMOLECULAR ANALYSIS; LANDSCAPE AND ENVIRONMENTAL RECONSTRUCTION; PALEODIETARY ANALYSIS; PALEONUTRITION

Further Reading

Ambrose, Stanley H., and M. Anne Katzenberg, eds. 2001. *Biogeochemical Approaches to Paleodietary Analyses.* New York: Plenum Press.
Hoefs, Jochen. 2009. *Stable Isotope Geochemistry.* Berlin: Springer-Verlag.

■ MARY ANNE TAFURI

STAR CARR (ENGLAND)

Star Carr, a Mesolithic-period settlement in Yorkshire, was excavated between 1949 and 1951 by J. G. D. Clark. The site, dating to ca. 9000 BC, was occupied over several hundred years, and current theories suggest that it was a very large site on which a variety of activities would have taken place. Remains of bones and plants found within the peat were used to interpret subsistence practices at the site. Large quantities of faunal remains were excavated. Red deer, roe deer, elk, aurochs, and wild boar were the predominant species and have tended to dominate this and subsequent analyses; however, the range of species represented was much broader and included hedgehog, beaver, hare, pine marten, badger, fox, dog, and a number of different bird species. Although there was no direct evidence for plant consumption, Clark suggested that plant food probably contributed a small part of the diet. Using ethnographic examples, Clark even suggested that inhabitants may have eaten the partly digested plant contents from the stomachs of the animals they killed.

Previous interpretations are being reexamined, however. Although Clark thought he had excavated the whole site, recent research has demonstrated that less than 5 percent of the site has been uncovered; in addition, a significant number of animal bones has been found in the backfill of some of Clark's trenches, suggesting his quantitative analysis is skewed. Many new analyses of the Star Carr data have focused on calorific value, ranking in terms of importance of species, and seasonality of occupation. New avenues of inquiry have examined the range of possible foodstuffs, rather than concentrating on dominant species, in order to investigate variability in diet. Researchers also seek to identify species that are missing to determine whether Star Carr's residents had specific food taboos. Additional research focuses on how people were processing foods (smoking, cooking, boiling) and whether there is evidence for communal consumption or for symbolic or ritual treatment of the remains, as practiced by many modern hunter-gatherers. Finally, new excavations and spatial patterning analysis through 3D recording and GIS help identify different areas of consumption activities.

See also HUNTER-GATHERER SUBSISTENCE; MESOLITHIC DIET; SPATIAL ANALYSIS AND VISUALIZATION TECHNIQUES; ZOOARCHAEOLOGY

Further Reading

Clark, J. G. D. 1954. *Excavations at Star Carr.* Cambridge: Cambridge University Press.

Conneller, Chantal, Nicky Milner, Barry Taylor, and Maisie Taylor. 2012. Substantial Settlement in the European Early Mesolithic: New Research at Star Carr. *Antiquity* 86(334):1004–20.

Milner, Nicky. 2009. Mesolithic Consumption Practices: Food for Thought. *Journal of Nordic Archaeological Science* 16:49–63.

Milner, Nicky, Barry Taylor, Chantal Conneller, and Tim Schadla-Hall. 2013. *Star Carr: Life in Britain after the Ice Age.* York: Council for British Archaeology.

■ NICKY MILNER

STARCHES, ROLE OF

Starch is the most common carbohydrate in human diets and occurs in large amounts in staple foods. It is also used as a minor ingredient, for example, to thicken soups and stews or stabilize custards. Archaeological starch (figure 56) provides an important line of evidence for seed staples (e.g., maize, rice, millets, wheat, barley), and, perhaps more important, it is often the only indicator of root crop exploitation. Edible tubers, roots, and corms (underground plant stems that serve as food storage organs) are central to both tropical (e.g., manioc, sweet potatoes, taro, yam, arrowroot) and temperate diets (e.g., potato) because they are relatively easy to cultivate and generate high yields.

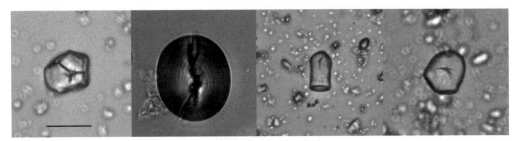

Figure 56. Left to right: Archaeological starch granules from a pop or flint variety of maize (*Zea mays*), common bean (*Phaseolus* sp.), squash (*Cucurbita* sp.), and manioc (*Manihot esculenta*) (in plane polarized light). All are common staple foods among New World tropical societies. The detection of starch granules through residue analysis allows archaeologists to identify food-related utensils, vessels, and cooking surfaces and provides another line of evidence in studying the domestication and spread of agricultural crops. Photomicrographs by Stephanie R. Simms.

Most starchy plants are difficult to digest without processing, a feature that produces abundant opportunities for them to enter the archaeological record. In addition to improving digestibility, processing might be undertaken to remove toxins (e.g., bitter manioc, acorns), enhance nutritional value, or alter taste, texture, or other properties according to cultural preferences. Grinding, peeling, grating, leaching, fermenting, cooking, storing, and other practices result in starch deposition on artifacts and in domestic activity areas. When recovered from sediments, starch can also reveal aspects of ancient land use, and starch recovered from dental calculus or coprolites provides direct evidence for consumption of plant foods. For example, Dolores Piperno and Tom Dillehay recovered squash, peanut, bean, and pacay (a tree crop with edible pods) starch from the teeth of Ñanchoc preceramic culture villagers in northern Peru (ca. 7500–5700 cal BC); these foods represent a mixed subsistence economy that included agriculture.

Owing to its durability, archaeological starch provides some of the earliest evidence for the role of plants in human diets and human evolution, as well as artifact function. In most societies, women perform food-processing labor, so starch is also associated with gender and household dynamics. Interdisciplinary methods, including artifact use–wear analysis and experimental studies, continue to reveal the cultural and natural processes that link past human behaviors with archaeological starch remains, facilitating even more nuanced interpretations of human–plant interactions.

See also ARCHAEOLOGY OF COOKING; BIOMOLECULAR ANALYSIS; CEREALS; EXPERIMENTAL ARCHAEOLOGY; FOODWAYS AND GENDER ROLES; LANDSCAPE AND ENVIRONMENTAL RECONSTRUCTION; ÑANCHOC VALLEY; PALEODIETARY ANALYSIS; PLANT PROCESSING; RESIDUE ANALYSIS, STARCH; ROOT CROPS/TUBERS; TOOLS/UTENSILS, STONE; USE-WEAR ANALYSIS, LITHICS

Further Reading

Food and Agriculture Organization (FAO) of the United Nations. 1990. *Roots, Tubers, Plantains and Bananas in Human Nutrition*. FAO Food and Nutrition Series 24. Rome: FAO.

■ STEPHANIE R. SIMMS

STATUS

See FOOD AND STATUS

STORAGE

See FOOD STORAGE; STORAGE FACILITIES

STORAGE FACILITIES

A variety of storage facilities have been used by hunter-gatherers and farmers from many different regions of the world from the Paleolithic to the present day. Storage facilities can generally be separated into two categories: aboveground and belowground. Aboveground facilities include granaries, stone piles, platforms, storehouses, containers such as baskets, and wooden and ceramic vessels. Animals that are kept, cared for, and fed in order to be eaten at a later date also can be classed as aboveground storage. Belowground storage facilities largely consist of caches or pits where food can be stored directly or first placed in a container and then into the pit. Storage pits and caches can be lined and capped with a variety of materials including matting, basketry, or clay to aid successful storage. At the early Jōmon site of Sabota, Japan (5,200–5,000 BP), there is evidence of a variety of pit storage methods, including baskets used to store nuts in pits and nut-storage pits lined with matting, indicating the significant role that nuts played in Jōmon subsistence strategies.

Storage facilities can be located at permanent settlements, temporary settlements, within buildings, outside of buildings, within the communal or private areas of a settlement, along route ways, or at the gathering/processing site. Caches and pits can be open (where the location is obvious) or closed (hidden and the location only known by a few). The location of storage facilities depends on the type of food stored, duration of storage, environmental conditions, and cultural traditions.

Although storage is often linked with plant domestication (e.g., the large-scale storage of cereal grain) and the increase in sedentism, storage was also practiced by mobile communities. Storage played a significant role in the subsistence strategies of both hunter-gatherers and farmers but in different ways: for mobile communities, storage facilities aided travel and mobility; for farmers who needed to store cereals for later planting, we see not only an increase in storage facilities but also sedentism, social hierarchy, and exchange networks.

See also AGRICULTURE, PROCUREMENT, PROCESSING, AND STORAGE; ANIMAL HUSBANDRY AND HERDING; DHRA'; FOOD PRESERVATION; FOOD STORAGE; HUNTER-GATHERER SUBSISTENCE; SEDENTISM AND DOMESTICATION

Further Reading

Cunningham, Penny. 2011. Caching Your Savings: The Use of Small-Scale Storage in European Prehistory. *Journal of Anthropological Archaeology* 30(2):135–44.

Habu, Junko. 2004. *Ancient Jomon of Japan*. Cambridge: Cambridge University Press.

Morgan, Christopher. 2012. Modeling Modes of Hunter-Gatherer Food Storage. *American Antiquity* 7(4):714–36.

■ PENNY CUNNINGHAM

STORES/MARKETS

People have acquired comestibles and accompanying paraphernalia by trade, barter, cash, credit, and theft at all kinds of stores and markets for millennia. Markets and stores have long served essential functions—social, political, religious, and economic—and markets could be among the earliest commercial sites studied by archaeologists. Key research questions center on physical layout and activity areas, availability of goods, trade networks, community development, and consumption, among others.

This entry emphasizes places and times where archaeology is aided by written and graphic records that help us understand the role of food and food distribution in complex societies. Cuneiform tablets of clay were used by Sumerian temple clerks and priests more than 5,000 years ago to record tribute (including food) paid to the priest-king. The famous temple ziggurats were partly stores of barley, dates, and palm oil from which food and other goods were redistributed to the people according to rank. In this way, food and religion combined to help maintain Sumerian social structure. In addition, retail shops in cities sold a variety of foods. Barley and dates were staple foods. What texts describe as "bread" was sold by volume. Archaeologists believe this was a dry substance that was mixed with water to create flat pancake-like loaves. Wine was made of dates rather than grapes, while bas-reliefs show a great range of fruits and vegetables. The milk of sheep, goats, and cattle was sold as butter, curd, and cheese. Retail transactions in food shops were not based on the familiar fixed price system but the personal relationship between buyer and seller, and how much the former was willing to pay. The Assyrian term for "seller" was "he who gives," while the buyer was "he who fixes the price." One could buy a measure of dates for a weight of lead, silver, copper, or iron, or exchange commodities of equal value (barter).

The volcanic eruption that buried Pompeii and Herculaneum nearly 2,000 years ago left a record of food shops, marketplaces, and inns in graffiti, shop signs, painted friezes, scenes of everyday life depicted on tessellated pavements, and the actual remains of food and drink. Food shops and inns where travelers could buy bread, cheese, wine, and fruit lined streets adjoining the main city gates. The city also was known for *garum*, a ubiquitous sauce made of liquefied fermented fish. This pungent condiment was often made and sold on the same premises where the owner and his family lived. Amphorae, the conical-based ceramic containers found in quantity in the remains of Pompeii, stored *garum*, wine, and honey, among other liquids. Bakers lived above their shops, milling the grain and baking and selling the bread from the same building or from stalls in the street. The forum (called a *macellum* or market) was the center of public life, politics, socializing, and eating. It contained the official standard weights and measures that shopkeepers were supposed to reproduce. The forum was also the center of the Roman version of modern café society, where one could sit in a formal restaurant or buy finger foods cooked over a brazier at a temporary stall.

Consumer behavior is an important research area for historical archaeologists facing the explosion of durable goods produced by the Industrial Revolution in the 19th century. It is axiomatic, however, that without a basic understanding of what people could have purchased, one cannot assess the significance of what they did. Documentary sources, such as newspapers and catalogues, supply important background data on price. British potters' price fixing lists and invoices from the Kwong Tai Wo store in California (USA) are but two examples of documentary data that can be directly connected with artifacts commonly found on archaeological sites.

The range of goods available at a particular time and place is poorly understood. Creating an index of local availability is an essential prerequisite to most interpretations of domestic archaeological sites. Fires, floods, and other natural disasters contribute to the archaeological record by creating time capsules of individual stores on a particular date. In the United States, the early-19th-century Darrach Store in Delaware, the Stranahan Store in Florida, and Anthony Winan's Store in Manhattan provide but a few examples.

Gold Rush California offers two excellent case studies of stores that provide the backdrop for wider studies of community and consumption. William Hoff's ship's chandlery burned in 1851 in one of the many fires that plagued early San Francisco. The site provides a fascinating glimpse into Gold Rush cuisine. Merchants had imported a wide range of preserved and packaged goods into a newly rich community that could not feed itself from local foods. Merchandise included many luxury goods but no fresh produce: wine, champagne, beer, canned oysters, tinned sardines, dried fruit, nuts, beans, packaged cake, crackers, pickled and preserved food, and salt pork by the barrel. Butchering patterns reconstructed from pork bones aid faunal analysts in their interpretations related to status.

A hundred miles away and a year later, the W. S. Cothrin Building burned down along with much of early Sacramento. Archaeologists reconstructed the store layout and found not as much variety as expected. From English tableware, in particular, it appeared that exporters dumped unfashionable goods on California consumers happy just to have the essentials at most any price in a time of scarcity. Certainly, for a brief time merchants provided Gold Rush Californians with what they could amass and transport quickly by boat.

A pioneering ethnoarchaeological study of Bill Wilson's Store in rural Washington (USA) combined oral history and archaeology to explore community life in one small, early-20th-century town and reconstruct the residents' hierarchy of economic and social networks tying them to the nation and world.

As stores evolved into capitalist ventures where distribution's function was connected to its price, those with the ability to pay could purchase most anything they wanted in certain venues, while others continued in the long-standing modes of barter, trade, credit, and theft.

See also AMPHORAE; BAKERIES; CONDIMENTS; DOCUMENTARY ANALYSIS; FOOD AND CAPITALISM; FOOD AS A COMMODITY; FOOD PRODUCTION AND THE ORIGINS OF WRITING IN MESOPOTAMIA; HERCULANEUM AND POMPEII; INFORMAL ECONOMIC EXCHANGE; MARKETS/EXCHANGE; MATERIAL CULTURE ANALYSIS; ORAL AND FOLK NARRATIVES; SPATIAL ANALYSIS AND VISUALIZATION TECHNIQUES; TRADE ROUTES

Further Reading

Beard, Mary. 2008. *The Fires of Vesuvius*. Cambridge, MA: Harvard University Press.
Carson, Gerald. 1954. *The Old Country Store*. New York: Oxford University Press.

■ ADRIAN PRAETZELLIS AND MARY PRAETZELLIS

STOVES
See OVENS AND STOVES

SUBEIXI CEMETERIES (CHINA)

The Turpan Basin is characterized by a typical continental desert climate, preserving many mummies and plant remains over thousands of years. During the Late Bronze to Early Iron Ages (3,000–1,900 BP), the ancient Gushi people inhabited the Turpan Basin. The Subeixi site, associated with the Gushi culture (Subeixi culture), lies in the Tuyugou Valley and contains three groups of cemeteries and a residential area. Desiccated foodstuffs, including noodles, cakes, and a bowl of grains, were excavated from the cemeteries (500–300 cal BC) (figure 57). Starch grains and phytolith analyses showed that both the noodles and the cakes were made from the ground fruit or caryopses of common millet

Figure 57. Desiccated foodstuffs excavated from the Subeixi Cemeteries, China (500–300 cal BC). The noodles (left) and cakes (center) in these earthenware bowls were made from processed millet (*Panicum miliaceum*). Right: Caryopses of common millet (*Panicum milliaceum*). Experiments to investigate cooking techniques indicate that the caryopses were boiled (Gong et al. 2011). Photographs by Prof. Enguo Lü, Xinjiang Institute of Archaeology.

(*Panicum miliaceum*), while the unprocessed grains in the bowl were also common millet. Based on cooking experiments like boiling, steaming, and baking, researchers concluded that the noodles had been boiled while the cakes were baked. The millet grains in the bowl would have been boiled like the noodles.

Common millet was a very important crop at that period, and agricultural activities were an indispensable part of daily life for the indigenous people. Other excavated items include woolen textiles, leather clothes, as well as bows, arrows, and the bones of goats/ sheep, indicating that stockbreeding and hunting were also important parts of their subsistence, and that some inhabitants still led a seminomadic lifestyle. The vegetal food remains show that both boiling and baking technologies, which were popular in the East and the West, respectively, were accepted and adopted by the ancient inhabitants of the Subeixi site, and that Turpan played an important role in cultural exchange between the East and the West, including the diffusion of domesticated cereals and cooking technologies, more than 2,000 years ago.

See also ARCHAEOLOGY OF COOKING; EXPERIMENTAL ARCHAEOLOGY; FOOD TECHNOLOGY AND IDEAS ABOUT FOOD, SPREAD OF; MILLETS; OFFERINGS AND GRAVE GOODS; PHYTOLITH ANALYSIS; RESIDUE ANALYSIS, STARCH; TRADE ROUTES

Further Reading

Gong, Yiwen, Yimin Yang, David K. Ferguson, et al. 2011. Investigation of Ancient Noodles, Cakes, and Millet at the Subeixi Site, Xinjiang, China. *Journal of Archaeological Science* 38(2):470–79.

■ JIANG HONGEN

SUBSISTENCE MODELS

Subsistence models represent idealized ways of procuring or creating food and thus are useful tools to help archaeologists understand the essentials of subsistence practices. All subsistence models—from foraging to hunting and gathering to agriculture—cover a huge range of variation, however. There are vast differences between rice cultivation in Java compared to mechanized cereal farming in North America in the modern world, for example. Similarly, concepts such as animal husbandry encapsulate a wide range of possibilities.

Within archaeology, one of the biggest transitions is that between hunting and gathering and agriculture, and here we can see both the power and the problems represented by the use of models. Since the 1960s it has been accepted that hunter-gatherer subsistence can be a perfectly successful economic strategy in its various forms, providing ample leisure time as within some African groups such as the Hadza or the !Kung, or even sustaining quite complex societies such as the Tlingit on the American Northwest coast. Such modern societies have been used to provide basic models for the past, with African hunter-gatherers providing a model for generic past hunter-gatherer lifeways, and the Northwest coast people for more complex societies such as the Ertebølle in Mesolithic northwest Europe or the Natufian in southwest Asia. The insights generated by such comparisons led to significant advances in archaeological thinking, moving us on from previously held views that hunter-gatherer lifeways were nasty and primitive, and that farming was not necessarily an obvious "upward" step.

Other models have provided useful tools for thinking about how subsistence can be structured. The Broad Spectrum Revolution represented an important step forward in understanding how and why hunter-gatherer economies might change. Use of optimal foraging and niche construction theories also has played a significant role in developing a deeper appreciation of human subsistence behavior and its adaptation to changing environments.

At the same time, because the core subsistence models represent ideal states, they generate a number of problems of their own. To start, there is a constant risk that we generalize too far, and simply impose our models on the enormously varied archaeological evidence, re-creating the present in the past. Stereotyping the past through the simplistic use of subsistence models can provide an illusion that we understand a society. Modern hunter-gatherers are highly developed modern societies, superbly adapted to their specific environments. Some have even abandoned farming in the past, and all are part of a global economy. Populating the ancient past with such societies is clearly anachronistic. Similar problems affect early food-producing societies. To describe, for example, early Middle Eastern pastoralists as "paleo-bedouin" masks enormous variation in animal husbandry practices.

Equally problematic is that these models describe fixed states, and they are not ideal for examining change—a key archaeological focus. Especially once we have established that farming is not an obvious goal for a hunter-gatherer, the gulf between living on wild foods and producing food from domesticated resources appears to become enormous and difficult to cross. In the modern world, despite the availability of domesticated resources, most hunter-gatherers make minimal use of them, while farmers rely almost exclusively on them. In the past there must have been economic systems in between for which we no longer have analogs at all. One key concept that has been developed is of *low-level food production*. This encompasses subsistence economies where people have begun to significantly manipulate wild resources. The most common examples are the cultivation of wild cereals (sometimes described as incipient cultivation) in the earliest Neolithic societies and the management of wild herds. Both are necessary steps on the route to domestication, and both make the hard-and-fast distinction between hunting-gathering and farming less sharp. Conventionally, domestication was identified by the morphological changes in plant and animal remains, but these are now understood to substantially postdate the development of management practices. It is consequently less clear when we should now talk of domestication, or even of agriculture and pastoralism. Low-level production should not be used as an additional static model, but as a way of understanding change and transition.

An important aspect of developing these models within archaeological thought is that modeling subsistence is closely connected to modeling society. While many of the subsistence models are based within the more scientific end of archaeology, both in their use of ecological models and on the nature of the evidence (e.g., the close understanding of animal and plant behavior, morphological traces, isotope analysis, dental wear patterns, and so on), the impact of these models is tightly linked to social behavior and archaeology as a social science. The development of food production can have very pragmatic effects on population, not only in the simple quantity of food available, for example, but in the production of foods that allow earlier weaning. But there are also the ethnographically informed connections, for example, between foragers and egalitarian societies. There are a range of ideas connected with the creation of wealth and, consequently, hierarchies through the production of food surpluses and the provision of feasts, or through differential access to the best resources and developing ideas of ownership through increasing investment of labor into food production. Perhaps the most elaborate connections are made in ideas that food cannot be domesticated without substantial social changes, and the domestication of society is a necessary preliminary step before plant and animal control can be envisaged. Such a close intertwining of subsistence and society moves into theories that relate the development of formal religion with food-producing societies.

See also Agriculture, Origins of; Animal Husbandry and Herding; Broad Spectrum Revolution; Cultivation; Ethnoarchaeology; Food Production and the Formation of Complex Societies; Foraging; Hunter-Gatherer Subsistence; Plant Husbandry; Sedentism and Domestication

Further Reading

Binford, Lewis R. 1980. Willow Smoke and Dogs' Tails: Hunter-Gatherer Settlement Systems and Archaeological Site Formation. *American Antiquity* 45(1):4–20.
Price, T. Douglas, and Anne Birgitte Gebauer, eds. 1995. *Last Hunters, First Farmers: New Perspectives on the Prehistoric Transition to Agriculture*. Santa Fe, NM: School of American Research Press.
Smith, Bruce D. 2001. Low-Level Food Production. *Journal of Archaeological Research* 9(1):1–43.
———. 2007. Niche Construction and the Behavioral Context of Plant and Animal Domestication. *Evolutionary Anthropology* 16(5):188–99.
Winterhalder, Bruce, and Douglas J. Kennett. 2006. Behavioral Ecology and the Transition from Hunting and Gathering to Agriculture. In *Behavioral Ecology and the Transition to Agriculture*, edited by Douglas J. Kennett and Bruce Winterhalder, 1–21. Berkeley: University of California Press

■ BILL FINLAYSON

SUCROSE

Sucrose, or sugar, is an odorless, crystalline powder used primarily as a sweetener in food but also as a preservative or decorative material. Sucrose is derived from plants, principally sugarcane (*Saccharum officinarum*) and sugar beets (*Beta vulgaris*). Cane sugar accounts for 80 percent of the world market. Unlike honey, maple sugar, fruit, or other natural sweeteners, refined cane or beet sugar sweetens without imparting an additional taste.

Sugarcane was domesticated in Southeast Asia—New Guinea or Indonesia—as early as 8000 BC. Two thousand years later it spread to the Philippines and India. By AD 500, cane was cultivated in southern Persia and thereafter spread rapidly around the Mediterranean in the wake of the Arab conquests following the founding of Islam in AD 622. In Europe, sugar was used as a medicine through the medieval period. As a sweetener, it was a luxury commodity until the 17th century, when demand for the commodity increased; by the 19th century, however, sucrose had become a part of the working-class diet. The demand for sugar is strongly connected to the history of conquest and colonial expansion around the Mediterranean, the Atlantic islands (Madeira, the Canary and Cape Verde Islands, and São Tomé), and, after 1494, the Americas.

Sugarcane is propagated asexually by planting a section of the stalk or *sett* containing at least one node. In optimum conditions, sugarcane takes eight to nine months to ripen, depending on the variety of cane. Climate is the most important factor in determining the viability of cane cultivation; while hot, humid climates are best, some varieties can be grown in cooler climates. Cane cultivation also requires large quantities of water, either from rainfall or irrigation. The northern extent of sugar cultivation during the Middle Ages was the Mediterranean coasts of Iberia and southern Italy; cane grown in these marginal zones did not mature fully, however, and therefore produced less juice.

Mature cane must be milled within a few days of being cut to avoid loss of sugar by evaporation; therefore, the harvest season can extend over a period of four to six months, depending on the labor supply for harvesting and the capacity of the mill. Where, how, and when cane juice was first refined into crystalline sugar is still a matter of conjecture, but most scholars accept Sanskrit references as proof of its widespread use in India as a sweetener by 300 BC. This process involved boiling and reducing the juice to a thick syrup that was then poured into cone-shaped ceramic molds. Sugar molds typically had a plugged hole at the narrow end that was unstopped after crystallization had taken place to allow any remaining liquid (molasses) to drain into a syrup jar or trough. Until the 17th century, molasses was used in cooking or as an additive to animal fodder, but it later became the principal ingredient in the distillation of rum.

Milling cane prior to the 17th century was a two-stage, labor-intensive process wherein the cane was first cut into small pieces and fed between the grinding stones of a mill. The partially crushed stalks were then placed in a press to release the remaining juice. Milling technology for sugar changed remarkably little from its first application in the seventh century AD until the early 17th century, when the vertical-roller sugar mill was invented in Brazil. Milling was entirely manual until the late Antique era, after which mechanized milling techniques using animal or hydraulic power were employed.

Although sugar production involved substantial capital investment in land, mills, machinery, and irrigation, landholding arrangements and models of labor extraction for cane cultivation in the Mediterranean and Atlantic islands ranged widely during the Middle Ages. Sugar was one of many crops grown on large estates or small farms, by independent farmers, tenant peasantry, sharecroppers, and temporary wage laborers. Monocropping was not the norm, and the use of slaves in the later phases of the Mediterranean and Atlantic sugar industries was largely confined to the milling operations. Research also demonstrates there was a separation between agricultural and manufacturing activities, with many mills being centrally located near ports or in towns. The archaeology of the medieval sugar industry on the island of Cyprus is rich and well preserved. Additionally, a few mills have been excavated in the Middle East. Any investigation of 16th-century production in the Americas must consider how its Mediterranean and Atlantic antecedents structured both the industry's physical remains, as well as its social and economic organization.

Columbus introduced sugar to the Caribbean in 1494, but it did not become a major industry until 1520 when placer mining in the region declined. The Portuguese started to produce sugar in Brazil by the 1530s. Archaeological research in the Caribbean has demonstrated that during the early decades of the 16th century, the sugar industry was not uniformly prefigured as large-scale plantation production based on slave labor. By the mid-16th century, however, the production of sugar was instrumental in creating a slave-owning aristocracy with the power to influence local, regional, and colonial policy. A plantation production model was adopted by the other European nations when they established colonies in the region in the 17th century.

Sugar production defined the economic, social, and physical landscape of the Caribbean and northern Brazil more than any other industry. The production of sugar and molasses contributed to the formation of an elaborate network of commercial, governmental, regional, and intercolonial relationships that would eventually evolve into the European capitalist system. Fifteenth- and 16th-century archival documentation provides limited details on the industrial, social, and economic aspects of the sugar industry in Spain and its Atlantic and Caribbean colonies, and only one mill in Spain and two mills in the Caribbean have been excavated from this transitional period. Most archaeological research has focused on late 17th- to 19th-century colonial sugar plantations and their attendant slave villages. Industrial archaeologists have studied the evolution of mills and specialized machinery, but only a limited number of studies have been published in Europe on the topic of ceramic sugar molds.

See also Agricultural/Horticultural Sites; Distilled Spirits; Factories; Food and Capitalism; Food and Colonialism; Food as a Commodity; Industrialization of Food and Food Production; Milling

Further Reading

Deerr, Noel. 1949. *The History of Sugar*. 2 vols. London: Chapman and Hall.
Galloway, J. H. 1989. *The Sugar Cane Industry: An Historical Geography from Its Origin to 1914*. Cambridge: Cambridge University Press.
Mintz, Sidney. 1985. *Sweetness and Power*. New York: Penguin.
Vieira, Alberto, ed. 1996. *Slaves With and Without Sugar*. Funchal, Portugal: Atlantic History Study Center.

■ ROBYN P. WOODWARD

SUGAR

See Sucrose

SUSTAINABILITY

Where does food come from? Separating food from the social institutions that facilitate its production, distribution, and consumption is impossible, but what kinds of "natural" environments accommodate its immediate growth and its continuous harvesting over time? What actually sustains food production? At its most fundamental, sustained food production involves the human manipulation of solar energy, water availability, and soil types to accommodate our food supply. In the ancient past, societies altered their environments by enhancing the availability of food-friendly landscapes by way of terracing soils, canalizing and ponding water (reservoirs), and creating microenvironments that enhanced measured exposure to solar radiation given scalar light requirements of both conserved and domesticated plants. Given the mobility of animals, kept species frequently occupied a human niche provided by these same plant-altered, engineered landscapes that synergistically complemented societal work routines (e.g., scheduling and calendars), especially with the advent of agriculture.

Sustainability is a complicated term, but in the context of food generation, food demands a high degree of reproducibility and predictability in terms of its quality and quantity. Quality is frequently assessed by way of nutritional sustenance, but foods that are healthy can be dismissed if they are not considered tasty or appropriate (i.e., food taboos) by the societies that consume them. Sustainable food stores also are a challenge. Because of the seasonal availability of food and the organic decomposition process, food quality frequently requires rapid consumption upon harvesting, paths or roads to move it quickly to consumers, and degrees of storage—the latter an institutionally developed condition with the advent of agriculture. In tropical settings this can be as simple as leaving root crops in the ground for several years—yams in Southeast Asia or manioc in Central and South America—or salting fish, while in arid regions, storage pits appear well before horticulture. By the fourth millennium BC in the Near East, mass-produced, bevel-rimmed bowls from Uruk suggest ration allotments from sizable stores of barley, while early room sealings at Susa also indicate grain stocks to feed the first experiments in urban living.

See also FOOD PRESERVATION; FOOD STORAGE; INDUSTRIALIZATION OF FOOD AND FOOD PRODUCTION; IRRIGATION/HYDRAULIC ENGINEERING; MANURING AND SOIL ENRICHMENT PRACTICES; WATER SUPPLY AND STORAGE

Further Reading

Costanza, Robert, Lisa J. Gramlich, and Will Steffen, eds. 2007. *Sustainability or Collapse? Integrated History and Future of People on Earth (IHOPE)*. Cambridge, MA: MIT Press.

Fisher, Christopher T., J. Brett Hill, and Gary M. Feinman, eds. 2009. *The Archaeology of Environmental Change: Socionatural Legacies of Degradation and Resilience*. Tucson: University of Arizona Press.

Scarborough, Vernon L. 2010. The Archaeology of Sustainability: Mesoamerica. *Ancient Mesoamerica* 20(2):197–203.

Scarborough, Vernon L., and William R. Burnside. 2010. Complexity and Sustainability: Perspectives from the Ancient Maya and the Modern Balinese. *American Antiquity* 75(2):327–63.

Scarborough, Vernon L., and Y. Yasuda, eds. 2014. *Water and Humanity: Historical Overview*. History of Water and Civilization 7. Paris: UNESCO, International Hydrological Programme.

■ VERNON L. SCARBOROUGH

SWEET POTATO

Sweet potato (*Ipomoea batatas*) is a domesticated root plant indigenous to the Americas. Archaeological evidence for sweet potato cultivation includes charred or dessicated macroremains, starch grains and other residues from tools, and starch grains from archaeological sediments and paleofecal matter. Theories for the primary domestication of sweet potato have ranged from a tropical origin between the Yucatán in Mexico and the Orinoco River in Venezuela, to a Central American origin, to a South American origin in Colombia, Ecuador, or an area north of Peru. While the greatest genetic diversity occurs in Mexico, the earliest archaeological evidence for the use of sweet potato comes from the Peruvian highlands 8,000 years ago, though it is unclear whether this was a wild or domesticated tuber.

The origin of sweet potato in the Americas is unquestioned; thus its presence in prehistoric archaeological contexts in Polynesia has posed a problem for researchers. Multiple prehistoric and historical dispersals have been proposed based on archaeological, linguistic, and historical data, as well as ocean drift models, but the tripartite hypothesis has had the greatest longevity. This hypothesis suggests an initial prehistoric migration via Polynesian contact with South America, now confirmed by archaeological evidence dated to AD 1200–1300, followed by two separate historical dispersals, one with Spanish explorers and traders who crossed the Pacific in the 16th century, and one with the Portuguese who traveled east across the Atlantic and Indian Oceans to the Pacific. A 2013 study using modern plants and herbarium specimens collected between the 17th and 20th centuries found genetic differences that support this hypothesis.

The sweet potato plant produces storage roots that are generally baked, boiled, roasted, or fermented. The roots can be processed for starch or made into flour and used for other products. Leaves and shoots are also eaten. An important global crop, sweet potato is grown as a subsistence food in many countries. It is valued as a source of vitamins A and C, iron, potassium, and beta-carotene, but also for its adaptability to marginal environments, high temperatures, and humidity; some varieties show resistance to high-moisture stress, and others to drought, for example.

See also ARCHAEOBOTANY; COLUMBIAN EXCHANGE; PACIFIC OCEANIC EXCHANGE; PALEOFECAL ANALYSIS; ROOT CROPS/TUBERS; RESIDUE ANALYSIS, STARCH

Further Reading

Denham, Tim. 2013. Ancient and Historic Dispersals of Sweet Potato in Oceania. *Proceedings of the National Academy of Sciences USA* 110(6):1982–83.

Horrocks, Mark, Ian W. G. Smith, Scott L. Nichol, and Rod Wallace. 2008. Sediment, Soil and Plant Microfossil Analysis of Maori Gardens at Anaura Bay, Eastern North Island, New Zealand: Comparison with Descriptions Made in 1769 by Captain Cook's Expedition. *Journal of Archaeological Science* 35:2446–64.

Kirch, P. V., A. S. Hartshorn, O. A. Chadwick, et al. 2004. Environment, Agriculture, and Settlement Patterns in a Marginal Polynesian Landscape. *Proceedings of the National Academy of Sciences USA* 101(26):9936–41.

Loebenstein, Gad, and George Thottappilly, eds. 2009. *The Sweetpotato.* New York: Springer.
Roulliera, Caroline, Laure Benoit, Doyle B. McKey, and Vincent Lebota. 2013. Historical Collections Reveal Patterns of Diffusion of Sweet Potato in Oceania Obscured by Modern Plant Movements and Recombination. *Proceedings of the National Academy of Sciences USA* 110(6):2205–10.

■ KAREN BESCHERER METHENY

SYMBOLISM

See CARVINGS/CARVED REPRESENTATIONS OF FOOD; COMMENSALITY; FEASTING; FOOD AND IDENTITY; FOOD AND RITUAL; FOOD SHARING; FOODWAYS; FOODWAYS AND RELIGIOUS PRACTICES; MORTUARY COMPLEXES; OFFERINGS AND GRAVE GOODS; ORAL AND FOLK NARRATIVES; PREFERENCES, AVOIDANCES, PROHIBITIONS, TABOOS; REPRESENTATIONAL MODELS OF FOOD AND FOOD PRODUCTION; ROCK ART; WALL PAINTINGS/MURALS

T

TABOOS
See PREFERENCES, AVOIDANCES, PROHIBITIONS, TABOOS

TARO
Before the modern era, taro (*Colocasia esculenta*) was likely the Old World's most popular starch crop, having been grown in the tropics from West Africa to Oceania and in temperate Asia and Europe. Today, it is best known from the Hawaiian dish poi, a thick paste made from corms (the underground portion of the plant resembling a tuber or bulb) that have been peeled, cooked, mashed, and fermented. Its origin is unknown, but the distribution of wild varieties points to tropical Southeast Asia or the islands of Near Oceania. Starch recovered on artifacts dated to the Late Pleistocene and early Holocene has been attributed to taro, but it is unclear if the granules are from wild or domesticated varieties.

Finding direct evidence for cultivation can be problematic since taro grows well in unmodified wetlands. Abandoned fields do survive in the archaeological record as clusters of associated irrigation ditches and terraces, but they look similar to those built and used for rice. There is surviving documentary evidence relating to taro, including advice on planting and recipes from ancient Rome, Han Dynasty China, and elsewhere, and there have been efforts to reconstruct the crop's history through linguistics. Ancient DNA would help clarify many of these issues, but intact taro DNA has yet to be recovered from archaeological deposits.

In Hawai'i, irrigated taro farming provided a high yield-to-effort ratio with a low long-term impact on soil nutrients. Large irrigated field systems were prized by elites, whose desire to control surplus was a driving force in the archipelago's history. More research is required to determine to what degree these same factors shaped the histories of the many other groups who relied on taro as a staple food.

See also AGRICULTURAL FEATURES, IDENTIFICATION AND ANALYSIS; DNA ANALYSIS; FOOD AND STATUS; IRRIGATION/HYDRAULIC ENGINEERING; RESIDUE ANALYSIS, STARCH; ROOT CROPS/TUBERS; STARCHES, ROLE OF

Further Reading

Matisoo-Smith, Elizabeth, and K. Anne Horsburgh. 2012. *DNA for Archaeologists*. Walnut Creek, CA: Left Coast Press.

McCoy, Mark D., Anna T. Browne Ribeiro, Michael W. Graves, et al. 2013. Irrigated Taro (*Colocasia esculenta*) Farming in North Kohala, Hawai'i: Sedimentology and Soil Nutrient Analyses. *Journal of Archaeological Science* 40(3):1528–38.

Spriggs, Matthew, Dave Addison, and Peter J. Matthews, eds. 2012. *Irrigated Taro (*Colocasia esculenta*) in the Indo-Pacific: Biological, Social and Historical Perspectives*. Osaka: National Museum of Ethnology.

■ MARK MCCOY

TAVERNS/INNS

Inns and taverns have served vital functions for travelers and as centers of community social interaction for millennia. These institutions often gave travelers their first taste of local cuisine and became vital places for human exchange and negotiation. Thus archaeologists can explore a range of social, economic, political, and cultural activities using food remains, artifacts related to food preparation and service, dining, drinking, smoking, and entertainment, along with documentary and architectural evidence. Recent work has used soil chemistry to test a tavern floor in Italy in order to identify activity areas. Most data currently derive from excavations in Britain and the Americas, but inns and taverns existed worldwide and comparative evidence comes from Australia, Europe, and the Middle East.

In Britain and North America, the terms *inn*, *ordinary*, *tavern*, *ale-house*, and *saloon* describe different institutions that vary over time. Inns were often called ordinaries in the colonial era, offering lodging, food, and drink. *Ordinary* derives from the fixed rate set by the government for an ordinary meal. Taverns began as dispensers of wines, ale-houses sold brewed beverages, and distilled drinks predominated in saloons. *Ordinary* and *inn* were subsumed by the term *tavern* during the 18th century; the saloon appeared in the 19th century. Women often ran inns, and men and women were customers in the 1600s and early 1700s. By the 19th century, taverns and saloons were largely male domains. Foodways clearly differed according to the type of institution and time period, as well as customer status, cultural setting, and geographic location. In general, the foods consumed reflected the agrarian economies of the inn's surroundings; in one example, however, a Bolivian colonial inn shows that an Iberian meat diet was maintained, despite the harsh environment of the high Andes.

Tavern faunal assemblages have been a particular focus of study. Excavated animal bones from inn and tavern sites of the 17th and 18th centuries show domestic meats predominated, with beef, pork, and mutton the most important. Meat was considered a primary measure of a meal in the early modern period, and the consumption of large quantities was a status marker. Animal bones provide insights about procurement, butchery, and preparation methods including boiling, broiling, and roasting of meat. Samples from taverns in Paternoster Square in London showed a high frequency of high-meat-value cuts and juvenile animals, a pattern also seen at some North American taverns. Meats were served as a main course as well as in stews or potages. Excavations in the Chesapeake and New England regions of North America provide a corpus of data on 17th- and 18th-century inns/taverns that show regional and rural/urban variations. While beef and pork were most prominent, lamb and mutton were popular at inns. Garrett Van Sweringen kept sheep at his elegant inn at St. Mary's City, Maryland (USA), in the 1680s as a ready source of fresh meat for guests, as did Henry Wetherburn in 1750s Williamsburg, Virginia (USA). Archaeology shows that sheep were even more important in urban settings in England and New England. Domestic fowl were common at most sites and allowed quick preparation of a meal with a protein base of meat or eggs. Wild animals, although usually present in small quantities, indicate that many tavern keepers served deer, rabbit, turtle, fish, and wildfowl to ensure a supply of fresh meat and offer seasonal diversity. There may have been more game consumed in rural than urban settings, but fresh domestic meat, specific cuts, and some game were more consistently available from active urban markets. A comparison of animal remains from four saloons in Virginia City, Nevada (USA), from the second half of the 19th century suggests ethnic and class variability. Notable differences in the faunal assemblages were evident between a German, two Irish, and an African American saloon, with the lowest quality beef and mutton meat cuts most frequent in one of the Irish establishments and the highest quality cuts in the African American saloon.

Alcoholic drinks were a key part of the inn/tavern offering in North America, with a mug of cider or beer served with the meal. Beer was more common in the northern colonies. Imported wines, rum, and brandy were also offered. Many drinks were consumed with sugar, especially in wine. Punch made with citrus juice, sugar, and rum or brandy was popular at later 17th- and 18th-century inns/taverns. Drinking vessel forms like tankards, wine glasses, and punch bowls are evidence of the types of beverages consumed. Hot beverages of tea and coffee were added to tavern offerings by the late 1700s, as demonstrated by the recovery of quantities of cups, saucers, and teapots at sites like Kings Arms Uxbridge in Britain and Tweeds Tavern in Delaware (USA). Inns also served bread, fruit, and cheese. From privy pits and other deposits, excavators have recovered seeds of peach, cherry, apple, different berries, and occasionally grape or even fig. At Wetherburn's Tavern in Williamsburg, archaeologists uncovered intact wine bottles containing perfectly preserved 18th-century cherries.

Despite their significance as major social institutions, comparative archaeological research on the foodways of inns and taverns has been relatively limited. Yet the few studies demonstrate that valuable insights can come from exploring the ethnic and class differences among inn, tavern, and saloon sites, and from considering how cuisines varied by culture, geographic setting, and time. In the absence of documents, it is still difficult to distinguish these institutions archaeologically from one another or from domestic households. This is because inn/tavern activities are essentially similar to those of dwellings. It is the amount of food consumption, drinking, and smoking activity that differs, suggesting that the study of quantitative distinctions may be the most fruitful approach. Better definition of their archaeological signatures remains a key research problem.

See also ARCHAEOBOTANY; BEER; BREWING/MALTING; COMMENSALITY; DISTILLED SPIRITS; FEASTING; FOOD AND IDENTITY; FOOD AND STATUS; FOOD AS A COMMODITY; MACROREMAINS; MATERIAL CULTURE ANALYSIS; LATRINES AND SEWER SYSTEMS; SAN GENESIO, MEDIEVAL TAVERN SITE (SAN MINIATO, PISA); WINE; ZOOARCHAEOLOGY

Further Reading

Dixon, Kelly J. 2005. *Boomtown Saloons: Archaeology and History in Virginia City*. Reno: University of Nevada Press.

Ehrman, Edwina, Rory O'Connell, Jacqui Pearce, et al. 2003. *London Eats Out, 1500–2000: 500 Years of Capital Dining*. London: Philip Wilson.

Rice, Kym S. 1983. *Early American Taverns: For Entertainment of Friends and Strangers*. Chicago: Regnery Gateway.

■ HENRY M. MILLER

TEA

Tea (chá or chai), the aromatic beverage commonly prepared by pouring hot water over (often dried) tea plant leaves (*Camellia sinensis*), is currently the world's most consumed beverage after cold water. It is generally assumed that tea originates from South Asia and in particular from China, where it was known by the tenth century BC. Probably first used as a medicinal beverage, tea was already a common drink in the third century BC during the Qin Dynasty and became widely popular during the Tang Dynasty (AD 618–907).

In the 16th century, the drink was introduced in China to Portuguese priests and merchants, who spread it to other parts of the world. During the next century, tea became a luxury drink among wealthy European households, and porcelain cups and teapots were exclusively designed for the drinking of the liquid. In the 19th century tea trickled down to all levels of British society as its price fell sharply. Today, the tea habit is considered to be a typical part of British culture. Tea is also the most prevalent drink in most cultures in the Middle East, and in Arab culture it is the focal point for social gatherings. Ceremonies have developed with ritualized techniques and protocols of brewing and serving tea, especially in China and Japan.

Archaeological studies of tea brewing equipment and serving vessels range from the brown- and black-glazed stoneware bowls used in medieval China and Japan (known as *temmoku* in Japanese) to transfer-printed whiteware cup-and-saucers found on 19th-century American domestic sites. The Russian tea samovar (self-boiler) is also a focus of study. The samovar is thought to have been introduced from Holland by Czar Peter the Great (1672–1725) or developed from an ancient boiler (*authepsa*) in Byzantium and introduced into Russian culture via the Orthodox Church.

See also FOOD AND DINING AS SOCIAL DISPLAY; FOOD AND RITUAL; MATERIAL CULTURE ANALYSIS; OLD WORLD GLOBALIZATION AND FOOD EXCHANGES

Further Reading

Rousmanière, Nicole C. 2002. The Tea Ceremony, Tea Utensils and Ceramics. In *Japan's Golden Age: Monoyama*, edited by Money L. Hickman, 305–35. New Haven, CT: Yale University Press.

Vroom, Joanita. 2012. Tea and Ceramics: New Perspectives on Byzantine Pottery from Limyra. In *40 Jahre Grabung Limyra*, edited by Martin Seyer, 341–55. Vienna: Österreichisches Archäologisches Institut.

Weinberg, Bennet A., and Bonnie K. Bealer. 2002. *The World of Caffeine: The Science and Culture of the World's Most Popular Drug*. New York: Routledge.

■ JOANITA VROOM

TEETH, DIET, AND HUMAN EVOLUTION

Determining what triggered the origin and early evolution of our biological genus, *Homo*, is an important step toward the deeper understanding of what makes us human. For paleoanthropologists, this question almost always involves the search for a change in diet, driven by the spread of savannas across eastern and southern Africa during the Early Pleistocene. Many theories have been put forth. Hunting meat or scavenging marrow made us human. Gathering underground storage organs or other plant parts made us human. Dietary versatility owing to tools for gathering and processing new foods made us human. Cooking made us human. There are many elegant and well-reasoned models in the literature. Some are based on nutritional analyses and direct analogy to living peoples or nonhuman primates. Others use contextual evidence, such as archaeological remains and paleoenvironmental indicators suggesting potential foods available.

Each of these models of diet is important, but what can the fossilized remains of the extinct hominins themselves teach us? There are four principal groups to consider: the Mio-Pliocene hominins including *Ardipithecus*, the Pliocene genus *Australopithecus*, and the early Pleistocene species of early *Homo* and *Paranthropus*. Most diet-related studies of these hominins rely on teeth. Not only are they the most common elements in vertebrate fossil assemblages, but they are the only durable parts of the digestive system that contact food. Teeth also offer many types of evidence, both adaptive (tooth size, structure, and shape) and nonadaptive (tooth chemistry, dental microwear).

Differences between hominin species in tooth size, measured as occlusal area (biting surface) of the premolars and molars, are reasonably clear. *Australopithecus* has larger cheek teeth than *Ardipithecus*, those of many *Paranthropus* are larger still, and those of *Homo* are reduced over time, especially from *H. erectus* onward. Traditional theory holds that larger cheek teeth mean more surface area to process bulky, low-quality foods. If so, hominins ate more of these through the Pliocene, with *Paranthropus* continuing in this direction in the Pleistocene and *Homo* reversing the trend. But this approach has its caveats. First, the error bars on our body size estimates make it difficult to put tooth size in proper context. Second, the relationship between tooth size and diet is actually very complex. Leaf-eating colobine monkeys, for example, should have larger teeth relative to body size than fruit-eating cercopithecines, but the opposite is true.

Tooth structure, especially enamel thickness, also has been considered. Many have thought that thick enamel evolved for life on the open savanna. It could be to compensate for wear in the abrasive environment: the thickest-enameled hominins also tend to have the steepest wear gradients between the first and last molars. Or perhaps it is to strengthen teeth against breakage, given a diet of hard, brittle foods like roots and nuts. Hard-object-feeding monkeys today tend to have thicker enamel than soft-fruit eaters. *Australopithecus* and especially *Paranthropus* have thicker enamel than *Ardipithecus*, and while early *Homo* has been said to have thinner enamel, recent work suggests this varies greatly, in part depending on how enamel thickness is measured. Also, enamel strength is not just a matter of thickness but also distribution, microstructure, and chemistry. Enamel thinness can be selected for, too, for surface sculpting to form sharp edges when wear breaks through to the softer dentin.

For tooth shape, there is a fairly consistent relationship between form and function in living primates. Tough-leaf eaters have longer shearing crests and more occlusal relief than primates that eat hard nuts, bark, and palm fronds. Those that consume soft fruits or have mixed diets are often in between. Theoretically, cheek teeth with longer crests and more topographic relief are better at slicing tough foods, whereas those with rounded, hemispherical cusps can transmit more stress to crush hard, brittle foods without themselves breaking in the process. There are, as with the other lines of evidence, differences among the hominins in tooth shape. Early *Homo* tends to have more relief and sharper biting surfaces than *Australopithecus* and especially *Paranthropus*. This may mean less hard-object feeding or more tough food consumption, perhaps including meat, by early *Homo*. But, as with other categories of evidence, there are caveats. Tooth shapes (and size and structure) all measure potential for breaking foods with different properties. They tell us more about natural selection among hominin species than actual behaviors of individuals.

Tooth chemistry is different. The ratio of ^{13}C to ^{12}C in tooth enamel, for example, depends on the ratio of these stable isotopes in the raw materials (food) used to make those teeth. Open-country tropical grasses and sedges (C_4 plants) have higher ratios than trees, bushes, shrubs, or forbs (herbaceous flowering C_3 plants), and animals do too if they eat them during growth and development. *Ardipithecus* evidently ate mostly C_3 plants, whereas *Australopithecus* isotope ratios range from one end of the C_3–C_4 food spectrum to the other. *Paranthropus* species vary from a mixed diet to mostly C_4 plants. Early *Homo* specimens show a mixed diet, with a combination of C_3 and C_4 plant parts or the animals that eat them.

Finally, patterns of microwear, or microscopic patterns of use-wear, also reflect diet. Hard-object feeders tend to have heavily pitted, complex microwear surfaces, whereas tough-food eaters more often have scratches running in parallel as opposing teeth slide past one another during shearing. *Australopithecus* species tend to have scratchier surfaces, whereas *Paranthropus* species range from scratchy to pitted. Early *Homo* individuals, especially *H. erectus*, vary in their microwear surface textures, suggesting a varying, versatile diet, though not one including the extremely hard objects likely eaten by some *Paranthropus*.

The dental evidence in aggregate suggests that *Australopithecus* likely ate mostly softer or tougher foods, like fruits and leaves, in a mixed setting, but that they could subsist on a fairly broad diet. There seems to have been an evolutionary fork in the road at the Plio–Pleistocene boundary, with our specialzed *Paranthropus* cousins having different diets in different places. Some ate tough savanna foods like grasses or sedges, whereas others consumed more hard items, like nuts and seeds, in a mixed setting. Our early *Homo* ancestors had less specialized teeth and probably a broader or more variable diet including both savanna and forest resources. Judging from the archaeological record, this may have included more meat.

See also BIOARCHAEOLOGICAL ANALYSIS; DENTAL ANALYSIS; DIGESTION AND HUMAN EVOLUTION; OLDUVAI GORGE; PALEODIETARY ANALYSIS; PALEOLITHIC DIET; STABLE ISOTOPE ANALYSIS

Further Reading

Ungar, Peter S. 2012. Dental Evidence for the Reconstruction of Diet in Early *Homo*. *Current Anthropology* 53(S6):S318–S329.
Ungar, Peter S., and Matt Sponheimer. 2011. The Diets of Early Hominins. *Science* 334(6053):190–93.

■ PETER S. UNGAR

TEHUACÁN VALLEY (MEXICO)

The impact of archaeological work in the Tehuacán Valley, Puebla, is widely recognized. Excavations by R. S. MacNeish's team in four rockshelters and numerous open-air sites documented the transition between food collecting and food production in Mesoamerica over thousands of years. MacNeish's work also marked the beginning of interdisciplinary archaeological science in Mesoamerica.

The Tehuacán Valley is known for its arid climate and tropical deciduous forest. The early evolution of no fewer than five major crop plants is documented here. Maize (*Zea mays* L. ssp. *mays*) appears around 5,510 cal BP and persists through 220 cal BP in rockshelters. Maize appears in fully domesticated form throughout the Tehuacán sequence. Tepary beans (*Phaseolus acutifolius*) appear first around 2,360–2,300 cal BP. Scarlet runner beans (*P. coccineus*) appear around 480 cal BP. Common beans (*P. vulgaris*) appear ca. 2,280 cal BP and persist until 1,580 cal BP. Tepary and common beans were domesticated prior to introduction into the Tehuacán Valley. A small-seeded, possibly domesticated cucurbit (*Cucurbita pepo*) appears around 5,930 cal BP. *Cucurbita argyrosperma* appears around 2,070 cal BP and, like *C. pepo*, continues into the historical period. A single chili pepper (*Capsicum annuum*) seed was recovered in deposits dated ca. 8,400 cal BP. Avocados (*Persea americana*) were common from 6,750 cal BP and are frequent throughout the sequence thereafter. It is not currently known whether either plant was wild or domesticated.

A significant number of other food plants were recovered from Tehuacán archaeological deposits. Many have not been directly dated. Most are still very significant food crops in urban and rural plazas of Mesoamerica today, including annual herbs, *quintonil* (*Amaranthus* spp.), *tomate* (*Physalis* sp.), peanut (*Arachis hypogaea*), tropical trees, *guaje* (*Leucaena esculenta*), *coyol* (*Acrocomia mexicana*), *zapote blanco* (*Casimiroa edulis*), *copalcojote* (*Cyrtocarpa procera*), *jocote* (*Spondias mombin*), *tempesquite* (*Bumelia laetevirens*), *tempisque* (*Sideroxylon tempisque*), *zapote negro* (*Diospyros digyna*), and *pitaya* (*Stenocereus stellatus*). The extremely useful *maguey* (*Agave* spp.) was present throughout the sequences and, like the tropical tree crops, is still used today.

See also AGRICULTURE, ORIGINS OF; ARCHAEOBOTANY; BEAN/COMMON BEAN; GUILÁ NAQUITZ; HUNTER-GATHERER SUBSISTENCE; MAIZE; MESOAMERICAN ARCHAIC-PERIOD DIET; PLANT DOMESTICATION; ROCKSHELTERS/CAVES

Further Reading

Byers, Douglas S., ed. 1967. *The Prehistory of the Tehuacán Valley*. Vol. 1, *Environment and Subsistence*. Austin: University of Texas Press.

MacNeish, Richard S. 1981. Tehuacán's Accomplishments. In *Supplement to the Handbook of Middle American Indians*, vol. 1, *Archaeology*, edited by Victoria R. Bricker and Jeremy A. Sabloff, 31–47. Austin: University of Texas Press.

■ BRUCE F. BENZ

TEL REHOV (ISRAEL)

Tel Rehov is a ten-hectare site located in the Jordan Valley in northern Israel. It was established as a Canaanite city in the 15th century BC and became an Israelite city during

Figure 58. The apiary at Tel Reḥov, Israel. The apiary dates to ca. 900 BC. Left: General view of the apiary, looking to southeast. Right: Detail of a hive with a clay lid. Photographs by Amihai Mazar, Tel Reḥov Expedition, The Hebrew University of Jerusalem.

the tenth to ninth centuries BC. An apiary was discovered in the midst of this city during excavations and remains the only one known from an archaeological context (figure 58).

Radiocarbon dates indicate that the apiary was in use ca. 900 BC. It was well planned, with three rows of hives constructed parallel to each other (figure 59). Each hive was made of a horizontal cylinder (0.4 meters in diameter, 0.7 meters long) made of unfired mud; one side had a small "flying hall" while the other side had a portable lid, enabling the harvesting of honeycombs. About 30 hives were preserved in three tiers, and there probably were 100–200 hives at one time. It is estimated that 100 hives could produce 0.5 tons of honey and about 60 kilograms of bees' wax. Similar hives are known from artistic depictions in ancient Egypt and from ethnographic parallels throughout the Middle East. Remains of bees found in the hives were identified as the subspecies *Apis mellifera anatoliaca*, which is known in Turkey as particularly fertile and convenient to raise but is foreign to Israel. Based on this identification and Assyrian textual sources, it was suggested that bee swarms were imported from southern Turkey to Israel at that time.

Honey production in apiaries is well known in ancient Egypt and the land of the Hittites but is not mentioned in the Bible. Though the Bible defines the Land of Israel as a "Land of Milk and Honey," scholars previously interpreted this honey (*Dvash*) as fruit syrup. Yet textual studies and the discovery at Tel Reḥov perhaps indicate that bees' honey and wax were important commodities in biblical Israel.

See also DOCUMENTARY ANALYSIS; ETHNOGRAPHIC SOURCES; HONEY AND NECTAR

Further Reading

Bloch, Guy, Tiago M. Francoy, Ido Wachtel, et al. 2010. Industrial Apiculture in the Jordan Valley during Biblical Times with Anatolian Bees. *Proceedings of the National Academy of Sciences USA* 107(25):11240–44.

Mazar, Amihai, and Nava Panitz-Cohen. 2007. It Is the Land of Honey: Beekeeping at Tel Reḥov. *Near Eastern Archaeology* 70(4):202–19.

■ AMIHAI MAZAR

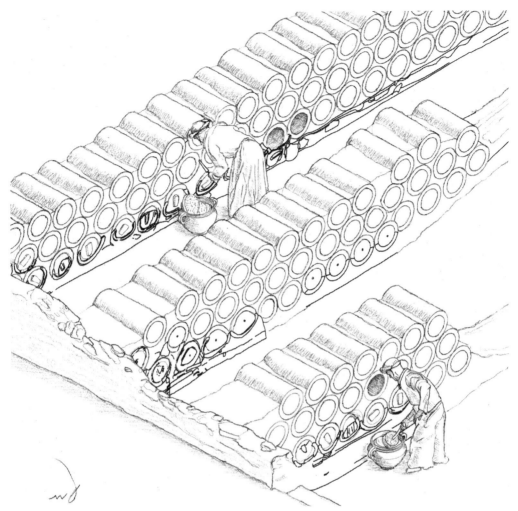

Figure 59. Artist's reconstruction of the apiary at Tel Reḥov. Drawing by Ana Yamim for the Tel Reḥov Expedition, The Hebrew University of Jerusalem.

TEXTUAL SOURCES
See DOCUMENTARY ANALYSIS

TOBACCO

Tobacco (*Nicotiana* sp., from the Solanaceae or nightshade family) is a potent intoxicant plant that has a very long history of use by humans. Tobacco was widely regarded as a sacred plant by native peoples throughout the Americas and is one of the earliest New World domesticates; its use was intimately entwined with ritual and religious life, a spiritual connection that persists among many to this day. Its ancient history and popularity among humans is linked to its physiological effects when ingested. Tobacco contains addictive psychotropic alkaloids, including nicotine, that act as stimulants, producing effects including euphoria, increased heart rate, heighted mental acuity or alertness, suppression of hunger and thirst, and an increased sense of calm. In large doses tobacco can cause out-of-body experiences, hallucinations, or visions, effects that were sought after by shamans or doctors in vision quests, curing, and other religious and ritual practices. The first people to discover these qualities and exploit tobacco were the ancient Americans, and we are just beginning to trace its long history of use and path of domestication.

At the time of European contact, tobacco was the most widely exploited intoxicant plant throughout the Americas. Native peoples ingested tobacco most often by smoking but also by chewing (often with lime), by sniffing powdered tobacco, and, while rare, also by enema. Farming societies throughout South America, Mesoamerica, the Caribbean, the eastern United States, and parts of the American Southwest raised the domesticated species *N. rustica* and *N. tabacum*. Many species of wild (or coyote) tobacco were also widely exploited, for example, by hunter-gatherers throughout the North American west.

Tracking ancient tobacco use is challenging, although we have learned quite a bit through recent advances in archaeological science. Tobacco use is often inferred by the presence of durable stone or clay pipes or smoking paraphernalia (e.g., snuff trays, grinding implements); however, many species of plants were used by native peoples. Thus direct evidence through the recovery and identification of seeds is important. Charred tobacco seeds are quite rare in the archaeological record, however, and are very hard to identify due to their exceedingly small size. Chemical residue analysis involving gas chromatography–mass spectrometry (GC-MS) provides an alternative means to trace the origins and spread of tobacco and other smoke plants. GC-MS tobacco studies were pioneered by Sean Rafferty and have been employed by a handful of scholars. To date the technique has been used to identify tobacco use through the identification of the biomarker nicotine extracted from residues associated with pipes, the ash content of pipes, and samples of human hair from South American mummies. Another innovative application, employed by Zagorevski and Loughmiller-Newman, identified nicotine in a Mayan ceramic flask dating to between AD 600 and 900, suggesting use as a tobacco container; the flask was marked with codex text translating to "the home of his/her tobacco" (figure 60).

Key research questions centering on tobacco use revolve around the antiquity of its use, artifact function and ritual activity, and the history of domestication, cultivation, management, and anthropogenic range extension. At its most basic level, archaeological investigations can help us better understand when and why people first began using tobacco. Archaeologists hypothesize that tobacco was first domesticated around 4,000 years ago in the Andes region of South America. It likely reached eastern North America, the Caribbean, and parts of the American Southwest by about 2,500 years ago. Much remains unknown about the timing and trajectory of species domestication, however.

In many parts of western and northern North America the antiquity of tobacco smoking is debated. Some believe it to have been a very recent practice brought by Euro-American traders, while others argue that the practice has very ancient origins. Wild tobacco is believed to have spread into the arid zones of the American Southwest,

Figure 60. Residue analysis of a Maya flask using GC-MS revealed traces of nicotine in the vessel. The glyph has been translated as *yo-'OTOT-ti 'u-MAY-ya*, spelling *y-otoot 'u-mahy* ("the home of his/her tobacco"). The flask dates to ca. AD 700. Photograph by Jennifer A. Loughmiller-Cardinal. Kislak Collection, Library of Congress.

California, and Great Basin by the end of the Early Pleistocene. If true, it is certainly plausible that native peoples living in these areas would have readily recognized the intoxicant qualities of tobacco and would have incorporated the plant into their ritual and medicinal complex.

There is abundant documentary evidence that tobacco was cultivated or managed in areas outside of its natural range, yet the antiquity of these practices is debated. Some scholars have hypothesized that its range in North America was expanded through management of wild tobacco, possibly leading to the creation of new species. At contact, tobacco was cultivated by many otherwise nonfarming peoples in many parts of the American West through the preparation of plots, burning, sowing of seeds, and pruning.

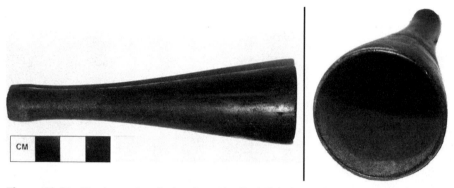

Figure 61. Steatite (soapstone) pipe from the Red Elderberry Site (CA-DNO-26), northwest California. The pipe tested positive for nicotine residues using GC-MS. Nicotine is a biomarker for tobacco. Photograph by Shannon Tushingham.

Along the Pacific Northwest coast, where tobacco is a nonnative plant, human management of wild tobacco as far north as British Columbia is viewed as a dramatic case of anthropogenic range extension. Recent GC-MS analysis of pipes from Northern California by Tushingham and colleagues demonstrates that tobacco was indeed used in the Pacific Northwest by at least AD 860 (figure 61).

The intoxicant qualities of tobacco were sought out by humans, who had an active hand in the spread of tobacco and the creation of new species. Tobacco domestication ultimately had profound consequences for humankind. Spanish explorers introduced tobacco to Europe in the early 1500s, and it spread quickly throughout the Old World: in less than 100 years the plant was traded throughout the Ottoman Empire and beyond. Tobacco use exploded during the Industrial Revolution with the advent of commercial cigarettes. Originally used by the indigenous peoples of the Americas, primarily in sacred and religious contexts, recreational tobacco use has reached epidemic proportions. Today, despite enormous health consequences, tobacco remains one of the most widely used addictive substances; according to the World Health Organization there are currently over one billion tobacco users around the globe, and it is the leading cause of preventable death.

See also ARCHAEOBOTANY; BIOMOLECULAR ANALYSIS; COLUMBIAN EXCHANGE; GAS CHROMATOGRAPHY/GAS CHROMATOGRAPHY—MASS SPECTROMETRY; PLANT DOMESTICATION; PSYCHOACTIVE PLANTS

Further Reading

Echeverría, Javier, and Hermann M. Niemeyer. 2013. Nicotine in the Hair of Mummies from San Pedro de Atacama (Northern Chile). 2013. *Journal of Archaeological Science* 40(10):3561–68.

Rafferty, Sean M., Igor Lednev, Kelly Virkler, and Zuzana Chovanec. 2012. Current Research on Smoking Pipe Residues. *Journal of Archaeological Science* 39(7):1951–59.

Tushingham, Shannon, Dominique Ardura, Jelmer W. Eerkens, et al. 2013. Hunter-Gatherer Tobacco Smoking: Earliest Evidence from the Pacific Northwest Coast of North America. *Journal of Archaeological Science* 40(2):1397–1407.

Wilbert, Johannes. 1987. *Tobacco and Shamanism in South America*. New Haven, CT: Yale University Press.

Winter, Joseph C., ed. 2000. *Tobacco Use by Native North Americans: Sacred Smoke and Silent Killer*. Norman: University of Oklahoma Press.
Zagorevski, Dmitri V., and Jennifer A. Loughmiller-Newman. 2012. The Detection of Nicotine in a Late Mayan Period Flask by Gas Chromatography and Liquid Chromatography Mass Spectrometry Methods. *Rapid Communications in Mass Spectrometry* 26(4):403–11.

■ SHANNON TUSHINGHAM

TOOLS/UTENSILS, DECORATED

Nothing is more ordinary than food and drink, yet people have expended an extraordinary amount of time and resources on the implements used for its enjoyment. Decorated eating and drinking utensils were frequently made of perishable materials like wood, bone, and horn. Such forms rarely survive except under ideal conditions, as at Çatalhöyük in Anatolia (7500–5700 BC) where utensils such as wood and bone spoons were preserved in carbonized form after their incomplete burning by fire, or at Herculaneum in Italy (AD 62–79), which was buried under hot volcanic ash. The majority of preserved utensils recovered from archaeological contexts are made of clay, stone, and metal, such as those unearthed from burials at Ur in Mesopotamia (third millennium BC). Residue, use-wear, lithic, and metallographic analyses of utensils, supplemented by visual (paintings, seals) and literary evidence (inscriptions, texts), have contributed to our knowledge about diet, technology, trade, ritual, and, in particular, social behavior.

Today we have a large variety of utensils at our disposal, yet for most of history our hands have conveyed food to our mouths. Utensils like spoons carved from wood and bone were known as early as Paleolithic times (13,500–12,000 BP), whereas knives and two-tined forks were used only for preparing and serving food. The Romans (first century AD) were the first to employ specialty spoons (*cochleare, ligula*) for eating extravagant fare like shellfish and snails. This culminated in the widespread acquisition of the silver service (*ministerium*), which is attested by the elaborate finds unearthed in the towns devastated by the eruption of Mount Vesuvius (AD 79), but also further afield in Germany and Britain. A refinement of dining customs in Renaissance Europe (17th century) led to the introduction of the table knife and fork, as well as the production of flatware in precious metals and exotic materials, as at Sheffield, England.

Particular care has always been lavished on utensils used for consuming beer and wine, no doubt because of the social and ritual importance of such beverages. Drinking tubes used in funerary feasts in the Near East and Egypt, like those from Ur (third millennium BC), were made of silver and gold. In Greece (fifth century BC), the majority of utensils for private use were produced in painted clay (figure 62), though exquisite silver ladles and strainers are found in the tombs of Scythians and Thracians in Russia and Bulgaria. Private wealth in the Hellenistic period (fourth–first century BC) led to more elaborate metal utensils—for example, those from Vergina, Greece. This decadent tradition, upheld by the Romans, later culminated in wind-up mechanisms (*automata*) that dispensed alcoholic beverages. Such devices were meant to impress as well as to entertain the diner.

See also ÇATALHÖYÜK; FOOD AND DINING AS SOCIAL DISPLAY; FOOD AND RITUAL; FOOD AND STATUS; FOOD AS SENSORY EXPERIENCE; HERCULANEUM AND POMPEII

Figure 62. Red figure askos with strainer, excavated in 1937 from a well in the ancient Athenian Agora in Greece. Illustrated are a dog and a griffin facing one another and, on the opposite side, a crouching lion. The molded spout is the lion's head. Late fifth century BC. Inventory number P 10017. Photograph by Craig Mauzy. Courtesy of the American School of Classical Studies at Athens, Agora Excavations.

Further Reading

Boger, Ann C. 1983. *Consuming Passions: The Art of Food and Drink*. Cleveland: Cleveland Museum of Art.

Maeir, Aren M., and Yosef Garfinkel. 1992. Bone and Metal Straw-Tip Beer-Strainers from the Ancient Near East. *Levant* 24(1):218–23.

Oliver, Andrew. 2004. The Changing Fashions of Roman Silver. *Record of the Art Museum, Princeton University* 63:2–27.

Strong, D. E. 1966. *Greek and Roman Gold and Silver Plate*. Ithaca, NY: Cornell University Press.

■ JOANNA PAPAYIANNIS

TOOLS/UTENSILS, GROUND STONE

Stone tools have been used since prehistoric times to process foodstuffs and a variety of other materials. Ground stone tools include grinding slabs/querns and handstones—known in the New World as *metates* and *manos*—as well as mortars, pestles, pounders, abraders, and many other artifact types. Grinding slabs and querns have been identified in archaeological contexts as early as the Epipaleolithic in the Levant and appear in greater frequency in the Neolithic period in the context of early permanent settlements and increasing reliance on cereal agriculture. Millstones and various other types of ground stone tools continue to be used in contemporary societies, thus ethnographic data, as well as experimental studies and other techniques, provide useful information for reconstructing aspects of tool manufacture and use in the past.

Archaeologists and other researchers have traditionally paid less attention to ground stone than to other artifact categories, like lithics and pottery, despite the fact that ground stone tools are the most visible and durable artifacts that inform on the daily activities necessary for human survival. Reasons for this disparity include their association with mundane, female-associated activities; the widespread belief that their functions in the past are self-evident; the inability to use them as chronological indicators in many regions; and their size and weight, which make collection, analysis, and curation difficult. Recent studies by ground stone specialists working at sites around the world demonstrate, however, that this overlooked class of material culture can inform a variety of research questions related to food production and consumption, the sexual division of labor, and organization of craft production, among others.

The term *ground stone* is problematic because it can refer either to the method used to make a tool—through grinding—or to the way a tool was used, such as to grind grain. Ethnographic and experimental studies have shown, however, that ground stone tools can be made using a variety of techniques, including flaking, pounding, and drilling, while some artifacts, like vessels, axes, and hoes, have little or nothing to do with grinding plant foods and other substances. Although ground stone tools can be made from a variety of raw materials, rough-grained, igneous stones like basalt seem to be a preferred material for making grinding implements like slabs and querns. Experimental studies demonstrate the superior cutting and self-sharpening properties of basalt. Ethnographic studies inform on the practice of pecking or roughening grinding implements made of smoother material, like flint and limestone, to make them more efficient. Provenance analyses have been used to identify the origins of raw stone materials and show the movement of raw materials or finished artifacts over great distances. These studies challenge the belief that raw stone material was acquired from the closest available source and that only semiprecious stones were exchanged over great distances. Geochemical studies of basalt artifacts and outcrops in the Southern Levant, for example, hint at the complex physical and social factors that influenced the choice of raw material and subsequent artifact manufacture in this region.

The assumed function of tools such as grinding slabs and querns, handstones, mortars, and pestles is to grind and pound agricultural products, primarily cereal grains, although various lines of evidence demonstrate the use of tools in a variety of processing activities. A further complicating factor in the study of ground stone tools is their unique durability: they can remain in use for a very long time and are frequently reused, often for a different function. Documented cases from archaeological contexts include examples from Neolithic Çatalhöyük in Anatolia, where the fragments of broken ground stone artifacts were stained with pigment, suggesting their reuse as part of a painting toolkit.

A range of methods may be necessary to identify the types of processing activities for which ground stone tools were used in the past. In addition to ethnographic studies, experimental approaches such as replicative studies may permit the identification of tool function. Use-wear analyses allow for the identification of macroscopic and microscopic wear patterns that correspond to specific processing activities, like maize grinding. Analysis of chemical residues and microbotanical remains on stone tools, including blood, lipids, and starches, allows for the identification of some of the actual materials processed with ground stone tools. Identification of the remains of starch grains, phytoliths, and fern and lily starch on a ca. 27,000-year-old grinding slab from southeastern Australia, for example, is very important in developing models of subsistence strategies and resource use in the region during this period.

These studies show that artifact form does not equal function. For example, some hide-processing stones are similar in shape to some *manos*, but use-wear analysis can distinguish the wear patterns resulting from stone-against-stone food grinding from those created by rubbing hide against a stone surface. Further, the same set of grinding tools can be used to process a variety of different materials; in addition, they reveal that a single tool can have multiple functions. As a result of increased attention to the analytical potential of this artifact class and the use of new techniques and approaches, however, scholars are generating more sophisticated and highly nuanced studies concerning the manufacture and use of these ubiquitous artifacts.

See also ARCHAEOBOTANY; BEDROCK FEATURES; ETHNOARCHAEOLOGY; ETHNOGRAPHIC SOURCES; EXPERIMENTAL ARCHAEOLOGY; MILLING; PLANT PROCESSING; RESIDUE ANALYSIS, STARCH; STARCHES, ROLE OF; USE-WEAR ANALYSIS, LITHICS

Further Reading

Adams, Jennie L. 1996. *Manual for a Technological Approach to Ground Stone Analysis.* Tucson, AZ: Center for Desert Archaeology.

Fullager, Richard, Judith Field, and Lisa Kealhofer. 2008. Grinding Stones and Seeds of Change: Starch and Phytoliths as Evidence of Plant Food Processing. In *New Approaches to Old Stones: Recent Studies of Ground Stone Artifacts*, edited by Yorke M. Rowan and Jennie R. Ebeling, 159–72. London: Equinox.

Rutter, Graham, and Graham Philip. 2008. Beyond Provenance Analysis: The Movement of Basaltic Artifacts through a Social Landscape. In *New Approaches to Old Stones: Recent Studies of Ground Stone Artifacts*, edited by Yorke M. Rowan and Jennie R. Ebeling, 343–58. London: Equinox.

Wright, Katherine I. 2008. Craft Production and the Organization of Ground Stone Technologies. In *New Approaches to Old Stones: Recent Studies of Ground Stone Artifacts*, edited by Yorke M. Rowan and Jennie R. Ebeling, 130–43. London: Equinox.

■ JENNIE EBELING

TOOLS/UTENSILS, METAL

Cooking over an open hearth, as was typical in ancient times, required cooking utensils that could withstand heat, and these were typically made from ceramic or metal. Pottery was cheaper and therefore much more common, but metal was more durable and, in some societies, conveyed status. European societies, from the Bronze Age onward, used simple metal spits to roast meat, while Iron Age excavations have produced examples of iron pots or cauldrons. These could be suspended on chains from tripods or bars or used directly on the hearth. Bronze beaked wine flagons have been recovered from burials in Italy and temperate Europe from the sixth–fourth centuries BC, and wine equipment reached a high point with the great wine mixing crater from Vix (ca. 500 BC), an extraordinary vessel that clearly had a social value far beyond the price of the material from which it was made.

Roman metal vessels were more common, and more utilitarian. Bronze saucepans have been recovered from both military and civilian contexts and would have been a standard part of many Roman kitchens; the use of lead is also known, and must have been the cause of lead poisoning before this hazard was recognized. Iron tripods and gridirons from Roman contexts show that cooking took place over charcoal fires, sometimes at waist height. Trivets to support vessels taken off the fire are also known from early medieval contexts, as are flat griddle plates for baking oatmeal and small cakes. Double-ended or S-hooks and fragments of chains that might have been used to suspend cooking vessels over hearths continue unchanged from Iron Age contexts.

Shallow open forms, such as flat-bottomed dishes, frying pans, or skillets, also have been recovered, with several coming from Viking Age contexts. An almost complete example (65 millimeters deep, 350 millimeters in diameter) was found in a tenth-century context in York (figure 63). Its handle was missing, but the vessel had been patched and repaired on several occasions, with both iron and lead patches riveted onto the sides and base. The vessel was made from a single sheet of iron beaten into shape. Similar examples, together with others made from several plates riveted together, are known from Viking Age Scandinavia. The effort to repair the vessel, seen also on a comparable vessel from Winchester, demonstrates the value of such items to their owners.

Metal cooking implements also have been recovered and had several functions in the kitchen. A good example is a flesh hook. These two- or three-pronged metal hooks have curved prongs to ensure a safe hold while extracting meat from hot liquids or removing it from a spit, and their form changes very little over time. Similarly, spoons are a recognizable functional form although there is considerable variation in size and style. Among those recovered from Viking Age York are small tin-plated, double-ended spoons (figure 63); one bowl is spatulate, suggesting use with solid or viscous materials, rather than liquids. Their decoration raises them from the purely utilitarian and suggests a role beyond the kitchen. This also may be true for a single-bowl example with gilding recovered from tenth-century Birka in Sweden. More obviously functional (though the functions of knives were many and varied, including craft activities, weaponry, and butchery) are the knife blades recovered from archaeological sites from the Iron Age onward. Ladles and colanders (metal containers with holes pierced through the sides and base) are known from among Roman household equipment, and the fragment of a perforated disc from Viking Age levels in York might be part of a strainer. Metal buckets or pails are known but are rare, as these items are commonly made of wood with metal supporting hooks. The recovery of metal handles (usually iron), suspension loops, and other fittings is evidence of composite utensils made from bone, horn, stone, pottery, glass, and wood, though only the iron has survived.

Through prehistory and into the medieval period, metal utensils are comparatively rare. In pre-Christian times, they are occasionally found in burials, attesting to their role in conveying status or prestige, but broken or discarded items also could have been recycled and the metal content retrieved for reuse. Metal cooking utensils appear commonly as

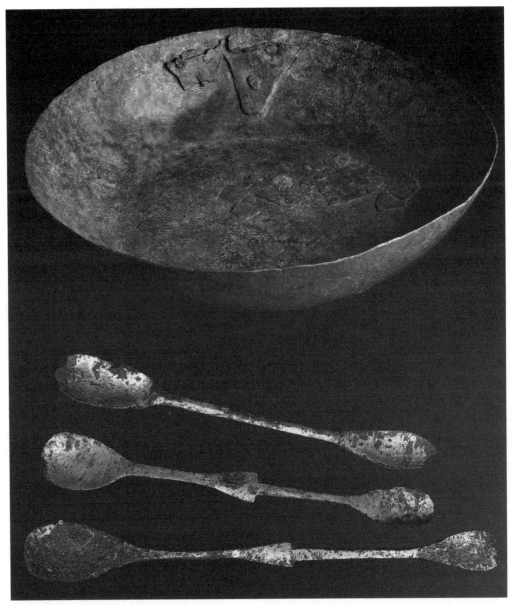

Figure 63. Excavations at Coppergate in York, England, from 1976 to 1981 uncovered numerous tools and utensils from the Viking period. Top: An iron vessel that most probably had a riveted metal handle and was repaired several times with patches of iron and lead and with riveted iron sheets. Bottom: Double-ended spoons made of iron with tin plating were probably used for measuring spices, drugs, or ointments rather than liquids and may have been produced on site. Photographs by Michael Andrews. © York Archaeological Trust.

items listed in medieval wills and inventories and passed down to favored family members and neighbors, once again suggesting an emotional as well as functional value.

The recovery of metal tools and utensils from archaeological sites of this period is quite rare. This is the result not only of recycling but also of the fact that metal itself does not always survive well in many soils. Items made from nonferrous materials (such as copper alloy, lead alloy, silver, and gold) generally survive well, but ferrous (iron) items will corrode badly in many soils. It is only when conditions are right, such as in water-logged, anaerobic deposits, that ironwork will survive well. Often the corrosion products will mask the original character of the objects, but this can still be revealed by radiography and careful conservation treatments. Techniques of manufacture and evidence of use, such as wear and repair, can be revealed, while various types of analyses can identify the metal composition. After cleaning, metal items need to be kept or displayed in a stable, dry atmosphere to prevent further deterioration.

The introduction of steel, and particularly stainless steel, has meant that tools and utensils are regularly recovered from postmedieval and historical-period contexts. The Sheffield cutlery industry has been a particular focus of study. Textual sources such as mail order catalogues document the proliferation of forms in the 19th and 20th centuries. Interestingly, though new types of metal cooking utensils have been introduced (the rotary egg beater, for example), other basic forms have remained largely unchanged in form and function (e.g., knives, spatulas).

See also ARCHAEOLOGY OF COOKING; MATERIAL CULTURE ANALYSIS; TOOLS/UTENSILS, DECORATED; TOOLS/UTENSILS, ORGANIC MATERIALS; USE–WEAR ANALYSIS, METAL

Further Reading

Allason-Jones, Lindsay, ed. 2011. *Artefacts in Roman Britain: Their Purpose and Use.* Cambridge: Cambridge University Press.

Brown, Peter, ed. 2001. *British Cutlery: An Illustrated History of Design, Evolution and Use.* York: York Civic Trust.

Cool, H. E. M. 2006. *Eating and Drinking in Roman Britain.* Cambridge: Cambridge University Press.

Egan, Geoff. 2010. *The Medieval Household: Daily Living c. 1150–c. 1450.* Woodbridge, UK: Boydell Press.

Hyer, Maren Clegg, and Gale R. Owen-Crocker, eds. 2011. *The Material Culture of Daily Living in the Anglo-Saxon World.* Liverpool: Liverpool University Press.

Symonds, James, ed. 2002. *The Historical Archaeology of the Sheffield Cutlery and Tableware Industry, 1750–1900.* Sheffield, UK: ARCUS.

■ AILSA MAINMAN

TOOLS/UTENSILS, ORGANIC MATERIALS

From Paleolithic times, tools and utensils for the procurement, preparation, and consumption of food were frequently made from materials that were once living organisms, such as wood, bone, horn, and shell. The inedible parts of animals were repurposed to make implements, which meant that almost nothing was squandered. Tools made of organic materials—as opposed to those fashioned from stone—have survived at relatively few sites

Figure 64. Viking Age lathe-turned wooden cups and bowls used for food preparation and consumption, from the 1976–1981 excavations at Coppergate in York, England. One bowl was held together with metal staples, suggesting that bowls were often repaired rather than discarded when the wood split or broke. The cups, some of which had traces of paint, were most likely used for drinking beer, which was consumed daily during this period. The Viking settlement at York (Jorvik) dates from 866–1066 AD. Photograph by Michael Andrews. © York Archaeological Trust.

since they are more susceptible to decomposition. Ideal conditions for the preservation of organics are those that hinder bacterial decay, such as the desert-like environment of Egypt or the arctic cold of Siberia. Waterlogged, flooded sites also preserve organic materials, for example, the Viking settlement of Jorvik (York, UK) (figure 64). The peat bogs of northern Europe, Russia, and China, where acidic, oxygen-deficient water and low temperatures inhibit decomposition, also provide excellent preservation conditions. At the site of Hemudu, China (5000–3300 BC), the marshy environment has led to remarkable discoveries of wood and bone farming tools and eating utensils. Destructive events have fortuitously preserved organics as well. At Herculaneum and Pompeii, Italy, the sudden, intense heat of the pyroclastic material from the eruption of Mount Vesuvius (AD 79) carbonized many wood and bone household implements. Less catastrophic events, such as the incomplete burning of organic materials in hearths at Çatalhöyük in Anatolia (7500–5700 BC), also preserve perishable artifacts.

Organic artifacts can be dated relatively by means of their physical characteristics (typologies), but also can be more precisely dated through dendrochronology (tree ring dating) and radiocarbon dating. Use-wear and residue analyses of tool surfaces have been particularly helpful in identifying the function of implements. These analyses are often supplemented by visual (paintings, seals) and literary evidence (inscriptions, texts), as well as by experimental archaeology, which tests the function of tools by replicating various activities with similar implements. The analysis of both ordinary utensils and more specialized tools has greatly contributed to our understanding of agriculture, technology, nutrition, trade, and even social behavior.

Specialized wooden and bone implements employed for hunting and fishing, such as spears, points, and harpoons, occur at Paleolithic sites in Africa and Europe—for example, in the peat bogs in Hanover, Germany (400,000 BP) and the cave sites of La Madelaine, France (16,000 BP), and Gough's Cave, Britain (12,000 BP). Tools and implements are more abundant and more developed at Mesolithic sites, such as at Star Carr, Britain (8,500 BP), and Vela Spila, Croatia (7,380–7,080 BP), where bone needles for extracting shellfish were found. The bone tool industry saw its peak in the Natufian culture of the Levant (13,000–9800 BC). Cave sites such as Hayonim, Israel, have produced farming and fishing implements such as sickles and fishhooks, as well as cooking tools such as spatulas. The site of Çatalhöyük (7500–5700 BC) offers some of the best-preserved organic finds from the Neolithic period, such as bone, wood, and antler sickles, fishhooks, harpoons, spoons, and ladles. Tools made from mollusk shells also occur at Neolithic sites such as Esh Shaheinab in the Sudan (ca. 4000 BC) and the Shandong Peninsula of China (3500–2000 BC), where food procurement implements like fishhooks and sickles were unearthed. Other subsistence-related tools include early cultivating and farming implements—for example, wooden hoes, plows, sickles, and winnowing forks, such as those from New Kingdom Thebes (ca. 1550–1292 BC) and the Roman Fayum (first to fourth centuries AD) in Egypt, as a result of the desertlike conditions that impede decomposition.

Fermented beverages, like barley beer, were an early development in the Near East. Visual representations of beer drinking show that it was common to drink beer through a tube or straw with a strainer attached to filter out any residue from barley husks or wild yeasts, most of which would float to the surface. Physical examples of straws rarely survive, perhaps because these were made from reeds, though the strainer tips, which were usually made of bone, are found at numerous sites in the Near East and Egypt. In the burials at Gesher, Israel (2000–1750 BC), hollow bone implements about six centimeters long with perforations at one end were found, including one inside a jar (figure 65), suggesting that they had been employed for consuming an unfiltered drink, in all probability beer.

Specialized tools for eating are a comparatively recent development. Spoons, the oldest man-made utensils, occur from Paleolithic times (13,500–12,000 BP), perhaps because these were shaped most like the human hand. The Romans (first century AD) first employed specialty spoons (*cochleare*, *ligula*) for eating delicacies at banquets. Examples occur

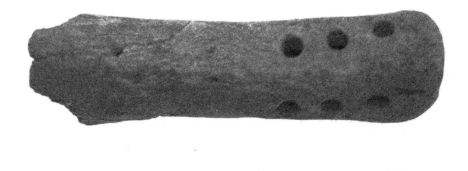

Figure 65. Bone implement from a Middle Bronze Age II cemetery (29th century BC) at the site of Gesher, Israel. Grave 7 contained three artifacts: a ceramic juglet, a jar, and, inside the jar, a perforated, hollow bone implement with nine drilled holes. Its association with the jar and its similarity to other forms, both metal and bone, suggest that this implement served as a straw-tip strainer for consuming fermented beverages. Length: 5.4 centimeters. Width: 1.3–1.4 centimeters. Photograph by Gabi Laron. Courtesy of Yosef Garfinkel, The Hebrew University of Jerusalem. Reprinted from Maeir and Garfinkel 1992 (fig. 14) with permission of Maney Publishers through Copyright Clearance Center, Inc.

in wood, bone, and ivory throughout the Classical world and, in particular, at Herculaneum and Pompeii (AD 62–79), where such implements were recovered from household cabinets and chests. Knives and forks were used only for preparing and serving food until the introduction of tableware in Renaissance Europe. In Asia, chopsticks originated in China during the Shang Dynasty (1766–1122 BC) but only attained widespread use during the Ming Dynasty (AD 1368–1644). These long bamboo or wooden sticks (*kuaizi*) acted as extensions of the fingers and were in line with the teachings of Confucius, who believed that sharp utensils at the dinner table evoked violence.

See also AGRICULTURE, PROCUREMENT, PROCESSING, AND STORAGE; ARCHAEOLOGY OF COOKING; BEER; ÇATALHÖYÜK; FISHING; HERCULANEUM AND POMPEII; MATERIAL CULTURE ANALYSIS; RADIOCARBON DATING; SHIPWRECKS; STAR CARR; TOOLS/UTENSILS, DECORATED; TOOLS/UTENSILS, METAL; TOOLS/UTENSILS, STONE; WINE

Further Reading

Bar-Yosef, O., and E. Tchernov. 1970. The Natufian Bone Industry of Hayonim Cave. *Israel Exploration Journal* 20(3–4):141–50.

Hurcombe, Linda. 2008. Organics from Inorganics: Using Experimental Archaeology as a Research Tool for Studying Perishable Material Culture. *World Archaeology* 40(1):83–115.

Janick, Jules. 2002. Ancient Egyptian Agriculture and the Origins of Horticulture. *Acta Horticulturae* 582:23–39.

Maeir, Aren M., and Yosef Garfinkel. 1992. Bone and Metal Beer-Strainers from the Ancient Near East. *Levant* 24(1):218–23.

Russell, Nerissa. 2005. Çatalhöyük Worked Bone. In *Changing Materialities at Çatalhöyük: Reports from the 1995–99 Seasons*, edited by Ian Hodder, 339–368. Çatalhöyük Research Project 5. BIAA Monograph 39. Cambridge: McDonald Institute for Archaeological Research and British Institute at Ankara.

■ JOANNA PAPAYIANNIS

TOOLS/UTENSILS, STONE

Food procurement has always been one of the most important types of human economic activity. Hunting, fishing, animal husbandry, and agriculture have served as main nutritional resources. Food remains are a rare find in archaeological contexts, however, and there are few direct data on human diet for the Stone Age period. Paleozoology and paleobotany provide us with considerable information on the range of foods available to past populations. The stone, bone, and antler tools associated with food procurement and processing are another important source of information on Stone Age diet. This entry focuses on the study of stone tools and utensils. Traceological analysis, first introduced by S. A. Semenov, helps to identify the function of tools used for food procurement and processing. This method is based on microscopic identification of specific use-wear on tool working edges. Residue and starch grain analyses complement this research. Finally, to test hypotheses about tool use, experimental replication with ethnographic and modern analogs and written source data are often used.

The opportunistic use of lithic materials as tools can be dated to early *Homo*. The Oldowan industry, the first named tool industry, includes crude choppers and hammers used to cut flesh and break bone. Increased sophistication in tool manufacture and use is typically correlated with cognitive advances in hominins, and the Acheulean tool industry, which includes highly sophisticated hand axes, is seen as the next evolutionary stage in tool manufacture. It is in the Upper Paleolithic, however, that the tool kit expands rapidly. Flint butcher knives, flint and bone fish-scaling knives, fishing hooks, sinkers for fishing nets, and other tools for meat and fish processing have been found on various Eurasian Stone Age sites (e.g., the Upper Paleolithic sites of Kostenki and Malta, Russia; the Mesolithic site of Ivanovskoe-7, Russia). Plant gathering and consumption in the Mid-Upper Paleolithic are confirmed by traces of plant grinding and starch residues on ground stone tools (e.g., Pavlov VI, Czech Republic; Bilancino II, Italy; Kostenki-16, Russia).

Plant foods played a key role in the diet of the Neolithic period (7000 BC) with the beginning of cereal cultivation. Agricultural toolkits included antler hoes and sickles with stone inserts in the antler and wooden handles. Composite sickles could have different construction. The earliest sickles from the Near East and central Asia (e.g., Beidha, Jordan; Chopan-depe, Turkmenistan) have straight handles with continuous blades made with several flint inserts. Later, new forms appeared with curved handles and inserts set in one line or obliquely, forming a denticulate edge. One of these forms, named "Karanovo type," is widely known from the prehistoric sites of southeastern Europe (numerous Neolithic and Eneolithic sites in Bulgaria, Romania, Moldova, and Ukraine) as well as in Anatolia and the Near East (Turkey, Syria, Iraq, Iran). Of particular interest are sickles with handles made from animal jawbones and obsidian inserts, such as those found in the Caucasus (e.g., Shomu-tepe, Azerbaijan). In some areas sickles consisting of one large denticulate implement or crescent-shaped sickles fully made of flint bifacial inserts survive up to the Bronze Age.

Sickles have been the subject of considerable ethnographic and experimental study. In experimental cereal harvesting with different types of sickles, modern iron tools slightly surpassed in productivity tools with curved handles and flint inserts. Characteristic sickle use-wear presents a mirrorlike polish covering the tool's working edge. Its continuity and location (along the edge or oblique) are defined by the handle construction. The particular pattern of fine linear striations and bright polish helps us to clearly distinguish between sickles and reed-processing knives.

For grain threshing, a large variety of tools and methods were used, including special threshing sledges (*tribulum*) with flint inserts (figure 66). This agricultural tool was distinguished for the first time by its specific use-wear in the chipped stone assemblages of Bulgarian and Middle Eastern sites (e.g., Durankulak and Golyamo Delchevo, Bulgaria; Tell 'Atij, Syria). In the Caucasus area the remains of similar threshing sledges were found in the burial grounds of the Bronze and Iron Ages (e.g., Atkhala, Armenia; Hanlar, Azerbaijan). Items of similar construction were used in several Eurasian regions up to the middle of the last century (e.g., Romania, Bulgaria, Turkey, Greece, Georgia, Spain). One threshing sledge could be used by several households. Special areas or threshing floors ("harman" in Bulgaria) were prepared, usually on the edge of the village. These areas were carefully leveled, watered, dried, and swept. The ears of cereal crops were laid in the center. Oxen or horses pulled the sledge, which was weighed down by a person sitting on the sledge. Flint inserts cut the straw and separated the grains from the stems or leaves and, in some cases, the husks that protect the grain.

A variety of stone tools and utensils were used to process cereals and other foodstuffs. Grinding stones were used to process grains. Experiments have shown that eight ounces of grain could be turned into flour in about 20 minutes using this method. Inside the houses of ancient farmers, grinding stones were put in a special zone. The grain was prepared with stone mortars and pestles of various forms and sizes. Starch grain and phytolith analyses may indicate the species of plants that were used but may also provide some evidence for how and where plants were stored, processed, and cooked prior to consumption.

Other archaeological finds provide insight into specific technologies and methods of stone tool use associated with grain procurement and processing (e.g., sculptural images, rock paintings, images on walls of the Egyptian tombs, and seal impressions). For example, one of the most ancient images of a threshing sledge is known from a clay seal impression from Arslantepe (Turkey).

See also AGRICULTURE, PROCUREMENT, PROCESSING, AND STORAGE; BONE FAT EXTRACTION; BUTCHERY; ETHNOARCHAEOLOGY; ETHNOGRAPHIC SOURCES; EXPERIMENTAL ARCHAEOLOGY; GESHER BENOT YAʿAQOV; KABAH, MAYA ROYAL KITCHEN; OLDUVAI GORGE; PHYTOLITH ANALYSIS; PLANT PROCESSING; RESIDUE ANALYSIS, BLOOD; RESIDUE ANALYSIS, STARCH; TOOLS/UTENSILS, GROUND STONE; USE-WEAR ANALYSIS, LITHICS

Figure 66. Threshing sledges have been used to process harvested grain stalks for millennia. Top: Ethnographic and ethnoarchaeological studies indicate that sledges were pulled by draft animals over stone or dirt threshing floors, as seen in this photograph from the archives of the Bulgarian ethnographer H. Vakarelskiy (Skakun 1999). Bottom left: Sledges were fitted with flint blades to separate the grain from the straw. Bottom right: Microwear studies of flint inserts show use patterns that can be distinguished from those on blades used as sickle teeth. The sledge in this example is thought to have originated in the Balkans or Turkey. Photographs by Michael Hamilton. Courtesy of Curtis Runnels, Boston University.

Further Reading

Anderson, P. C., ed. 1992. *Préhistoire de l'Agriculture: Nouvelles approches expérimentales et ethnographiques.* Monographie du CRA 6, éds. Paris: CNRS.

Kardulias, P. Nick, and Richard W. Yerkes. 1996. Microwear and Metric Analysis of Threshing Sledge Flints from Greece and Cyprus. *Journal of Archaeological Science* 23(5):657–66.

Revedin, Anna, Biancamaria Aranguren, Roberto Becattini, et al. 2010. Thirty-Thousand-Year-Old Evidence of Plant Food Processing. *Proceedings of the National Academy of Sciences USA* 107(44): 18815–19.

Semenov, S. A. 1964. *Prehistoric Technology: An Experimental Study of the Oldest Tools and Artefacts from Traces of Manufacture and Wear.* Translated by M. W. Thompson. New York: Barnes & Noble.

Skakun, Natalia. 1993. Agricultural Implements in the Neolithic and Eneolithic Cultures of Bulgaria. In *Traces et fonction: Les gestes retrouvés*, edited by P. C. Anderson, S. Beyries, M. Otte, and H. Plisson, 361–68. Centre de Recherches Archéologiques du CNRS. Liège: Etudes et Recherches Archéologiques de l'Université de Liège.

———. 1999. Evolution of Agricultural Techniques in Eneolithic (Chalcolithic) Bulgaria: Data from Use-Wear Analysis. In *Prehistory of Agriculture: New Experimental and Ethnographic Approaches*, edited by Patricia C. Anderson, 199–210. Institute of Archaeology Monograph 40. Los Angeles: University of California, Los Angeles.

———. 2003. Threshing Sledges in the Caucasus from Prehistory to the Present. In *Le traitement des récoltes: Un regards sur la diversité, du néolithique au présent*, edited by Patricia C. Anderson, Linda S. Cummings, Thomas K. Schippers, and Bernard Simonel, 389–99. XXIIIe recontres internationales d'archéologie et d'histoire d'Antibes. Antibes: Éditions APDCA.

———. 2008. Comprehensive Analysis of Prehistoric Tools and Its Relevance for Paleo-Economic Reconstructions. In *"Prehistoric Technology" 40 Years Later: Functional Studies and the Russian Legacy*, edited by Laura Longo and Natalia Skakun, 9–20. BAR International Series 1783. Oxford: Archaeopress.

■ NATALIA SKAKUN

TRACE ELEMENT ANALYSIS IN HUMAN DIET

In archaeological research, trace element analysis can be used to identify the general dietary patterns in prehistoric humans. These patterns are measured from skeletal or dental tissues using a variety of analytical techniques and can provide information regarding diet during different stages of an individual's life. The ability to distinguish dietary trends between individuals from a skeletal sample is a major advantage of trace element analysis in paleodietary studies. This method has been widely used since the 1970s as a stand-alone method to assess the relative dietary contributions of meat, plants, and seafood but has been applied more recently in conjunction with isotopic analysis.

In paleodietary applications, trace elements define a range of chemical elements that are found in low concentrations within skeletal tissues. For example, concentrations of strontium (Sr), barium (Ba), lead (Pb), and zinc (Zn) in the human body are particularly sensitive indicators of differences in diet and are typically measured in parts per million (ppm) or as a ratio (Sr/Ca, Ba/Sr). These elements are not naturally found in the body and are therefore not physiologically regulated. Instead, the trace element levels are generally accumulated in proportion to the type of food ingested. The majority of the trace element retained in the body is then stored in the mineral component of skeletal tissue.

This method has been used on skeletal remains of various ages and from a wide range of different site types around the world. Archaeologists have used trace element analysis to examine significant aspects of prehistoric societies, such as migration, social status, the adoption of agriculture, and hominid foraging ranges, by identifying dietary variation within and between skeletal samples. Attribution of trace element data to diet can be somewhat problematic, however. This is largely the result of potential chemical contamination of skeletal tissue from the burial environment (diagenesis) and the uneven movement of some trace elements through the food chain. These issues do not preclude the use of this method in paleodietary research but define the limits of its applicability.

See also BIOARCHAEOLOGICAL ANALYSIS; PALEODIETARY ANALYSIS; STABLE ISOTOPE ANALYSIS

Further Reading

Burton, James H., and T. Douglas Price. 2000. The Use and Abuse of Trace Elements for Paleodietary Research. In *Biogeochemical Approaches to Paleodietary Analysis*, edited by Stanley H. Ambrose and M. Anne Katzenberg, 159–71. New York: Kluwer Academic.

■ BEN SHAW

TRADE ROUTES

For millennia, large expanses of both the Old and New Worlds were linked in a series of complex, ever-changing spheres of trade and interaction. While it is more challenging to document ancient trade and trade routes involving foodstuffs than to find archaeological evidence for exchange in more durable goods such as metals or ceramics, it is not only equally important but has potential to reveal the more nuanced cultural, social, and political implications of trading activities.

Perhaps the best known and glamorous manifestation of the movement of foods across the ancient world is the famous Spice Trade, driven by desires for luxuries such as sugar, pepper, ginger, cardamom, cinnamon, and other expensive delicacies (as well as exotic nonedible aromatics such as frankincense). The so-called Spice Trade was not a single phenomenon or route, however, but involved dynamic networks that spanned the Old World from South Asia to the Mediterranean from at least the late centuries BC through the early modern period, by which time its circles had grown to encompass the New World.

To limit archaeological investigations of food trade only to expensive exotic goods, however, would miss many far greater impacts of exchanges of foodstuffs across the ancient world. Trade in food at a more mundane level has long supplemented and expanded human diet, supported specialized producers, facilitated sociopolitical machinations, and allowed human colonization of agriculturally or ecologically marginal lands.

The seemingly most obvious means to establish that a food was involved in trade is the archaeological recovery of the foodstuff itself in a location distant from the region in which it was known to have been grown, raised, or produced. Archaeological identification of trade and trade routes involving foodstuffs requires the marshaling of multiple lines of interrelated evidence at different scales, however. What constitutes sufficient evidence will vary depending on the context but can generally be divided into several main categories.

First, as with any archaeological study of foodways, researchers must establish the presence of the food. Direct evidence includes macroscopic and microscopic archaeobotanical remains (e.g., charred, dessicated, or waterlogged seeds and fibers, starches, pollen, or phytoliths), zooarchaeological specimens, and organic residues. Indirect evidence for the ancient consumption, processing, or transport of a food can include specialized vessels or tools associated with that food item—for example, fragments of wine amphorae in the ancient circum-Mediterranean world. Such indirect evidence may be compelling; however, without actual organic remains or associated artistic representations or textual references to the foods in question, it may be impossible to rule out reuse of such vessels or implements for other purposes.

The archaeological contexts and chronology of the food remains must be evaluated carefully to assess whether they were traded or produced and consumed locally. In some cases, establishing trade activities can be relatively straightforward, such as when a food is found in a location where it could not feasibly have been produced. A clear example of this is the large quantities of dried black pepper, a tropical plant from India, found at the Roman-period port city of Berenike on the Egyptian Red Sea coast.

Establishing that archaeological food remains are the result of long-distance trade activities usually requires extensive corroborating knowledge of local production and an overall understanding of the entire archaeological assemblage and associated contexts. In addition, many foods first traded into a region were later incorporated into local production strategies. While the spread of crops, domesticated animals, agricultural knowledge, and culinary skills has profoundly transformed life on this planet throughout human history, it is not a simple matter to determine exactly when a food ceased being a trade item and became integrated into local production strategies.

Foods found in regions beyond their natural zone may have in fact never been a trade item in the first place. Debate continues on many fronts. Theories regarding the introduction of agriculture into ancient Europe, or the spread of maize into southeastern North America, for example, diverge over whether crops first arrived via trade, by some other form of cultural contact, or through migrations of farmers bringing their crops with them into new regions.

Establishing the presence of a food at a location distant from its origin does little on its own to define the routes, transport mechanisms, or traders' hands by which the item arrived. The actual locations of trade routes, whether by land or by sea, can be reconstructed at wide scales by combining evidence for production and consumption zones with archaeological remains of the network of routes connecting them such as shipwrecks, caravan stops, trade colonies, roads, and port towns. Perhaps the best archaeological evidence for food trade comes from the recovery of food remains from such a trade- or transport-specific context—for example, the recovery of pomegranate fragments from the 14th-century BC Uluburun shipwreck off the coast of Turkey. It is likely that most trade and exchange in foods, especially bulk goods or animals, took place within relatively limited distances, however; thus strategies to collect evidence for the trade in foodstuffs must also look to local exchange networks.

To fully understand the complexities of ancient food economies, including the subtleties of food trade from local to global scales, the depth and breadth of research into food and foodways must be expanded. Archaeological knowledge of food trade must be constructed and strengthened by multiple related lines of evidence from production, distribution, and consumption contexts, and analyzed across different scales, from starch on a grinding stone or charred grains in a hearth to the landscapes of entire regions.

See also AMPHORAE; COLUMBIAN EXCHANGE; FOOD AND POLITICS; FOOD AS A COMMODITY; FOOD TECHNOLOGY AND IDEAS ABOUT FOOD, SPREAD OF; GLOBALIZATION; INFORMAL ECONOMIC EXCHANGE; MARKETS/EXCHANGE; OLD WORLD GLOBALIZATION AND FOOD EXCHANGES; QUSEIR AL-QADIM; SHIPWRECKS; SPICES; STORES/MARKETS

Further Reading

Cappers, Rene. 2006. *Roman Foodprints at Berenike: Archaeobotanical Evidence of Subsistence and Trade in the Eastern Desert of Egypt*. Los Angeles: Cotsen Institute of Archaeology, UCLA.

■ KRISTA LEWIS

TRASH DEPOSITS
See MIDDENS AND OTHER TRASH DEPOSITS

TUBERS
See ROOT CROPS/TUBERS

U

UMAMI/GLUTAMATES

Taste is linked to human survival as it signals both the nutritive nature of foodstuffs and the presence of harmful substances. Umami is one of five known basic tastes, together with sweet, bitter, sour, and salty. It is often described as savory and is associated with nutrient-dense foods such as meat and fish. Umami taste develops with ripening, aging, and certain food processing methods and is particularly strong in foods such as aged cheese, dried mushrooms, concentrated broths, cured meats, and fermented fish sauce. It is also present in plant-based food sources, including ripe tomatoes, seaweed, and soy sauce. Foodstuffs in prehistoric times and throughout human history have been processed in manners that promote umami taste.

Taste is the result of the interaction between molecules present in foods and receptor cells in humans and other animals. The amino acid L-glutamate interacts synergistically with two other food molecules, the nucleotides 5'-inosine monophosphate and 5'-guanosine monophosphate, to elicit the taste of umami. As components of foods break down, these umami molecules are freed from their parent structures and become available to interact with taste receptor cells. These breakdown processes occur naturally but are also set in motion by certain food-processing techniques. Techniques used in prehistoric and historical times that favored development of umami taste include cooking, drying, fermenting, and curing.

Archaeological, ethnographic, and historical records provide examples of foodstuffs rich in umami molecules that were cooked, dried, fermented, and cured. Remains of hearths with charred animal bones are evidence that meat cooking began in the Paleolithic period. There are indications that in the Neolithic period meat drying or curing may have been used as a preservation method. Evidence of wine production dates back to at least 4000 BC, while Egyptian pottery sherd residues and Sumerian tablets demonstrate that grains were fermented to produce beer. The archaeological record also shows remains of large-scale production of fermented fish products in ancient Rome, while ancient Roman writings describe the process used to cure pork. Each of these products of food processing would have had significant levels of the molecules responsible for umami taste and were important nutritional contributions to the human diet.

See also CONDIMENTS; FERMENTATION; FOOD PRESERVATION

Further Reading

Kurihara, Kenzo. 2009. Glutamate: From Discovery as a Food Flavor to Role as a Basic Taste (Umami). *American Journal of Clinical Nutrition* 90(3):719S–722S.

Ninomiya, Kumiko. 2002. Umami: A Universal Taste. *Food Reviews International* 18(1):23–38.

Yamaguchi, Shizuko, and Kumiko Ninomiya. 1998. What Is Umami? *Food Reviews International* 14 (2–3):123–38.

■ VALERIE RYAN

USE-ALTERATION ANALYSIS

See Use-Wear or Use-Alteration Analysis, Pottery

USE-WEAR ANALYSIS, LITHICS

Use-wear analysis of lithic artifacts is used to understand the function of an implement or tool. Traces resulting from the use of a stone tool can indicate its function. Forms of surface alteration include edge rounding, scarring, polishing, smoothing, striations, sickle gloss, and beveling. The mode of use is also of importance (e.g., transverse or perpendicular motion direction, the extent of rounding or beveling). This information helps to determine which task a particular stone tool was used for. Research over the last several decades also has shown the interdependency between use-wear and residue analyses. For instance, studies have found that many lithic flakes with scarce or ambiguous evidence of use-wear had starchy residues that differed in composition from surrounding soils. It could then be deduced that the presence of this starch indicated that the lithic flakes were used in the processing of plant food. The same can be true for the processing of meat; cutting or slicing meat may not leave clear interpretable traces on the stone edge or surface, while blood, protein, collagen, and bone residues point to butchering or meat-processing activities. Obtaining information about how stone tools were used assists in answering questions about food procurement, food processing, resource availability, and behavior of people.

Important questions about plant domestication, transport of plants, the nature of plant use, hunting, and changes to activities through time can be addressed through integrated use-wear and residue analyses. In particular, studies of starch residues have brought to light new information about the onset of plant use and domestication. An example for early plant use is the identification of two types of taro starch residues found on stone tools in the Solomon Islands dating to 28,000 BP. Analyses of 30,000- to 37,000-year-old stone tools found at Cuddie Springs in New South Wales, Australia, reveal animal meat and plant food processing occurred at this site. Grass seed grinding, identified by use-wear and residues on grindstones from Cuddie Springs, indicates a response to climate change 30,000 years ago as humans adapted to a harsher environment and the extinction of megafauna.

On some stone artifacts, wear patterns are macroscopically visible—for example, on bungwall pounders, the wedge- or chopper-shaped implements found in Australia's southeast Queensland and northeastern New South Wales. Ethnographic reports and experimental use-wear studies suggest the implements were used to process the *Blechnum indicum* rhizome, a plant growing in swamps and known as bungwall. The beveled edges of such implements show smoothing likely resulting from pounding and bruising the rhizomes as part of food processing.

Ideally, use-wear patterns are found in association with use-related residues, such as wood residues located in edge-damaged scars on the working edge of a scraper. Samples taken from the soil surrounding the artifacts can help to determine whether residues are use related or simply adhering to the stone tool because they were part of the soil matrix in which the artifact was embedded. Often patterns of use-wear are visible only after the removal of residues, which suggests a thorough recording of residues on stone tools is a necessary first step. In general the low-power method of stereomicroscopes with magnification ranges from 5x to 100x is used. Various residues (e.g., resin, wood, plant tissue, hair) and use-wear (e.g., edge rounding, polish, scarring) become visible and can be recorded. High-power analysis, usually carried out under an incident-light compound microscope at magnifications up to 1,000x, allows further observation of residues such as starch grains, phytoliths, and raphides (crystalline structures of calcium oxylate) and, after residue removal, makes use-wear traces such as striations more visible. The use of scanning electron microscopy (SEM) and energy dispersive analysis of X-rays (EDX), methods that reveal the elementary composition of the residue, are helpful for the identification of some residues such as resins. Further analyses such as the Hemastix test can assist in the detection of blood residues.

Experimental studies have helped to resolve questions about the relationship between wear patterns and the use of the contact material and give information about residue preservation and distribution on stone tools. Recent studies have concentrated on integrating new methods to document layering of residues and to identify and remove non-use-related, post-depositional, or modern residues (i.e., contamination). The latter is significant because studies that seek to date organic residues through accelerator mass spectrometry (AMS) can be compromised as a result of the tiniest amount of contamination by extraneous carbon.

Use-wear and residue analyses have become an independent and continuously growing sector in archaeological science. These studies have shown that many stone tools were multifunctional and used for various tasks despite their particular morphology or type. Future research in the field will continue to develop in specialized areas and reveal more information about function, use, and age of lithic artifacts.

See also BIOMOLECULAR ANALYSIS; BUTCHERY; ETHNOARCHAEOLOGY; EXPERIMENTAL ARCHAEOLOGY; PLANT PROCESSING; RADIOCARBON DATING; RESIDUE ANALYSIS, BLOOD; RESIDUE ANALYSIS, STARCH; SCANNING ELECTRON MICROSCOPY; STARCHES, ROLE OF; TOOLS/UTENSILS, STONE; WEAPONS, STONE

Further Reading

Fullagar, Richard. 2006. Residues and Usewear. In *Archaeology in Practice: A Student Guide to Archaeological Analyses*, edited by Jane Balme and Alistair Paterson, 207–33. Oxford: Blackwell.

Gillieson, D. S., and J. Hall. 1982. Bevelling Bungwall Bashers: A Use-Wear Study from Southeast Queensland. *Australian Archaeology* 14:43–61.

Loy, Thomas H., Matthew Spriggs, and Stephen Wickler. 1992. Direct Evidence for Human Use of Plants 28,000 Years Ago: Starch Residues on Stone Artefacts from the Northern Solomon Islands. *Antiquity* 66(253):898–912.

Pawlik, Alfred F., and Jürgen P. Thissen. 2011. Hafted Armatures and Multi-Component Tool Design at the Micoquian Site of Inden-Altdorf, Germany. *Journal of Archaeological Science* 38(7):1699–1708.

Torrence, Robin, and Huw Barton, eds. 2006. *Ancient Starch Research*. Walnut Creek, CA: Left Coast Press.

Yates, A., A. M. Smith, J. Parr, et al. 2014. AMS Dating of Ancient Plant Residues from Experimental Stone Tools: A Pilot Study. *Journal of Archaeological Science* 49:595–602.

■ ANDREA BETTINA YATES

USE-WEAR ANALYSIS, METAL

Surfaces and edges of metal tools and weapons can be studied for use-wear traces by comparing them to results from archaeological experiments. Use-wear traces include bluntness, depressions, or indentations (and contortion) and striations, which archaeologists try to distinguish from manufacturing and post-depositional traces. Microscopes can be used to study these use-wear traces, while high-magnification imaging techniques are used to study microwear traces, such as interference patterns in polished metal surfaces.

Metal objects remain greatly understudied for use-wear when compared to lithics and pottery. There are several reasons for this. Metal corrosion is a significant problem. Corrosion layers can sometimes be removed to expose original surfaces, though these are often corrupted and do not entirely preserve the fine evidence of use- and microwear. Traces of sharpening often can be found on edged tools and weapons, removing any previous use-wear evidence, especially those with a utilitarian function. Studies of metal weaponry largely have been limited to use in warfare and manufacturing traces, though many have looked at wood processing. Archaeologists have also concluded that some Chalcolithic daggers and knives from burial contexts show little evidence of use because their functionality overlapped with their symbolic roles in animal sacrifice, skinning, and defleshing.

The use of metal tools and objects in subsistence is indirectly confirmed by the cut and puncture marks imparted on animal remains, which have been studied using experimental and ethnoarchaeological approaches and through microscopic study of the faunal remains.

See also ETHNOARCHAEOLOGY; EXPERIMENTAL ARCHAEOLOGY; TOOLS/UTENSILS, METAL; WEAPONS, METAL; ZOOARCHAEOLOGY

Further Reading

Christidou, Rozalia. 2008. An Application of Micro-Wear Analysis to Bone Experimentally Worked Using Bronze Tools. *Journal of Archaeological Science* 35(3):733–51.

Dolfini, Andrea. 2011. The Function of Chalcolithic Metalwork in Italy: An Assessment Based on Use-Wear Analysis. *Journal of Archaeological Science* 38(5):1037–49.

Gordon, Robert B. 1985. Laboratory Evidence of the Use of Metal Tools at Machu Picchu (Peru) and Environs. *Journal of Archaeological Science* 12(4):311–27.

Xiuzhen, Janice Li, Marcos Martinón-Torres, Nigel D. Meeks, et al. 2011. Inscriptions, Filing, Grinding and Polishing Marks on the Bronze Weapons from the Qin Terracotta Army in China. *Journal of Archaeological Science* 38(3):492–501.

■ THOMAS E. BIRCH

USE-WEAR OR USE-ALTERATION ANALYSIS, POTTERY

The primary function of pottery containers in prehistory is food processing. Certainly, pottery can and did perform a number of other functions as well, such as storage, transport, group identification, or many other roles that any piece of material culture can play in a society. But the primary advantage of pottery compared to other containers is that it can be placed over a fire to boil food. Prior to pottery, boiling with watertight containers and hot stones was effective, but it is not a method that works well for long-term boiling, which is necessary to make a number of grains and domesticated cultigens palatable. Pottery use-alteration traces (attrition, carbonization, and residue) provide evidence about what was cooked and the use activities associated with a vessel throughout its life history.

All vessels are designed for a particular use—their intended function. Potters can control a number of technical properties (e.g., surface treatment, temper, firing temperature) to suit a particular function. For example, cooking pots often are low-fired, heavily tempered, and have a textured exterior surface because these properties greatly improve thermal shock resistance, which is a primary performance characteristic of cooking pots. Thus archaeologists can examine prehistoric pottery, reconstruct the technical choices made by the potter, and draw inferences about the intended function of the vessel (e.g., storage, serving, boiling, ritual). These inferences, though useful, provide only general information about vessel function. For a number of reasons, it is important to determine the actual function of a vessel, which is accomplished by performing a use-alteration study of the traces left on the vessel as a result of use. This type of analysis not only provides more specific information about pottery use behavior, but also can contribute to an understanding of the vessel's use life.

There are three primary forms of use-alteration traces: carbonization, attrition, and residue. Exterior carbonization is the deposition of soot from the cooking fire, and interior carbonization is caused by the charring of food on the surface of the vessel. Wood or some other fuel creates combustion products (soot) that include ash along with tars and resins. Two types of soot are deposited on cooking vessels: ashy soot that is easily rubbed or worn away, and a resinous soot that becomes affixed to the ceramic surface and can survive for thousands of years in the depositional environment. Soot deposition is dependent primarily on the temperature of the ceramic surface. If the surface is above 300 to 400°C, soot will not be deposited, but on cooler surfaces, which often happens with pots used to boil food, the resinous soot will adhere to the surface. Consequently, the exteriors of cooking pots have patches of soot and oxidation that occur in patterns dependent on the type of hearth, what is being cooked, and distance from the fire, among other variables.

Interior carbonization is created by the charring of food particles that adhere to the surface. For charring to take place, the interior surface must reach 300 to 400°C, at which time the contents of the vessels can burn and leave a remnant patch on the surface. If a vessel is used to boil food, the temperature of the surface below the water line will not exceed 100°C and thus food will not char. But just above the water line, sometimes referred to as the scum line where fats and food particles float on the surface, the surface will exceed the combustion temperature and the food will char. Consequently, a telltale pattern of boiling food is a ring of carbonization at the waterline.

Attrition is defined as the removal of ceramic material on the surface that occurs in a variety of use and nonuse contexts throughout a vessel's life history. Attrition can be caused by a variety of abrasive (e.g., vessel contact with dirt floors, impact from utensils and covers) or nonabrasive processes (e.g., fermentation and salt erosion). Attrition is created by repeated vessel use activities that start with individual attritional traces, such as pits or scratches, and then grow into patches. Various kinds of use activities can be inferred from attritional patches, as can sundry attritional processes that can occur after deposition and can provide clues to the vessel (and sherd) life history. Nonabrasive forms of attrition such as spalls are also instructive. Rising and expanding gases associated with fermentation create spalls on the surfaces of permeable earthenware vessels. Spalls on the exterior of pots are also caused by salt erosion, particularly on water vessels, as salts crystallize in evaporating water.

A third type of use-alteration trace occurs when various forms of organic residue either adhere to or become absorbed inside the vessel wall. This organic material often survives and provides direct clues as to what was cooked or stored in a vessel. One of the most profitable areas of analysis has been with lipids, which occur in different combinations and amounts in every species and thus can serve as a means to infer vessel contents. Lipids, especially those that have become entombed in the permeable vessel walls, have been shown to survive long periods and thus have been used successfully with archaeological samples. One of the most common methods of analysis involves separating residue components with gas chromatography and then analyzing them with a variety of spectrographic techniques. These lipid profiles can then be compared to a lipid library of various plant and animal species, and specific identifications sometimes can be made.

See also BIOMOLECULAR ANALYSIS; COOKING VESSELS, CERAMIC; FIRE AND THE DEVELOPMENT OF COOKING TECHNOLOGY; GAS CHROMATOGRAPHY/GAS CHROMATOGRAPHY–MASS SPECTROMETRY; INFRARED SPECTROSCOPY/FOURIER TRANSFORM INFRARED SPECTROSCOPY; MATERIAL CULTURE ANALYSIS; OVENS AND STOVES

Further Reading

Arthur, John W. 2006. *Living with Pottery: Ethnoarchaeology among the Gamo of Southwest Ethiopia*. Salt Lake City: University of Utah Press.
Rice, Prudence M. 2006. *Pottery Analysis: A Sourcebook*. Chicago: University of Chicago Press.
Skibo, James M. 2013. *Understanding Pottery Function*. New York: Springer.

■ JAMES M. SKIBO

UTENSILS

See TOOLS/UTENSILS, DECORATED; TOOLS/UTENSILS, GROUND STONE; TOOLS/UTENSILS, ORGANIC MATERIALS; TOOLS/UTENSILS, METAL

V

VEGETABLES

Most of us will know what is meant by *vegetable*, but, ironically, no watertight definition exists. Botanists tend to emphasize which part of the plant is eaten, and "vegetables" are thus defined as plants of which the leaves, stem, root, or tuber are eaten, in contrast to "fruits," which are plants of which the usually sweet and fleshy fruit (the mature ovary and other flower parts) are consumed. There are, however, plenty of exceptions: artichoke is regarded by most as a vegetable even though it is the fleshy flower head that is eaten, while cucumber, tomato, and aubergine are also technically fruits, yet are regarded by some as vegetables, probably because they are not sweet. This brings us to the culinary definition, in which vegetables are regarded as plants that are eaten as part of the main meal and fruits as plants eaten as part of a dessert or as a snack. This definition is also fraught with problems as there are strong cultural differences in how and when certain foods are consumed. This is further exacerbated by the fact that it is not always known exactly which part of the plant was used in the past or how it was used, nor whether people in antiquity distinguished between main meals and desserts in the same way that we in the West do today. Additionally, there is a considerable overlap between culinary and other uses: many plants also have medicinal, ritual, and industrial (e.g., textiles, oils, dyes) applications, and some are used as both food and fodder.

Vegetables, in the widest sense, are nutritionally important. While cereals grains and some root crops provide important carbohydrates and thus energy, vegetables contribute vitamin C, beta-carotene, folic acid, iron, as well as other essential minerals and antioxidants, all vital to health and nutrition. For example, a diet high in vegetables from the cabbage family may lower the risk of developing cancer or heart disease because of the properties of certain compounds (glucosinolates) within their leaves.

Despite their importance in human diet, we know little about which vegetables were consumed in early human societies. This is because vegetables tend not to preserve well in the archaeological record. Most plants found on excavations are preserved through charring (carbonization), but vegetables have a lower chance of contact with fire than, for example, grain crops. Moreover, their leafy plant parts rarely survive such contact, in contrast to grains, seeds, and nutshells. Most archaeological finds of vegetables thus consist of remains preserved in waterlogged conditions, such as fragments of leaf epidermis of leek (*Allium porrum*) from early medieval York, England, or arid environments, such as the

528

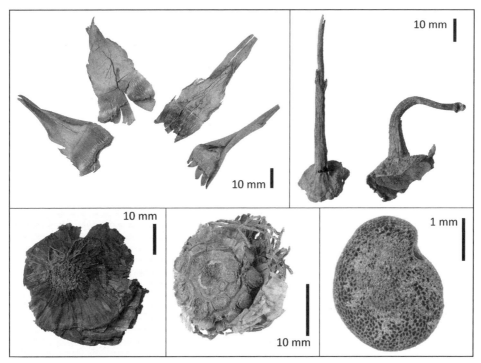

Figure 67. Plant remains preserved through desiccation at Mons Claudianus and Mons Porphyrites, both Roman quarry settlements located in the Eastern Desert of Egypt, and Quseir al-Qadim, an important Roman and medieval port of trade on the Red Sea coast of Egypt. Top row, left to right: Artichoke bracts (*Cynara cardunculus*, cf. ssp. *scolymus*, Roman) from Mons Claudianus and aubergine calyx (*Solanum melongena*, medieval) from Quseir al-Qadim. Bottom row, left to right: Onion (*Allium cepa*, Roman) from Quseir al-Qadim; garlic baseplate (*Allium sativum*, Roman) from Mons Porphyrites; aubergine seed (*Solanum melongena*, medieval) from Quseir al-Qadim. Photographs by Jacob Morales. After Van der Veen and Tabinor 2007, fig. 4.14; Van der Veen 2011, fig. 3.10 and plate 12; and Van der Veen 2001.

bracts of artichoke (*Cynara cardunculus*, cf. var. *scolymus*) from Roman Mons Claudianus, Egypt, the cloves and baseplate of garlic (*Allium sativum*) from Roman Mons Porphyrites, Egypt, and the aubergine calyxes (*Solanum melongena*) and skin and roots of onion (*Allium cepa*) from medieval Islamic Quseir al-Qadim (figure 67).

The leaves, roots, stems, and fruits of wild plants have been consumed by people throughout the ages, but the domestication and cultivation of vegetables is a relatively late phenomenon. Prehistoric populations began to domesticate many cereals and pulses some 10,000 years ago, but the earliest evidence for the domestication of vegetables dates to ca. 4,000 years ago (in the Old World, e.g., in Egypt and Mesopotamia). Some of the earliest vegetables and fruits found archaeologically (botanical remains and paintings) are those from Pharaonic tombs, such as that of Tutankhamun (e.g., lettuce, leek, lentil, garlic, onion, watermelon, and coriander). By the late first millennium BC, a wide range of cultivated vegetables was available in the Mediterranean region, as witnessed by both archaeological evidence and ancient, classical texts (e.g., Theophrastus and Pliny).

In northwestern Europe there is archaeological evidence for cultivated, rather than wild, vegetables from the late first millennium BC, when contact with the Mediterranean and especially incorporation into the Roman Empire brought a large variety of new food plants—vegetables, as well as fruits, nuts, herbs, and spices—into this region, thus significantly enriching diet and cuisine. These newly introduced vegetables include cabbage, carrot, leaf beet, leek, and cucumber. While the first three of these are actually native to northwestern Europe, the earliest evidence of their cultivation currently dates to the Roman period. Large-scale cultivation of vegetables—horticulture or market gardening—tends to develop in societies with large population groups not directly involved in farming, and such cultivation is thus often found in and around towns where there is a ready market for such produce and where supply routes are short (modern refrigerated transport has, of course, changed that).

Vegetables were an important part of Roman cuisine, and a wide variety of recipes survive that called for greens, roots, and pulses. An example of their cultural importance comes from the Roman stone quarry site at Mons Claudianus, located in a remote part of the Eastern Desert of Egypt. The columns adorning the portico of the Pantheon in Rome, Italy, originate from this quarry site. While most of the food for the workmen and officers in charge of the quarries was brought in on regular caravans from the Nile Valley, both the botanical and textual evidence from the site indicate that some fresh greens were grown in small gardens in the desert.

In the Roman world vegetables were part of the everyday meal, served as side dishes with meat and cheese, or included in single-course dishes, but also as appetizers in banquets. In contrast, medieval Islamic recipes rarely employ vegetables on their own. Here a great variety of vegetables were used, but these were usually incorporated in stews. While this highlights how vegetables played varying roles in past cuisines—a phenomenon still known today—their importance in human health and nutrition has remained constant through time.

See also AGRICULTURAL/HORTICULTURAL SITES; ARCHAEOBOTANY; CARVINGS/CARVED REP-RESENTATIONS OF FOOD; GREENS/HERBS; MARKETS/EXCHANGE; PALEODIETARY ANALYSIS; QUSEIR AL-QADIM; TRADE ROUTES; WALL PAINTINGS/MURALS

Further Reading

Hepper, F. Nigel. 2009. *Pharaoh's Flowers: The Botanical Treasures of Tutankhamun.* 2nd edition. London: Gainsborough House.

Van der Veen, Marijke. 2001. The Botanical Evidence. In *Survey and Excavations at Mons Claudianus 1987–1993,* vol. 2, *The Excavations, Part 1,* edited by Valerie A. Maxfield and David P. S. Peacock, 174–247. Documents de Fouilles 43. Cairo: Institut Français d'Archéologie Orientale du Caire.

———. 2011. *Consumption, Trade and Innovation: Exploring the Botanical Remains from the Roman and Islamic Ports at Quseir al-Qadim, Egypt.* Journal of African Archaeology Monograph 6. Frankfurt: Africa Magna Verlag.

Van der Veen, Marijke, Alexandra Livarda, and Alistair Hill. 2008. New Food Plants in Roman Britain—Dispersal and Social Access. *Environmental Archaeology* 13(1):11–36.

Van der Veen, Marijke, and Helen Tabinor. 2007. Food, Fodder and Fuel at Mons Porphyrites: The Botanical Evidence. In *The Roman Imperial Quarries: Survey and Excavation at Mons Porphyrites 1994–1998,* vol. 2, *The Excavations,* edited by Valerie Maxfield and David Peacock, 83–142. London: Egypt Exploration Society.

Zohary, Daniel, Maria Hopf, and Ehud Weiss. 2012. *Domestication of Plants in the Old World.* 4th edition. Oxford: Oxford University Press.

■ MARIJKE VAN DER VEEN

VISUALIZATION TECHNIQUES
See SPATIAL ANALYSIS AND VISUALIZATION TECHNIQUES

WALL PAINTINGS/MURALS

Never merely decorative, food in archaeological murals reflects the ideology of the culture and time period in its different purposes. Murals with depictions of food in some cases illustrate the world of the living, whether elites or commoners, in contexts that display abundance and wealth; at other times they depict a supernatural or mythological world, in which the food acts as the link between humans and the afterlife or the realm of deities.

Some of the earliest surviving depictions of food belong to Old Kingdom Egyptian tombs of the late third millennium BC, but they continue into the New Kingdom (ca. 1550–1070 BC) and comprise wall murals, painted reliefs, and decorated coffins with scenes that convey vibrant, naturalistic vignettes of daily life with people tending crops in fields, processions with carriers of provisions and drink, and presentations of foodstuffs on a table of offerings before the deceased. The images of preparation and presentation of food contribute to a funerary banquet intended to sustain the departed in the afterlife and were typically accompanied by offerings of actual food in the tomb. The illustrations portray an abundance of provisions that include crops in the field as well as harvested plants bundled and in baskets, jointed carcasses of animals, fowl tied up and even plucked, fruits, loaves of bread, and jars for other consumables and liquids.

The same perception of abundance extends to other Old World murals depicting food, but unlike the private funerary contexts of royal and subroyal tombs in Egypt, frescoes of Roman Pompeii decorated the houses of patrician landowners and wealthy middle-class merchants. These murals included food as a display of wealth and often adorned the peristyle gallery walls; other examples include depictions of bucolic gardens replete with fruit trees and birds; still others decorated the *triclinia*, or dining rooms, where people entertained guests and showed off their good fortune.

In the New World, murals with representations of food encompassed both religious ceremony in cosmological context and consumption and exchange in daily life. Dating to approximately the same time period as much of the Pompeii corpus, the Maya murals of San Bartolo in the jungles of Guatemala show a first-century BC rendition of a basket of tamales and a gourd of water or other drink, offered by the Maize God to a primordial couple in a scene depicting the origins of human life (figure 68). On other scenes of the same mural, the gods are presented with offerings of fish, deer, and a turkey on tripods

San Bartolo Mural, North Wall detail.
Painting by Heather Hurst, copyright 2004.

Figure 68. Top: Ancestral couple with food and drink from the gods: basket of tamales and gourd of water. From the San Bartolo mural, Maya Late Preclassic period (first century BC). Bottom: Serving and drinking of *atole*, or maize gruel, labeled as *ul* in hieroglyphic Mayan, from Calakmul mural, Maya Classic period (seventh century AD). Drawing by Simon Martin, Proyecto Arqueológico Calakmul. Reprinted from Martin 2012, fig. 6.

smoking with fire, establishing a relationship of sustenance and veneration from gods to humans and vice versa that links the natural and supernatural worlds through food.

Additional Mesoamerican murals illustrate maize, in some cases together with other precious food items like cacao, such as in the Red Temple at Cacaxtla. Whether depicted as a growing plant or a prepared food that takes on several different forms, these images fundamentally communicate the idea of sustenance as a divine gift. The Tlalocan scene in the Tepantitla residential complex at Teotihuacán is one of the best known among the many murals at this Classic Mesoamerican site, depicting a lively scene of people engaged in a ballgame and other activities set in a mythical paradise of flowering plants, maize, and fruits.

The most recent New World discoveries of foods in mural painting come from the site of Calakmul in Mexico, where an earthly scene of Maya commoners depicts women, men, and children engaged in marketlike exchanges of known and unidentified foodstuffs, some labeled as salt, tobacco, and *atole*, or maize gruel, stocked in vessels and baskets, handed out on platters, or poured into bowls with ladles (figure 68). The seventh-century AD paintings adorn the exterior platform walls of a pyramid adjoining a plaza that may have served as an actual market area. In contrast with the funerary setting of food for the afterlife, the display of wealth in strictly elite contexts, and the cosmological framework of religious veneration, the Calakmul murals are a unique representation of people with cooking implements in a public setting, interacting with each other over food.

Representations of food are a visual stand-in for the most perishable and often missing categories of material culture and food remains. In the absence of these remains, pictorial representations provide an illustrated record of the material culture of a people as well as what they ate, what they valued, and how they served it.

See also Architectural Analysis; Carvings/Carved Representations of Food; Food and Dining as Social Display; Food and Identity; Food and Ritual; Food and Status; Foodways and Religious Practices; Herculaneum and Pompeii; Markets/Exchange; Mortuary Complexes; Offerings and Grave Goods; Representational Models of Food and Food Production; Rock Art

Further Reading

Carrasco Vargas, Ramón, and María Cordeiro Baqueiro. 2012. The Murals of Chiik Nahb Structure Sub-1-4, Calakmul, Mexico. *Maya Archaeology* 2:8–59.

De La Fuente, Beatriz, Leticia Staines Cicero, Maria Teresa Uriarte, et al. 1999. *The Pre-Columbian Painting Murals of the Mesoamerica*. Milan: Editoriale Jaca Book.

Dunbabin, Katherine M. D. 2003. *The Roman Banquet: Images of Conviviality*. Cambridge: Cambridge University Press.

Martin, Simon. 2012. Hieroglyphs from the Painted Pyramid: The Epigraphy of Chiik Nahb Structure Sub 1-4, Calakmul, Mexico. *Maya Archaeology* 2:60–81.

Saturno, William A., Karl Taube, and David Stuart. 2005. The Murals of San Bartolo, El Petén, Guatemala, Part 1: The North Wall. *Ancient America* 7.

Taube, Karl, William A. Saturno, David Stuart, and Heather Hurst. 2010. The Murals of San Bartolo, El Petén, Guatemala, Part 2: The West Wall. *Ancient America* 10.

Tiradritti, Francesco. 2008. *Egyptian Wall Painting*. New York: Abbeville.

■ ASTRID RUNGGALDIER

WATER

Water is such a biological necessity that its functions in relation to food are often taken for granted. As a beverage, it has been historically appreciated for its origin (river, rain, cave, etc.), state (still, sparkling, cold, etc.), or taste. Humankind has invented several techniques to improve its quality, from boiling and decanting to filtering—using, for instance, stone drip jars. Water is consumed on its own or in conjunction with specific foods or drinks, such as wine or spirits. Its material culture includes objects that can hold and pour liquids (e.g., pitchers, bottles, jugs, jars); these forms may not always be specialized but sometimes are. During food preparation, water acts as both a medium and an ingredient. Cooks can use it to thaw, wash, soak, brine, ferment, pickle, or rehydrate their ingredients. Many dishes call for foods to be boiled, blanched, coddled, infused, or steeped in water. Water is also a thermic agent in indirect cooking methods, such as bains-marie or steaming, and a component of liquid or semiliquid recipes, including beverages, soups, and porridges. In some places, water also represents a source of salt. In addition, it often plays an important role in the maintenance of objects and in food preservation. For instance, it can help season ceramic cookware. Cleaning pots and dishes after a meal is best done with water. Scalding glass storage containers helps preserve their contents. Water can create a physical barrier against crawling insects and extend the freshness of some ingredients, such as herbs or leafy greens. It is therefore likely that in most settings, cooking and other food practices involved its use. Devoting effort to identify its traces in the archaeological record, as well as to reflect on its absence or shortage, could be productive. Most studies, however, emphasize issues of supply and distribution, and often at the community scale. Adding analysis about its usage might put water at the center of the study of food.

See also ARCHAEOLOGY OF COOKING; ARCHITECTURAL ANALYSIS; FIRE AND THE DEVELOPMENT OF COOKING TECHNOLOGY; FOOD PRESERVATION; FOOD STORAGE; WATER SUPPLY AND STORAGE

Further Reading

Arcangeli, Myriam. 2015. *Sherds of History: Domestic Life in Colonial Guadeloupe.* Gainesville: University Press of Florida.
Coleman, Ronald A. 2001. Dripstones: Rudimentary Water Filters on Ship and Shore in the 18th Century. *Bulletin of the Australian Institute for Maritime Archaeology* 25:113–20.

■ MYRIAM ARCANGELI

WATER SUPPLY AND STORAGE

Agro-pastoral practices require water. The effects of droughts and floods on food production need to be mitigated. In addition, waterways can be used to process and transport food. This partially explains why societies began to devise active means to control and manage water during the Neolithic period. In the Levant, man-made dams, wells, and terrace walls existed by 3600 BC. At the site of Choga Mami, a Samarran settlement in northern Mesopotamia, archaeologists have found traces of what is considered to be the earliest irrigation system, a series of ditches that brought water from a nearby river to fields of wheat or barley. There is ample evidence that all of the major civilizations of the past have used hydraulic systems to either improve agricultural yield or amend the livability of their land. This allowed humans to settle in a great variety of environments and climates, from arid deserts to tropical areas. Large-scale irrigation systems were essential to ancient Egypt, Mesopotamia, the Indus Valley, and Imperial China. Cultures as diverse as the Nabataeans in Jordan, the Minoans in Crete, the Khmers in Southeast Asia, the Maya in Mesoamerica, the Inca in South America, and the Hohokam in the American Southwest undertook extensive water management. More recently, archaeologists have uncovered the remains of irrigation systems in less-studied areas, such as highland Yemen, eastern Africa, Ethiopia, Polynesia, and central Asia. Since water management is critical to urbanization, archaeologists also have tried to map and understand the water supplies of cities and, in particular, those with long histories, such as Athens, Rome, Constantinople, or Jerusalem.

These efforts have shown that water systems come in many forms because they respond to local needs and conditions. Still, it is possible to classify hydraulic engineering techniques in two main categories: the technologies that rely on flow—through features such as channels, canals, dikes, ditches, pipes, or aqueducts—and the technologies that are based on storage, using dams, reservoirs, tanks, cisterns, pools, wells, terraces, and so on. In many cases, water systems combine several of these solutions to harness the sources of water that are available at any one locale, whether from rainfall, runoff, flash floods, rivers, springs, or underground aquifers. For instance, the water management technologies developed at Tikal by the Maya and at Petra by the Nabataeans allowed their populations to thrive in environments that lacked permanent sources of water. Both settlements used storage strategies and thrived on a supply that was exclusively fed by rainfall and runoff.

Rarely are water systems well documented in documentary sources—including in early modern times—so archaeology often represents the best, if not the only, method of study. Archaeologists employ an array of techniques for surveying and mapping waterworks. Traditional field surveys and excavations are nowadays enhanced by an array of remote sensing techniques, from aerial photography to space shuttle imagery, and GIS mapping, which allows for all kinds of data to be integrated together on maps. The first goal of these surveys is often to record the scale of these systems and understand how they articulate with the local geography and settlements. In some cases, complementary data sets can also be marshaled from other sources—for instance, paleoecology, micromorphology, or paleoethnobotany—and by analyzing iconography, architecture, or ceramics.

A number of important archaeological theories reflect on the role of irrigation systems in societies. In the 1930s, the sinologist Karl Wittfogel proposed a particularly thought-provoking thesis, namely, that large-scale irrigation systems spurred, in hydraulically compact societies such as ancient China or Mesopotamia, the rise of centralized bureaucracies and despotic rulers. Since then, many archaeologists working in various areas of the world have tried to test, disprove, or refine Wittfogel's hydraulic hypothesis. These studies demonstrate that hydraulic systems may generate or enhance an elite's power, but that they can also be managed through heterarchical, communal, or corporate structures, as in the southwestern Hohokam communities. It also has become apparent that water control is a source of major political, economic, or social change in human history. Water can even inspire spiritual or religious mutations, through water-related rituals or ideologies. More directly in relation to food, the evolution of water management can explain how certain foods, such as rice, were domesticated, or how agriculture arose in various parts of the world.

Because they often reflect on the relationship between water and power, many archaeological publications discuss the role of rulers and of the elite. They also emphasize the work of engineers, builders, planners, water managers, or water distributors, but they rarely consider what happens to water once it has arrived at a destination. Remarkably, the story of water users is the most underdeveloped aspect of this field, even in the case of food producers. Given that in many places to this day women are responsible for provisioning and managing the household's domestic supply, attention to these themes could lead to a compelling re-engendering of water history. Moreover, archaeologists have favored issues of quantity over quality, even though there is evidence that water quality also influenced people's behaviors and technologies. For instance, the Maya improved the quality of their reserves by transforming their reservoirs into wetland biospheres, where weeds, bacteria, and algae helped purify their supply. The water lilies that thrived in these environments were later incorporated into the symbolic iconography used by their royalty. Other common purifying strategies, such as decantation or filtering, would certainly leave traces in the archaeological record. In the end, what this field further reveals is that we all share a common concern with water, which provides, in Steven Mithen's words, a "mental unity to humankind."

See also FOOD AND POLITICS; FOOD AND POWER; FOOD AND RITUAL; FOODWAYS AND GENDER ROLES; IRRIGATION/HYDRAULIC ENGINEERING; LANDSCAPE AND ENVIRONMENTAL RECONSTRUCTION; RICE; SUSTAINABILITY; WATER

Further Reading

Lucero, Lisa J., Joel D. Gunn, and Vernon L. Scarborough. 2011. Climate Change and Classic Maya Water Management. *Water* 3(32):479–94.

Mithen, Steven. 2012. *Thirst: Water and Power in the Ancient World*. Cambridge, MA: Harvard University Press.

■ MYRIAM ARCANGELI

WEAPONS, BONE/ANTLER/IVORY

Points for hunting weapons have been made from bone, antler, and ivory throughout time. Projectile points from osseous materials appear in Europe at the beginning of the Upper Paleolithic. Various types of projectile points are associated with the Upper Magdalenian (13,500–12,000 cal BC), for example, the cave sites of Isturitz and La Vache in the Pyrenees. Although osseous materials were more important in the Stone Age, bone and antler points also appear in Bronze and Iron Age Europe. Weapons from osseous materials have been especially numerous among the northern peoples in America and Eurasia—for example, at the Walakpa site in Alaska (USA), occupied during the Birnirk and Thule periods (AD 500–1600).

Archaeologists have studied extensively the manufacturing technologies, types and functions, and durability of weapons made from these raw materials. Bone, antler, and ivory are tough and resilient materials. Barbs could be cut or sawn into the material and holes drilled to fix shafts. Experiments carried out to estimate the effectiveness of projectile points have proven that bone and antler arrowheads break less frequently than stone arrowheads. The shape of bone projectiles depended on their function. Points with expanding cross-sectional perimeters opened the wound and caused bleeding, thereby weakening the prey. Blunt antler arrowheads were used for hunting waterfowl. Marine mammals were hunted with harpoons, the heads of which separated from the shaft upon contact (figure 69). A line was attached to the head, while barbs on the harpoon head were secured in the flesh of the prey animal. Toggle harpoon heads also detached from the shaft and turned sideways in the animal. Harpoons from osseous materials have a wide distribution, but the most complex harpoon forms were developed among the Inuit.

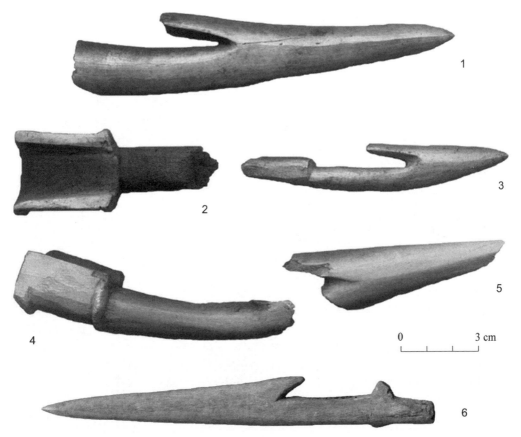

Figure 69. Antler (1–5) and bone (6) harpoon heads used for seal hunting from the Late Bronze Age site of Asva, Estonia (900–500 BC), a fortified site on the coast; though not waterlogged, bone and antler were well preserved as a result of the constant moisture level in the soil (AI 4012: 113; 4366: 642; 3307: 298; 4366: 1863, 1942; 3994: 580). Photo by Heidi Luik. Courtesy of the Institute of History, Tallinn University.

Bone and antler preserve well in anoxic (e.g., waterlogged) or frozen environments but decompose rapidly under acidic conditions. Thus the presence or absence of bone weapons at particular sites depends on the soil conditions.

See also FORAGING; HUNTER-GATHERER SUBSISTENCE; MARINE MAMMALS; MATERIAL CULTURE ANALYSIS; PALEOINDIAN DIET; PALEOLITHIC DIET; TOOLS/UTENSILS, ORGANIC MATERIALS; WEAPONS, METAL; WEAPONS, STONE

Further Reading

Arnold, Charles D. 2004. Arctic Harpoons. *Arctic* 42(1):80–82.

Knecht, Heidi, ed. 1997. *Projectile Technology*. New York: Plenum.

Pétillon, Jean-Marc. 2009. What Are These Barbs For? Preliminary Study on the Function of the Upper Magdalenian Barbed Weapon Tips. *Palethnologie* 2009(1):66–97. http://www.palethnologie.org/wp-content/uploads/2009/en-GB/Palethnology-2009-GB-04-Petillon.pdf.

■ HEIDI LUIK

WEAPONS, METAL

The earliest hunting weapons made with metal were not all that different from their stone counterparts, showing similar stylistic characteristics and function. The principal difference was the longer functional life of metal weapons, which could be maintained through repair and resharpening and were less prone to breakage. Casting copper alloys or forging steel permitted new shapes and constructions that exceeded the constraints imposed by lithic raw materials; weapons could become longer, sleeker, and formed into more elaborate shapes. While some weapons were used interchangeably for warfare, hunting, or sport, two long-standing achievements in hunting weaponry that stem from the emergence of metallurgy are the sword and firearms.

The first weapons with metal components were made using naturally occurring metals, such as copper and iron, requiring no form of extractive metallurgy. These metals required little more than reworking by hammering and heating to produce small knives, arrowheads, and projectile points. Native copper artifacts, including weapons, were widespread in the Near East by the seventh millennium BC. Prehistoric hunter-gatherers in the American northeast were making weapons and tools from native copper by the fifth millennium BC, whereas its occurrence in South America (Peru) is considerably later (fifth century BC) after a long tradition of precious metalworking.

Telluric iron (native iron) only exists in a few major sources, such as Kassel (Germany) and the Disko Bay area (Greenland), where it was mostly used by the Inuit to make knives and *ulus* (moon-shaped skinning tools). The more abundant form, meteoritic iron, was in fact extraterrestrial in origin. This iron could be worked by hammering and was used by the Nama (South Africa) as well as by the Inuit in the north circumpolar region to make knives and harpoon points.

The working of native metals to make the earliest weapons was opportunistic. The proliferation of metal weaponry only occurred with the advent of extractive metallurgy, where metals were extracted from their constituent ores in a process known as smelting.

The first evidence for copper smelting and casting comes from the Vinča culture (eastern Serbia) around 5000 BC. Smelted copper is relatively soft but could be hardened by hammering the metal when it was cold in a process known as work hardening.

A much harder and more durable metal could be achieved by adding small amounts of tin to copper, creating the alloy known as bronze and partly defining what we now call the Bronze Age (beginning around 3300 BC in the Near East). Copper alloys were cast into a variety of hunting weapons, including axes, spearheads, and arrowheads. The ability to standardize weaponry had its advantages, allowing replication of forms that lent themselves to repeatable action (muscle memory) and thus precision. Stunning bolts, some of which were standardized forms, were found widely across the Near East; these were essentially blunt arrowheads (club shaped) used for hunting birds (fowling). Copper alloys also can be cast to shape, allowing for an almost infinite number of possible forms and paving the way for the creation of moving mechanics in ancient weaponry. Although typically considered a military weapon, crossbows were also used for hunting, developed during the Spring and Autumn and Warring States periods (770–221 BC) in ancient China. Other metals could be cast, such as lead for slingshot or, much later, rifle shot.

Iron played an increasingly important role in hunting weaponry. The earliest direct evidence for iron smelting comes from a metal production site in Jordan dating to 900 BC, and arguably earlier in Georgia, though indirect evidence suggests this technology emerged several centuries earlier. Because of the high melting temperature of iron (1,538°C), it had to be worked by hand, forged into shape by a combination of heating and hammering. Iron can be relatively soft but may be hardened by adding carbon, producing the tougher alloy steel. During the early Middle Ages, many knives across Europe were made using an iron blade forged with a steel edge, creating a hard and durable cutting edge. Steel arrowheads were less easily blunted compared to iron, allowing them to be easily reused. There is a large repertoire of iron hunting weapons, but other forms include traps used to capture game and cages used to transport and store live animals, either for delayed consumption or later sport.

The arrival of gunpowder marks a significant change in hunting technology. The marriage of metallurgy and explosives led to the development of firearms by the 14th century AD. The blast furnace spread across Europe at this time, allowing for the production of cast iron (a process achieved considerably earlier in China). Gun barrels, the main component of any firearm, could be made from bronze or steel. Various metals were used to produce ammunition, such as lead shot, as well as numerous fittings, fixtures, moving parts, and decorative pieces. Firearms became a key component of modern hunting on land but also at sea for whaling and fishing (e.g., harpoon guns).

Archaeometallurgy, the study of ancient and historic metals and their associated technologies, may be used to learn about the manufacturing process of a weapon through examination of the metal's microstructure. Use-wear analysis of its edges can provide insights into function. Chemical composition can be used to identify the metal and learn about its technological origin. As is the case with native copper, some metals can be tied to a specific geographical source, what archaeometallurgists refer to as provenancing.

Metals react with their depositional environment and become badly corroded, in some cases disappearing entirely. Thus archaeologists also rely on textual sources as well as indirect evidence for weaponry in artistic representations, wood carvings, and cave art (e.g., North America). Experimental approaches using replica weapons are directed toward specific research questions; one recent revelation is that Early Iron Age swords did not perform demonstrably better than those made from bronze. Similarly, experimental studies of cut marks through use-wear studies can identify the use of metal edges as well as characterize their form.

See also EXPERIMENTAL ARCHAEOLOGY; MATERIAL CULTURE ANALYSIS; RESIDUE ANALYSIS, BLOOD; USE-WEAR ANALYSIS, METAL; WEAPONS, BONE/ANTLER/IVORY; WEAPONS, STONE

Further Reading

Bjorkman, Judith Kingston. 1972. Meteors and Meteorites in the Ancient Near East. *Meteoritics* 8(29):91–132.

Blackmore, Howard L. 1972. *Hunting Weapons: From the Middle Ages to the Twentieth Century*. New York: Walker.

Buchwald, Vagn Fabritius. 1992. On the Use of Iron by the Eskimos in Greenland. *Materials Characterization* 29(2):139–76.

Genz, Hermann. 2007. Stunning Bolts: Late Bronze Age Hunting Weapons in the Ancient Near East. *Levant* 39:47–69.

Greenfield, Haskel J. 1999. The Origins of Metallurgy: Distinguishing Stone from Metal Cut-Marks on Bones from Archaeological Sites. *Journal of Archaeological Science* 26(2):797–808.

Latta, Martha A., Paul Thibaudea, and Lisa Anselmi. 1998. Expediency and Curation: The Use and Distribution of "Scrap" Trade Metal by Huron Native Peoples in Sixteenth-Century Southern Ontario. *Wisconsin Archeologist* 79(1):175–84.

Tylecote, Ronald F. 1976. *A History of Metallurgy*. London: Metals Society.

■ THOMAS E. BIRCH

WEAPONS, STONE

Stone-tipped weapons are a major development in the evolution of humans because they permitted consistent access to meat. Attaching a sharp stone to the tip of a spear, dart, or arrow increases weapon effectiveness by increasing wound size and bleeding. Hafting a stone tip to a shaft involves multiple materials including gums or bindings, with important cognitive implications because it requires multiple steps and significant planning.

Our evolutionary ancestors used stone to acquire scavenged meat for more than three million years; there is no evidence prior to ~500 KYA, however, that the sharp edges of stone were being used as hunting weapons. The earliest evidence for stone-tipped weapons comes from Kathu Pan, South Africa, where triangular stone points with damage patterns indicative of use as weapon tips were recovered from sediments dated to ~500 KYA.

By ~300 KYA, stone points are common in many archaeological contexts in Africa and Eurasia and were often used to tip hunting weapons. These points are usually removed from stone cores that are carefully prepared in a manner that helps predetermine the shape of the detached flake, ensuring that it is large, regular, and symmetrical in form. Cores prepared in this way are called Levallois cores. Levallois technology was widespread across much of Africa and Eurasia between ~300 and 40 KYA. Sometimes flakes were further shaped into a point after being detached from the core by removing small flakes from one (unifacial) or both (bifacial) edges, a process called retouch. Experimental studies show that points used as weapon tips develop characteristic fracture types at their tips. Near the base of the point where it contacts the shaft, the point may become polished or fractured. These use-wear signatures have been observed on Levallois points, indicating that early points served as weapon tips.

The earliest hafted hunting weapons were likely handheld, thrust, or thrown spears, but modern humans used various types of stone-tipped weapon technology, including projectiles. The term *projectile* is often restricted to technologies that significantly increase the distance between the hunter and the prey, such as atlatl/dart and bow/arrow technology. The atlatl, also called a spear thrower, is a wooden or bone shaft that acts as a lever for propelling a dart, increasing its distance and velocity. The shaft is held in one hand; the butt of the dart is supported and propelled from a spur at the opposite end. Indigenous Australians used atlatls, called *woomera*, with stone-tipped darts.

The bow involves a flexible material bound at both ends by string (animal sinew or skin). When the string is pulled back and then released, the flexion in the bow is transformed into energy to propel an arrow. An arrow usually consists of a stone or bone arrowhead on one end of the shaft, and fletching and a nock (for resting on the string) on the other. Poison can be put on the arrowhead to increase its killing power. !Kung San hunter-gatherers in southern Africa used combinations of plant and animal toxins on the stone tips of their light-duty arrows to slow down large game, which they sometimes followed for days as the toxin slowly took effect.

The earliest evidence for projectile technology, recovered from several South African archaeological sites, is about 70 KYA and consists of small standardized stone tool forms, known as backed blades, with impact damage. Backed blades are elongated stone pieces that have been blunted along one edge. The blunting serves to facilitate hafting into a handle or shaft and to impart a regular geometrical shape onto numerous tools. There are many methods of hafting. For arrow and dart tips, small backed blades can be hafted longitudinally or axially at the tip of the weapon to aid in penetration, for example, or they can be attached to the sides of the weapon to serve as barbs. One weapon may have an individual backed blade insert or multiple inserts. Some of the earliest backed blades from South African sites have plant and ocher residue, which could have been ingredients in the mastic (resin) used to attach these pieces to weapon tips. A projectile function for these tips as opposed to spears is indicated mainly by their small size. Ethnographic examples of spears generally have tips with a much larger size than darts and arrows, and arrow tips have the smallest size.

Based on ethnographic sources, the type of weapon used for hunting game is dependent on historical and cultural traditions, as well as functional and adaptive considerations. Researchers have found that spears are predominately used on large game where the terrain enables driving strategies or encounters with naturally disadvantaged prey. Atlatls and darts are predominately used on smaller game and ambush hunting. Bow-and-arrow technology is used for a greater diversity of game sizes and hunting strategies. For these and other reasons, the invention of complex projectile technology was a major advance for early modern humans and could be connected to our capacity to colonize new environments and spread across the globe.

Weapon tip shape across many recent tribal and hunter-gatherer societies is variable and influenced in part by function and in part by cultural and symbolic traditions. Some tool types have distinct spatial and temporal distributions and are therefore used by archaeologists as chronological or cultural markers. For example, Aterian points are characterized by a tanged or stemmed proximal end that would have been inserted into a socket on a wooden shaft or handle and are restricted to parts of northern Africa between ~120 and 50 KYA. Clovis points are finely made bifacial points with characteristic fluting that runs up the center of the point near the base. They are known across much of North America in contexts dating to ~13 KYA and are often associated with mammoth and other megafauna kill sites.

See also COOPERATIVE HUNTING; ETHNOARCHAEOLOGY; ETHNOGRAPHIC SOURCES; EXPERIMENTAL ARCHAEOLOGY; HUNTER-GATHERER SUBSISTENCE; MATERIAL CULTURE ANALYSIS; PALEOINDIAN DIET; PALEOLITHIC DIET; USE-WEAR ANALYSIS, LITHICS; WEAPONS, BONE/ANTLER/IVORY; WEAPONS, METAL

Further Reading

Churchill, Steven E. 1993. Weapon Technology, Prey Size Selection, and Hunting Methods in Modern Hunter-Gatherers: Implications for Hunting in the Palaeolithic and Mesolithic. *Archeological Papers of the American Anthropological Association* 4(1):11–24.

Lombard, Marlize. 2005. Evidence of Hunting and Hafting during the Middle Stone Age at Sibudu Cave, KwaZulu-Natal, South Africa: A Multianalytical Approach. *Journal of Human Evolution* 48(3):279–300.

Shea, John. 2006. The Origins of Lithic Projectile Point Technology: Evidence from Africa, the Levant, and Europe. *Journal of Archaeological Science* 33(6):823–46.

Villa, Paola, Paolo Boscato, Filamena Ranaldo, and Annamaria Ronchitelli. 2009. Stone Tools for the Hunt: Points with Impact Scars from a Middle Paleolithic Site in Southern Italy. *Journal of Archaeological Science* 36(3):850–59.

Wilkins, Jayne, Benjamin J. Schoville, Kyle S. Brown, and Michael Chazan. 2012. Evidence for Early Hafted Hunting Technology. *Science* 338(6109):942–46.

■ JAYNE WILKINS

WEEDS

Weeds are plants out of place or those that have volunteers in cultivated plots alongside the intended sown crop. Weeds also may be referred to as synanthropes because of their close association with human occupation and activities. While many weeds may be edible, used as salad greens, herbs, or famine foods, the key distinction is that these species were not sown intentionally from seed stores. Some weeds may actually be inadvertently sown as they are contaminants of stored crops. Other weeds derive from a soil seed bank or from belowground perennating organs (small tubers) that were not destroyed by tillage. In general, more advanced tillage technology (true plows that turn over soil) destroys most of these perennial weeds. Weeds are often divided into segetals, those that occur in the midst of planted crops, and ruderals, which occur on field margins, pathways, and other anthropogenically disturbed areas, such as middens, but not within tilled fields. Over the long term, species have probably moved from being segetals to ruderals as cultivation techniques have improved and helped to eliminate taxa from among the segetals. At the same time, new species of segetal weed flora have been recruited as agriculture spread into new environments or as weeds have been translocated with the long-distance movement of people and crops. Weeds are often classified by their conjectural history into apophytes (those considered native to a regional flora), archaeophytes (weeds introduced to a region in ancient times, prior to AD 1400), and neophytes or kenophytes (weeds introduced since European colonial expansion, after AD 1400).

The archaeobotanical investigation of weed flora is of growing importance, as the ecology of weed taxa reveals aspects of arable ecology from which agricultural practices can be inferred. For example, highly manured fields or those with long fallows will have more nitrophilous weeds, while continuously farmed plots may have taxa more tolerant of depleted soils, such as nitrogen-fixing legumes. The seasonality of cultivation may also be reflected in the weed flora, although there may be confounding factors as autumn-sown crops may appear more nitrogen-depleted than spring-sown crops. Wet or irrigated versus drier field conditions also will be reflected in the weed flora, and recent work has indicated that weed flora can be used to distinguish different cultivation systems for rice, such as between flooded paddies and rain-fed dry rice. In addition to the study of weed flora from preserved weed seeds that enter the archaeological record through crop-processing residues, phytolith assemblages may reflect the prominent weed flora within the dominant crop.

Weed flora have become especially important in the study of agricultural origins, as early arable fields created new habitats that were colonized by arable weeds even before the crop plants had evolved morphological divergence from their wild form. Thus inferred arable weed assemblages have been used to infer predomestication cultivation. This raises the question of the origins of weeds, as these taxa or closely related ancestors must have existed in naturally disturbed wild settings, or co-occurred with the wild progenitors of crops, before colonizing the new niche offered by early cultivation. However, for some of our better-known weeds, wild populations outside cultivation may be rare or nonexistent; this raises the question of whether their original habitats have been destroyed and the extent to which they have evolved obligate anthropogenic species.

See also AGRICULTURAL FEATURES, IDENTIFICATION AND ANALYSIS; AGRICULTURE, ORIGINS OF; AGRICULTURE, PROCUREMENT, PROCESSING, AND STORAGE; ARCHAEOBOTANY; LANDSCAPE AND ENVIRONMENTAL RECONSTRUCTION; MANURES AND OTHER FERTILIZERS, IDENTIFICATION AND ANALYSIS; PHYTOLITH ANALYSIS; PLANTS

Further Reading

Bogaard, A., C. Palmer, G. Jones, et al. 1999. A FIBS Approach to the Use of Weed Ecology for the Archaeobotanical Recognition of Crop Rotation Regimes. *Journal of Archaeological Science* 26(9):1211–24.

Fuller, Dorian Q, and Ling Qin. 2009. Water Management and Labour in the Origins and Dispersal of Asian Rice. *World Archaeology* 41(1):88–111.

Jones, G., M. Charles, A. Bogaard, and J. Hodgson. 2010. Crops and Weeds: The Role of Weed Func-
    tional Ecology in the Identification of Crop Husbandry Methods. *Journal of Archaeological Science*
    37(1):70–77.
Weisskopf, Alison, Emma Harvey, Eleanor Kingwell-Banham, et al. 2014. Archaeobotanical Implications
    of Phytolith Assemblages from Cultivated Rice Systems, Wild Rice Stands and Macro-Regional
    Patterns. *Journal of Archaeological Science* 51:43–53. doi:10.1016/j.jas.2013.04.026.
Willcox, George. 2012. Searching for the Origins of Arable Weeds in the Near East. *Vegetation History
    and Archaeobotany* 21(2):163–67.

■ DORIAN Q FULLER

WHEAT

Historically, wheat is the chief crop of Western civilization. Its importance for bread
making is reflected in a number of religious symbolisms and everyday expressions (e.g.,
"separate the wheat from the chaff," "bread riot," "*matzah* bread"). It is one of the most
nutritive cereals because of its very high carbohydrate (60–80 percent) and protein (8–15
percent) content. Its dough has exceptional rising and baking properties owing to specific
gluten proteins that capture the carbon dioxide produced by fermentation when yeast is
added to produce leavened bread.

The common term *wheat* includes different species within the *Triticum* genus, each
having distinct end uses, biology, and cultural meanings. All are self-pollinated annual
plants. Although the taxonomy of the genus *Triticum* is debated, cultivated wheats can be
best grouped according to (1) ploidy level (the number and type of chromosome sets or
genomes each cell possesses) and (2) threshability.

Einkorn (*T. monococcum*) is the only domesticated diploid, or species containing two
sets of a single genome (represented as AA). Tetraploid wheats have two sets of diploid
genomes, either AABB or AAGG. Among the former is *T. turgidum*, which includes
durum (ssp. *durum*), emmer (ssp. *dicoccum*), Polish (ssp. *polonicum*), and rivet (ssp. *turgidum*)
wheats. Among the AAGG type is *T. timopheevii*. The hexaploid group (AABBDD) includes the species *T. aestivum* with its subspecies bread (ssp. *aestivum* = *T. vulgare*), spelt
(ssp. *spelta*), club (ssp. *compactum*), and Indian-dwarf wheat (ssp. *sphaerococcum*). Some of
these wheats are hulled, that is, the grains are protected by husky glumes that do not
break during threshing (e.g., einkorn, emmer, spelt). Others are naked or free-threshing, with thin glumes that release the naked grain during threshing (e.g., durum, rivet,
Polish, club, and bread wheat).

Only bread and durum wheat are still significant crops today. Bread wheat is used to
make wheat beer and flour-derived products like bread and cakes. The hardness and low
gluten content of durum makes it more suitable for semolina-derived products like pasta,
couscous, and bulgur. Other wheats had historical significance but are now relic crops,
cultivated only in remote areas and consumed in the form of bread and porridge or used
for animal feed.

Wheat domestication occurred in the Near East, a well-studied process with some
as-yet-unresolved details. Einkorn was domesticated from wild einkorn (*T. monococcum*
ssp. *aegilopoides* = *T. baeoticum*). All the other wheats originated from a different lineage.
Emmer was domesticated after selection of wild emmer (*T. turgidum* ssp. *dicoccoides*) plants

with desirable traits. Naked tetraploid wheats (i.e., durum) evolved from hulled emmer. Hexaploid forms (bread wheat and spelt) emerged from the spontaneous cross between an already domesticated tetraploid—emmer or durum—and the diploid wild grass *Aegilops tauschii* (donor of the D genome). It is not clear if spelt evolved from bread wheat or vice versa. The goat grass's D genome conferred bread wheat its broad-range adaptability.

Wheat was one of the first plants to be domesticated. Use of wild einkorn and wild emmer is documented in the Near East Epipaleolithic sites of Ohalo II, Israel (23,000 cal BP); Abu Hureyra, Syria (12,700–11,100 cal BP); Mureybit, Syria (11,800–11,300 cal BP); and Chogha Golan, Iran (12,000–9,800 cal BP). It is unclear if wheat was domesticated only once and in a single area of the Near East or if domestication occurred in different places based on local wild populations. The tempo and mode of the domestication process is still contentious; some researchers propose a quick domestication process and others suggest a protracted model lasting three to four millennia. Early sites with evidence of domesticated wheat include Tell Aswad, Syria (10,500–10,200 cal BP), and Çayönü, Turkey (10,250–9,550 cal BP). The first naked tetraploids appear at the sites of Tell Aswad and Can Hasan III, Turkey (9,450–8,450 cal BP). Bread wheat is assumed to have emerged in Transcaucasia or the Caspian Belt around 8,000–7,000 BP. As agriculture spread outside the Near East, wheats were always present in the crop assemblage. With time, farmers selected varieties with desirable traits and good performance under their regions' environments, resulting in a number of independent lines characteristic of each region (landraces). From the late 19th century to the present, scientific wheat breeding resulted in the replacement of traditional landraces with high-yield commercial varieties, with a consequent narrowing of the crop's biodiversity. Seed banks have preserved thousands of wheat landraces that can still be used for food security purposes in the face of climate change and soil degradation.

Information on wheat domestication and history comes from archaeobotanical data, historical documents, art depictions, agricultural tools, spatial analysis, and ethnography. Archaeobotanists consider the shape of grain, ear, spikelets, and rachis (the spine of the ear holding the spikelets) fragments to distinguish wheat from other cereals and to identify the remains' wild or domesticated status, their ploidy, and threshability. Distinction between tetraploid and hexaploid naked wheats is not always possible. Ancient DNA retrieved from archaeological remains and genomic analysis of landraces has provided valuable insights about the crop's domestication process and its spread in prehistoric and historical times. This research benefits from recent advances in DNA sequencing technologies.

Farming communities in different times and regions have adopted different wheat species, either a single species (for example, emmer was the only wheat cultivated in ancient Egypt up to the Hellenistic period) or preferred types (durum wheat was preferred in south Europe whereas hulled wheats were preferred in north Europe). Types of wheat cultivated sometimes varied from one period to the next because of migrations, social dynamics, trade, environmental cues, and resilience strategies (e.g., the progressive replacement of hulled wheats for naked types in most of Europe; the association in some cultures of white flour with wealth and purity). Distinct communities also espoused diverse methods and technologies to cultivate, process, store, and use wheat. These differences are sharper if hulled or naked wheat was used. Hulled wheats were traditionally considered all the same crop (e.g., the use of the word *farro* or *escaña* in Italian and Spanish, respectively, to refer indistinctively to emmer, einkorn, or spelt).

The importance of wheat for the sustenance of many Western cultures is reflected in the use of the word *bread* as a synonym of *food* in many languages, even though it presently ranks fourth among world crops after sugarcane, maize, and rice.

See also Agriculture, Origins of; Archaeobotany; Biomolecular Analysis; Bread; Cereals; DNA Analysis; Fermentation; Neolithic Package; Ohalo II; Old World Globalization and Food Exchanges; Plant Domestication; Wild Progenitors of Domesticated Plants; Yeast

Further Reading

Bjørnstad, Åsmund. 2012. *Our Daily Bread: A History of Cereals*. Oslo: Vidarforlaget.
Fuller, Dorian Q, George Willcox, and Robin G. Allaby. 2012. Early Agricultural Pathways: Moving outside the "Core Area" Hypothesis in Southwest Asia. *Journal of Experimental Botany* 63(2):617–33.
Shewry, P. R. 2009. Wheat. *Journal of Experimental Botany* 60(6):1537–53.
Zohary, Daniel, Maria Hopf, and Ehud Weiss. 2012. *Domestication of Plants in the Old World*. 4th edition. Oxford: Oxford University Press.

■ HUGO R. OLIVEIRA

WILD PROGENITORS OF DOMESTICATED PLANTS

Domesticated crop species are the product of evolution in which the cultivated populations of wild species are transformed into those adapted to cultivation and harvesting by humans. Thus a complete understanding of the domestication process requires the identification of wild progenitors. In addition, as the domestication process invariably involved a genetic bottleneck, the genetic diversity within living populations of wild progenitors is normally significantly higher than that in the crop and offers potentially important genes for modern breeding to improve crops, especially in traits relating to disease or pest resistance. Strictly speaking, although the closest living wild relatives are usually referred to as wild progenitors of crops, it should be kept in mind that these modern wild populations have had just as long to evolve from the early Holocene populations as crops have, and some populations that might have been important in domestication may have since become extinct. Nevertheless, the distribution and habitats of modern wild populations provide the best approximation to where geographically these species were first taken into cultivation by the hunter-gatherer populations that became Neolithic food producers.

The identification of wild ancestors of crops and the mapping of their distribution are generally botanical research problems. Plant taxonomy, increasingly enhanced by molecular genetics, aims to relate domesticated crops to the closest living wild populations, their wild progenitors. The contrasts between these wild relatives and domesticated crops normally include a range of morphological traits, termed the domestication syndrome, that characteristically have evolved during domestication. The comparisons between modern wild progenitors and crops provide a baseline for traits that can be expected to mark the domestication process in archaeobotanical remains. The geographical range of wild populations should be mapped, ideally by targeted field botany and collecting, but in some cases this can be drawn from regional floristic studies. While the wild progenitors are well established and mapped for many crops, especially those from better-studied regions (e.g., the cereals and pulses of the Near East, the pulses and grain crops of Africa, or the wild relatives of maize), in many other cases wild progenitors are underresearched, as is the case in many South and Southeast Asian crops. A wild progenitor species may be widespread, but that does not mean that domestication processes were widespread. A key research problem then is to determine where within wild distribution there is evidence for local domestication processes. This is made difficult by the likelihood that introduced domesticated forms also hybridized with local wild populations, when available, and acquired regional adaptations from local wild populations through introgression (the transfer of genes by cross-pollination from wild populations to crops). This appears to have happened in species such as rice, where wild populations provide a diverse range of regional adaptations, and is also likely in sorghums across Africa.

In general, we might divide the current status of wild progenitors into four categories. First, there are those wild populations that are well documented and likely have a roughly similar geographical range today as they did in the earlier Holocene when they were first domesticated. Examples include wild wheats and barley in western Asia's Fertile Crescent, and teosinte, the Mesoamerican wild ancestor of maize. Second, there are those wild progenitors that have modern distributions that are altered, usually reduced, from what they would have been at the time of domestication. Examples include Asian rice, which has been extirpated from central China and much of the Yangtze Valley where it was domesticated. Sunflowers also are likely to have been more widespread as a wild species in the American Midwest in the past. Third, there are taxa for which the wild progenitor is extinct (or still undiscovered). Examples include the fava bean, an early domesticate of the Fertile Crescent, and tree cotton, which originated in southern Asia (probably modern Pakistan), although wild forms are now unknown. In cases such as these, habitat transformation through human action is the most likely cause of extinction, although climate change may have also played a role. Fourth are cases of trans-domestication, when the wild ancestral distribution is quite distinct from the region of domestication. In such cases the wild form would have been translocated through human action, as a weed or incidental, and then subsequently domesticated from these weedy populations. In such cases the domestication represents a secondary genetic bottleneck after that related to the translocation. Examples include oats, wild in the eastern Mediterranean but domesticated in Europe in the Late Bronze Age from weeds of wheat or barley; the gaur bean, a native of eastern Africa, domesticated in the Indus region within the past 1,000 years; and the tomato, which is regarded as a domesticate of Mesoamerica despite its wild diversity and occurrence in nonanthropogenic habitats in the Andes.

The study of wild relatives of crops is essential to understanding domestication processes and thus origins of agriculture. An additional challenge is to document the use of the wild forms by preagricultural hunter-gatherers and to explain why these particular species, among the many edible plants in a region, were brought into cultivation and domesticated.

See also AGRICULTURE, ORIGINS OF; CEREALS; CULTIVATION; PLANT DOMESTICATION; PLANT HUSBANDRY; PLANTS

Further Reading

Fuller, Dorian Q. 2006. Agricultural Origins and Frontiers in South Asia: A Working Synthesis. *Journal of World Prehistory* 20(1):1–86.

Harlan, Jack R. 1992. *Crops and Ancient Man.* 2nd edition. Madison, WI: American Society for Agronomy and Crop Science Society of America.

Hymowitz, T. 1972. The Trans-Domestication Concept as Applied to Guar. *Economic Botany* 26(1):49–60.

Piperno, Dolores R., and Deborah M. Pearsall. 1998. *The Origins of Agriculture in the Lowland Neotropics.* San Diego, CA: Academic Press.

Smartt, J., and N. W. Simmonds, eds. 1995. *Evolution of Crop Plants.* 2nd edition. Harrow, UK: Longman.

Zeven, A. C., and J. M. J. De Wet. 1982. *Dictionary of Cultivated Plants and Their Regions of Diversity.* Wageningen, the Netherlands: Centre for Agricultural Publishing and Documentation.

Zohary, Daniel, Maria Hopf, and Ehud Weiss. 2012. *Domestication of Plants in the Old World.* 4th edition. Oxford: Oxford University Press.

■ DORIAN Q FULLER

WINE

Wine is part of religious and cultural traditions from prehistory and has played a major role in the lives of the ancient Mediterranean people. It is a naturally fermented beverage produced from grapes and other fruits (e.g., dates, figs) and grains by the action of yeasts that transform sugar into alcohol. Archaeological evidence for the production of wine includes iconography, texts, artifacts (wine jars, strainers, cups), wine presses, and organic material (grape berries, wood, wine residues).

The cultivation and domestication of the grape vine appears to have occurred between 7000 and 4000 BC. Archaeological and historical evidence suggests that grape primo-domestication occurred in the Near East. Domesticated vines gradually spread to adjacent regions such as Egypt and Lower Mesopotamia, with subsequent dispersal around the Mediterranean region. The ancestral cultivars and diversification process of grape varieties through time are not well known, and it is uncertain whether secondary independent domestications also may have occurred. Recent advances in studies of morphological diversity of seeds and ancient DNA (aDNA) analysis of grapes might reveal the extent and origin of genetic diversity.

Although it is still unclear exactly where wine was first made, the earliest archaeological evidence for wine comes from Haji Firuz Tepe in the Zagros Mountains (Iran) ca. 5400 BC and from a winery in Areni (Armenia) ca. 4000 BC. Wine-making facilities, wineries, and storerooms are frequently found in the archaeological record of the ancient Mediterranean. In addition, amphorae have been recovered from shipwrecks in the Mediterranean Sea—for instance, those of two Phoenician boats (ca. 750 BC) whose cargo of wine was still intact—and from graves, such as the intact wine cellar in Tutankhamun's tomb (ca. 1323 BC) (figure 70). Residue analysis of archaeological samples using liquid chromatography–mass spectrometry (LC-MS/MS) identified tartaric acid, a grape marker, and syringic acid, a red grape marker that is derived from malvidin 3-glucoside, the main anthocyanin that gives the red color to grapes and wine.

Figure 70. Top: Grape harvest and wine making depicted in the tomb of Nakht at Thebes, 18th Dynasty (1539–1292 BC). On the right, workers pick the grapes by hand and put them in baskets. On the left, four men press the grapes with their bare feet. A red juice flows from the vat. Above, center, are sealed amphorae. Photograph © Irep en Kemet Project (www.wineofancientegypt.com). Bottom: Tutankhamun's amphora JE 62303, Carter No. 486. The inscription reads: "Year 4, wine of the Estate of Aten, l.p.h., of the Western River, chief vintner Nen." The abreviation "l.p.h." means "life, prosperity, and health," and it is always found after the name of the god. Photograph © Maria Rosa Guasch Jané, with permission of the Egyptian Museum in Cairo.

Wine making also has a considerably history in other regions. Archaeological residues of pottery jars from China, at the site of Jiahu (between 7000 and 6000 BC), using Fourier transform infrared spectroscopy (FTIR) and high performance liquid chromatography (HPLC), show a mixed fermented beverage made from rice, honey, and possibly a fruit. The earliest known archaeological example of grape wine dates to the Han Dynasty (206 BC–AD 220). The earliest grape seeds and skins in the Aegean have been found at the Late Neolithic site (ca. 4500 BC) of Dikili Tash in Greece. In ancient Greece and Rome, resins and plants were added to wines for preservation and to give flavor. Phoenician and Greek trade networks distributed wines throughout the Mediterranean region. Wine was a drink of the gods in ancient Egypt (Osiris), Greece

(Dionysus), and Rome (Bacchus) and was enjoyed in banquets. Athenaeus of Naucratis (a Greek city in the Nile Delta) discussed the essence of drinking wine in *Deipnosophistae* (Philosophers at Dinner) in the third century BC. The world's oldest textual sources describing of the role of wine in medicine are ancient Egyptian papyri and Sumerian tablets dating back to 2200 BC. The Greek Hippocrates (ca. 460–370 BC) recommended wine as part of a healthy diet.

One of the world's oldest and most extensive records for wine production comes from ancient Egypt. In Egypt, wine was a prestigious drink consumed mainly by royalty and the elite, offered to gods in daily temple rituals, and used in medical treatments and the pharaoh's resurrection ritual for the afterlife. From the Predynastic period (ca. 3800 BC) onward, wine jars were placed in graves as funerary offerings. Inscriptions on pottery jars dating to the Early Dynastic period (ca. 3300 BC) indicate the wine's geographic origin. From the Old Kingdom period (2680–2160 BC) through to the Greco-Roman period (332 BC–AD 395), wall paintings depict viticulture and wine-making scenes in private tombs, such as the mastaba of Iymery at Giza and the tomb of Nakht at Thebes (figure 70). During the New Kingdom period (1550–1069 BC), wine jars (amphorae) were inscribed in hieratic writing to indicate harvest year, product, quality and sweetness, provenance, ownership, and the wine maker's name and title. Egyptian mythology from the Old Kingdom accorded significance to the red color of wine; no textual references to white or red wine have been found from the Dynastic period (3100–343 BC). For many years, the only known evidence for wine from the New Kingdom was the representation of red grapes in tombs and the myths that connected red wine with the blood of Osiris, the god of the underworld. Recent chemical analysis through the identification of wine markers has now revealed three kinds of wine in the New Kingdom period: red, white, and a third wine named *Shedeh*. The *Shedeh*, a distinct type of red wine, was mentioned in the Salt papyrus 825 (BM 10051) of the Late Dynastic period (715–332 BC); this text described filtering and heating, but because the papyrus was damaged, a list of its raw ingredients did not survive. Chemical analysis of a unique sample identified the presence of the two markers for red wine, however.

See also ARCHAEOBOTANY; ARENI; BIOMOLECULAR ANALYSIS; CARVINGS/CARVED REPRESENTATIONS OF FOOD; DNA ANALYSIS; DOCUMENTARY ANALYSIS; FERMENTATION; FOOD AND RITUAL; FOODWAYS AND RELIGIOUS PRACTICES; HIGH PERFORMANCE LIQUID CHROMATOGRAPHY; INFRARED SPECTROSCOPY/FOURIER TRANSFORM INFRARED SPECTROSCOPY; MORTUARY COMPLEXES; OFFERINGS AND GRAVE GOODS; REPRESENTATIONAL MODELS OF FOOD AND FOOD PRODUCTION; RESIDUE ANALYSIS, TARTARIC ACID; SHIPWRECKS; TRADE ROUTES; WALL PAINTINGS/MURALS; WINERIES; YEAST

Further Reading

Guasch-Jané, Maria Rosa. 2008. *Wine in Ancient Egypt: A Cultural and Analytical Study*. BAR International Series 1851. Oxford: Archaeopress.

———. 2011. The Meaning of Wine in Egyptian Tombs: The Three Amphorae from Tutankhamun's Burial Chamber. *Antiquity* 85(329):851–58.

Guasch-Jané, Maria Rosa, Cristina Andrés-Lacueva, Olga Jáuregui, and Rosa M. Lamuela-Raventós. 2006a. First Evidence of White Wine in Ancient Egypt from Tutankhamun's Tomb. *Journal of Archaeological Science* 33(8):1075–80.

———. 2006b. The Origin of the Ancient Egyptian Drink *Shedeh* Revealed Using LC/MS/MS. *Journal of Archaeological Science* 33(1):98–101.

Guasch-Jané, Maria Rosa, Sofia Fonseca, and Mahmoud Ibrahim. 2013. "Irep en Kemet" Wine of Ancient Egypt: Documenting the Viticulture and Winemaking Scenes in the Egyptian Tombs. In *ISPRS Annals of the Photogrammetry, Remote Sensing and Spatial Information Sciences, Volume II-5/W1, 2013 XXIV International CIPA Symposium, 2–6 September 2013, Strasbourg (France)*:157–61.

McGovern, Patrick E. 2003. *Ancient Wine: The Search for the Origins of Viniculture*. Princeton, NJ: Princeton University Press.

This, Patrice, Thierry Lacombe, and Mark R. Thomas. 2006. Historical Origins and Genetic Diversity of Wine Grapes. *Trends in Genetics* 22(9):511–19.

■ MARIA ROSA GUASCH-JANÉ

WINERIES

Wineries are facilities specifically constructed for the production of wine from grapes (*Vitis vinifera*). The vinification process appears to have developed at the beginning of the Neolithic in the Fertile Crescent, from which location it spread through Southeast Asia, North Africa, and Europe. In colonial times the technique was imported into the Americas, South Africa, and Australia. In an archaeological context, wineries are primarily identified by the presence of the seeds or stalks and stems of grapes in combination with the remains of an installation to press grapes, installations to collect and process the resulting juice, or fermenting vessels. The inference of wine production can be corroborated through chemical analysis by showing the presence of malvidin, the anthocyanin that gives grapes and wines their red color and preserves because of its tendency to polymerize over time; tartaric acid ($C_4H_6O_6$), an organic acid especially common in grapes that can be preserved in the form of potassium and calcium salts; or compounds that are likely from tree resins that were used to make ceramic vessels less porous or were added to wine to enhance its flavor or act as preservative. Fermentation can sometimes be supported by showing the presence of yeast, either microscopically or by finding the DNA of yeast microbes. The earliest winery (4223–3790 cal BC) that has been identified to date is in the Areni cave complex in modern Armenia. As this is fully developed, it must have been the result of a much longer tradition, also indicated by isolated evidence of wine in, for instance, Dikili Tash (Greece), Gadachrili Gora (Georgia), and Godin Tepe (Iran).

See also ARENI; BIOMOLECULAR ANALYSIS; DNA ANALYSIS; FERMENTATION; MACROREMAINS; RESIDUE ANALYSIS, TARTARIC ACID; WINE; YEAST

Further Reading

Barnard, Hans, Alek N. Dooley, Gregory Areshian, et al. 2011. Chemical Evidence for Wine Production around 4000 BCE in the Late Chalcolithic Near Eastern Highlands. *Journal of Archaeological Science* 38(5):977–84.

McGovern, Patrick E., Benjamin P. Luley, Nuria Rovira, et al. 2013. Beginning of Viniculture in France. *Proceedings of the National Academy of Sciences USA* 110(25):10147–52.

■ HANS BARNARD AND GREGORY E. ARESHIAN

WONDERWERK CAVE (SOUTH AFRICA)

Wonderwerk Cave, located in the Northern Cape Province, South Africa, is the site of one of the oldest and longest human occupation sequences known to date (figure 71). The cave has been the subject of archaeological investigation since the 1970s. The earliest artifacts are of the Oldowan tradition and date to about 1.7 MYA. The site has produced the earliest evidence of (1) cave occupation (Oldowan); (2) use of fire (Acheulean); and (3) collection and exploitation of pigment ores (Fauresmith, about 500,000 years ago). The unique archaeological and environmental evidence from Wonderwerk Cave is producing a detailed, diachronic understanding of early human subsistence practices.

Wonderwerk Cave is a ~140-meter-long karstic cave that formed in the Precambrian dolostone of the Kuruman Hills. Peter Beaumont carried out extensive archaeological excavations from the 1970s to the 1990s in seven different areas within the cave. Beaumont's ~2-meter-deep sounding, in Excavation 1, located ~25 meters from the cave entrance, immediately behind a large, active stalagmite, covers an area of ~43 square meters. The assemblage resulting from this large excavation area provided a solid basis for describing

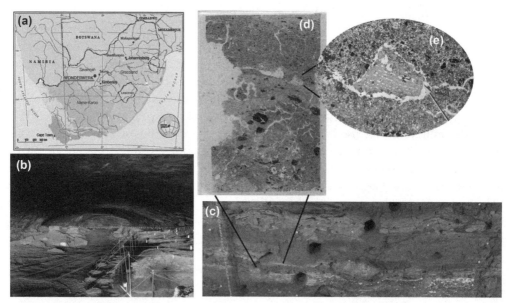

Figure 71. Wonderwerk Cave: (a) map of South Africa and location of Wonderwerk Cave; (b) internal view of Wonderwerk Cave; (c) layers composing Stratum 10, Excavation 1; (d) petrographic thin section processed from an intact sediment block sampled from Stratum 10 and showing the presence of several living surfaces; (e) close-up (micrographs) of a fragment of heated bone lying on one of the living surfaces of Stratum 10. Photograph credits: Michael Chazan (b, c) and Paul Goldberg (d, e).

the archaeological and paleontological sequence and for dating its origin to the early phases of the Earlier Stone Age (ESA).

In 2004, a new team coordinated by Michael Chazan and Liora Kolska Horwitz renewed field- and lab work to reanalyze the archaeological record, reconstruct site formation processes, and perform chronometric dating. The new work showed that in Excavation 1 the archaeological sequence begins in basal Stratum 12 with a small lithic industry attributed to the Sterkfontein-like Oldowan. The sediment associated with this assemblage was dated to ca. 1.7 MYA using several techniques, including biostratigraphic analysis and paleomagnetic data. Sediment burial ages also were estimated by measuring the residual amount of the cosmogenic isotopes ^{10}Be and ^{26}Al contained in sand grains. (These cosmogenic isotopes are produced at a known rate by the collision of cosmic rays with the atoms of silicon and oxygen in the quartz grains of rock and sediments exposed on the earth's surface and decay with time). The overlying Acheulean sequence shows developments from proto hand axes (Stratum 11) to hand axes with noninvasive retouch (Stratum 10) and more refined Victoria West–like hand axes (Stratum 9).

The site formation processes at the cave were investigated by microscopic analysis of intact sediment blocks processed into petrographic thin section slides (micromorphological analysis). The sediments at the bottom of Excavation 1 are characterized by sterile phreatic deposits (deposits immersed in an active water table) that formed when the cave was still closed to the external landscape. Stratum 12, the earliest archaeological occupation (Oldowan), is associated with low-energy, water-deposited sand and fine gravel, probably introduced into the cave by sheet flow. At the top of Stratum 12 (Oldowan), the depositional processes changed dramatically and involved the accumulation of aeolian material composed of fine sand and characteristic rounded aggregates composed of silt and clay. This kind of aggregate typically forms in drying lake environments such as that clearly present outside the cave in the past. In the Oldowan and lower Acheulean strata (Stratum 12 to 10), the aeolian sand and aggregates appear reworked by gravity and trampling, indicating the presence of stable surfaces that hosted human and animal occupation.

The microscopic analysis of the sediments and the use of infrared spectroscopy on bones and sediment demonstrated the presence of in situ fire associated with Acheulean artifacts in Stratum 10 (dated to ~1 MYA) 25–30 meters inside the cave. The nature and spatial distribution of specific microscopic and macroscopic evidence (i.e., heated bone, heated lithic stone artifacts, and microscopic fragments of ashed plant remains) suggests the presence of several small campfires fueled with twigs, leaves, and grass (figure 71). The temperature of these fires, assessed by the heat-alterations detected in bone, stone, and sediment, is estimated at between 400 and 700°C. The combined evidence from the Acheulean level of Wonderwerk Cave suggests that humans, most probably groups of *Homo erectus*, could control fire and cook their food. Currently, these two hypotheses are being tested by renewed excavation and the application of multidisciplinary investigation.

See also FIRE AND THE DEVELOPMENT OF COOKING; FIRE-BASED COOKING FEATURES; INFRARED SPECTROSCOPY/FOURIER TRANSFORM INFRARED SPECTROSCOPY; ROCKSHELTERS/CAVES; SOIL MICROTECHNIQUES; TOOLS/UTENSILS, STONE; WEAPONS, STONE

Further Reading

Berna, Francesco, Paul Goldberg, Liora Kolska Horwitz, et al. 2012. Microstratigraphic Evidence of In Situ Fire in the Acheulean Strata of Wonderwerk Cave, Northern Cape Province, South Africa. *Proceedings of the National Academy of Sciences USA* 109(20):E1215–E1220.

Chazan, Michael, D. Margaret Avery, Marion K. Bamford, et al. 2012. The Oldowan Horizon in Wonderwerk Cave (South Africa): Archaeological, Geological, Paleontological and Paleoclimatic Evidence. *Journal of Human Evolution* 63(6):859–66.

Chazan, Michael, Hagai Ron, Ari Matmon, et al. 2008. Radiometric Dating of the Earlier Stone Age Sequence in Excavation I at Wonderwerk Cave, South Africa: Preliminary Results. *Journal of Human Evolution* 55(1):1–11.

Matmon A., H. Ron, M. Chazan, et al. 2012. Reconstructing the History of Sediment Deposition in Caves: A Case Study from Wonderwerk Cave. *Geological Society of America Bulletin* 124(3–4):611–25.

■ FRANCESCO BERNA

WORK CAMPS

Historical archaeologists study work camps around the world. These camps provided for workers employed by private or public developers (e.g., transportation or water systems) or extractors of local resources (e.g., lumber, minerals, crops). The food experiences of industrial laborers in these settings varied by the remoteness of the camp, the social and economic status of the participants, and their ethnicity in often contested relationships of power and control. The food itself, often considered part of the workers' wages, varied considerably. When skilled labor was scarce, the camp serving the best food got the best workers. Industries not requiring skilled labor generally supplied the worst food, emphasizing beans, and left their workers to forage for variety. Dining facilities and environments also varied. Larger camps tended to be more institutional and formal, small ones more idiosyncratic and accommodating.

Three late-19th-century work camps in the Sierra Nevada of California (USA) supply some points on this continuum. The remains of James Nelson's small sawmill suggest an austere environment mitigated by the frequent and liberal use of alcohol, no attempt at a formal Victorian after-work environment, and trash simply pitched out of the cookhouse door. The Pioneer Mine owned two closely sited boardinghouses: the Thomas House and the China House. The Thomas family, which supplied food and lodging for the white miners, attempted a formal Victorian dining experience and discarded their waste in a discretely hidden dump. The Thomas daughters organized teas and social events. Meals were substantial—oatmeal or cornmeal mush, bacon or ham and eggs, toast or hotcake, and coffee, a tin pail with lunch, choice of two meats, a soup, vegetables, fruit, pie or cake, and tea or coffee. Wine and liquor were discouraged. Local merchant Yee Ah Tye supplied China House residents with Chinese foodstuffs in Chinese stoneware jars, Chinese liquor, and opium. Chinese miners lived in and around the house in a dispersed settlement and left their refuse in place.

See also ARCHITECTURAL ANALYSIS; DOCUMENTARY ANALYSIS; FOOD AND INEQUALITY; FOOD AND POWER; HOUSEHOLD ARCHAEOLOGY; MIDDENS AND OTHER TRASH DEPOSITS

Further Reading

Conlin, Joseph R. 1986. *Bacon, Beans, and Galantines: Food and Foodways on the Western Mining Frontier.* Reno: University of Nevada Press.

HARD Work Camps Team and Caltrans Staff. 2013. *Work Camps: Historic Context and Archaeological Research Design.* Sacramento: California Department of Transportation. http://www.dot.ca.gov/ser/guidance.htm#workcamp.

■ MARY PRAETZELLIS AND ADRIAN PRAETZELLIS

Y

YAM

Yams are starchy edible tubers produced by perennial vines belonging to the genera *Dioscorea* (about 95 percent of the family Dioscoreaceae) and have been the dietary mainstay of numerous societies across the tropical zones for millennia. Yams derive from the "yam zones" of West Africa, South and Southeast Asia, and the Pacific, as well as the Americas. Yam crops are also important in the sociocultural life of societies where they occur. There are around 600 varieties of yams, but only a few are economically important and repeatedly cultivated. Agriculture involving the domestication and exploitation of yams has occurred in areas where seed-based agriculture has not been viable. Today, 90 percent of yam production comes from West Africa. Tubers are harvested every season, and stocks are replenished by replanting part of the unprocessed tuber or from perennial species. Some *Dioscorea* tubers contain compounds that affect palatability, specifically alkaloids, tannins, and saponins, and require complex processing to render them edible. Tubers can be stored for up to six months; some are dried and subsequently milled for flour.

Yam domestication occurred over a similar time period as grain crops. Some of the earliest evidence for systematic exploitation of yams comes from Kuk Swamp in highland New Guinea and dates to the Early Holocene. The persistence of the remains of yams, either as macro- (plant cell tissue including vascular elements such as xylem or phloem) or microfossils (starch) in cultural deposits for many thousands of years, has only recently been realized. At Niah Caves in Borneo, charred parenchyma (cell tissue) identified as a toxic yam tuber (cf. *Dioscorea hispida*) was recovered from Last Glacial Maximum deposits. Stone tools from cultural deposits dated to ca. 45,000–50,000 cal BP in the highlands of eastern New Guinea have yielded use-related starch residues consistent with *Dioscorea alata*, a species now thought to be endemic to the region. Functional studies of stone artifacts, particularly residue analysis (low and high power microscopy), greatly improve our ability to identify yams in archaeological contexts. As these new data add detail to the larger picture of settlement histories, so will our understanding of the evolution of *Dioscorea* species in relation to the emergence of agriculture in the tropical zone.

See also AGRICULTURAL/HORTICULTURAL SITES; AGRICULTURE, PROCUREMENT, PROCESSING, AND STORAGE; ARCHAEOBOTANY; MACROREMAINS; NIAH CAVES; PLANT DOMESTICATION; PLANT PROCESSING; RESIDUE ANALYSIS, STARCH; ROOT CROPS/TUBERS; TOOLS/UTENSILS, STONE

Further Reading

Barton, Huw, and Victor Paz. 2007. Subterranean Diets in the Tropical Rainforest of Sarawak, Malaysia. In *Rethinking Agriculture: Archaeological and Ethnoarchaeological Perspectives*, edited by Timothy P. Denham, José Iriarte, and Luc Vrydachs, 50–77. Walnut Creek, CA: Left Coast Press.

Lebot, Vincent. 2009. *Tropical Root and Tuber Crops: Cassava, Sweet Potato, Yams and Aroids*. Crop Production Science in Horticulture 17. Oxfordshire, UK: CABI Group.

Summerhayes, G., M. Leavesley, H. Mandui, et al. 2010. Refocusing the Boundaries: Human Adaptation and Use of Plants in Highland New Guinea from 49–44,000 Years Ago. *Science* 330:78–81.

■ JUDITH H. FIELD

YEAST

Yeasts are microorganisms or microbes that typically grow in moist environments; together with molds and mushrooms, they are placed in the kingdom Fungi (L. *Saccharomyces*). Yeasts are widely distributed in nature, and many have the ability to transform soluble nutrients, such as sugars and amino acids, into alcohol and carbon dioxide. Yeast cells have the ability to enlarge, and several yeasts have been harnessed for the production of food and drinks; others have been used for medicinal purposes. Early humans were dependent on spontaneous yeasts. It is unknown when the conscious selection of yeasts started, and within the archaeological context, processes of microbe (yeast) domestication remain obscure. Fermentation yeasts (that make food palatable) pass the winter in the soil; in spring they are disseminated by bees, dust, and other agents.

In ancient Mesopotamia and Egypt, beer was made from staple cereal crops. In Egyptian tombs and settlements, archaeologists have discovered yeast residues in brewing vats, pottery vessels, and prepared foods (e.g., charred breads) throughout Pharaonic times (ca. 3100–332 BC). Beer was prepared from stored cereals (emmer and barley), and as it could not be kept for more than a few days, it was prepared on demand. Yeast is very common on the skin of grapes and other fruits and berries that do not keep well, and wine was produced immediately. During Greco-Roman times, bread wheat, which was uniquely suited for leavened bread, began to replace traditional cereals and milling technologies. The Greeks probably leavened sourdough bread with wild yeast (Athenaeus describes more than 70 different bread loaves), and the Romans further developed the application of yeasts. Preserved bread loaves were recovered from Pompeii AD 79. From Neolithic to early medieval times, and throughout Europe, remains of several types of yeasts have been excavated from archaeological sites.

See also BAKERIES; BEER; BREAD; BREWING/MALTING; CEREALS; FERMENTATION; FUNGI; HERCULANEUM AND POMPEII; WHEAT; WINE

Further Reading

Boulton, Christopher M., and David Quain. 2006. *Brewing Yeast and Fermentation*. Hoboken, NJ: Wiley-Blackwell.

Jones, Martin. 2007. *Feast: Why Humans Share Food*. Oxford: Oxford University Press.

Samuel, Delwen. 2000. Brewing and Baking. In *Ancient Egyptian Materials and Technology*, edited by Paul T. Nicholson and Ian Shaw, 537–76. Cambridge: Cambridge University Press.

■ KARIN VANEKER

YORK (ENGLAND)

Large-scale excavations in the city of York have yielded rich assemblages of food remains that establish an almost 2,000-year-old sequence of changing food practices within the city. Remains from highly organic sediments were preserved through anoxic waterlogging. Less organic deposits yielded a sparser, but still informative, record.

Food remains reflect the establishment of a Roman military fortress at the site of York in the first century AD and its transition into the major city of northern Britannia. Throughout the second to fourth centuries, dietary staples predominate: six-row barley (*Hordeum vulgare*), spelt (*Triticum spelta*), and, to a lesser extent, bread/club wheat (*T. aestivo-compactum*); mature beef and young pork; hazelnuts (*Corylus avellana*); blackberry and other *Rubus* fruits; sloe and other *Prunus* species. These resources represent what the surrounding countryside could supply. Imports provided distinctively Mediterranean elements such as olive (*Olea europaea*), fig (*Ficus carica*), grape (*Vitis vinifera*), coriander (*Coriandrum sativum*), and stone pine (*Pinus pinea*). Evidence for the local production of fish sauce (*garum, liquamen*) also reflects Mediterranean tastes. Sheep were mostly eaten as mature mutton; groups of young lambs found together may represent seasonal sacrifice.

The immediate Post-Roman period is poorly represented in York until the late ninth- to tenth-century Scandinavian resettlement. Staple foods from this latter period are beef and cereals such as barley, bread wheat, oats (*Avena sativa*), and rye (*Secale cereale*). There is additional evidence for legumes and pulses, including peas (*Pisum sativum*) and beans (*Vicia faba*), and vegetables, including carrots (*Daucus carota*) and leeks (*Allium porrum*). Some sites have revealed diverse flavorings: celery (*Apium graveolens*), hop (*Humulus lupulus*), and summer savory (*Satureja hortensis*). These three, with linseed (*Linum usitatissimum*) and bilberry (*Vaccinium* spp.), are characteristic of this period in York, together with wetland wildfowl and copious fish remains, predominantly herring (*Clupea harengus*) and eel (*Anguilla anguilla*).

Archaeological data also reveal changing preferences through medieval and later periods that reflect altered provisioning systems, the increased social importance of conspicuously fine dining, the ethnic mix of York's people, the productive local hinterland, and the city's fluctuating articulation with international trade.

See also ARCHAEOBOTANY; CEREALS; CONDIMENTS; FISH/SHELLFISH; FOOD AND DINING AS SOCIAL DISPLAY; FOOD AND IDENTITY; FRUITS; LEGUMES AND PULSES; MEAT; TRADE ROUTES; VEGETABLES; ZOOARCHAEOLOGY

Further Reading

Hall, A. R., ed. 1976–1995. *Archaeology of York*. Vol. 14, *The Past Environment of York, Fascicules 1–7*. York: Council for British Archaeology.

O'Connor, T. P., and Bond, J. M. 1984–1998. *Archaeology of York*. Vol. 15, *The Animal Bones, Fascicules 1–5*. York: Council for British Archaeology.

White, Eileen, ed. 2000. *Feeding a City: York*. Totnes, UK: Prospect Books.

■ ALLAN HALL AND TERRY O'CONNOR

Z

ZOOARCHAEOLOGY

Zooarchaeology, or faunal analysis, is the study of animal remains from archaeological sites. The nature of archaeological preservation means that hard tissues of animals—bones, teeth, and shells—are what usually survive to be recovered and studied. These faunal remains are often the trash left from animals that were eaten and thus can provide very direct evidence for past diet and foodways.

Faunal analysis spans all time periods and geographic areas. Many of the earliest archaeological sites in the world are collections of animal bones and a small number of stone tools. At the oldest sites in Africa, faunal remains are key to understanding the diet, ecological niche, and adaptive strategies of human ancestors. At more recent sites across the globe, zooarchaeologists study animal remains to understand human hunting, fishing, and foraging practices; the origins of domestic animals; animal husbandry practices of farmers; the development of complex food systems supporting early cities; and ultimately the commodification of animal products and rise of industrial systems of food production and marketing. In all these instances, archaeologists are interested in the interplay of social and cultural factors and consumption of animal food products.

Archaeologists identify faunal remains with reference to published guides to animal anatomy and modern comparative collections of animal skeletons. This analysis can include identification of the species of animal, the skeletal part, surface modifications to the bones, or indications of the animal's size, age, or sex. Identification of the animals at a site relies on classification of specimens into biological taxonomies with assignment of family, genus, and species names. Skeletal part representation is often studied in detail to understand the processing and transportation of the carcasses and the cultural uses and values of specific parts of animals.

The study of taphonomy, or the processes of bone assemblage formation, is central to faunal analysis. A key concern is differentiating human actions from natural forces in the creation of bone assemblages. Many researchers have documented patterns of density-mediated attrition, where destructive forces acting on bones tend to preferentially remove the least dense specimens, changing the relative representation. Archaeologists have undertaken a variety of experimental and observational studies to record how human butchery, animal gnawing, weathering, and other factors pattern faunal collections. Surface modifications to bones that result from these processes are commonly analyzed to understand the variety of factors acting on the bones, strengthening cultural interpretations of faunal remains.

Specific methods of quantifying the faunal specimens play an important role in the analysis. In the most basic sense, archaeologists frequently try to translate counts of bone specimens into other measures, such as the number of animals represented. This measure is the minimum number of individuals (MNI), literally the number of animals that had to be present to account for all of the bones. To understand diet and foodways, analysts often try to estimate the amount of meat or other products the animals might have provided and the relative dietary importance of the different animal foods. This is sometimes estimated using the MNI and the potential meat weight of animals, or by calculating biomass, which statistically relates the bone weights to live animal weights. While these measures are generally imprecise, they do help archaeologists to move conceptually from counts of bones to estimates of food.

Faunal analysts study the growth of animals' bones and shells and tooth eruption and wear to determine the ages of animals at death. With many common food animals the patterns of age-related growth are well known, including detailed stages of tooth wear for some species. Animal age data assist reconstruction of past hunting practices by showing the effectiveness, strategies, and intensity of human hunting. Specific animal husbandry practices also are reflected in age data, especially for domestic animals that are used for purposes beyond meat, such as their secondary products. For pastoralists raising sheep and goats, faunal analysts have developed models for the age and sex structure of animal herds being raised for milk, meat, or wool. These types of models provide a comparative framework for assessing archaeological data.

The analysis of faunal remains includes seasonality studies that interpret when during the year animals were killed. These studies draw on specific seasonal behaviors of animals, such as migratory routes or the development and shedding of antlers. Seasonal growth patterns in the microstructure of animal tooth tissues or shells also are analyzed to help determine the season of death. Patterns in the seasonal use of animals contribute to our understanding of mobility practices of hunter-gatherers, site settlement systems and the origins of permanent settlements, and seasonal agricultural cycles. In these examples detailed information on animals' life histories, interpreted from faunal remains, is used to help understand human behavior.

Specialized analytical tools continue to expand the range of faunal analysis. Stable isotopes, while more commonly examined in human remains, are also being investigated in animals. These studies have led to complex interpretations of animal diet, trade in animal products, weaning of young livestock by farmers, and foddering regimes, among other topics. Similar advances are being made through DNA analysis, which has helped differentiate closely related taxa and increased our understanding of the development of specific breeds. At the same time, researchers studying animal use in complex societies are increasingly pushing the interpretive emphases beyond diet and subsistence to a broader range of social issues, especially how social stratification and differentiation are created, maintained, or challenged through differential access to and consumption of animal products. The continuing development of scientific analytical tools, coupled with increasingly sophisticated contextual and interpretive approaches, promises to keep faunal analysis at the center of archaeological studies of food.

See also ANIMAL DOMESTICATION; ANIMAL HUSBANDRY AND HERDING; BUTCHERY; DNA ANALYSIS; ETHNOARCHAEOLOGY; EXPERIMENTAL ARCHAEOLOGY; INDUSTRIALIZATION OF FOOD AND FOOD PRODUCTION; HUNTER-GATHERER SUBSISTENCE; MEAT; PALEODIETARY ANALYSIS; SECONDARY PRODUCTS REVOLUTION; STABLE ISOTOPE ANALYSIS; SUBSISTENCE MODELS

Further Reading

Landon, David B. 2009. An Update on Zooarchaeology and Historical Archaeology: Progress and Prospects. In *International Handbook of Historical Archaeology*, edited by Teresa Majewski and David Gaimster, 77–104. New York: Springer.

O'Connor, Terry. 2000. *The Archaeology of Animal Bones*. College Station: Texas A&M Press.

Reitz, Elizabeth J., and Elizabeth S. Wing. 1999. *Zooarchaeology*. Cambridge Manuals in Archaeology. Cambridge: Cambridge University Press.

■ DAVID B. LANDON

INDEX

Abu Hamid (Jordan), 359
Abu Hureyra (Syria), 23, 339, 445, 545
Abydos (Egypt), 47
accelerator mass spectrometry (AMS) dating, 45, 245, 292, 432, 475, 524
Acha Man, Atacama Desert (Chile), 330
Acheulean tool industry, 242, 515, 552–53
acorns (*Quercus*), 70, 91, 146, 218, 235, 245, 269, 284, 313, 334, 343, 347, 361, 411, 480
aerial photography, 3, 19, 274, 535
African-American foodways, 134–35, 181, 188, 465, 495; "soul food," 135, 181–82, 191
African diaspora foodways, 123–25, 134–35, 180–81, 188, 415, 463–67
Agate Basin, Wyoming (USA), 207
agave (*Agave* spp.), 1, 22, 245, 304, 311, 423, *426*, 499
Agora, Athens (Greece), *506*
agricultural features, 18–22, 111, 159, 183, 209–10, 229, 272–74, *273*, 278–79, 300–3, 306, 333, 366, 385, 399, 405, 409, 436–37, 452–53, 470, 490, 493, 516, *517*, 534–35; identification of, 2–6, 286–87. *See also* *chinampas*; irrigation/hydraulic engineering; terraces
agricultural/horticultural sites, 2–6, 18–22, 24–25, 40, 111, 159, 224, 229, 249–50, 265, 278–79, 286–87, 300–3, 306, 344, 380, 385, 399–400, 409, 463–66, 490, 493. *See also* gardens; kraals; orchards; pastures; vineyards
agricultural strategies, 2, 7, 14, 18–21, 57–58, 269, 278, 286, 291–92, 300–3, 311, 321, 384, 436–37, 442–44, 467–69, 542–43; crop rotation, 20–21, 291, 543; intensification, 18–20, 111, 182, 194, 196, 209, 240, 436, 453 polycropping, 7, 45, 278, 296, 311, 413, 499; tilling, 14, 20, 409, 442, 453, 542–43. *See also* manuring and soil enrichment practices; swidden agriculture
agricultural tools, 8, 18–22, *20*, 31, 56, 306, 318, 365, 445, 452, 513, 515, 545; plow, 20, 56, 287, 451–54, 513, 542; sickle, 19–20, 96, 126, 150, 445, 513, 515, 523; threshing sledge, 21, 404, 516, *517*; wheeled vehicle, 451–54
agriculture, origins of, *xxvii*, 6–18, 30, 126–27, 222, 229, 269, 296–99, 309–11, 338–40, 365–67, 371, 374, 415–16, 441–45, 457, 470, 474–76, 491–93, 499, 502, 543–48, 556, 559; centers of domestication, 7,

9–10, 18, 69, 98, 113, 126, 161, 209, 291–92, 296–97, 310–11, 365, 393, 413, 454, 475; theories of, 6–17, 80–81, 158, 182, 193–94, 286, 339, 408–10, 451–52, 454–56, 535
Aguadulce (Panama), 299
Akoris (Egypt), 360
Akrotiri, Santorini (Greece), 38–39, 271, 293
Alaca Höyük (Turkey), 445
alcohol. *See* beer; distilled spirits; fermented beverages; mead; wine
Ali Kosh (Iran), 173
almonds (*Amygdalus communis*), 104, 229–30, 251, 351, 353; wild, 91, 235, 240, 343
alpaca (*Vicugna pacos*), 26, 105, 111, 452
Alto Salaverry (Peru), 333
Amaranthaceae, 10, 209, 336, 466, 499
Amarna (Egypt), 42, 47, 271, 359
amino acids, 50, 59, 165, 252, 297, 416, 522, 557
amphibians, 34, 234, 276, 381
amphorae, 23–24, 112, 239, 250, 252, 264, 359, 434–35, 459–61, *460*, 471, 483, 520, 548–50, *549*
Amud Cave (Israel), 338
anemia, 14–15, 51, 55, 383, 388, 394, 467
Angkor (Cambodia), 3
animal domestication, 25–29, 93, 162, 209, 226, 309–10, 328, 333, 339–40, 365–66, 374, 402, 406–7, 428, 451–52, 454–55, 486–87, 559; wild progenitors, 26, 328, 455, 457
animal enclosures, 28, 468
animal fodder, 106, 210, 212, 269–70, 292, 322, 350, 361, 384, 444, 473, 488, 528, 530, 560; foods classified as, 269–70, 361
animal husbandry and herding, 25–29, 52, 58, 61, 91–93, 111, 126, 146, 148–50, 160, 193, 214, 220, 225, 229, 240, 247–48, 250, 283, 287, 317, 320–21, 350–53, 374, 393, 395, 400–402, 418, 421, *421*, 457, 467, 473, 478, 485–86, 515, 559–60
animal processing, 34, 87–88, 92, 150, 164, 172–73, 207, 234–35, 242–43, 248, 254, *254*, 258, 280–81, 303, 357, *357*, 370, 376–78, 430, 432, 466, 471, 494–95, 509, 515, 523, 525, 559. *See also* bone fat extraction; butchery practice

ABOUT THE EDITORS AND CONTRIBUTORS

EDITORS

Karen Bescherer Metheny, PhD, is a Visiting Researcher in the Department of Archaeology at Boston University and Lecturer for the Gastronomy Program, Metropolitan College, Boston University, where she teaches courses in the anthropology and archaeology of food, food history and food culture of New England, and method and theory in food studies. She is the author of *From the Miners' Doublehouse: Archaeology and Landscape in a Pennsylvania Coal Company Town* (2007) and coeditor of *Landscape Archaeology: Reading and Interpreting the American Historical Landscape* (1996, with Rebecca Yamin). Her current research interests include food mapping and other visualization techniques, historic-period cookbooks and foodways, and the cultural significance of maize in colonial New England.

Mary C. Beaudry, PhD, is Professor of Archaeology, Anthropology, and Gastronomy at Boston University. She is the author or coeditor of numerous published works, including *Findings* (2006), *Archaeologies of Mobility and Movement* (2013, coedited with Travis Parno), and *The Oxford Handbook of Material Culture Studies* (2010, coedited with Dan Hicks). She teaches courses on archaeological theory, historical archaeology, and material culture, including "Pots and Pans: The Material Culture of Cookery and Dining," combining her interests in foodways and material culture to examine technological and material change in the kitchen and at the table.

CONTRIBUTORS

Umberto Albarella, PhD, Reader in Zooarchaeology, Department of Archaeology, University of Sheffield, United Kingdom

Robin G. Allaby, PhD, Associate Professor, School of Life Sciences, University of Warwick, United Kingdom

Penelope M. Allison, PhD, Reader in Archaeology and Ancient History, School of Archaeology and Ancient History, University of Leicester, United Kingdom

Adauto Araújo, MD, PhD, Senior Researcher, Escola Nacional de Saúde Pública, Fundação Oswaldo Cruz, Brazil

Myriam Arcangeli, PhD, Independent Scholar, United States

Gregory E. Areshian, PhD, Adjunct Associate Professor of Near Eastern Archaeology, Department of Near Eastern Languages and Cultures, and Director, UCLA Program in Armenian Archaeology and Ethnography, University of California, Los Angeles, United States

Hans Barnard, PhD, Adjunct Assistant Professor of Archaeological Sciences, Department of Near Eastern Languages and Cultures, and Assistant Researcher, Cotsen Institute of Archaeology, University of California, Los Angeles, United States

Ofer Bar-Yosef, PhD, George Grant MacCurdy and Janet G. B. MacCurdy Professor of Prehistoric Archaeology, Emeritus, Department of Anthropology, Harvard University, United States

Karl-Ernst Behre, Prof. Dr. rer. nat., Niedersächsisches Institut für historische Küsten-forschung, Germany

Bruce F. Benz, PhD, Professor of Biology, Texas Wesleyan University, United States

José María Bermúdez de Castro, PhD, Profesor de Investigación, Centro Nacional de Investigación sobre la Evolución Humana, Spain

Francesco Berna, PhD, Assistant Professor, Department of Archaeology, Simon Fraser University, Canada

Carrie Anne Berryman, PhD, Independent Scholar, United States

Thomas E. Birch, PhD, Postdoctoral Researcher, Institut für Archäologische Wissen-schaften der Goethe-Universität, Germany

Nicole L. Boivin, PhD, Senior Research Fellow, Research Laboratory for Archaeology and the History of Art, University of Oxford, and Senior Research Fellow in Archaeology, Jesus College, University of Oxford, United Kingdom

Aimee C. Bouzigard, MA, Staff Archaeologist, Historic Preservation Division, Georgia Department of Natural Resources, United States

Tamara L. Bray, PhD, Professor, Department of Anthropology, Wayne State University, United States

Stephen A. Brighton, PhD, Associate Professor, Department of Anthropology, University of Maryland, United States

Terry Brown, PhD, Professor of Biomolecular Archaeology, Faculty of Life Sciences, Manchester Institute of Biotechnology, University of Manchester, United Kingdom

William Bruce, PhD Candidate, Department of Classics, University of Wisconsin–Madison, United States

Peggy Brunache, PhD, Instructor/Graduate Faculty, Department of Anthropology, University of Alabama at Birmingham, United States

Maria C. Bruno, PhD, Assistant Professor, Department of Anthropology/Archaeology, Dickinson College, United States

Tammy Y. Buonasera, PhD, Visiting Scholar, Department of Anthropology, University of Arizona, United States

Domenico Camardo, PhD, Chief Archaeologist, Herculaneum Conservation Project, Italy

Rachel N. Carmody, PhD, Postdoctoral Fellow, Hooper Research Foundation, University of California, San Francisco, and Visiting Fellow, Department of Human Evolutionary Biology, Harvard University, United States

Sergio J. Chávez, PhD, Professor of Anthropology, Department of Sociology, Anthropology, and Social Work, Central Michigan University, United States

Cheryl Claassen, PhD, Professor, Department of Anthropology, Appalachian State University, United States

Mark Nathan Cohen, PhD, University Distinguished Professor of Anthropology and Distinguished Teaching Professor of Anthropology, State University of New York, Plattsburgh, United States

Patricia Colunga-GarcíaMarín, PhD, Profesora-Investigadora Titular, Unidad de Recursos Naturales, Centro de Investigación Científica de Yucatán, México

Sarah Court, MA, Heritage Specialist, Herculaneum Conservation Project, Italy

Oliver Craig, PhD, Reader in Archaeological Science, University of York, United Kingdom

Alison Crowther, PhD, Postdoctoral Research Fellow, School of Social Science, University of Queensland, Australia

Andrea M. Cuéllar, PhD, Associate Professor, Department of Anthropology, University of Lethbridge, Canada

Linda Scott Cummings, PhD, Director/Founder, PaleoResearch Institute, Golden, Colorado, United States

Penny Cunningham, PhD, Honorary University Fellow, Department of Archaeology, University of Exeter, United Kingdom

L. Antonio Curet, PhD, Curator, Smithsonian Institution, National Museum of the American Indian, and Adjunct Curator, Field Museum, Chicago, United States

Robyn E. Cutright, PhD, Assistant Professor, Department of Anthropology, Centre College, United States

Jeff A. Dahlberg, PhD, Director, Kearney Agricultural Research and Extension Center, University of California Division of Agriculture and Natural Resources, United States

A. Catherine D'Andrea, PhD, Professor, Department of Archaeology, Simon Fraser University, Canada

Kristin De Lucia, PhD, Visiting Instructor, Department of Anthropology, University of Illinois at Urbana-Champaign, United States

Michael W. Dee, PhD, Leverhulme Trust Early Career Fellow and Junior Research Fellow, St Edmund Hall, Research Laboratory for Archaeology and the History of Art, School of Archaeology, University of Oxford, United Kingdom

James A. Delle, PhD, Associate Dean, College of Arts and Sciences, Shippensburg University, United States

Tim Denham, PhD, Convenor and Senior Lecturer, Masters of Archaeological Science Program, Australian National University College of Arts and Social Sciences, Australia

Caroline A. Dezendorf, MA, Department of International Studies, University of Oregon, United States

Oliver Dietrich, PhD Candidate, Freie Universität Berlin, and Research Assistant, Deutsches Archäologisches Institut, Orient-Abteilung, Germany

Thomas D. Dillehay, PhD, Rebecca Webb Wilson University Distinguished Professor of Anthropology, Religion, and Culture and Professor of Anthropology and Latin American Studies, Department of Anthropology, Vanderbilt University, United States

Merryn Dineley, BA, MPhil, Independent Scholar, Scotland

Manuel Domínguez-Rodrigo, PhD, Professor, Departmento de Prehistoria, Facultad Geografía e Historia, Universida Complutense de Madrid, Spain

Frank M. Dugan, PhD, Research Plant Pathologist, United States Department of Agriculture, Agricultural Research Service, Washington State University, United States

Jennie Ebeling, PhD, Associate Professor of Archaeology, Department of Archaeology and Art History, University of Evansville, United States

Thomas E. Emerson, PhD, Director, Illinois State Archaeological Survey, University of Illinois, United States

James G. Enloe, PhD, Professor, Department of Anthropology, University of Iowa, United States

Gary M. Feinman, PhD, MacArthur Curator of Mesoamerican and East Asian Anthropology, Field Museum of Natural History, Chicago, United States

Judith H. Field, PhD, Honorary Senior Lecturer, School of Biological, Earth, and Environmental Sciences, University of New South Wales, Australia

Bill Finlayson, PhD, Director, Council for British Research in the Levant, United Kingdom

Scott M. Fitzpatrick, PhD, Associate Professor, Department of Anthropology, University of Oregon, United States

Rowan K. Flad, PhD, Professor, Department of Anthropology, Harvard University, United States

James L. Flexner, PhD, ARC Postdoctoral Fellow, School of Archaeology and Anthropology, Australian National University, Australia

Brendan P. Foley, PhD, Research Specialist, Department of Applied Ocean Physics and Engineering, Woods Hole Oceanographic Institution, United States

Sarah L. Fordyce, PhD, Postdoctoral Researcher, Department of Forensic Medicine, University of Copenhagen, Denmark

Ellery Frahm, PhD, Research Associate, Feinberg Research Group, Departments of Anthropology and Earth Sciences, University of Minnesota–Twin Cities, United States

Maria Franklin, PhD, Associate Professor, Department of Anthropology, University of Texas at Austin, United States

Rita E. Freed, PhD, John F. Cogan Jr. and Mary L. Cornille Chair, Art of the Ancient World, Museum of Fine Arts, Boston, United States

Dorian Q Fuller, PhD, Professor of Archaeobotany, Institute of Archaeology, University College London, United Kingdom

Sabine Gaudzinski-Windheuser, PhD, Director, MONREPOS Archaeological Research Centre and Museum for Human Behavioural Evolution of the Römisch-Germanisches Zentralmuseum, and Professor, Department of Pre- and Protohistorical Archaeology, Johannes Gutenberg-University Mainz, Germany

Jonny Geber, PhD, Postdoctoral Fellow, Department of Archaeology, University College Cork, Ireland

Pascale Gerbault, PhD, Research Associate in Human Evolutionary Genetics, Molecular and Cultural Evolution Laboratory, Research Department of Genetics, Evolution, and Environment, University College London, United Kingdom

Geneviève Godbout, PhD Candidate, Department of Anthropology, University of Chicago, United States

Naama Goren-Inbar, PhD, Professor, Institute of Archaeology, Hebrew University of Jerusalem, Israel

Rebecca L. Gowland, PhD, Senior Lecturer in Human Bioarchaeology, Department of Archaeology, Durham University, United Kingdom

Sarah R. Graff, PhD, Honors Faculty Fellow, Barrett Honors College, Arizona State University, United States

Haskel J. Greenfield, PhD, Professor, Department of Anthropology, St. Paul's College, University of Manitoba, Canada

Kristen J. Gremillion, PhD, Professor, Department of Anthropology, Ohio State University, United States

Amy S. Groesbeck, MSc, Marine Ecologist, Natural Resources Department, Tulalip Tribes, United States

Amy B. Groleau, PhD, Curator of Latin American Collections, Museum of International Folk Art, Santa Fe, New Mexico, United States

Leore Grosman, PhD, Professor, Institute of Archaeology, Hebrew University of Jerusalem, Israel

Maria Rosa Guasch-Jané, PhD, Director, Project Irep en Kemet, University of Barcelona, Spain

Eric Guiry, PhD Candidate, Department of Anthropology, University of British Columbia, Canada

Guo Wu, PhD, Associate Professor, Institute of Archaeology, Chinese Academy of Social Sciences, China

Jon Hageman, PhD, Associate Professor, Department of Anthropology, Northeastern Illinois University, United States

Allan Hall, PhD, Senior Research Fellow, Retired, Department of Archaeology, University of York, United Kingdom

Paul Halstead, PhD, Professor of Archaeology, University of Sheffield, United Kingdom

Yannis Hamilakis, PhD, Professor of Archaeology, Faculty of Humanities, University of Southampton, United Kingdom

John P. Hart, PhD, Director, Research and Collections Division, New York State Museum, United States

Michelle Hastings, MLA, Gastronomy Program, Metropolitan College, Boston University, and Exhibit Curator, Custom House Maritime Museum, Newburyport, Massachusetts, United States

Mark W. Hauser, PhD, Associate Professor, Department of Anthropology and Associate Director, Center for African American History, Northwestern University, United States

Frances M. Hayashida, PhD, Associate Professor of Anthropology, University of New Mexico, United States

Barbara J. Heath, PhD, Associate Professor of Anthropology, University of Tennessee, Knoxville, United States

Andreas G. Heiss, PhD, Postdoctoral Researcher, Vienna Institute for Archaeological Science (VIAS), University of Vienna, Austria

John S. Henderson, PhD, Professor of Anthropology, Cornell University, United States

Amanda G. Henry, PhD, Max Planck Research Group on Plants in Hominin Dietary Ecology, Max Planck Institute for Evolutionary Anthropology, Germany

Edward W. Herrmann, PhD, Research Scientist, Department of Geological Sciences and Research Affiliate, Department of Anthropology, Indiana University, United States

Matthew G. Hill, PhD, Associate Professor, Department of Anthropology, Iowa State University, United States

W. Jeffrey Hurst, PhD, Principal Scientist, Hershey Company Technical Center, United States

William H. Isbell, PhD, Distinguished Professor of Anthropology, Department of Anthropology, State University of New York at Binghamton, United States

Stefanie Jacomet, PhD, Professor of Archaeobotany, Institut für prähistorische und naturwissenschaftliche Archäologie, Universität Basel, Switzerland

Dennis L. Jenkins, PhD, Senior Archaeologist, Museum of Natural and Cultural History, University of Oregon, United States

Jiang Hongen, PhD, Associate Professor, Department of Scientific History and Archaeometry, Graduate University of Chinese Academy of Sciences, China

Jennifer R. Jones, PhD, Postdoctoral Research Associate, School of Archaeology and History, Cardiff University, United Kingdom

Richard Jones, PhD, Senior Lecturer in Landscape History, Centre for English Local History, University of Leicester, United Kingdom

Sharyn Jones, PhD, Associate Professor of Anthropology, Department of Sociology, Anthropology and Philosophy, Northern Kentucky University, United States

David Kaniewski, PhD, Université Paul Sabatier-Toulouse, CNRS EcoLab (Laboratoire d'Ecologie Fonctionnelle et Environnement), and Institut Universitaire de France, France

Arunima Kashyap, PhD, Departmental Affiliate, Department of Anthropology, Portland State University, United States

Gerald K. Kelso, PhD, Independent Scholar, United States

Elizabeth A. Klarich, PhD, Assistant Professor, Department of Anthropology, Smith College, United States

Lucy Kubiak-Martens, PhD, BIAX Consult, Biological Archaeology and Landscape Reconstruction, the Netherlands

David B. Landon, PhD, Associate Director, Fiske Center for Archaeological Research, Department of Anthropology, University of Massachusetts Boston, United States

Robert H. Layton, PhD, Professor, Department of Anthropology, Durham University, United Kingdom

Steven A. LeBlanc, PhD, Associate of the Peabody Museum of Archaeology and Ethnology, Harvard University, United States

Christina Lee, PhD, Associate Professor in Viking Studies, School of English, University of Nottingham, United Kingdom

Dana Lepofsky, PhD, Professor, Department of Archaeology, Simon Fraser University, Canada

Krista Lewis, PhD, Associate Professor of Anthropology, Department of Sociology and Anthropology and Middle Eastern Studies Faculty, University of Arkansas at Little Rock, United States

Nili Liphschitz, PhD, Botanical Laboratory, Institute of Archaeology, Tel-Aviv University, Israel, and Fellow of the International Academy of Wood Science

Diane L. Lister, PhD, ERC Post-Doctoral Research Associate, McDonald Institute for Archaeological Research, University of Cambridge, United Kingdom

Amanda L. Logan, PhD, Assistant Professor, Department of Anthropology, Northwestern University, United States

Heidi Luik, PhD, Senior Research Fellow, Institute of History, Tallinn University, Estonia

Rachel MacLean, PhD, Honorary Research Fellow, Department of Archaeology, University of Manchester, United Kingdom

Aren M. Maeir, PhD, Professor of Archaeology, Martin (Szusz) Department of Land of Israel Studies and Archaeology, Institute of Archaeology, Bar-Ilan University, Israel

Ailsa Mainman, PhD, Research Associate, York Archaeological Trust, and Department of Archaeology, University of York, United Kingdom

Frank Maixner, PhD, Coordinator, Institute for Mummies and the Iceman, EURAC-European Academy Bolzano, Italy

Paula Marcoux, BA, Independent Scholar, United States

Marjan Mashkour, PhD, Senior Research Fellow, Sociétés, Plantes et Animaux en Asie et en Afrique, CNRS/Muséum national d'Histoire naturelle, France

Amihai Mazar, PhD, Professor Emeritus of Archaeology, Institute of Archaeology, Hebrew University of Jerusalem, Israel

Mark McCoy, PhD, Associate Professor, Department of Anthropology, Southern Methodist University, United States

Larry McKee, PhD, Project Manager, Archaeology, TRC Environmental Corporation, United States

Richard H. Meadow, PhD, Senior Lecturer, Department of Anthropology, and Director, Zooarchaeology Laboratory, Peabody Museum of Archaeology and Ethnology, Harvard University, United States

Marco Meniketti, PhD, Associate Professor, Department of Anthropology, San Jose State University, United States

Timothy C. Messner, PhD, Assistant Professor, Department of Anthropology, State University of New York at Potsdam, United States

Hayley L. Mickleburgh, PhD, Postdoctoral Researcher, Faculty of Archaeology, Leiden University, the Netherlands

Christopher Miller, PhD, Dr. rer. nat., Juniorprofessor für Geoarchäologie, Institut für Naturwissenschaftliche Archäologie and Senckenberg Centre for Human Evolution and Palaeoenvironment, Eberhard-Karls Universität Tübingen, Germany

Henry M. Miller, PhD, Director of Research, Historic St. Mary's City, United States

Naomi F. Miller, PhD, Consulting Scholar, Near East Section, University of Pennsylvania Museum, and Adjunct Associate Professor, Department of Anthropology, University of Pennsylvania, United States

Nicky Milner, PhD, Professor, Department of Archaeology, University of York, United Kingdom

Daniel E. Moerman, PhD, William E. Stirton Professor Emeritus of Anthropology, University of Michigan–Dearborn, United States

Lisa Moffett, MSc, MPhil, Archaeological Science Advisor, English Heritage, and Honorary Research Fellow, Institute of Archaeology and Antiquity, University of Birmingham, United Kingdom

Salvatore F. Monaco, PhD, Independent Scholar, Italy

Christopher T. Morehart, PhD, Assistant Professor, School of Human Evolution and Social Change, Arizona State University, United States

Kathleen D. Morrison, PhD, Neukom Family Professor in Anthropology and of Social Sciences in the College, and Director, South Asia Language and Area Center, Department of Anthropology, University of Chicago, United States

Isabella Mulhall, MA, Assistant Keeper, Irish Antiquities Division, National Museum of Ireland, Dublin, Ireland

Paul R. Mullins, PhD, Professor, Department of Anthropology, Indiana University–Purdue University, Indianapolis, United States

Natalie D. Munro, PhD, Professor, Department of Anthropology, University of Connecticut, United States

Dani Nadel, PhD, Professor of Archaeology, Zinman Institute of Archaeology, University of Haifa, Israel

Kit Nelson, PhD, Chair of Integrated Sciences, New Orleans Center for Creative Arts and Tulane Science Scholars Program, Tulane University, United States

Mark Nesbitt, PhD, Curator of Economic Botany Collections, Herbarium, Royal Botanic Gardens, Kew, Honorary Senior Lecture, University College London, and Honorary Research Fellow, Department of Anthropology, University of Kent, United Kingdom

Jens Notroff, PhD Candidate, Ludwig-Maximilians-Universität München and Research Assistant, Deutsches Archäologisches Institut, Orient-Abteilung, Germany

Gustavo Adolfo Novelo Rincón, BA, Archaeologist, Instituto Nacional de Antropología e Historia-Centro Regional Yucatán, Mérida, México

Terry O'Connor, PhD, Emeritus Professor of Archaeological Science, University of York, United Kingdom

Hugo R. Oliveira, PhD, Postdoctoral Researcher, Research Centre in Biodiversity and Genetic Resources, Universidade do Porto, Portugal

Kenneth M. Olsen, PhD, Associate Professor, Biology Department, Washington University in St. Louis, United States

Rintaro Ono, PhD, Associate Professor, Department of Maritime Civilizations, School of Marine Science and Technology, Tokai University, Japan

Ingvild Øye, PhD, Professor of Archaeology, Department of Archaeology, History, Cultural Studies, and Religion, University of Bergen, Norway

Eva Panagiotakopulu, PhD, Lecturer in Palaeoecology, School of GeoSciences, University of Edinburgh, Scotland, United Kingdom

Michael C. Pante, PhD, Assistant Professor, Department of Anthropology, Colorado State University, United States

Joanna Papayiannis, PhD, Lecturer, Program in Material Culture at Victoria College, University of Toronto

Victor Paz, PhD, Professor, Archaeological Studies Program, University of the Philippines, Diliman, the Philippines

Alessandra Pecci, PhD, Postdoctoral Researcher, Dipartimento di Biologia, Ecologia, e Scienze della Terra, Università della Calabria, Italy

Linda Perry, PhD, Foundation for Archaeobotanical Research in Microfossils and Department of Geography and Geoinformation Science, George Mason University, United States

William J. Pestle, PhD, Assistant Professor, Department of Anthropology, University of Miami, United States

Adrian Praetzellis, PhD, Professor of Anthropology and Director, Anthropological Studies Center, Department of Anthropology, Sonoma State University, United States

Mary Praetzellis, MA, Associate Director, Anthropological Studies Center, Sonoma State University, United States

Sean M. Rafferty, PhD, Associate Professor, Department of Anthropology, State University of New York at Albany, United States

Elizabeth DeRidder Raubolt, PhD Candidate, Department of Art History and Archaeology, University of Missouri, United States

Karl J. Reinhard, PhD, Fulbright Scholar and Professor of Environmental Archaeology and Forensic Science, School of Natural Resources, University of Nebraska–Lincoln, United States

Simone Riehl, PhD, Senior Researcher, Institute for Archaeological Science and Senckenberg Centre of Human Evolution and Palaeoenvironment, Eberhard-Karls Universität Tübingen, Germany

Charlotte A. Roberts, PhD, Professor, Department of Archaeology, Durham University, United Kingdom

Flor Rodríguez, PhD, RTC Phylogeneticist, International Potato Center, Peru

Enrique Rodríguez-Alegría, PhD, Associate Professor, Department of Anthropology, University of Texas at Austin, United States

Danny Rosenberg, PhD, Senior Lecturer and Research Director, Laboratory for Ground-Stone Tools Research, Zinman Institute of Archaeology, University of Haifa, Israel

Kirsten Rowell, PhD, Burke Museum of Natural History and Culture and Department of Biology, University of Washington, United States

Astrid Runggaldier, PhD, Senior Lecturer, Department of Art and Art History and Researcher, The Mesoamerica Center, University of Texas at Austin, United States

Hannah Russ, PhD, Consultant and Research Fellow in Archaeological Science, Department of Social Sciences and Oxford Brookes Archaeology and Heritage, Oxford Brookes University, United Kingdom

Nerissa Russell, PhD, Professor, Department of Anthropology and the Cornell Institute of Archaeology and Material Studies, Cornell University, United States

Valerie Ryan, MLA, Part-Time Lecturer, Gastronomy Program, Metropolitan College, Boston University, and Food Correspondent, *Boston Globe*, United States

Anne K. Salomon, PhD, Assistant Professor, School of Resource and Environmental Management, Simon Fraser University, Canada

Dennis M. Sandgathe, PhD, Lecturer, Department of Archaeology and Human Evolution Studies Program, Simon Fraser University, Canada

Manon Savard, PhD, Professeure régulière en géographie and Co-directrice du Laboratoire d'archéologie et de patrimoine, Université du Québec à Rimouski, Canada

Vernon L. Scarborough, PhD, Distinguished University Research Professor and Charles Phelps Taft Professor in Anthropology, Department of Anthropology, University of Cincinnati, United States

Klaus Schmidt[†], PhD, Adjunct Professor, Institute for Prehistory, Erlangen-Nürnberg University, and Senior Research Fellow, Deutsches Archäologisches Institut, Orient-Abteilung, Germany

Cynthia Shafer-Elliott, PhD, Assistant Professor of Hebrew Bible, Department of Bible and Theology, William Jessup University, United States

Ruth Shahack-Gross, PhD, Researcher, Kimmel Center for Archaeological Science, Weizmann Institute of Science, Israel

Madeline Shanahan, PhD, Archaeology Department, University College Dublin, Ireland

Ben Shaw, PhD Candidate, School of Archaeology and Anthropology, Australian National University, Australia

Payson Sheets, PhD, Professor, Department of Anthropology, University of Colorado Boulder, United States

Lisa-Marie Shillito, PhD, Research Fellow, School of History, Classics and Archaeology, University of Edinburgh, United Kingdom

Laura Short, PhD Candidate, Anthropology Department, Texas A&M University, United States

Emilie Sibbesson, PhD, Lecturer in Archaeology, School of Humanities, Canterbury Christ Church University, United Kingdom

Stephanie R. Simms, PhD, Postdoctoral Researcher, Charles E. Young Research Library and Center for Digital Humanities, University of California, Los Angeles, United States

Natalia Skakun, PhD, Senior Scientific Researcher of the Institute for the Material Culture History of the Russian Academy of Sciences, St. Petersburg, Russia, and President of the Scientific Commission (A 17) "Functional Studies of Prehistoric Artifacts and their Social-Economical Influence on Past Societies," Union Internationale des Sciences Préhistoriques et Protohistoriques

Penelope M. Skalnik, MLA, Gastronomy Program, Metropolitan College, Boston University, United States

James M. Skibo, PhD, Professor of Anthropology, Illinois State University, United States

Andrew B. Smith, PhD, Professor Emeritus, Department of Archaeology, University of Cape Town, South Africa

Frederick H. Smith, PhD, Associate Professor, Department of Anthropology, College of William and Mary, United States

Monica L. Smith, PhD, Professor, Department of Anthropology, University of California, Los Angeles, United States

Robert N. Spengler, PhD, Research Associate, Department of Anthropology, Washington University in St. Louis, United States, and Volkswagen and Mellon Foundations Postdoctoral Fellow, Eurasia Department, German Archaeological Institute (DAI), Germany

John E. Staller, PhD, Research Associate, Botanical Research Institute of Texas, United States

David R. Starbuck, PhD, Professor of Anthropology and Sociology, Plymouth State University, United States

Mary C. Stiner, PhD, Regent's Professor, School of Anthropology, University of Arizona, and Curator of Zooarchaeology, Arizona State Museum, University of Arizona, United States

Alice Storey, PhD, Project Manager, Archer CRM Partnership, Canada

Beverly Straube, PhD, Research Associate, James River Institute for Archaeology, United States

Aaron Jonas Stutz, PhD, Associate Professor of Anthropology, Oxford College of Emory University, United States

Mark Q. Sutton, PhD, Professor of Anthropology, Emeritus, California State University, Bakersfield, and Statistical Research Inc., United States

Paul Szpak, PhD, Killam and SSHRC Postdoctoral Research Fellow, Department of Anthropology, University of British Columbia, Canada

Paul S. C. Taçon, PhD, Chair in Rock Art Research, Director of PERAHU (Place, Evolution, Rock Art, and Heritage Unit), and Professor of Archaeology and Anthropology, School of Humanities, Griffith University, Australia

Mary Anne Tafuri, PhD, Lecturer, Dipartimento Biologia Ambientale, Sapienza, Università di Roma, Italy

Mark G. Thomas, PhD, Professor of Evolutionary Genetics, Research Department of Genetics, Evolution and Environment, University College London, United Kingdom

Alston V. Thoms, PhD, Associate Professor, Department of Anthropology, Texas A&M University, United States

María de Lourdes Toscano-Hernández, BA, Archaeologist, Instituto Nacional de Antropología e Historia-Centro Regional Yucatán, Mérida, México

Heather B. Trigg, PhD, Senior Research Scientist, Fiske Center for Archaeological Research, Department of Anthropology, University of Massachusetts Boston, United States

Shannon Tushingham, PhD, Assistant Director, Museum of Anthropology and Department of Anthropology, Washington State University, United States

Katheryn C. Twiss, PhD, Associate Professor, Department of Anthropology, Stony Brook University, United States

Peter S. Ungar, PhD, Distinguished Professor, Department of Anthropology, J. William Fulbright College of Arts and Sciences, University of Arkansas, United States

Soultana Maria Valamoti, PhD, Associate Professor, School of History and Archaeology, Aristotle University of Thessaloniki, Greece

Elise Van Campo, PhD, Laboratoire d'Ecologie Fonctionnelle et Environnement, Université Paul Sabatier-Toulouse, and CNRS, France

Marijke van der Veen, PhD, Professor of Archaeology, School of Archaeology and Ancient History, University of Leicester, United Kingdom

Amber M. VanDerwarker, PhD, Director, Integrative Subsistence Laboratory and Associate Professor, Department of Anthropology, University of California, Santa Barbara, United States

Patricia Vandorpe, PhD, Research Associate, Institut für prähistorische und naturwissenschaftliche Archäologie, Universität Basel, Switzerland

Karin Vaneker, BA, Independent Scholar, the Netherlands

Joost Van Itterbeeck, PhD, Independent Scholar, the Netherlands

Joanita Vroom, PhD, Associate Professor, Faculty of Archaeology, Leiden University, the Netherlands

Timothy J. Ward, PhD, Professor and Associate Dean of Sciences, and Director, W. M. Keck Center for Instrumental and Biochemical Comparative Archaeology, Millsaps College, United States

Jane Webster, PhD, Senior Lecturer in Historical Archaeology and Head of Archaeology, School of History, Classics, and Archaeology, Newcastle University, United Kingdom

Christine D. White, PhD, Professor and Canada Research Chair in Bioarchaeology and Isotopic Anthropology, Department of Anthropology, University of Western Ontario, Canada

Jayne Wilkins, PhD, Lecturer, Department of Archaeology, University of Cape Town, South Africa and Visiting Scholar, School of Human Evolution and Social Change and Institute of Human Origins, Arizona State University, United States

David Williams, PhD, Visiting Senior Research Fellow and Emeritus Professor, Department of Archaeology, University of Southampton, United Kingdom

Jim Wood, PhD, Professor of Biological Anthropology and Demography, Department of Anthropology and Population Research Institute, Pennsylvania State University, United States

Robyn P. Woodward, PhD, Adjunct Professor, Department of Archaeology, Simon Fraser University, Canada

Patti J. Wright, PhD, Associate Professor, Department of Anthropology, Sociology, and Languages, University of Missouri–St. Louis, United States

Andrew R. Wyatt, PhD, Assistant Professor, Department of Sociology and Anthropology, Middle Tennessee State University, United States

Andrea Bettina Yates, PhD Candidate, Southern Cross GeoScience, Southern Cross University, Australia

Anne E. Yentsch, PhD, Independent Scholar, United States

Zhang Linhai, PhD, Professor, South China Botanical Garden, Chinese Academy of Sciences, China

Albert R. Zink, PhD, Head of Institute, Institute for Mummies and the Iceman, EURAC-European Academy Bolzano, Italy

Daniel Zizumbo-Villarreal, PhD, Profesor-Investigador Titular, Unidad de Recursos Naturales, Centro de Investigación Científica de Yucatan, México

Sharon Zuckerman[†], PhD, Lecturer, Institute of Archaeology, Hebrew University of Jerusalem, Israel